When the Machine Stopped

When the Machine Stopped

A Cautionary Tale from Industrial America

Max Holland

Harvard Business School Press
Boston, Massachusetts

Library of Congress Cataloging-in-Publication Data

Holland, Max.
　　When the machine stopped　:　a cautionary tale from industrial
America　/　Max Holland.
　　　p.　　cm.
　　Bibliography: p. 317
　　Includes index.
　　ISBN 0-87584-244-5
　　1. Burgmaster Corporation—Management—History.　2. Machine-tool
industry—United States—Management—case studies.　3. Consolidation
and merger of corporations—United States—Case studies.　4. Machine-
tool industry—Government policy—United States.　5. Machine-tool
industry—Government policy—Japan.　6. Competition, International—
Case studies.　　I. Title.
HD9703.U54B875　　1989
338.7'621902'0973—dc19　　　　　　　　　　　　　　　　　　88-31566
　　　　　　　　　　　　　　　　　　　　　　　　　　　　　　　　　CIP

HD
9703
.U54
B875
1989
c.1
91000176

93 92 91 90　　　　5 4 3 2 1

To my father, who machined only one "anchor" in 29 years

*Divide each problem into as many
parts as possible; that each part
being more easily conceived,
the whole may be more intelligible.*

—Descartes, *Discourse on Method*

CONTENTS

When the Machine Stopped

PREFACE

The idea that eventually became this book first occurred to me in 1983.

That April, after a year of deliberation, the Reagan administration finally turned aside a novel petition for trade relief from Houdaille Industries. The Florida-based conglomerate wanted the administration to erect barriers against imports of Japanese machine tools. The loss of its market shares, Houdaille charged, was the direct result of unfair collusion between Japan's government and industry.

The reason I was fascinated with the case was that Houdaille was not just another company to me. The year before, my father had retired after working twenty-nine years for Houdaille's second-largest machine tool manufacturer. It was a Houdaille division called Burgmaster.

I was struck by the yawning gap between the Washington debate and what I knew about Burgmaster through my father's eyes. In Washington, Houdaille was an efficient, state-of-the-art machine tool builder, beset by unfair foreign competition. I had an entirely different perspective, one suggesting that many of Houdaille's and Burgmaster's wounds were self-inflicted.

I began to seek out other former Burgmaster employees, and based on interviews with them, wrote a long magazine piece that attempted to reconcile the Washington debate with my father's account. The result was an awkward beast. The article was too long for most magazines. On the other hand, it was far too short to do justice to all the subjects and themes it attempted to cover.

Lawrence Wechsler was the first to recognize that perhaps I had unwittingly spawned a book rather than just an article. But turning that manuscript into this book was by no means a solo effort. The breadth of the history compelled me to explore several unfamiliar subjects. Joel Rogers provided the foundation for understanding, and I doubt I will ever be able to repay his contribution in kind. Jeff and Anabela Frieden gave me a concentrated seminar (and bibliography) in Japanese industrial policy. Mark Hulbert was a sure-footed guide to the mysteries of the capital markets, and a willing sounding board for ruminations on trade, manufacturing, and industrial policy. Tom Ferguson, Harvey Feigenbaum, Russell Borthwick, William Burr, Abby Smith, Fred Branfman, and David Corn also offered encouragement and important suggestions along the way.

My agent, Elaine Markson, sensed the potential of the Burgmaster saga, and skillfully matched me with a publisher. Through her and David DeVoss, I also managed to find a magazine outlet for a concentrated version of the story. John Brownell and the staff of the *Los Angeles Times Magazine* made the major surgery relatively painless.

Expanding the initial draft also required reinterviewing former Burgmaster employees, not just once, but two and three times. Everyone associated with Burgmaster was unfailingly helpful and patient, but I should single out several persons for their assistance, namely, Joe Burg, Pete Ives, Bob French, Ed Merk, Alex Alvarado, Dave Balbirnie, Bob Doyle, Frank Maggiorino, and Gil Torres, a Steelworkers Union official. Norm and Blanche Ginsburg deserve special thanks for helping me understand Burgmaster's beginnings, among many other aspects.

Several key Houdaille executives, including Jerry Saltarelli, Phil O'Reilly, Ken Slawson, Tom Norton, Allan Folger, and George Delaney, shared their recollections over many hours of interviews. Carl Green and Richard Copaken, the lawyers involved on opposite sides of the Houdaille petition, were also generous with their time. However, two requests for an interview with the senior partner at the investment banking firm of Kohlberg, Kravis and Roberts failed to elicit any response.

Glyn Finley, the statistical director at the National Machine Tool Builders' Association, went out of his way to help when I needed old facts. Elaine Essman performed a similar function by supplying me with *American Machinist*'s annual surveys of the leading machine tool builders since 1965. Numerous officials inside the government also shared their time and knowledge. Ed Levy helped me grasp the process and politics of trade petitions. Tom Gallogly showered me with more information about the machine tool industry than I thought I would ever use. By the end, I found I needed it all. Their employer, the Commerce Department, responded to my Freedom of Information Act request with a diligence that is all too rare in the government. The Securities and Exchange Commission did the same. Jim Callear at the National Labor Relations Board went to great lengths to dig up some long-buried information on Burgmaster. And in the Senate, Charles Grassley's staff retrieved some retired files that were instrumental to my understanding of the Houdaille trade case.

The published sources that were consulted can be found in the Bibliography. I would be remiss, however, if I failed to single out three scholars whose writing on machine tools so informed my own. This book would be crippled without David Noble's history of NC technology, Seymour Melman's work on the effects of military spending on machine tool economics, and David Friedman's serendipitous book about the rise of the Japanese machine tool industry. In addition, Dr. Carolyn Kay Brancato's timely research and writing on leveraged buyouts saved me from an enormous amount of work, and two Washington think tanks, the Economic Policy Institute and Rebuild America, provided me with some invaluable insights.

When the pages did not seem to be coming out fast enough, Sally Cammack bolstered my confidence, soothed my exasperation, or did whatever else was necessary to help me take the book one day at a time. Victor Navasky also provided sage counsel when I needed it most. Helen Chen, my research assistant, reliably collected information I needed to expand and revise the original manuscript. Tom Cammack also helped fill in some of the holes.

No one was more instrumental in seeing this book through to completion than Barbara Ankeny, my editor. Time and again she crystallized hazy thoughts. Though the book was delivered well beyond deadline, her patience seemed endless and her enthusiasm never flagged. Most important, she shared my vision for the book and was not willing to settle for less.

Lastly, although this book is dedicated to my father, Bernhard, even that tribute does not begin to portray the extent of his contribution. He introduced me to former Burgmaster employees, and spent countless hours explaining the intricacies of the trade to a novice. His explanation of technical terms and concepts will be found in the footnotes as well as the text. He also scoured newspapers and trade journals for articles on Burgmaster, Houdaille, and machine tools. More than once I taxed his patience by insisting that he try and remember events from a decade or more ago. Not many people had his vantage point. For twenty-nine years, he worked at and observed Burgmaster, as a tool-and-die maker, union steward, and machine shop foreman.

In many ways this story is his, though I am solely responsible for the interpretations, conclusions, and any errors.

Washington, D.C.   Max Holland
July 1988

INTRODUCTION

O nce, manufacturing and the U.S. economy were almost synonymous. The "American system" of manufactures, or mass production, was the chief emblem of an economy that was both the wonder and envy of the world.

Today, the U.S. economy is remarkable primarily for its debits, including a chronic merchandise trade deficit. American products cannot keep pace with foreign manufactures, either in the United States or abroad. Rich and powerful American companies have been humbled, sometimes permanently, as have whole sectors of the U.S. manufacturing economy, most prominently, automobiles, electronics, machine tools, and steel.

The eclipse of American industry has not escaped notice, and the reasons for it have been hotly argued. Over the years, the debate has continued under many different rubrics: "industrial policy," "unfair trade practices," "foreign industrial targeting," and "competitiveness." But underneath, the issue is always the same.

Yet these debates often seem to generate more heat than light. As a result, the reasons why America cannot compete seem to recede from understanding, until they almost appear unfathomable. Meanwhile, the crisis deepens and protectionist barriers are erected. In 1981, when the Reagan administration took office, 20 percent of America's manufactured goods (by value) were protected in some way from international competition. By 1988, this figure rose to 35 percent, and in 1986 America registered its first high-tech trade deficit.

When faced with a difficult problem, a celebrated philosopher once advised, divide it into many parts and analyze one, so that the whole may be more comprehensible. That is the axiom of this book. Rather than provide an abstract account, leaving the reader with equally vague answers, this book pares the problem down to the rise and demise of a single company. The purpose is to make specific, compelling, and understandable at least some of the reasons for the decline in manufacturing.

This goal should not be construed as explicit or implicit criticism of many earlier efforts by other writers to make sense of the problem. Their work provides much of the intellectual framework for explaining the experience of a single company, and their contributions will be found in every chapter. Nor, it should be added, is it claimed that the rise and fall of one manufacturer explains everything. The story is unique in several respects, and we must be careful about which conclusions to draw. Nevertheless, the saga is not a parochial one.

The first division of the problem yields the U.S. machine tool industry. Machine tools have been described as the "machines nobody knows," and for good reason. By almost any measure, machine tools are a small part of the manufacturing economy. The industry is not as primal as steel, nor are its products as obvious as the automobile. And the standard definition of a machine tool is too dry to lend much insight: "a powered device, not hand-held, which cuts, forms, or shapes metal."

Even when the ubiquity of the industry begins to sink in, machine tools remain forbidding to the average person. Lathes and milling, drilling, or grinding machines—all of which are machine tools—are ungainly slabs of steel and iron that cut metal using brute force. But they vary, as one industry expert liked to say, "as much in power, size, and complexity in the field of metal cutting as do elephants and earthworms in the animal kingdom."[1]

Yet despite these off-putting characteristics, it would be hard to overstate the importance of machine tools to contemporary life. If we adapt the old question—which came first, the chicken or the egg—to manufacturing, the answer would be a machine tool. Most Americans think of General Motors, Westinghouse, and Boeing as being synonymous with industry in America. Perhaps so, but machine tool companies like Cincinnati Milacron, Ingersoll Milling Machine, and Brown & Sharpe, though they may be relatively unknown, constituted the industrial backbone.

Machine tools are in fact the "mother" or "master" machines, the machines that make all machines. *Every manufactured product is made either by a machine tool or by a machine that was made by a machine tool.* Machine tools, for example, take all the metal forgings that go into an automobile and fashion them into a finished car. But unlike cars, or any other machines they make, machine tools also *reproduce* themselves. Thus, at the heart of the industrial health of any nation is its machine tool industry, and for decades this industry was the very badge of U.S. manufacturing prowess. The correspondence between the emergence of the American machine tool industry and the American economy in the twentieth century was no coincidence.

It is also no coincidence that the erosion of the U.S. machine tool industry parallels the decline in domestic manufacturing. In 1965, U.S. tool builders were the most productive anywhere, with more than 28 percent of total worldwide production. By 1986, the U.S. share was less than 10 percent, and foreign manufacturers supplied 49 percent of all the machine tools used in the United States. In five short years, from 1981 to 1986, the number of U.S.

machine tool plants shriveled by one-third because of bankruptcies, take-overs, and reductions in capacity. That figure, moreover, does not include the number of firms that went "hollow," that is, became importers and salesmen for machines produced in Asia and elsewhere.[2]

There is another reason for focusing on the machine tool industry: it typifies the kind of protectionism and trade politics ascendant in the United States, especially during the Reagan presidency. Most trade disputes have a tortured history, but even by that measure the struggle to gain protection for the U.S. machine tool industry was extraordinarily bitter. After temporizing for more than four years, in December 1986 the Reagan administration uni-laterally imposed "voluntary" quotas on imports of machine tools from Japan, Switzerland, Taiwan, and West Germany. The program was similar to pre-vious agreements restricting imports of textiles, steel, and, most prominently, automobiles.

It would not be in keeping with the Cartesian prescription to look at the entire industry. Fortunately, the choice of which company to single out pre-sents itself. Long before the industry as a whole decided to press for import relief, one company, Houdaille Industries, took up the banner against Japa-nese machine tools, the most serious threat to domestic tool builders.

Houdaille (pronounced WHO-dye) was not the largest domestic ma-chine tool company, but it usually ranked among the top twelve in an annual survey conducted by *American Machinist*, the industry trade magazine. In May 1982, Houdaille filed a unique claim for trade relief. The petition asserted that Japan's government, in close concert with industry, had created an inter-national cartel bent on devastating American competitors. Houdaille asked for a presidential finding that would unilaterally brand as "unfair" the Japanese method of organizing their industrial economy, and penalize imports of Japanese tools.

Over the next year, Houdaille Industries, theretofore a little-known, Florida-based corporation, became notorious in Japan. Domestically, the Houdaille petition became the focal point for a titanic struggle between protec-tionists in the Reagan administration (also known as the "Jap-bashers") and the partisans of free trade (called the "White Hats"). The Departments of Defense, Commerce, State, Treasury, Transportation, and Labor, along with the National Security Council, Office of Management and Budget, Central Intelligence Agency, and the president's Special Trade Representative, all participated in the Washington equivalent of trench warfare. The intragovernmental clash was so acrimonious, and Houdaille's claim so novel, that the media and the Congress seized upon the case as well. Houdaille and machine tools became the subject of lead editorials in the *Washington Post* and *New York Times*. Congressmen delivered impassioned speeches on the subject, and half a dozen committees held hearings on the threat posed by Japanese penetration. By the time Reagan rejected Houdaille's petition in April 1983, what began as an obscure trade case had become worthy of its own segment on "60 Minutes."

Reverberations from Houdaille's petition continued long after it was defunct. As U.S. trade frictions with Japan increased, a torrent of books appeared on trade, manufacturing, and competitiveness, and many writers cited the Houdaille petition as evidence for their argument. Most quoted it to demonstrate the fecklessness of U.S. trade policy and Japan's controlled march toward economic domination. Only a few authors took a critical view.[3] The Houdaille case was also one reason why lawmakers became determined to overhaul U.S. trade statutes. In 1987, four years after the petition failed, Houdaille's president, Phillip O'Reilly, was still testifying before Congress.

Houdaille is certainly worth closer scrutiny, if only to examine dispassionately the merits of its unprecedented petition. But the paring down of the original problem is not yet complete. Houdaille was not solely a builder of machine tools, although their manufacture did account for a large portion of the company's business. Rather, Houdaille was a modest conglomerate, with interests in a dozen disparate areas, ranging from construction materials to auto bumpers. Although conglomerate ownership might seem to disqualify Houdaille from consideration, in fact it makes the company all the more appropriate. Such ownership is (or was) a dominant tendency in the machine tool industry. Although some of the larger machine tool companies were not in any other business, most big builders were controlled by larger, parent corporations.

The solution then is to pick one of Houdaille's machine tool companies. Houdaille's machine tool group, as it was called, actually comprised five separate entities: the Burgmaster, Di-Acro, Powermatic, Strippit, and Universal divisions. Of these, only two—Strippit and Burgmaster— were substantial machine tool builders in their own right. Of these two, the Burgmaster Corporation was the division that suffered the most damage from Japanese competition.

Burgmaster was located in Gardena, California, about ten miles south of Los Angeles. It was an unlikely place for a major machine tool builder. Befitting a mature industry, nearly all the large machine tool companies are "east of the Mississippi, and north of the Ohio" rivers. That fact was well known to the forty-eight-year-old Czechoslovakian immigrant named Fred Burg who founded the company in 1944. But entering the machine tool business had been a lifelong dream.

He started the company in his garage, and with the aid of his son and son-in-law built Burgmaster into the largest machine tool company west of the Mississippi by the mid-1960s. Burg's enterprise bore all the attributes of that typically American vision: the rags-to-riches saga of an immigrant who had a better idea. Yet his state-of-the-art company came to a disquieting end. In January 1986, the entire Burgmaster plant was sold at public auction, proof of America's inability to compete. If Burgmaster's rise was a quintessentially American tale, its demise also struck an increasingly familiar chord.

A book about Burgmaster then is not simply the tale of one company. It is also about the destruction of U.S. manufacturing, and the reasons for its failure to innovate and to survive fierce competition in a global economy. There are few, if any villains. Instead, the Burgmaster story reveals a whole system out of kilter: a corporate mind-set that mismanages capable and willing American workers; a government incapable of sustaining a sound economy, leading to a climate where speculation replaces enterprise; and, finally, Wall Street's ability to win big even as a company is being irrevocably damaged.

Everyone acts logically. Only the result is illogical, but unmistakable. The American blueprint for a sound and equitable economy is fading fast.

1
THE FOUNDING OF BURG TOOL
(1943–1954)

F red Burg was a deeply frustrated man in the fall of 1943. He felt like he was wasting his life.

He owned and managed a small department store in Cicero, Illinois. Yet his passion was for all things mechanical. Burg was an inveterate tinkerer and inventor, a man who always had machines and mechanisms on his mind. He sorely missed the beauty of fitting different parts together to produce a predictable result. He only "did dry goods" to support his family, and with great reluctance.[1]

Burg liked to say he was "born a machinist," and figuratively that was true. He had grown up in Czechoslovakia, one of nine children in a poor family. All the children had to learn a trade as soon as possible. And since he liked to play with tools, in 1906, when Burg was ten years old, it was decided he should be apprenticed to a locksmith.

It took some time, however, to find one who would take him on. Back then a locksmith did much more than fix locks and make keys. He had to make everything himself from scratch, which meant he had to forge as well as cut, or machine, metal. Such tradesmen usually wanted husky boys, because their primary job was to feed the fires necessary to make forgings. Burg was short and skinny. But the bigger obstacle was that he was Jewish. Eventually, one locksmith was persuaded to hire him, and Burg quickly proved to be a handy apprentice. He liked to work, and soon the locksmith set up a lower vise just so Burg could use it.

In 1911, when Burg was fifteen years old, he joined the stream of immigrants who were leaving the troubled Austro-Hungarian empire for America. He settled in Chicago, where his father and two sisters were already living, and immediately landed a job in a small factory near an International Harvester plant. He assembled ball bearings. Few Jewish immigrants saw their future in such factory work, but to Burg, being "in the trade" was the most important thing.

He subsequently found better-paying work as a lathe machinist. Burg clearly had an aptitude for taking a raw piece of round metal stock, making the crucial first cut, then another, and another, until the floor was littered with metal shavings and he held a finely honed shaft. A good lathe operator carried a certain status, for he was responsible for making the basic cut from which all other operations were measured. If the first cut was bad, the piece was scrap. Nevertheless, lathe work, or "turning," was just one of many machining skills. Ambitious and talented, Burg worked hard until he was capable of performing all the basic metal-cutting functions, namely, turning, drilling, milling, grinding, and planing.[2]

He did not stop until he mastered the top of his profession: the skills of a tool-and-die maker. Such an appellation was reserved only for those machinists who could produce any part, requiring any combination of machine operations, *and* make any of the tools or dies needed to make the part. In other words, if one of the operations called for a hole to be drilled, Fred Burg could not only drill the hole but also *make* the drill. In an industrial age, no manual skill was more demanding.

It became obvious during these years that Burg's dexterity was exceeded only by his uncommonly inventive mind. Ideally, he would have quit work and gone to engineering school. But that was out of the question. Nevertheless, here and there he began to pick up the rudiments of machine design. While working at Columbia Snap Fasteners, he helped build the first machine designed expressly to make fasteners for clothes. Later, he helped design and manufacture one of the first machines to make zippers.

Marriage and the responsibility of raising his own family took him away from machines in the early 1920s. Some relatives were relatively well-to-do in the dry goods business, the owners of a small chain called the Leader Stores. The business had started as a typical *shmata* (Yiddish for "rag") business, a venture common among newly arrived Jewish immigrants. A basement in one of the stores was not being used, and his relatives persuaded him to open a new department devoted to house furnishings. Reluctantly, Burg agreed. The job promised to pay more than any work he could do with his hands.

Burg proved a capable manager in a competitive trade. The Leader Stores could not hope to rival the fancy displays or special services offered by bigger chains like Marshall Fields. They had to concentrate on selling similar goods for less. Burg learned not only to keep his costs as low as possible but also how to do so. He relied on his employees for suggestions and set a firm example. More than once he picked up a paper clip from the floor so that is could be reused.

Yet the dry goods business never absorbed him, and he often toyed with the idea of leaving. He came close to doing so in the late 1920s, when the Leader chain was sold to the Goldblatt brothers, Jewish immigrants from Poland who were also in the dry goods business. Burg was sorely tempted to use his portion of the proceeds to "get back to the trade." But the Goldblatts wanted him to work for them. Staying in dry goods promised greater security for his family, which by then included a son, Joe, and a daughter, Blanche. So Burg decided to remain.

He did not stay with the Goldblatts for very long. Burg was strong-willed, intense, and opinionated, and could not abide doing something he thought was wrong or inadvisable. The Goldblatts, of course, were intent on asserting their authority, and so a parting of the ways was inevitable after a few years. Burg was left with another chance, or so it seemed, to get back to machines.

By the early 1930s, however, depression gripped the economy and it was no time to take risks. If Burg wanted to work for himself—and that was an absolute condition—he had to stay in the business where his chances of success were best. He opened his own, three-story dry goods store in Cicero, outside Chicago. The soundness of his decision seemed to be confirmed shortly afterward, when Burg fell ill with a mysterious high fever for several weeks. The illness went away just as inexplicably as it had come, except that the thigh muscles in his left leg were permanently atrophied. From then on he had to use a cane to walk. No one would realize for years that he had in fact suffered a mild attack of polio.

For one reason or another, there were always cogent arguments against going back to machines and making things. Burg resigned himself to his fate by using his spare time to invent. Almost every night and most weekends, he puttered around in his garage, trying out ideas that came to mind. One of his early brainstorms was to adapt refrigerator technology to air-condition automobiles. He was stymied when he could not find anyone who manufactured a suitable compressor. He also tinkered with an idea for an electric toothbrush. Failure never bothered him. His interests were so numerous that sometimes it seemed as if his tinkering was not compensation for staying in dry goods, but a way to get out.

The weakness in his left leg prompted one of his best ideas. In the early 1930s, he invented what he called a clutchless "Gear Shifting Mechanism" to obtain different speeds in an automobile—in other words, an automatic transmission. It took more than a year to design, engineer, and painstakingly build the unwieldy mechanism. He even went to night school to learn how to render mechanical drawings. Burg outfitted his own car with the electrically powered automobile shift, taking the three-speed gearbox out of his Hudson Terraplane. On the first test drive the transmission broke down ten blocks from home. Never one to give up, Burg fixed the defect and was soon proudly driving around Chicago without using his left foot. On April 5, 1932, he filed for his first patent.[3]

No American manufacturer was offering anything more advanced than the General Motors "Synchromesh," so Burg tried to get an audience for his invention, hoping to sell it. In 1936, Charles Kettering, the engineering wizard in charge of all industrial research for General Motors, directed his engineers to confer with Burg. They spent hours firing questions at him. He managed them all, but the engineers seemed oddly unimpressed with the accomplishment. After some delay, they finally dismissed the idea as impractical.

In 1938, GM's Oldsmobile division, the most technically advanced in the company, came out with an automatic gearbox as an option. The Oldsmobile version used hydraulic instead of electrical power, but otherwise the concept was quite similar. After that experience, Burg swore "he would not do any more inventing unless he could build it himself." He did not necessarily believe that GM had appropriated his idea, but he thought the GM engineers had treated him disingenuously, at the very least.

To invent and build: that was the desire that nagged at him. By the early 1940s, the industrial economy was thriving again, during a war that depended on machines more than any before it. Yet Burg was playing no part and his tolerance for the compromise of the last twenty years was beginning to erode. He was too far removed from his passion, and he began to dread each day at the dry goods store. That fall, with his son in the army, Burg decided he finally had the opening he needed to make a change.

But what could he do, at the age of forty-seven, to get work with machines? It would be unseemly to trade a profitable store for a worker's hourly wage. The best pretext Burg could muster was retirement. He had saved enough money, he explained to inquiring family and friends, to quit working and move to a hospitable climate. He intended to indulge his love for machines by tinkering in his free time.

With the full support of his wife, Erna, Burg sold all his stock to a rival merchant and made arrangements to move to California. On December 15, 1943, he closed his department store for the last time. To Burg, leaving in the middle of a retailer's busiest season simply underscored his determination and liberation.

No one who knew Fred Burg believed that he was genuinely headed for retirement. He had too much energy and ambition, although it was far from clear where it would lead. He chose Los Angeles for his family's new home, partly because his sister Vilma lived there, partly because of its climate. In addition, it had a booming war economy. That meant machines and, to Burg, opportunity, however vague.

Many people come to Los Angeles to make movies. Fred Burg came to make machines.

Retirement lasted all of four months. Although Burg had claimed he had enough money to retire on, it soon became apparent that he did not. The path was now clear for him to seek work as a machinist. Given wartime demand, he had no difficulty finding a job as a tool-and-die maker. He began working at Hydro-Air, a small Hollywood company that had a government contract to produce mounts for grenade launchers. Fred Burg had surrendered his own business, and a clean one at that, for a dirty job in a noisy factory, where he had to punch a clock. But he was "back to the trade" after more than twenty years, and nothing mattered more.

One day, an idea came to him while he was setting up a lathe to ream a hold. Reaming was always the second step in making an exact hole in a piece of round metal stock. First, the hole had to be drilled slightly undersized; then the lathe operator had to use a reamer, which was more precise than a drill, to enlarge the hole to the required dimension.

The problem was that in the process of changing tools, from a drill to a reamer, a lathe operator could cause a slight misalignment. And if the reamer was not centered precisely on the axis of the hole, it would vibrate uncontrollably once it was brought to bear. A latheman who did not spend time making sure that no misalignment occurred was likely to produce a lot of scrap metal.

Burg conceived of a fist-sized tool holder that would grip the reamer, and be gripped by the lathe in turn, rather than having the lathe hold the reamer directly. His device would grasp the reamer firmly enough for machining, but a rubber or neoprene sleeve inside would allow sufficient play for the reamer to move, and automatically correct any slight misalignment. The reamer, in a sense, would "float" in the tool holder, so Burg dubbed his device the "Floating Tool Holder."

Several manufacturers already produced tool-holding mechanisms that accomplished the same thing. But all of them were complicated, expensive devices that needed careful maintenance. Burg's design was breathtakingly simple by comparison. Initially Hydro-Air permitted him to use their machines for his private endeavor, but eventually Burg had to work in his own garage. He bought an old but usable lathe to fashion the metal parts. Mrs. Burg, working in the kitchen, made the rubber sleeves. By July 1944, he was so confident his device would work that he applied for a patent.

And it did work—but not sufficiently well to sell in an industry that depends on precision and reliability. Undaunted, Burg worked to perfect his device until it reamed the forty-eighth hole as accurately as it reamed the first. He renamed the new, more durable version the "Flexible Tool Holder," or "Tool-flex," and began producing them in his garage at night and on weekends.[4]

He was not only the inventor and manufacturer but also the salesman. His years in the dry goods business had made him almost as good a salesman as he was a machinist. He hauled a suitcase full of the devices around to every manufacturer who used a lathe, from small "job" machine shops to massive aircraft companies. When he could not demonstrate the Tool-flex himself, he left a brochure. The orders began to pile up once machine shop foremen realized how much time could be saved by using a Tool-flex. Burg quit his job at Hydro-Air, and by early 1945 was in business for himself, turning out Tool-flexes that were snapped up as fast as he could make them.

The end of the war freed two servicemen Burg was determined to recruit for his growing business: Joe, his son, and Norm Ginsburg, a Chicago native who had married his daughter, Blanche, in September 1944. It took some convincing because neither one had worked as a machinist, studied engineering, or had any particular interest in machines. Both men, in fact, were planning to use the G.I. Bill to finish their college educations. Joe Burg had been a forestry major at the University of Illinois, and Ginsburg had completed three years of college in business administration.

No matter. The "old man," as he was called by both men, was not to be denied, not when he was so close to realizing his long-deferred ambition. The Burg family was close-knit, and still followed many European customs, including the notion that the patriarch was the final and absolute authority. Once Burg expressed his desire, it was almost inconceivable for either son or son-in-law to defy him. Nevertheless, it took some "hell-raising" before both men agreed to join the fledgling venture. Burg promised to release them if things did not work out within a year or two.

Within a few weeks of their discharge, both men and their wives moved into the Burgs' home in Hollywood. The garage no longer served as the factory for the Burg Tool Manufacturing Company, as Fred Burg dubbed his growing concern. He had rented a double garage in Florence, an industrial section of the city fifteen miles away. The three men drove in one car to the shop at 67th and San Pedro, ate sandwiches prepared at home for lunch, and worked six-day weeks. There was a large backlog of orders to fill.

The first few months of 1946 were the hardest. In addition to running the business, Fred Burg had to teach his new employees. Ginsburg became the first machinist to work for him, and the old man flattered his son-in-law by exclaiming that he ran a lathe "like he was born to it." Joe Burg learned to operate a small milling machine, and began to draw different Tool-flex designs under his father's tutelage. Blanche Ginsburg kept the books. Meanwhile, Fred Burg kept making his sales rounds. That was the one job that could not be entrusted to someone with little experience.

Even with the end of the war, Burg Tool's business kept burgeoning. By mid-1946 the company needed more machinists, and a few more used machines to keep pace with all the orders that were coming in. The Burgs began talking about finding a larger site for their machine shop. The lack of room was so acute, though, that it also set the old man to thinking about the time and space aspects of drilling holes in metal.

The problem was that no drilling machine could make more than one kind of hole at a time. All the power of the machine was harnessed to drive a single spindle, and that spindle could only grip one tool at a time.[5] Tools, of course, were expressly designed to be attached and detached so that the machinist could choose the most suitable one, in size or purpose, for the task at hand. The detachable quality also allowed worn tools to be sharpened, or replaced if broken. The seemingly unavoidable result, however, was that a machinist had to change the tool in the spindle five times if he was drilling five different-sized holes in a workpiece.

To a layman, changing tools might seem the most time-consuming aspect of a single-spindle drill. But as every machinist knew, the far greater problem was the single-spindle's effect on that inescapable factor in machining, namely, setup time. This term encompasses all the laborious preparations that have to be made prior to forcing metal against metal. Since every drill press (like all machine tools) performs its task by bringing to bear, with great force, a cutting tool on a workpiece, the latter has to be rigidly mounted and precisely aligned. Setting up is the most taxing aspect of machining, but has to be done to ensure accuracy, or "staying within tolerance" in machinist's jargon. Invariably, it takes longer to set up a part than to machine it. The inherent limitations of the single-spindle drill inevitably pushed the number of setups to the maximum in any production run of mass-produced parts. That's why drilling machines were often the cause of production bottlenecks.

Suppose a machinist needed to make the same five different-sized holes in twenty-five identical parts. The standard solution was to have five separate runs of all twenty-five parts. After each run the tool, or drill bit, would be changed, and a new setup made. This procedure was a verity of the trade that everyone followed, because it was the fastest and most accurate way to mass-produce the required parts. But it required loading each part onto the drilling machine five times. There was just no better way to do it.

For greater efficiency, a machine shop with five drilling machines might dedicate each to one of the five holes. But that was a costly alternative, reserved for factories with a lot of space, manpower, and money, and did not alter the procedure except to speed it up. All this made Burg think that if somehow more than one tool could be employed by a drilling machine, with no loss in accuracy, then the number of setups could be reduced drastically. The savings in time and money would be so dramatic that the potential market for such a machine would be vast.

He was brooding about this problem one day in early 1946 while he was selling the Tool-flex. Visiting one shop, he saw a turret lathe, and it suddenly dawned on him: here was the answer to his problem. What he had to do was adapt the concept of a turret lathe to a drill press. A turret lathe allowed its operator to switch tools, once the cutting tool was disengaged from the workpiece, simply by rotating the turret, a circular block that gripped several tools, usually six or eight, at one end of the lathe. In this manner, several tools could be brought to bear in rapid succession. Indeed, in the hands of a skilled machinist, this very feature created a fluidity of movement that seemed almost choreographed.

Fred Burg rushed back to Burg Tool, and called his son out of the office. "What would you say if you had a turret on a drill press?" he asked excitedly. Without waiting for an answer, and over considerable protest, he began to dismantle one of the shop's old turret lathes, all the while thinking about how he would reengineer its insides.

There was a considerable difference between the turret he had in hand and the one he had in mind. The turret from a lathe was a relatively unsophisticated mechanism, because its main function was to hold the tools rigidly. The turret he envisioned was far more complicated. A drill press operated on precisely the opposite principle from a lathe: on a drill press the workpiece was always stationary, and the tool revolved. This meant that the turret for a drill would have to be capable not only of gripping six tools but also of using the motor to drive each one. Moreover, it would have to do so while being as rigid and accurate as an ordinary drill press of equivalent size. In sum, the old man's idea represented no small engineering feat.

Working from a few rudimentary sketches, the Burgs painstakingly began to manufacture a prototype. As an intermediate step, they built a model out of wood. That was an easier material to work with, and allowed them to identify basic design flaws. Next came the metal prototype. They could not afford to order one-of-a-kind castings for the new machine, so they welded pieces of metal together when necessary. Throughout, the engineering progressed by trial and error; when something they thought would work did not, they simply remachined or, when necessary, redesigned the failing part.

In the midst of their ambitious project, the Burgs moved in the spring of 1946 to larger quarters, a thousand-square-foot shop near La Brea and Jefferson. They needed more room regardless of whether or not the turret drill panned out, and signed a five-year lease. More space allowed Burg Tool to hire two additional machinists, and a trained engineer who could help it develop the turret drill.

By late 1946 the prototype was finished. It had taken about ten months from conception to the first working model. It resembled, more or less, a common drill press except for a round turret, smack in the middle of the machine, which radiated tools in six different directions. There seemed little doubt that the old man's idea was workable. But now, having overcome that first hurdle, Burg Tool faced two others that were just as high: could Burg Tool make the machine, and would it sell?

Building an entire machine tool promised to be far more taxing than manufacturing the fist-sized Tool-flex. It would be a complicated and risky venture, one that would doubtless require going into debt and demand even harder work and longer hours. Moreover, even if Burg Tool proved capable of building a reliable machine that reduced setup time, there was no guarantee of a market. In the aftermath of the war, the industry's outlook was exceedingly bleak. More machine tools had been manufactured during the five years of war than had been produced during the previous forty years, and almost half were owned by the government. [6] Manufacturers who needed machine tools could obtain them from the U.S. government at bargain prices. In addition, the glut was compounded by excess production capacity among the long-established machine tool builders. The year 1946 was certainly not auspicious for a tiny, inexperienced, geographically isolated company to introduce a new product. The competition for whatever business did exist would be brisk, to put it mildly.

Albeit reluctantly, Fred Burg finally accepted these facts. With the livelihood of three families at stake, he agreed that the best course was to sell his invention to an established machine tool builder. He personally traveled back East to offer the turret drill to two of the premier companies in the industry: Giddings & Lewis, and the Cincinnati Milling Machine Company, often referred to as the General Motors of machine tools. For $25,000 both companies were offered all the manufacturing and patent rights to the turret drill.[7] Burg intended to use the proceeds to develop something a little less complicated to manufacture.

To Burg's chagrin, his invention generated little interest. The industry was on the cusp of a depression, with no end in sight, and the two companies apparently decided that the climate was too forbidding to undertake even a small risk. The younger partners in the venture called Burg Tool were merely disappointed. But Fred Burg was mad. Unlike most of his previous inventions, the turret drill was an innovation in an industry he knew. He had absolutely no doubt that the machine represented a significant advance, and he was asking a pittance for it. Burg imagined, rightly or wrongly, that his unhappy experience with General Motors was about to be repeated. In two or three years' time, Giddings & Lewis or Cincinnati would proudly announce and begin marketing a turret drill.

Burg resolved to build it after all, paying no heed to the machine tool economy, the difficulties inherent in manufacturing a precision tool, or his family's reservations.

Many years later, he would recall that if he had had any idea in 1946 of what was involved, "I would have been scared. But [instead] I was crazy." He borrowed $5,000 from his sister Vilma for working capital, and began to call on prospective customers. Ever the salesman, he decided he had to leave them with a memorable name for his yet-to-be-built turret drill. He printed sales brochures that promised to "master your drilling," so he advertised the machine as the "Drillmaster" and pledged to deliver it within a few months.

In mid-1947, the first machine, dubbed the "1A" model, was delivered to Beckman Instruments, a Pasadena-based manufacturer of scientific instruments. For a time, not a week went by without a trip to Pasadena to fix the first Drillmaster. The recurrent problem was getting the six-spindle turret drill to operate as reliably as a conventional, turretless, single-spindle drill press. "That was the trick," recalled Fred Burg, "to get accuracy out of six positions." But no setback, as usual, was ever sufficient to stop him. Eventually, the 1A achieved a tolerable level of reliability.

Throughout 1947 and 1948 orders for the turret drill only trickled in, and all three families continued to depend on profits from the Tool-flex. But Burg Tool survived, and it would soon thrive. For Fred Burg had unwittingly perpetuated one of the machine tool industry's oldest traditions: that of the lone inventor, who takes previously disparate elements and fuses them together in a classical and enduring combination.[8] In a few years, the same companies that had disdained his invention would ask to buy Fred Burg's company.

There are few branches of engineering, an Englishman once wrote, that are as attractive to a "mechanical enthusiast" as the building of machine tools: "though monetary reward may be inadequate, the continual overcoming of constantly increasing difficulties introduces an element of excitement and even of sport into the trade."[9]

Fred Burg had plenty of "grease in his blood," and no one enjoyed the challenges of the trade more. His advertising slogan, and preferred name for his turret drill, however, had run into a slight problem. A company that made hand drills already called its product the Drillmaster. So the old man promptly decided on a new name, one that reflected his fierce pride and was sure to be unique. He renamed the turret drill the "Burgmaster."

By 1949, the machine was finding ready acceptance by a diverse market, including aircraft parts manufacturers, textile machinery builders, and automotive parts suppliers.[10] Fred Burg overcame sales resistance by promising to back up his turret drills no matter what service problems arose. The biggest breakthrough occurred early that year, when he sold a Burgmaster to a Cleveland tool builder. It was tough to sell in the East because no one in the industry had much confidence in California products. Burg celebrated by getting drunk, because it meant he no longer would have to face skepticism about his young company.

Burg Tool's growth could not be labeled spectacular, except, perhaps, in comparison to the general depression afflicting the machine tool industry. In the three years since its founding in 1946, the number of machinists employed by Burg Tool had doubled, and the company now had an engineering department, consisting of one engineer and a secretary. Norm Ginsburg was no longer a lathe operator, but in charge of all manufacturing. Joe Burg oversaw sales and engineering. As for Fred Burg, his hand was felt in every aspect of the company.

By the spring of 1949, although the lease on the factory still had two more years to go, conditions were so cramped that Burg Tool had to find a larger space again, even if it meant buying out the lease. More space was necessary because Fred Burg was intent on completely redesigning the 1A model. He wanted to beef up the machine in dozens of ways, and make a new model that was more durable and capable of heavier tasks. The basic patent covering the Burgmaster, a "Machine Tool of the Drill Press Type Having Multiple Rotary Tools," was pending.[11] That protected Burg Tool's head start, but the old man had no intention of standing pat. The Burgmaster's potential was far from being fully exploited.

Burg Tool found a suitable building that was five times larger and just a few miles away, on Durango Avenue near Venice Boulevard. The week before the move was scheduled, the old man, then fifty-three, suddenly became sick and doctors were unable to diagnose the problem. All responsibility abruptly fell upon the junior partners, Norm Ginsburg and Joe Burg. They accomplished the move themselves, and to everyone's relief, Fred Burg recovered almost as quickly as he had been taken ill. But the episode left a lasting impression. It underscored, more than ever before, the fragility of the whole enterprise. The junior partners knew that without the old man, no matter how hard they worked, the Burg Tool Manufacturing Company could not survive.

With Burg Tool intact, however, there was every reason to be optimistic about the future. By early 1950, there were faint signs that the industry might be breaking out of its postwar doldrums. Several factors were contributing to the recovery, but the biggest shot in the arm was coming from military spending.

Following the end of World War II, the Truman administration had initially adopted the belief that America's atomic bomb monopoly would allow the government to keep a lid on the military budget.[12] That pleased no one more than Truman himself, who viewed military spending with a suspicious eye, dating back to his years as wartime chairman of the Senate Committee to Investigate the National Defense Program. He had in fact achieved his national reputation through the Truman Committee's exposure of military corruption and waste.

Yet, beginning in 1948, U.S. military spending began to rise. One important reason was interservice rivalries. The 1947 unification of the armed services, into a single Department of Defense, was supposed to reduce spending by eliminating duplication. Instead, bitter internal struggles persisted, albeit with a new twist. Rather than agreeing on how to divide their slice of the federal pie within the walls of the Pentagon, the services began to submit a unified claim for a larger slice.

The pressure within the government had a complement without: a vigorous campaign by the economically depressed aircraft industry to increase spending. Postwar civilian demand had turned out to be far less than anticipated, and aircraft manufacturers realized their industry needed military procurement. "The U.S. aircraft industry turns out to have only one effective customer—the Armed services of the national government," wrote *Fortune* magazine in early 1948.[13] Although the industry extolled the virtues of free enterprise, its business leaders nevertheless concluded that they could not remain solvent without a market underwritten by the government.

These two domestic factors coincided with an external circumstance, namely, the cold war. In 1949, two events of great moment occurred. First, Mao Tse-tung's forces seized power in China. Almost simultaneously, U.S.

visions of an atomic monopoly dissipated when the Soviet Union successfully tested its first A-bomb in late August 1949. With that explosion much of Truman's reluctance about military spending evaporated. In the wake of what was perceived as two terrible reverses, he ordered the State and Defense departments to reassess U.S. military strategy.

Military expenditures began to revive America's industrial might and, inexorably, the machine tool industry. The $1 billion Mutual Defense Assistance Program, designed to put military muscle in NATO, increased domestic production of military goods, and manufacturers began to order new machine tools. In April 1950, the industry received another boost when it was announced, in the interest of military preparedness, that "several thousand industrial plants now had explicit go-ahead agreements for production of war materials [and] that the number would be doubled by September 1st." That same month new machine tool orders, the best indicator of demand, reached a level last seen in 1945.[14]

Secretary of State Dean Acheson justified the emerging militancy of the United States by stating publicly that the only way to deal with the Soviet Union was to "create situations of strength." This public vow was secretly fleshed out in NSC-68, the classified result of Truman's request for a wholesale review of U.S. strategy. The study called for a global military presence and sharply higher military expenditures. Truman was still struggling over how to sell this proposal to Congress when a civil war broke out in Korea in June 1950. After that, the question no longer was how much the government could afford, but where to spend the military dollar.

To the general public, the evidence of military expenditures was in the manufactures pouring out of arsenals, weapons factories, and aircraft plants. Yet no industry felt the reverberations from Korea more than machine tools. "U.S. aircraft production lines are undergoing a tremendous and costly reorganization to meet the huge armament program," declared *Aviation Week* magazine in December 1950. Retooling meant new and more sophisticated machine tools. Almost overnight, the industry was expected to "race into high gear," as the Senate Small Business Committee put it two years later.[15]

The federal government's neglect of the industry now turned into an obsession about its health. At the outbreak of the Korean War, a machine tool shortage was not expected. Builders had plenty of idle capacity, and the government still had thousands of tools in reserve, even after years of selling off surplus machines. But 45 percent of the tools were more than ten years old, and to its dismay, the government found that

> existing tools [are] not adequate or satisfactory for new weapon production. The tools of 1940 [are] unable to manufacture the armament of 1950, particularly in the aircraft field, where jet engines [are] supplanting the piston type.[16]

As a consequence, new orders almost trebled overnight, and the ratio of unfilled orders to shipments rose from five to one, to twelve to one by December 1950. During World War II, machine tool production had been a serious problem, but the backlog had never exceeded thirteen months. Now machine tool production emerged as the "No. 1 bottleneck" in the war economy. By September 1951 there was a two-year wait for new machines.[17]

The crisis prompted the government to institute several programs to aid wartime production. Machine tool builders were given first call for scarce raw materials, and the "pool-order" program, which had worked successfully during World War II, was reinstated. The government again ensured that every machine made for a defense contractor would be purchased, even if the emergency ceased. The government also encouraged machine tool builders to expand their facilities. Firms that were willing to do so were granted accelerated depreciation on any new tools they acquired. Lastly, the government purchased new machines and leased them to builders. All told, the government's machine tool effort, in dollar value, became the largest single transaction authorized by the Defense Production Act of 1950.[18]

Along with hundreds of other builders, Burg Tool bought new machines to take advantage of the accelerated depreciation rates. But that was hardly the most significant change brought about by the war. Demand for virtually every machine tool was high, but especially for Burgmasters because of the increase in productivity they represented over conventional drilling machines. It is doubtful that any machine tool builder felt the war more than Burg Tool, although many were hit just as hard.

That the new "2A" model was entering production just as the surge began was a fortunate coincidence, or perhaps an instance of luck being the residue of design. Depending on the exact machining requirements, a Burgmaster 2A could produce the same number of mass-produced parts in 35 to 50 percent less time than a single-spindle drill. The Burgs' new factory on Durango, which had seemed almost cavernous in 1949 when they moved in, was bursting with activity—and thirty employees—a year later. Whereas Burg Tool had struggled to obtain a $10,000 loan from its bank a year earlier, suddenly another banker was willing to extend a $50,000 line of credit. Burgmasters became available nationally, through dealers or the manufacturer's representatives in the all-important cities of Cleveland, New York, and Chicago.

Nothing illustrated the hectic pace dictated by the war more than the sale of a 2A model to Kenyon Instrument Company on Long Island. In late January 1953, Kenyon placed a rush order for the machine, and in a month a standard 2A was ready for shipment. To Burg Tool's surprise, however, Kenyon then asked for the machine to be transported via air freight rather than rail—a costly and unheard-of undertaking, since the shipping weight was 1,925 pounds. Subsequently, a letter from Kenyon's president arrived, which began,

"The Burgmaster . . . arrived at our plant March 2nd and by noon on Tuesday, March 3rd, it was producing finished parts."

You may be curious as to why we asked you for the earliest possible delivery on the machine and also as to why we specified air freight shipment.

Late in January one of the largest producers of military aircraft in this country, for whom we make hydraulic control system assemblies, requested that we accelerate our delivery schedules to them by more than 50 percent starting in March. It so happened that the parts in question were not subject to subcontract, and at the same time our own machine shop was loaded almost to capacity. However, something had to be done, and fast. We gave the problem to our Production Control and Methods people, and in a few hours they came up with the answer that the schedules could be met provided we could get delivery on a Burgmaster Turret Drill early in March.

The rest of the story you know.[19]

The exigencies of war also forced Burg Tool to mature in one very important sense. Within the industry, one truism is that the easiest and surest profit comes from extended production runs of standard models. And Burg Tool was proving quite capable of cranking out virtually identical machines very quickly. But to be considered a significant machine tool builder, a company had to be able to meet requests for machines tailored to special needs.

During the war, for the first time customers came to Burg Tool for specially adapted versions of the 2A turret drill. Satisfying such requests represented whole new areas of risk. Making a machine according to unusual specifications meant tying up Burg Tool's best engineers and machinists. In addition, customized machines also carried the risk of not being profitable, or at least less profitable, if unforeseen engineering or machining problems arose.

One of the first special orders came from Boeing in Seattle. The aircraft manufacturer requested a 2A mounted on a carriage one hundred feet long so that the Burgmaster could drill holes in spars, the long lateral pieces that make up an airplane's framework.[20] This "special" taxed Burg Tool's small engineering and machining departments to their limits. But it was critical to respond for at least two reasons. For one, success was likely to breed more sales to Boeing. In addition, building to a customer's specifications forced the engineering department to innovate and the machine shop to develop its expertise. Such development was pivotal if Burg Tool was to grow and stay at the cutting edge of the machine tool industry.

No one was more convinced of the need to constantly innovate than the consummate inventor within the company, Fred Burg. In the midst of the wartime boom, he insisted that it was time to upgrade the 2A machine. The "2B" incorporated several changes that improved accuracy and durability. Most important, with a few additional parts, the 2B could be converted from a manual to a fully automatic "2BH" machine that employed hydraulic power. The chief advantage to hydraulic control was that it reduced operator fatigue and improved quality and productivity. A machinist running a 2BH was less prone to spoil parts because he would be far less tired near the end of the working day. No sooner was the 2BH in production than Burg began another project. He wanted to build a new model that had eight spindles in the turret instead of six.

By mid-1951, for the third time in five years, it was obvious that Burg Tool had to move. Not only was the Durango factory too cramped to fill the number of orders pouring in, it also did not have the room or the necessary facilities to manufacture the new machines the old man had in mind. He dreamed of building larger, better machines with moving tables, columns, and heads. To do so, he needed a larger engineering department, more and bigger machine tools to manufacture the new models, and more machinists. Such plans also entailed special facilities, designed specifically to accommodate the needs of a machine tool builder: a hoist, for example, to lift heavy castings from one machine to another; special wiring, to meet the high-voltage requirements of modern machine tools; and reinforced concrete floors, to bear the weight of the massive machines.

About the same time, the Burg family began thinking about the nature of their ownership of Burg Tool, and whether it made sense to change it. The three men were legal, though unequal, partners in their private enterprise, Joe Burg and Norm Ginsburg having become minority partners in 1950.[21] They hired a business consultant, who explained to them that it made sense to incorporate. This would allow them to retain more of their earnings for reinvestment, thus reducing Burg Tool's dependency on bank loans for which all the partners had to sign personally. Following his advice, the company became Burg Tool Manufacturing Company, Inc., in mid-1951.

After incorporation, they searched for land on which to build a new factory. In November, a suitable plot was located in an industrial section of Gardena, a suburb located about ten miles south of downtown Los Angeles. Burg Tool purchased the site on Figueroa Street for $18,000, and in 1952 hired an architect to draw up plans. The new factory was to be a twenty-thousand-square-foot facility—four times the size of the Durango plant. It took two years and $70,000 to build the new plant. It was ready for occupancy by late June 1954, and the Burgs prepared to move in over the Fourth of July weekend.

Ordinarily, the prospect of moving into a building expressly designed for Burg Tool would have been cause for celebration. Yet on moving day the Burgs felt the opposite. The machine tool industry had suddenly fallen into another slump, precipitated by the armistice in the Korean War. Half of the company's seventy employees had just been laid off. Even more worrisome, there was exactly *one* unfilled order on the books. Machinists and engineers still working there began to think about other job possibilities. And the Burgs rued the coincidence of their expansion with the industrywide recession.

Fred Burg tried to gloss over the uncertainty. He was prepared to alter a few facts if he thought it might encourage sales and dispel any rumors about his company's ill-timed expansion. In advertisements and statements to the press, the founding of the company was pushed back a few years, to 1942. The cost of the new plant and equipment was inflated to $300,000. And the nameplate on the prototype of the turret drill, now prominently displayed in the lobby of the new factory, read "First Burgmaster, 1943 Model." Burg was trying everything to make his company look older, and more stable.[22]

Years later, the Burgs and their employees would smile and joke about the inauspicious beginning on Figueroa. Many would recall it by repeating an anecdote that was perhaps apocryphal. Supposedly, just before the movers arrived, Fred Burg stood in the middle of his new plant, his voice echoing as he exclaimed, "What are we going to do with all this space?"

He need not have worried. On Figueroa, Burg Tool would succeed beyond even his ambitious dreams.

2
SUCCESS STORY (1954–1959)

The downturn after the Korean War lasted little more than two years, in contrast to the four-year slump following World War II. Nor was the decline nearly as steep. Demand for nonmilitary manufactured goods, especially automobiles, kept orders for machine tools from plummeting too far.[1] But another critical factor was the manner in which the government reduced its surplus stock of machine tools. Here, the Pentagon, Congress, and the industry exercised decisive influence, so as not to repeat the post–World War II debacle.

Many generals, most notably Dwight Eisenhower, had bitterly criticized the government for allowing the industry to fall into a prolonged recession in the late 1940s. Writing in the midst of the Korean War, Eisenhower observed:

> There seems to be a bad shortage of machine tools. When we get over this emergency I am going to take as one element of my personal ambitions, that of preaching of the need for machine tools as part of military preparation until some d— administration will take the necessary measures. I've heard the same story time after time and it seems to me we should learn.[2]

The Senate also held hearings during the war, and in 1952 the Small Business Committee issued a blistering report on machine tool shortages caused by official thoughtlessness:

> In retrospect, one of the gravest errors of the past decade, insofar as American Industry is concerned, and one in which many must share the blame, was the program to liquidate surplus machine tools after World War II. The almost promiscuous abandon with which they were distributed should have warned responsible officials of the dangers inherent in such a program. It should have been apparent that the flooding of the country with machine tools at 20 cents on the dollar and the loading of

real and pseudoeducational institutions with expensive high-production equipment at 5 cents and less on the dollar would dry up the machine tool market for years to come.[3]

This wartime criticism prodded the government to institute a careful procedure once it came time to dispose of surplus machine tools from its $6 billion stock. After the Korean armistice in 1953, the Defense Department, machine tool builders, and users cooperated to minimize the adverse impact of the surplus. A reprise of 1946–1947, when government-owned machine tools were sold for a fraction of their cost, simply did not occur.[4]

The government Office of Defense Mobilization, acting under the Defense Production Act of 1950, also extended some government incentives far beyond the end of hostilities in Korea. For one, the government bought about $100 million worth of machine tools in 1954, and another $100 million worth in 1955. Although the purchases were not enough to prevent a decline in shipments, undoubtedly they helped the industry weather the postwar decrease in orders until civilian demand picked up the slack, beginning in 1956.[5]

Along with other builders, Burg Tool rebounded in the mid-1950s. But its revival began before and far outpaced that of the industry as a whole. From 1954 to 1955, net sales almost exactly doubled, from $574,000 to $1,142,000, and net income rose 80 percent, from $35,000 to $63,000. In fact, 1955 marked the beginning of a decade of spectacular growth. By 1964, sales reached $7.4 million, thirteen times the 1955 figure, and Burg Tool employed more than 275 persons, up from 62.[6]

During this decade, the Burgs were besieged by offers from some of the most prestigious companies in the machine tool industry, builders like Giddings & Lewis, Kearney & Trecker, and Ex-Cell-O. All of them, at one time or another, inquired about whether or not the Burgs were interested in selling out.[7] They always refused. Instead, they concentrated on building the company, and the Figueroa plant underwent two major expansions. About 22,000 square feet was added in 1960, and 30,000 square feet in 1962, to accommodate the ever-growing needs of the engineering and machining departments.[8]

Several factors accounted for the unrelieved success of the decade, but none was more important than the product itself. The demand for Burgmaster turret drills was so constant that Burg Tool defied the cyclical, boom-and-bust nature that has long characterized the industry. With the exception of 1958, when a recession cast a pall over the whole economy, Burg Tool grew every year, even when orders were down or stagnant in the rest of the industry.[9] When the economy grew, manufacturers naturally wanted a Burgmaster to increase production. And when the economy slowed, manufacturers still put in orders because a Burgmaster promised to lower production costs dramatically. In effect, Burgmasters created "replacement" demand in companies that ordinarily would have used older or outmoded machine tools.[10] The savings from multiple tools on one machine was that persuasive.

The overwhelming logic of the multiple-tool concept, however, was not the only force behind Burg Tool's rapid growth from 1954 onward. An instrumental factor was the way the Burgs ran their enterprise, that is, how they managed. There were two main aspects to their management: how the three men worked together and how they treated the people who worked for them.

The old man as everyone now called Fred Burg, set the overall tone, and his basic approach never wavered. It was "hands-on," and nothing escaped his attention. He could do as much as, or more than, anyone else in the machine shop or engineering department, and was not adverse to rolling up his sleeves and doing it.

Just below his dominating presence were Joe Burg and Norm Ginsburg. Each was an extension of the old man in a sense, for each represented a distinct half of his makeup. Well aware of their different abilities, the old man designated his son, Joe, as Mr. Outside, and his son-in-law, Norm Ginsburg, as Mr. Inside.

Joe Burg had inherited his father's penchant for risk taking and salesmanship. "He was a bloody optimist not afraid to try," recalled Bob French, who began working at Burg Tool in 1954. Although Joe's style was probably not suited to all aspects of the company, it proved invaluable in the two departments he was responsible for: sales and engineering. He repeatedly obligated the company to develop something new because a customer wanted it. "Joe kept everyone really reaching," said Bob French. "He would have a machine sold before we even knew whether we could do it or not." If a company asked about a delivery date, Joe would respond, "When do you want it?" If a customer asked how a Burgmaster sized up against a competitor's machine, he answered, "Ours is better."[11]

His opposite in many ways was Norm Ginsburg. He was responsible for the manufacturing end of the business, from the purchase of castings and new machine tools for the machine shop, to assembly and quality control of finished Burgmasters. If Joe Burg was garrulous, Ginsburg was decidedly taciturn. He mirrored the old man's practical down-to-earth side, the one that made him weigh the risks carefully before spending money. He also followed, literally, Fred Burg's hands-on approach to manufacturing. At the end of the working day, Ginsburg's hands were invariably as dirty as any in the machine shop.

The working relationship among the three men was not a page taken from a storybook. There were occasional tensions and many disagreements, stemming from the dissimilar perspectives and needs of the departments they respectively managed. But the differences were creative ones, and honestly resolved. "The Burgs did the most arguing—the only good place they could argue—was the engineering department," recalled Bob French. "I swore more than once that one of them was ready to cold-cock [unexpectedly hit] the other in the middle of their heated arguments. Then the old man would look at his watch, say it's time for lunch, and the three of them would go off together as if nothing had happened."[12]

Engineering was the logical place to air differences because the department was the focal point for contrasting views. Ginsburg, reflecting a manufacturing bias and his more cautious personality, believed that Burg Tool should concentrate on producing standard bread-and-butter machines. Specials tended to clog up both engineering and manufacturing, he argued, and ought to be undertaken sparingly, when business was slower or when the modifications promised to attract new customers. Joe Burg just as convincingly argued the opposite. Any company that put in a special order was willing to pay a handsome premium, he noted. Besides, engineering and manufacturing had to be pushed constantly for the company to grow.

The final decision always rested with the old man. After Joe Burg explained his sale of a machine that had never been designed, much less made, Ginsburg would lay out all the reasons for turning down the order. Burg would turn to his father, knowing his tendency to accept a challenge and his fierce pride in the machines that carried his name. Joe would ask, "Do you want to turn down that order?" "Well," the old man would respond, hesitating. Usually that would be followed by, "I don't want to hear any more arguments. I just want to hear how we are going to do it."[13]

Burg Tool was committed. And the next day, after the wheels had been turning all night, the old man would come in with an idea. It might have a touch of Rube Goldberg, but his engineers would iron out any problems. And despite his initial, vehement protest, Ginsburg would find a way to deliver what Joe Burg had promised. "We got in some pretty tight spots," remembered Bob French, "but there were few times that the company got hurt." Far more often, "we did things *we* did not even believe we could do."[14]

The manufacture of the first "bridge" machine in 1960 typified Burg Tool's capacity for innovation. That year the National Machine Tool Exposition was scheduled to be held in Chicago. Eleven months before the exhibition, the old man called a meeting and told everyone that he intended to display a new machine at the Chicago show, the biggest Burgmaster ever made. This variation would feature a turret drill mounted on a bridge (a square, upside-down U shape), with a table that moved longitudinally between the pillars of the bridge.

The sales and engineering departments recognized that such a design promised to be very rigid, and therefore accurate, and might easily attract wide interest because of its versatility. It would be capable of light milling operations because of its rigidity, in addition to the usual drilling, boring, reaming, and tapping operations. But at the same time, the bridge machine presented an entirely new range of engineering and manufacturing difficulties. Burg Tool had never made a five-foot traveling table, let alone a bridge on which a turret drill moved vertically and horizontally. The risk was all the greater because no one had even ordered such a machine. It was being undertaken solely because the old man wanted to make a mark at the Chicago show, and was convinced that the bridge machine was the way to do it. He just "hoped like hell" that the machine would be sold during the exhibition.[15]

The bridge machine was designed, engineered, machined, and assembled in eleven months. "They were tightening the screws on it as it was going down the freeway" on its way to Chicago, recalled Bob French. Not only did the show model find a buyer, the bridge machine proved to be one of Burg Tool's most successful adaptations of the turret drill concept.[16]

With Joe Burg as dreamer, Norm Ginsburg as the voice of caution, and the old man as final arbiter, the three men were an effective, if at times contentious, triumvirate. Success, nevertheless, obviously required much more than their own efforts. The Burgs' entrepreneurial spirit could not have prospered without the relationship they nurtured between management and labor.

Maintaining a dedicated, capable work force was a prime consideration for every machine tool builder. The entire industry depended on the most skilled manual labor. Yet no builder had a more acute problem in this respect than Burg Tool because it operated in an adverse environment. Indeed, it was hard to imagine a worse place to locate a machine tool company than Los Angeles.[17]

It wasn't that good machinists or engineers were not available in Southern California. Quite the reverse. The problem was weaning them away from the aircraft (later aerospace) industry, which paid far higher salaries. Burg Tool could never hope to compete with these wage scales and remain in business. The company was in price competition with eastern and midwestern machine tool builders, who paid far less for their labor, and Burg Tool had to pay similar, not aircraft, wages.[18] Consequently, it had to furnish its workers more job security, something that was in short supply in the aircraft industry, which was even more cyclical than machine tools. Above all though, Burg Tool had to provide a more satisfying place to work.

Not that Burg Tool was run on a communal, or even consensus, basis. There were only two ranks at Burg Tool: the bosses and the workers, and there was no question about who was in charge. In fact, it was hard to imagine a more demanding set of bosses. The old man would prod everyone to the limit, and then some. He fancied himself a motivator of people, and thought by agitating them he obtained their best work. He thought nothing of giving an engineer or machinist a rush job that needed hours to complete, then coming back in fifteen minutes to peer over their shoulder and ask, "How is it going?"[19]

Ed Merk, upon joining the company in 1958, immediately noticed that Burg was very astute in his ability to handle people. He was "bullheaded and real hard-nosed." But if there was a disagreement and the old man was proved wrong, he would come back and admit, "Hey, I made a mistake," recalled Merk. "That's pretty rare in an individual." When employees realized that such candor came from the owner of the company, it encouraged them to be direct and honest in their dealings with the Burg family, as well as with each other.[20]

Joe Burg lacked some of his father's edge, but in his own way he was equally taxing, proposing new burdens for the engineering department every other month, or so it seemed. He wore out many chief engineers with the heavy demands he and his father imposed.[21] As for Norm Ginsburg, machinists often remarked about his uncanny ability to know which machines were running and which were not, even while he sat in his office. If janitors were not busy sweeping up metal chips and shavings, that meant machining had slowed down, and Ginsburg would promptly be out on the floor to find out why. His exalted rank did not prevent him from spending at least half his time there.

Yet the stiff demands made of Burg Tool employees were only half of the management-labor equation. The other half was that Burg Tool obviously valued its employees, their skills, and their ideas. There were few workers at Burg Tool who were not worth more on the outside. All a Burg Tool machinist or engineer had to do was open up the Sunday paper, and often he could find an advertisement for a similar job at Lockheed or Douglas Aircraft that paid a considerably higher wage. Naturally, over the years there were many employees who quit to make more money. But many stayed, because they appreciated forms of compensation other than money.

The sense of making a contribution toward a common effort was palpable because the Burgs listened to suggestions from everyone. Entry-level workers were accorded the same respect and seriousness given high-paid machinists and engineers. Even if at times some workers felt the old man tended to be a little too manipulative—he "loved to put that carrot out there," said Bob French— overall, his intensity evoked a high level of performance. One of his favorite sayings was "I grow, you grow."[22] And Burg Tool's workers believed him.

French, a design engineer who participated in many brainstorming sessions about possible new models, recalled how the old man got everyone to invest their energies in the company.

> When we designed new machines, he [Fred Burg] would bring in *everyone* he thought could contribute.
>
> I would sit there with colored pencils, thinking, what was I doing, a high-priced draftsman like me, drawing colored pictures. [Meanwhile] he would be asking for ideas from everyone who worked on machines, even scrapers. . . .
>
> He was preparing people down the line . . . if they felt they were part of the project, they would contribute to it. He was not only getting input, he was getting psychological benefit as well. But I didn't appreciate it fully at the time it was happening because I didn't really realize what was happening.[23]

None of this meant that it was the easiest thing in the world to go up to the old man and offer criticisms. Burg was always opinionated, and if an employee differed with a pet idea, he had better have a good reason for opposing it. "He didn't want yes men," remembered French. "But you didn't say no too damn loud. When you came up with a contrary idea he would often reject it at first. But then, come the next morning, damned if he wouldn't come up to you and tell you about the same idea you were trying to get across the day before."[24]

When it came time, in the early 1950s, to distribute year-end bonuses, though, the Burgs obviously remembered who had contributed what. There was no set formula for the bonuses, which had been a feature of the company since 1946, when Burg Tool hired its first employee from outside the family. Everyone, without exception, received a bonus in his or her last paycheck for the year. But the reward was clearly tied to performance. For salaried employees especially, December was often tense. In a good year, the bonus could amount to as much as 30 percent of annual income.[25] "People would be sweating blood," recalled Bob French. The Burgs purposely disbursed the bonuses annually because, "If you gave a little each week, a guy would forget," said Norm Ginsburg. "By giving it all at the end of the year, he would remember."

Beginning in 1956, the annual bonus was codified into a profit-sharing and pension system.[26] Payments were thereafter based on a formula rather than the discretion of the Burgs. The company had grown so much that the family no longer knew personally the contributions of every employee. Although this change presumably reduced some incentive, Burg Tool continued to benefit constantly from the suggestions of its workers. A machinist realized that if he had an idea that would decrease the percentage of scrap produced by the night shift, it meant money for him as well as for the Burgs.

The prospect of a tangible reward was not the only motive that prompted suggestions. Burg Tool employees also sought to contribute because it was personally satisfying. Employees respected the company the Burgs had built, and in turn sought respect and recognition from management for their own performance. The labor-management relationship, with its annual summer picnics, Thanksgiving turkeys, and Christmas dinners, was almost paternal. It seemed entirely natural for the Burgs to post bail, as they once did, for an employee who crashed into a telephone pole after drinking too much.

Mindful of his own beginning, Fred Burg was partial to hiring recent immigrants, and several people found their first job—and received on-the-job training—at Burg Tool. The old man shrewdly recognized that new immigrants often labored harder and for lower wages, at least initially, than many other workers. During the 1950s, immigrants from Eastern Europe were particularly plentiful. The company roster had a decidedly international flavor, with names on it like Joseph Braunstein, Ulrich Oesterle, Andy Kereskeny, Sandor Forizs, Shohichi Kato, Alex Alvarado, and Frank Maggiorino.

Sometimes newcomers were shocked by the frankness of the exchanges between the Burgs and their employees. Sandor Forizs was a Hungarian engineer who participated in his country's ill-fated 1956 revolt. After emigrating, he began working for Burg Tool in 1959. He was astounded at the way employees, especially young ones like Bob French, spoke to the Burgs. "He was fresh from Hungary, where he had been a freedom fighter," said French. "And I was in my twenties, and thought nothing of arguing tooth and nail with the old man. Sandor couldn't believe it. Here was a punk kid arguing with the owner of the factory!"[27]

Within the walls of Burg Tool during the 1950s, titles meant little, but a hands-on attitude meant everything. On one occasion, for example, a machinist working on a complicated part thought he recognized an error in the blueprint. He called over Norm Ginsburg, who was, typically, on the floor. After studying the blueprint, Ginsburg agreed with the machinist's assessment, and asked engineering to send someone down. The man chosen happened to be a relatively new employee.

After Ginsburg explained the problem, he asked the engineer to take the part to the engineering department, to show to a senior engineer. The employee responded, "I can't take the part back upstairs. It's going to make my hands dirty." Ginsburg, with a half-smile, looked at the machinist and then told the engineer, "I'll get you a towel." That was the last day the engineer worked at Burg Tool.[28]

The Burgs did not place undue emphasis on credentials probably because they had so few themselves. What mattered was not the number of degrees an employee had, or even the lack of one, but the person's ability to do a job. Bob French joined the company in 1954 as a draftsman. His plan to become an engineer had been stymied when he contracted tuberculosis right after high school, and his only credential was a certificate in tool design from a small technical school. But he was undeniably talented. At Burg Tool, he was permitted to learn by doing, and demonstrate his competence in tasks that might have been denied him elsewhere because he lacked a degree. Within a few years, he was the first person in the engineering department Fred Burg would talk to when an idea for a new machine popped into his head.

Nothing about the Burgs' attitude toward labor was codified. They did not read books about management, attend seminars, or ask their employees to. Their approach was instinctive, based on a thorough grounding in the business and a desire to have the people who worked for them share their dedication. Having been an hourly paid machinist himself, Fred Burg knew how deadening that job could be unless the worker viewed himself as something more than a cog. The most important thing, he believed, was to "get men interested in their work, make it something to look forward to." In his view, "interested people produce."[29]

In the mid-1950s, the Los Angeles–based Richfield Oil Corporation sponsored a thirty-minute television show every Friday evening at seven. Called "Success Story," the on-the-spot broadcast featured a local company that was doing well. The show was closer to Chamber of Commerce boosterism than anything else. One week it would showcase Fritos, a maker of corn chips; the next week a completely different kind of company. The only qualification was that the local business exemplify "our dynamic system of free enterprise."[30]

Richfield and its advertising agency were constantly on the lookout for companies that fit this mold. The wife of a Burg Tool employee worked at the agency, and she told them about her husband's employer.[31] The producers preferred to feature companies whose manufactures were immediately recognizable to a television audience, but she persuaded them that despite the complex nature of its product, Burg Tool was a quintessential American success story: the rags-to-riches saga of an immigrant who had a better idea.

Viewers who saw the May 18, 1956, broadcast were first given a tour of the factory. (Although Norm Ginsburg was usually only content when the floor was littered with shavings, for this show he was willing to tolerate a clean floor.) Then the moderator described Burg Tool's innovative product, how it was made, and the history of the company. The climax came when the camera moved to other factories to show what a Burgmaster was used for: at Douglas Aircraft, to drill a spar for an RB-66 reconnaissance bomber; at Parker Aircraft, (a subcontractor to North American), to machine the landing gear for an F-100 jet fighter; at Bendix Aviation, to make a part for "one of the new and dramatic bulwarks of our nation's defense . . . a fast-moving guided missile that stands ready to intercept any enemy who might try to invade and destroy our nation."[32]

The broadcast only gave a cursory explanation of Burg Tool's success, of course. It understandably concentrated on portraying, as vividly as possible, why these machines were important, and what was unique about the Burgmaster. There was insufficient time to touch upon the Burgs' management philosophy, even if they had been willing to articulate it. Yet visually, and by inference, the broadcast suggested the two remaining factors that were responsible for Burg Tool's growth: first, the attitude of the company toward its customers, and second, an unrelenting emphasis on innovation.

Joe Burg's facility for promises was a good sales technique, but the company would have floundered if there had been nothing more to its customer relations than promises. Not every buyer wanted a state-of-the-art machine. An equal, if not greater, number wanted only to know how reliable a standard machine was and when it could be delivered. Consequently, Burg Tool placed great emphasis on assuring that their machines performed "up to spec" once they were assembled, and stayed true after they were in the field. Quality control and field service received attention at the highest level of the company.

Fred Burg stepped in himself whenever necessary. On one occasion, Joe Burg recalled,

> We had just installed [a] machine. They claimed that it was not positioning correctly . . . that somehow, the drills were not making the holes in the right place.
>
> Dad flew in from California and saw that the drills were ground incorrectly. He then proceeded to regrind them himself, the old way, by hand. That was the start of [a] big break. They could not believe that he could grind the drills by hand.[33]

Whether it was the manner in which Burg Tool solved the problem, or that the president solved it, is immaterial. What mattered most was that Fred Burg acted as if he were still in the dry goods business, selling products worth only a few dollars. The competition then was so stiff that everything was done to make sure a customer was satisfied, lest he or she walk down the block and patronize another store. Burg gave companies that had spent $25,000 on one of his turret drills the same personal attention a department store salesman showed a housewife.

Peter Ives began working for Burg Tool in 1957, after spending eleven years with Pratt & Whitney Aircraft. The old man interviewed him personally for the job as field service representative for Burg Tool in the Chicago area. That region was one of the most important in the country, and the old man wanted to be sure he was hiring a capable, conscientious serviceman. Ives was all that, and more. But even Ives occasionally found himself amazed at Burg's demands. If the old man was passing through Chicago, he thought nothing of calling Ives up at 1:00 or 2:00 A.M., to see if Ives could arrange a visit to the Bendix Aviation plant in South Bend, Indiana, the next day. Bendix had twenty Burgmasters in that factory, and every year Burg wanted to see how well they were performing.[34]

Besides keeping customers satisfied, Burg's field trips served another important function throughout the 1950s. In 1946, walking into a job shop and seeing a turret lathe had given Burg his idea for a turret drill. He was thoroughly familiar with the operating principle of a turret lathe long before he walked into that shop. Yet until he actually saw the turret lathe, he could not imagine a solution to the problem he was brooding over. The old man never forgot how that experience catalyzed his thinking. From then on, field trips were an inseparable part of Fred Burg's emphasis on innovation, which was the last element in the cluster of factors responsible for Burg Tool's success.

The "Success Story" broadcast had illustrated, without explaining it in so many words, that Burg Tool constantly stressed research and development of new models. Viewers saw, not one or two kinds of Burgmasters, but a dizzying array of machines, ranging from the table-sized "O" model, suitable for small parts production, to behemoths like the "3BH," a hydraulic eight-spindle machine. Joe Burg's sales pitches were not the only reason why the engineering department was perpetually under pressure. One of the old man's favorite slogans was "A new model every year."[35]

The old man was aggressively inventive, and always preoccupied with improving the performance and features of his turret drill. From 1953 to 1960, he filed five patent applications for inventions designed to make his latest Burgmasters more capable than their predecessors.[36] But there also were sound economic reasons for innovation. Burg Tool could not control fundamental trends in the macroeconomy that buffeted the machine tool industry. By constantly improving its products, however, and developing new variations on the turret theme, the company could stimulate demand by introducing machines that promised to lower manufacturers' costs.

Innovation also allowed Burg Tool to exploit every market imaginable for the turret drill, no matter how competitive or small. The company recognized it had an unparalleled product, and sought to market the multiple-tool concept in every conceivable way. At the same time Burg Tool had its hands full developing state-of-the-art machines, Fred Burg insisted on bringing out the "O" model, a variation stripped to the barest essentials. He dubbed it the "Shopmaster," for he imagined there was a market for turret drills even among home hobbyists, if the machine was sufficiently inexpensive. He wanted to see a Burgmaster "in every garage."[37]

About 90 percent of all these ideas came from his field trips. The old man visited machine tool shows, customers who used Burgmasters, and manufacturers who did not. He would buttonhole everyone, from his own sales and repairmen to the machinists who used Burgmasters. He would pick their brains and more often than not return to the factory with an idea. "Three new castings and we've got a new machine," he would crow. The "2BR" or "radial" model was one of many machines that developed in this manner. The idea for the machine, which featured a swivel head that allowed it to accommodate bulky pieces, came to him after a trip to a Boeing plant.[38]

More than once, he appropriated concepts directly from competitors. Recalled Bob French, "He would go out and copy ideas. All his ideas would come to light after a trip to the East." French, when he was young and unschooled in the ways of the machine tool industry, initially thought there was something unethical about this. But it is generally accepted in the machine tool industry that patents are no match for engineering and innovation. The principles of machine tool design are well established. Traditionally, there have been few patents that cannot be easily circumvented, because talented engineers can devise several ways to achieve the same end. Fred Burg knew that what mattered was not who thought of an idea, but which builder could make it better.[39]

Nothing proved this maxim more than Joe Burg's discovery of an advertisement in an old magazine one day, many years after Burgmaster had become synonymous with turret drills. Leafing idly through a 1915 trade magazine, he came across a full-page advertisement for, of all things, a turret drill, manufactured by the A. E. Quint Company of Hartford, Connecticut. Use the Quint turret drill, said the ad, "for quick and accurate production of duplicate parts . . . will finish holes . . . at one setting without loss of time to change work or tools." Despite their outmoded features, the three belt-driven models depicted in the ad were all strikingly familiar.[40]

Fred Burg had not been the first to invent the turret drill after all.

In 1956, Joe Burg was intrigued by something else he read in a trade journal. The article described a new, automatic method of controlling machine tools; the method was called numerical control, or NC. In an NC system all the specifications for a movement of the tool and workpiece were placed on machine-readable cards, punched tape, or magnetic tape. The system promised to radically reduce scrap rates. Joe began to lobby his father, arguing that Burg Tool ought to investigate the new development. The old man, more concerned about making new machines, was against the idea at first. But he soon relented.[41]

No one at Burg Tool initially recognized the decision as a particularly momentous one. It seemed to be just another one of Joe's many ideas. But in fact, NC would catapult Burg Tool from the position of a small, though interesting, machine tool builder in 1956 into the front ranks of the industry in just a few years. In a sense, everything that had happened since 1946 was but a prelude to, and preparation for, the marriage of Burgmasters and numerical control in the late 1950s.

The application of controls to machine tools was the culmination of a trend dating back to Eli Whitney's time. Building skill into the machine, and demanding less of its operator, had long been characteristic of the American tool industry in particular.[42] Accounts differ as to who first conceived the notion of controlling a machine tool by coded instructions. But it is generally accepted that John C. Parsons, the owner of a company that manufactured helicopter rotor blades, did as much as or more than any other person to advance the concept in its early stages.[43]

Parsons approached the U.S. Air Force in the late 1940s because he was convinced that they would be interested in the "mathematical control" of machining operations. A future filled with jet fighters and rockets suggested unprecedented machining problems, and the air force was just beginning to investigate new manufacturing methods. In 1949, the air force awarded Parsons a $200,000 contract to build an automatic machine tool. Seeking help, he contacted the Servomechanisms Laboratory at the Massachusetts Institute of Technology, which had become famous for its wartime engineering achievements.[44]

MIT and the air force soon began to envision a much more ambitious project than the one Parsons proposed. Instead of concentrating on development of an efficient and economical method of automatic control, the project evolved into a vastly more complex undertaking. The MIT engineers were fascinated by theoretical possibilities, even if the result was not an immediately practicable machine. In addition, they recognized the commercial applications of numerical control, and were not disposed to let Parsons exclusively exploit the idea. The focus of the project changed from Parsons's modest goal to a universal system that would cut "any mathematically definable contour." Eventually Parsons himself was maneuvered out of the project he had initiated and MIT became the prime contractor.[45]

After three years of labor, in 1952, the MIT engineers publicly unveiled their achievement: an NC vertical milling machine. Now that NC had proved at least to be feasible, the air force hoped that the aerospace and machine tool industries would underwrite further research and development. But the approach developed by MIT was so unwieldy and expensive that no major machine tool builder or aerospace company was eager to follow suit. The former were especially leery about getting involved because of wartime demands, their inexperience with electronics, and the economic returns, which seemed uncertain.[46]

Extensive efforts were made to publicize and disseminate information about NC, but the air force could not overcome industry "aloofness." Following the MIT demonstration, two prominent machine tool builders, Giddings & Lewis (in association with General Electric) and Kearney & Trecker (with Bendix), agreed to construct NC milling machines for the aerospace industry. But in both instances the air force had to foot the bill. Even the end of the Korean War saw no rush by tool builders to try the new technology. Finally, in 1955, the air force decided to subsidize commercial development by creating a market. It announced procurement of more than one hundred NC milling machines, a decision that raised the federal government's NC investment to an estimated $62 million.[47]

The air force bid, which amounted to having the federal government underwrite transfer of the technology, achieved part of its desired effect. The attention of the machine tool industry was finally concentrated on NC. Yet in a sense the government program was a mixed blessing, for it created almost as many problems as it intended to solve. Most builders knew there was a big difference between machines for the government-subsidized aerospace industry and machines they might conceivably market to civilian manufacturers. There would be little incentive to keep costs down because aerospace industry profits were generally a percentage of costs. This would leave machine tool builders with products far more sophisticated than anything a civilian manufacturer might need, or be willing to pay for.[48]

Despite the air force's procurement bonanza, or perhaps because of it, shipments of NC machines during the mid-1950s stayed at a low level.[49] Worse, after many of these state-of-the-art machines reached their destination and were bolted into position, the builders and customers received a rude awakening. No one was quite prepared for the effect a factory floor—an "acutely hostile environment"—would have on NC machines. A typical machine shop was "hot, electrically noisy, the floors shook, [and] the air was full of physical and chemical contaminants." Inexperienced workers mishandled the coded tapes, or were otherwise ill prepared to operate or maintain the complex NC systems. Such factors caused more than one NC machine tool to literally tear itself apart. As one customer noted ruefully, "NC makes errors with greater authority than anything we are accustomed to."[50]

This was the environment that Joe Burg wanted Burg Tool to leap into in 1956. Burg Tool would not have the benefit of air force procurement to underwrite its venture into NC, if indeed that was a benefit. The government was still subsidizing the purchase of milling machines only. For that reason, and others, exploring NC would be a brash step, especially considering Burg Tool's relative youth. Other builders were becoming interested, but most of them could trace their genealogy back to the previous century, not just the previous decade.

Very soon after Burg Tool's engineers began looking into NC, it became obvious that such a marriage would be highly desirable. Drilling machines are traditionally the easiest machine tools to operate, as well as the most versatile. Computationally, drilling was also less difficult than milling, and Burg Tool could employ a far less sophisticated type of NC than the MIT system—one that would be cheaper, simpler, and easier to program. In addition, the synergy between NC and the multiple tools on a Burgmaster promised a breathtaking leap in machining productivity. Even in the late 1950s, the economic advantages of NC seemed dubious on some machine tools, given the nascent state of the technology and the costs involved.[51] That would not be true of an NC Burgmaster.

Through 1956 and 1957, Burg Tool experimented with a dizzying variety of controls, and every conceivable medium for the coded instructions, ranging from ten-inch-wide perforated paper tape to discarded movie film. By late 1957, little more than a year after Joe Burg first read about numerical control, the first NC Burgmaster, a 2BH model with GE controls, was sold to General Electric. Not only was it the first turret drill to employ NC, it was one of the earliest NC machines anywhere, and certainly the first one to be affordable and widely available.[52]

As one historian wrote, "The social and economic consequences of technological changes are a function of the rate of their diffusion and not the date of their first use. The critical social process . . . is that of diffusion."[53] By that, or any other measure, Burg Tool was a state-of-the-art manufacturer as the 1960s began.

3
HEYDAYS (1960–1964)

The 1960 National Machine Tool Exposition in Chicago was part show, part testimony. It was an opportunity for tool builders to display their wares, to their peers as well as to customers, at the most important exhibition in the trade. But the exhibition was also striking, tangible proof of American manufacturing prowess. Dozens of manufacturers vied for attention, and nearly one hundred varieties of NC machines were on display. The show was testimony to levels of productivity and technological ingenuity that were the envy of the world.

Not that the industry was without problems. For one, the feast or famine character of the business was unchanged. After the boom years of 1956 and 1957, sparked by retooling in the automobile industry, shipments had plummeted 47 percent during the 1958 recession. The year 1959 had not been much better, with only a 4 percent rise in shipments. And machine tools were also falling as a percentage of total investment in new plant and equipment. Many manufacturers were engineering metallic materials out of their products in favor of plastics or other synthetics.[1]

Nevertheless, there were many more reasons to be optimistic. After Korea's harsh lesson the U.S. government was no longer uninterested in the industry's health in peacetime. Although some believed its efforts were still insufficient, the Defense Department now procured machine tools worth tens of millions of dollars every year. By 1960, the government held three hundred thousand machine tools valued at more than $3 billion, or about 15 percent of the total American machine tool stock. The aim was to prevent a severe contraction in the industry; the effect was to make the government the industry's biggest customer on a sustained basis. It was more than symbolic when the National Machine Tool Builders' Association moved its headquarters from Cleveland to Washington in 1957.[2]

But finally winning the government's attention was probably not the main reason the future looked so rosy. A sustained boom seemed to be in the offing because demand from the auto industry was increasing at the same time that aircraft manufacturers wanted to retool, to produce new products like commercial jet airliners. In addition, the metalworking industries as a whole had permitted their machine tools to become obsolete. By the early 1960s, more than 60 percent of the machine tools in use were at least ten years old, and about one in five were more than twenty years old.[3]

Another reason tool builders were sanguine was that their home market, besides being the largest in the world, was also a captive one. American machine tools were renowned for their reliability and technology and had few peers. During boom times, U.S. customers desperate for a good standard lathe, drilling, or milling machine had little alternative to waiting months for an American tool. Buying from abroad was not really an alternative. As a percentage of domestic consumption, imports had never exceeded a minuscule 5 percent, because they fell by and large into two classes: extremely precise (and expensive) European machines that had no American equivalent, and rudimentary tools made in countries like Spain, Italy, or Japan. During a recession, even this low level of imports was sufficient to stir up American builders. But the industry's interest in tariffs or quotas invariably waned as soon as a recovery began.[4]

Insofar as exports went, they were five to seven times the volume of imports. The world, no less than U.S. industry, wanted American tools when they could get them, and many American tool builders were exploiting their technological edge to internationalize operations. They sought to license, subcontract, or even manufacture abroad so as to compete with rebuilt rivals, such as West Germany, on their own turf. By one estimate, nearly seventy American companies established some kind of overseas production arrangement by the early 1960s.[5]

The "macro" economic environment, of course, was as important to the industry as its internal, or "micro," economics. Here too American builders had ample grounds for optimism. Tool shipments rose and fell according to the level of capital investment, and nothing was more likely to reduce investment than uncertainty. But, if growth in the American GNP occasionally slowed, the overall trend was nevertheless healthy, and the economy was stable if not predictable. This climate was of immeasurable benefit to the machine tool industry and its customers.

If there was one flaw in the U.S. economy at the turn of the decade, it was the nagging balance-of-payments deficit. The dollar shortage of the early postwar years had been supplanted by a dollar glut, traceable to large U.S. military expenditures overseas and foreign aid.[6] Europe in particular was being flooded with more dollars than it could possibly use. Since the dollar was redeemable in gold, Europeans were exchanging excess currency for bullion, leading to a persistent decline in U.S. gold reserves.

That the dollar was no longer as good as gold was an early warning signal of a fundamental imbalance in the U.S. economy. The only connection between machine tools and this worrisome trend, however, was that tool exports helped to ameliorate it. The outflow of gold would have been considerably worse but for rising U.S. exports of capital goods to Europe; machine tools were an important component of such exports, especially because of wage and price inflation in Europe. Rising costs overseas during the early 1960s made American tools even more competitive than warranted by their sheer technological edge.[7]

If U.S. tool builders thought they were about to reap a windfall, the owners of Burg Tool were already enjoying theirs by 1960. After the 1958 recession, sales had risen a whopping 79 percent in 1959, the second-largest rise in Burg Tool's short history. An increase of 30 percent in 1960 seemed likely. The explosive growth was traceable, primarily, to Burg Tool's early exploitation of numerical control, which had resulted in a quantum leap in productivity. A Burgmaster NC turret drill reduced downtime for setups and retooling, and saved on inspection, rejection, inventory, and labor costs. It was perhaps the first NC machine to deliver reliably, at a reasonable cost, all the benefits promised by new technology.[8]

This was not mere sales talk. A 1962 article in *American Machinist* spelled out the dramatic gains achieved by General Electric, for example, after it purchased a numerically controlled "2BHT" Burgmaster. "One tape-controlled machine saved $10,000 in tooling and fixtures, plus $17,000 in labor costs on a single job at GE's Atomic Power Equipment Department," noted the article. The Burgmaster's job was to drill, bore, ream, chamfer, and then tap holes in stainless steel castings that fit over nuclear fuel rods. "Previously the job took eight hours per casting and rejects ran as high as two out of three pieces," said the article. "With the new setup, time has been cut in half and the reject rate is under 2 percent." Another, larger Burgmaster in the San Jose, California, plant machined aluminum plates that supported the fuel rods inside the reactor. Previously that task had taken two shifts a day, working ten hours each shift, six days a week, a total of three months to complete. The "3BHTL" NC Burgmaster finished the job in six weeks with only one ten-hour shift per day.[9]

Similar savings were the rule whenever Burg Tool installed an NC machine. At the Convair division of General Dynamics Corporation in San Diego, a 2BHT saved $40,000 in labor and operating costs in seven months. The same model, machining a cast-iron rocket bulkhead for Hughes Aircraft in Tucson, saved $3,000 in tooling costs and reduced the lead time necessary to make the part by five weeks. At a factory in Cedar Rapids, one machinist running two NC Burgmasters simultaneously saved Collins Radio $75,000 in tooling costs. No matter what the machining requirements, the invariable result was large gains in time, money, and quality.[10]

The advent of NC reopened a perennial controversy in the machine tool industry. The issue was whether this latest technological advance would be used as a pretext for "deskilling" machinists, and shifting responsibility for production from the factory floor to white-collar offices. And not surprisingly, an NC Burgmaster provoked the first such clash between management and labor. In 1960, General Motors installed an NC Burgmaster in Plant 21 of its Fisher Body division. Initially, GM put the operator of this machine in the same job category as a machinist who ran conventional Burgmasters. Simultaneously, all responsibility for programming, a relatively simple manual task, was assigned to a production engineer away from the shop floor.

In a precedent-setting grievance, the United Auto Workers contested GM's action on both counts. The UAW claimed that programming was simply a modern version of what machinists had done for decades, and should not be separated from the job description. The union also maintained that NC operators should be paid more because their job required programming skills. In its rebuttal GM insisted that programming was a managerial function, and that workers were asking for, in effect, a "measure of control over the methods, processes, and means of manufacture." In a landmark decision in 1961 an arbitrator ruled against GM on both counts.[11]

Such controversies aside, Burg Tool's success in the early 1960s was not going unnoticed within the machine tool fraternity. Three other large builders began to market turret drills: the Avey Drill Company (a division of Motch & Merryweather), Brown & Sharpe, and Cincinnati Milling Machine, the General Motors of the machine tool industry.[12] Burg Tool was an upstart compared to these venerable companies. But its reputation, as well as its technological lead, kept it ahead of all comers. Consumers of machine tools spent thousands of dollars according to whether a turret drill made the hundredth hole in a casting with the same precision as the first. Similarly, consumers wanted a machine that they could not only rely on when it worked but also rely on to work, shift after shift. After fifteen years, Burgmasters had proven dependable on both counts.

The other element that kept Burg Tool in front, its technological lead, was manifest in a number of ways. The company was far ahead in the marriage of NC to turret drills: 54 percent of its sales were NC machines, even though these machines cost two to four times their manual equivalents. None of Burg's competitors could boast a similar figure. The electronics divisions of Hughes, Bendix, and GE all competed vigorously to supply controls designed to Burg Tool's specifications. In addition, more than 65 percent of 1961 sales were of products introduced to the trade within the preceding three years— proof of the company's adherence to Fred Burg's cry of "a new model every year." Burg Tool's policy was to retain all earnings to finance growth and development; dividends were not paid to the company's three shareholders, although they benefited, as did every employee, from the profit-sharing plan.[13]

Significantly, Burg Tool's entire product line had been designed and developed in-house. An expenditure equal to at least 2.5 percent of annual sales was devoted to research and development. By the early 1960s, the company held twenty-two foreign and domestic patents, with fourteen new ones pending. Yet, reflecting the competitive, imitative nature of the machine tool industry, Burg Tool did not consider any one patent or group of patents "to be of fundamental importance to the overall business or to any major product category." Instead, the Burgs asserted, their success rested upon "technological leadership, know-how, trade secrets, manufacturing and sales capabilities, and a reputation for quality and customer service."[14]

Like that of almost every other builder, Burg Tool's prosperity was linked to the government's defense budget. In 1960, for example, although only 5 percent of sales were made directly to the government, approximately 30 percent were derived from contracts or subcontracts connected to defense spending. Burg Tool reduced this dependence by seeking to exploit every potential market. Its product line included NC machines that cost from $30,000 to $100,000 and weighed tons; hydraulic models costing from $8,500 to $20,000; manual machines that sold for $3,400 to $9,000; and bench models that cost as little as $600.[15] Burg Tool even continued to manufacture the $50 Tool-flex. Fred Burg was not willing to leave that small business to someone else.

Along with everything else, Burg Tool's labor force was growing rapidly. By 1960, the Burgs employed 155 workers at the Figueroa plant, up 120 percent in just two years. The company still enjoyed good labor relations, although labor and management were no longer as close-knit as in earlier days. The size of the work force prevented that. And it also produced a union, to the great anguish of Fred Burg.

Antiunionism had been a characteristic of the industry since World War I, and in this respect the old man was like most founders of machine tool companies.[16] Some of Fred Burg's perspective stemmed, not from his years as a boss, however, but from his own experience as a machinist and union member forty-five years earlier. He believed unions had a marked tendency to stifle individual initiative. More than once he had been criticized by fellow workers and his own union for working too hard in comparison to others.[17]

Union organizers had been eyeing Burg Tool ever since 1956, when the work force exceeded seventy employees for the first time. That year the United Auto Workers and International Association of Machinists, although both affiliated with the AFL-CIO, vied to gain recognition as the workers' bargaining agent. The IAM was the more logical representative, but since the UAW had initiated the organizing attempt, the IAM decided to withdraw six days before the May 28 election. The vote promised to be close, and apparently the AFL-CIO believed it was more likely to win if only one union was in the race.[18]

To the old man's great satisfaction, the first ballot went against the union by a healthy margin. The voting clearly split along old-timer and newcomer lines. The former voted against because they already received greater benefits than the union promised to bring. The Burgs often "red-lined" a machinist, that is, paid him twenty or twenty-five cents an hour more than he would receive under union scale.[19] Their motivation was twofold: reward productive employees and keep them sufficiently satisfied so they would not unionize.

The UAW promptly filed a protest, claiming that Fred Burg had violated labor laws by pressuring his workers unfairly. Anyone who knew the old man had no trouble believing that, but the hard evidence was lacking. Faced with a margin that was overwhelmingly against unionization, and recognizing that old-timers outnumbered newcomers, the UAW reconsidered and withdrew its demand for a new election. The AFL-CIO made it clear, however, that if Burg Tool continued to grow, the union intended to try again.

Four years passed before Burg Tool appeared ripe for unionization. For unknown reasons, the UAW declined to lead the second attempt, in 1960. Instead, the United Steelworkers of America, a UAW rival, decided to make the push. Well aware that the first attempt had failed miserably, the Steelworkers adopted more sophisticated tactics.

Outside the factory, Union representatives openly gathered the necessary signatures for another vote. Meanwhile, two skilled machinists, who also happened to be labor organizers, joined Burg Tool in the fall of 1960 and campaigned inside the company. In particular, they strenuously criticized red-lining because they correctly perceived it as an obstacle to winning certification.

This time, the criticism fell upon receptive ears. The Burgs paid below union scale to apprentices and workers with little experience. Unionization would mean money in the pocket to these workers, and that was more appealing than the distant promise of higher compensation. Then too, newer workers also felt somewhat slighted. They were seldom consulted by the Burgs as much as the older workers were.[20]

With newcomers far outnumbering old-timers, Fred Burg became extremely anxious about the upcoming vote. He called a meeting of all blue-collar employees and alternately threatened and pleaded with them not to unionize. He implied that he would rescind every benefit, such as the profit-sharing and pension plan, that went beyond the standard union contract if the vote went against him. The gathering was a blatant violation of National Labor Relations Board rules, which banned coercive attempts just before an election.[21]

The NLRB cited the old man for the infraction. But that was a minor irritant compared to how he felt after the Steelworkers won certification by two votes. He had always regarded the company as a "greater" family enterprise, and rightly or wrongly he felt betrayed. "The old man really never got over" the election, recalled Norm Ginsburg. Worse, during the contract talks that followed, Burg Tool experienced its first walkout, albeit a very short one. The union, bent on demonstrating that the workers had made the right decision, wanted to give them something tangible immediately. It demanded that the company pay out the sums the workers had vested in the profit-sharing and pension plan. (Under the original schedule, workers were only fully vested after ten years and forfeited the entire amount if they left Burg Tool before then.) Seeing his machinists walking back and forth in front of the factory instead of working inside was a picture that Fred Burg did not easily forget.

The family conceded the issue after a few days, and paid out all the monies. They also retaliated by canceling the entire plan for all blue-collar employees, and otherwise revoking all extraordinary benefits. The old man ordered management "not to go out of its way" for any worker. After a while he let up, privately telling the old-timers he still regarded them as friends. But he did so very warily.[22]

Although the old man's views were shared by his younger partners, they did not take the vote as personally. They simply thought the workers did not recognize their own best interests. "The workers were so dumb," said Ginsburg. "The union organizers came in with a line of bull, and they bought it. They would have gotten more without the union."[23] But in time, at least the younger partners in Burg Tool came to recognize that unionization was inevitable, if not in several respects desirable.

Once the labor force grew to more than four hundred employees by the mid-1960s, having a union meant that the Burgs could negotiate with an elected shop steward when grievances arose, and settle disputes according to an established procedure. Before, every complaint had to be handled on an individual, case-by-case basis. Then too, the Steelworkers' local proved far from militant, nor did it have any reason to be, during the contract negotiations held every three years. Unionism did not bring a rash of strikes or work stoppages at Burg Tool. A certain harmony was lost, but by most measures the company continued to have an enviable relationship between management and labor.

In 1961, the backlog of orders rose to $2.2 million, up more than 160 percent from the previous year.[24] It was the highest level ever, and this factor, among others, finally pushed Burg Tool into becoming what its accountants, financial advisers, and lawyers had been urging for some time: a publicly traded corporation.

The fundamental reason for undergoing such a transformation was the company's need for more capital to expand. And given demand for its product, there was no reason why Burg Tool could not raise the money through a stock offering, rather than paying more for the same capital from a bank.

There was an alternative, of course, to going public, namely, selling out to one of Burg Tool's persistent suitors. Corporations inside as well as outside the machine tool industry, including Bell Helicopter and Rockwell, had indicated a willingness to buy if the Burgs cared to sell. But the partners' unanimous feeling was that "Burg Tool was still going places" and they, especially the old man, did not want to let go just yet.[25] The Burgs began searching for an investment house skilled at raising equity capital.

A young, ambitious Wall Street investment banker heard about the interest of the West Coast tool builder in going public. John Shad was a partner at Shearson, Hammill in New York, in charge of corporate finance, merger, and acquisition activities. During a trip to Los Angeles, he was introduced to Fred Burg, and became intrigued with what clearly was a Horatio Alger story. He decided to investigate the company's prospects.

Shad himself was something of a success story. He had graduated from the Harvard Business School in 1949, a member of the first full postwar class, sometimes referred to as "the class the dollars fell on." Because there were only fifty thousand living M.B.A.'s in the country at the time, the class of '49 was considered to be in the prestigious vanguard of "scientific management in corporate America." Only 1 percent of the class, however, went straight to Wall Street like Shad. The majority entered corporations, and in due time many from the class of '49 would emerge as chief executives.[26]

Initially, Shad was concerned that the industry giant, Cincinnati Milling, might be able to preempt Burg Tool's market position. But as he investigated Burg Tool's finances, major customers, suppliers, competitors, and lenders, he developed a strong and positive impression. The company's track record and leadership in the application of NC persuaded him that it was competitive, and would continue to thrive. He agreed to serve as the company's chief financial adviser, and in turn, the Burgs invited him to become a director of their soon-to-be-public corporation.[27]

As the day of the offering approached, stockbrokers voiced one small reservation. They thought the "Burg Tool Manufacturing Corporation" was an unwieldy name, and that investors who tracked the machine tool industry would not necessarily associate it with Burgmaster turret drills. They lobbied for something that traded on the machine's enviable reputation. It was decided that Burg Tool's public successor would be named the Burgmaster Corporation.

On May 15, 1961, 190,000 shares of common stock were offered on the over-the-counter market by a group of underwriters, led by Shearson, Hammill. Of this total, 100,000 shares represented new financing, and the other 90,000 came from Fred Burg's holdings. Since the initial price had been set at $12 a share, that meant he was about to become a sixty-five-year-old millionaire. At the same time, majority control over the corporation would pass from his hands to the hands of his younger partners. The prospectus called for Joe Burg and Norm Ginsburg to each retain 25.7 percent of the outstanding shares.[28]

The year 1961 was known as a "hot new issue market" for shares in emerging companies that were anchored in rapidly growing areas of the economy. Some Wall Street wags were even calling it the "Furth-Burner Market."

> Take a nice little company that's been making shoelaces for 40 years and sells at a respectable six times earnings. Change the name from Shoelaces, Inc. to Electronics and Silicon Furth-Burners. In today's

market, the words "electronics" and "silicon" are worth 15 times earnings. However the real play comes from the word "furth-burners," which no one understands. A word that no one understands entitles you to double your entire score. Therefore, we have six times earnings for the shoelace business and 15 times earnings for the electronics and silicon, or a total of 21 times earnings. Multiply this by two for furth-burners and we now have a score of 42 times earnings for the new company.[29]

Burgmaster profited from this phenomenon but, unlike some companies, was no pretender to high technology. Within hours the stock was oversubscribed and trading at a premium. Buyers first bid it up to $18, and then $21, before the stock eased down to just under $15.[30]

By convention, the week between an offering and the closing, or actual exchange of stock for capital, is the time for the so-called cold comfort review. Auditors make a final check of the prospectus. To everyone's chagrin, on the last day of Burgmaster's cold comfort, auditors discovered a $24,739 error in the prospectus. All the sales figures listed were supposed to be based on the date of shipment—and most were, except for some figures in the very last column. Inadvertently, they reflected sales that had been invoiced but not shipped.[31]

The problem was primarily one of consistency, because there was nothing deceptive about using invoices as a basis for estimates. On March 31, a Friday, Burgmaster had invoiced $120,587 worth of machines, but they had not gone out until the next Monday, April 3, which happened to be the beginning of a new quarter. Consequently, Burgmaster's estimated net income had been overstated by $24,739.[32]

Everyone was mortified. The accountants and lawyers in Los Angeles called Shad at midnight in New York, and asked if he thought the difference was material. He recognized it as an "honest error," not intentional, and more important, one that did not genuinely misrepresent Burgmaster's sales or profits. Yet he realized that what amounted to a 50 percent overstatement was "obviously significant." It was decided that everyone—the Burgs, the lawyers, the accountants—should fly to New York the next day to decide what to do.[33]

After agonizing over the problem for twenty-four hours, Fred Burg decided to cancel the entire underwriting. The withdrawn offering (and the expense of a second one) personally cost him about $100,000.[34] But he wanted this rite of passage to be beyond reproach. *The Wall Street Journal* reported that veterans in the securities industry considered the cancellation unprecedented. No one on the Street or inside the Securities and Exchange Commission could ever recall a company, of its own volition, withdrawing an offering after trading had begun. "Calling off the issue took a lot of guts, but it also means a paperwork mess," one underwriter grumbled to the *Journal*.[35]

Shad prepared another registration statement, one that included a frank explanation of everything that had transpired. The way seemed clear to a second offering, but after the statement was submitted to the SEC someone suggested additional changes that had nothing to do with the accounting inconsistency. Shad did not look kindly upon the suggestions, and asked to see Manny Cohen, director of the Corporate Finance Division (and later head of the SEC). Cohen listened to Shad make his case and said, "You've bent over backwards in withdrawing the offering. Go ahead as you propose."[36]

In mid-June, the stock was offered to the public once again. The second solicitation was as successful as the first, and Burgmaster's subsequent performance did not disappoint its new investors. The years immediately following the offering were robust. From 1961 to 1964, Burgmaster annually registered new highs, and sometimes dramatic gains, in sales—up 31 percent in 1962, and about 9 percent in 1963 and 1964. Demand for the stock became sufficiently strong to warrant a switch from the over-the-counter market to the American Stock Exchange in mid-1963.[37]

If more sales each year did not always translate directly into increased earnings per share, it was because profits were retained for research, development, and growth. In 1962, Burgmaster added 14,400 square feet to its Figueroa plant. Most of the additional footage was reserved for the engineering department, which expanded by 40 percent.[38] Substantial investments also were made in new machines, including a large new milling machine. The tool enabled Burgmaster to relieve the pressure on its small milling machines, which were often operating twenty to twenty-two hours a day.[39]

Such expansion and investments helped Burgmaster capture about 80 percent of the turret drill market by the early 1960s, despite competition from such august builders as Cincinnati Milling. The Burgs had every intention of retaining this market share too, even in the face of cost cutting by the likes of Cincinnati. In short, Burgmaster was being managed for the long term.[40]

At the same time, the corporation underwent something of a reshuffle. In January 1962, Fred Burg retired as president and became chairman of the board. His son, Joe, Mr. Outside, succeeded him while Norm Ginsburg, Mr. Inside, remained as Burgmaster's vice president, treasurer, and general manager. In terms of how the company was actually run, however, these changes were nominal. Regardless of whether he owned 40 percent or 8 percent of the stock, the old man was still the "most equal" of the three partners.

Never content to stand pat, he kept Burgmaster moving. In 1962, the company introduced a new series of low-cost machines. The next year, Burgmaster began producing a series of expensive sliding head machines, priced from $56,000 to $90,000, and traveling column machines, which cost as much as $150,000. Besides these new models, incremental, unseen improvements were also emphasized. In 1962, Burgmaster introduced a new spindle design that permitted variable speeds, greatly increasing the turret drill's versatility.[41]

As usual, the Burgs instituted innovations with one goal in mind: to increase the reliability and capacity of the Burgmaster turret drill, so as to attract new and different customers. As a measure of their success, non-defense-related orders increased from about 67 percent to 80 percent by 1964, despite absolute increases in sales to defense contractors. Burgmaster was penetrating new markets, and could now count the big two auto makers, Ford and General Motors, among its customers.[42]

Few of the innovations occurred effortlessly, or without vexation. The development of the sliding head machines, in particular, brought a host of problems. Sometimes the machine shop found it exceedingly hard to machine newly designed parts to the required specifications. Other times the assembly department bore the brunt of a new model's problems. More than once faults only became apparent after a new model was already in the field, leading to expensive repairs and disappointed customers.

But if a continuous stream of new models meant unending headaches, solutions were just as inevitable at Burgmaster. When unforeseen problems arose, the company could respond quickly, with an ad hoc solution if necessary, because the lines of authority were clear and responsibility was shared. The number of employees was growing fast, but candor and coopera-tion still prevailed.

When they could, the Burgs instituted more systematic solutions to nag-ging problems. One lasting solution was a tough quality-control program, in-augurated in 1964, to resolve chronic problems caused by continuous in-novation.[43] To set up the new system, Fred Burg brought inside one of his best field repairmen, Pete Ives.

Ives had been longing to move to California for some time, and was full of ideas about how to improve Burgmaster's quality control. "Every time Fred Burg came out to Chicago, I would say to him, 'When are you getting me to California?'" recalled Ives. But he was so valuable in the field that every time Ives asked, the old man acted as if it were the first time he had heard the idea. Finally, Ives suggested that the old man's memory lapses were just too con-venient. Burg burst out laughing, forced to admit that he was boxed in. He asked Ives to prepare a letter outlining his ideas. Anticipating his request, Ives handed him a memo he had already prepared. He was on his way to Los Angeles.[44]

Shortly afterward Ives was devising a strict quality-control system, one that put all machines through a rigorous, thorough check. "At the time I did it," remembered Ives, "everyone was pissed off. No one likes a cop." But he had the full backing of the old man, and soon there was no kickup from the field, even though Burgmaster was shipping thirty to forty machines a month.[45]

There was only one truly jarring note during the early 1960s, a period of growth and growing pains. In late 1961, by accident, Burgmaster discovered that one of its turret drills was being manufactured abroad, specifically in Japan, without any permission. Someone sent the Burgs a picture of what seemed to be an O machine, the model suitable for drilling electronic parts. Instead of the familiar Burgmaster logo, the nameplate read "Chukyo." The Burgs had been in machine tools long enough to know that imitation was the industry's sincerest compliment. But from the picture, it appeared as if Chukyo Denki in Nagoya, Japan, had gone far beyond mere imitation. Their machine looked like an exact replica. Incensed, Fred Burg left within days for Tokyo to see the machine for himself, unfazed by the thought of trying to function in a strange culture.[46]

Upon arriving, the old man went directly to Nagoya. He wanted to have the satisfaction of confronting the company personally. The Japanese builder baldly denied infringing Burgmaster patents, which only served to heighten the old man's outrage and determination. That afternoon he took a train back to Tokyo, and began looking for a patent attorney. The one he eventually retained not only spoke English but also had written many of Japan's patent laws. Once all the arrangements to file suit were made, Burg left for home, bringing with him one of the Chukyo machines for his engineers to disassemble. They proved unable to tell the difference between that machine and one of Burgmaster's own.[47]

Burgmaster became one of the first American companies to win a patent infringement suit in Japan. In May 1962, an injunction prohibited Chukyo from manufacturing any more O machines. A month later Burgmaster succeeded on another count, winning substantial damages because of the machines previously manufactured without a license. It was many months before Burgmaster received any of the proceeds, however, because a special law had to be passed allowing that amount of currency to be taken out of Japan.[48]

Nevertheless, even this disturbing event eventually had a positive outcome. The old man initiated the suit with fire in his eyes. But after it was resolved in Burgmaster's favor, and after the prodding of both sides by Japan's Ministry of International Trade and Industry (MITI), the Burgs quickly became business partners with Chukyo. (One incentive for Burgmaster to do so was that MITI exercised great power, the Burgs soon learned, over the release of the infringement award.) In July 1962, MITI approved an agreement whereby Chukyo gained a license to manufacture several of the smaller models and sell them in Japan and the Far East. In return, Burgmaster received a one-time payment for its engineering know-how and an annual, guaranteed-minimum royalty. Soon afterward, the two companies reached a second agreement. Chukyo became the exclusive sales representative in the Far East for Burgmaster's larger-model machines.[49]

Japanese tool builders were not the only ones to infringe on Burgmaster patents, however. About the same time, a Spanish concern copied the "1D" model, and the Burgs found themselves embroiled in another lawsuit.[50] Although patent infringement was more of a nuisance than a menace, both instances left an impression, and accelerated a tendency already taking root at

Burgmaster. The company began to think in terms of global competition and markets.

Over the next few years, Burgmaster actively pursued licensing arrangements in the key machine tool markets overseas. By the mid-1960s, in addition to the arrangement with Chukyo, Burgmaster would have sales or coproduction agreements with Karl Huller, a Stuttgart tool builder, and with the English and German subsidiaries of the Ex-Cell-O Corporation, a major U.S. tool builder. Foreign sales subsequently rose from less than 2 percent of 1961 sales to approximately 9 percent by 1962.[51] In this respect, Burgmaster was part of an industrywide trend; most of the leading American tool companies were seeking overseas subsidiaries or outlets.

At the time Burgmaster began thinking globally, a serious challenge to its primacy at home arose. If it went unanswered, if Burgmaster could not meet it, the new development threatened to put at risk everything the Burgs had worked to build. For the early 1960s marked the moment when other tool builders finally began to catch up to the kernel of Burgmaster's success, the idea of one machine, multiple tools.

There were two ways in which to view Fred Burg's original innovation of 1946. The most obvious was to regard his machine as an advance on the simple drill press; the Burgmaster was a multiple-spindle drill press, capable of rapidly bringing up to eight tools to bear in succession on one workpiece. With this in mind, other and larger builders had been quick to manufacture clones of the Burgmaster once it proved successful. But none was better or less expensive than the original.

In simply imitating the Burgmaster design, however, these competitors had missed the most basic point of Burg's innovation. Stripped to its essence, the problem that Burg had solved better than any machine tool designer before him was the invariable need for more than one tool while machining a workpiece on a drill press. But Burg's solution—deploying six or eight spindles on a turret—was not the only way to solve the problem. In other words, the Burgmaster had actually initiated a new class of machines, soon to be designated as machining centers. And the monopoly that Burgmaster had enjoyed as the first in its class was fast coming to an end.

The venerable builder Kearney & Trecker was the first to prove it. At the Chicago show in 1960, K&T unveiled a whole new approach to the need for multiple tools, the instantly famous Milwaukee-Matic.[52] It too, like the Burgmaster, was a machining center, a phrase that suddenly was on the lips of every major machine tool builder. But the Milwaukee-Matic represented a drastically different solution. All the tools sat beside the machine in a carrousel. There was only one spindle, and after a machining operation was completed, a robotlike arm would remove the tool from the spindle, place it in the carrousel, and pick up another tool for insertion—all in the space of nine seconds.

When it came to actual machining, the M-M and an equivalent-sized

Burgmaster could both perform five distinct machining operations: drilling, boring, reaming, tapping, and light milling. In one respect, the Burgmaster was even superior. Its turret could index (revolve and lock into place) a tool much faster than the M-M could change one. But the M-M, defined as a tool changer to distinguish it from turret-style machining centers, enjoyed one striking advantage. It had at its disposal, not six or eight tools like a Burgmaster, but thirty, and already there was talk of putting as many as sixty tools on later models.

When married to NC, such tool changers could rapidly erode much of Burgmaster's market. The single most important indicator of a machine tool's value is the time it actually spends cutting metal. As everyone in the tool business knows, there are no profits in setting up workpieces. But when the metal chips are flying, money is being made. Standard machine tools were busy about 15 to 25 percent of the time. By contrast, an NC Burgmaster was generally "up and running" 40 to 60 percent of the time. Kearney & Trecker's tool changer, however, appeared to surpass even Burgmaster's accomplishment. "By minimizing setup and positioning time and by combining five operations in one machine," boasted Francis Trecker, K&T's president, "the M-M can be kept in operation well over 75 percent of the time."[53] The advertising copy of the M-M even sounded like Burgmaster's, only better.

No one doubted at Burgmaster that the machine tool business was about to get considerably tougher. For the time being, though, Burgmaster had some breathing room. For even though almost every workpiece needed to be machined by more than one tool, very few needed thirty-one separate operations. The Milwaukee-Matic, in its simplest configuration, also carried a hefty $140,000 price tag, and that was more than many customers would spend, even for a machine touted as "the most significant achievement of the machine tool industry in the last 50 years."[54] Nevertheless, the long-term implications of K&T's 1960 achievement were clear and could not be ignored, given the aerospace industry's penchant for ever more capable tools.

Predictably, no one was more conscious of the ramifications than Fred Burg. The old man, now in his midsixties, took charge of developing a radically new Burgmaster, one that would keep his company competitive in the market for machining centers. By late 1962, Burgmaster's engineers were hard at work on a new model, dubbed the "20T" and "designed specifically to fulfill the requirements of the aerospace industry in utilizing the exotic metals of the Space Age."[55]

Burg's answer dispensed with the ubiquitous turret that had become synonymous with Burgmaster. He also refused to follow K&T's design path, one that nearly every other competitor was hastily pursuing. K&T's patent on the most important feature of its machine, the tool-changing mechanism, was unusually tight. Burg and his engineering department realized that it might take years to get around the patent claims, and even then K&T might try to sue.[56]

The Wisconsin builder was making no secret of its intention to litigate at the slightest hint of infringement.

But the chief reason the old man stubbornly chose his own route was that he believed there was a third way. Burg thought, quite adamantly, that after a few years a tool changer's accuracy would be compromised. No machine could change tools dozens of times a day, withstand the strains of machining, and still grip its tools as rigidly in 1966 as it did in 1963. And true to the old man's conviction, this very problem plagued many builders for years.[57]

His alternative was to arrange twenty tools in twenty spindles around the edge of a rotating drum. When a different tool was needed, the drum would index within five seconds to the proper location, the spindle would engage, and machining would proceed. Burg calculated that twenty stations would be sufficient to meet the competition. Greater reliability at a lower cost, meanwhile, would compensate for the fewer number of tools. He thought he could bring the 20T in at a base price of about $87,500, one-third less than the Milwaukee-Matic.[58]

The 20T was the biggest, most complex, and most ambitious project ever attempted at Burgmaster. Curiously, none of the engineers, for varying reasons, shared the old man's enthusiasm for the machine. But his stature was such that despite their unanimous misgivings, Fred Burg could not be overruled. Besides, his instincts had often proved superior to any number of engineering degrees. The skeptics would have to await the pudding.

Until then, anyway, Burgmaster still had its hands full meeting all its orders for turret drills. By 1964, Burgmaster's success had become so conspicuous locally that it was the subject of a long feature article in the *Los Angeles Times.* Burgmaster was accurately billed as "the only machine tool producer of any significance on the West Coast." In the course of the article, Joe Burg mentioned that Burgmaster "was shooting for $8.5 million of sales" in fiscal 1965. That was very close to the absolute capacity of the Figueroa plant, which was about $10 million. Burg then acknowledged that Burgmaster was probably going to have to undergo another expansion in the near future.[59]

In fact, 1965 sales would climb by 29 percent to $9.6 million, the eighth consecutive new high, and expansion would become a matter of the utmost urgency by early 1965. A small building was leased a short distance from the main factory and devoted exclusively to assembly of the smaller models. Within a few weeks, however, the main Figueroa plant seemed as acutely congested as ever. Burgmaster had to have more room.

At this time, the Burgs received a discreet message from an East Coast corporation. It asked a familiar question, to which the answer had always been no. There was no reason to believe this feeler would prove any more attractive than had earlier offers. Nevertheless, the Burgs said they were willing to listen to what Houdaille Industries had in mind.

4
TAKEOVER (1965)

The Burgs soon recognized strong similarities between their company and the corporation that was wooing it. Like Burgmaster, Houdaille was largely the product of one man's vision and commitment to industrial manufacture.

In Houdaille's case, the responsible person was Ralph Peo, a man from Fred Burg's generation. A driven, and hard-driving, mechanical engineer turned corporate executive, Peo was a quintessential American industrialist, part of the breed that had manufactured the American victory during World War II and, afterward, the most productive economy in world history. "I have never worked eight hours a day in my life and I never expect to," he once observed. "I have worked 18 hours on so many days, it isn't funny. When you think the day's work is done, double it." The only thing he liked more than manufacturing was raising tulips, roses, and lilies in his garden.[1]

Peo had graduated in 1915 from the Mechanics Institute in Rochester, New York, and afterward devised his own postgraduate training program. Starting with the Packard Motor Car Corporation as a draftsman, he purposely changed jobs every year for the next five years. He left Packard to join the Dodge Brothers, and then jumped to Ford Motor, the Detroit Tool Company, and, finally, General Motors before deciding to settle down. "My five-year plan worked like a charm," he recalled years later. "I got broader experience that way than any other way I could have thought of."[2]

He cast his lot in the early 1920s with the Buffalo subsidiary of a corporation called Houdaille, which was based in Chicago.[3] The parent concern was named after Maurice Houdaille, the Frenchman who invented recoilless artillery during World War I. A standard, 75-mm. artillery gun was liable to spring back at least ten feet after being fired, greatly complicating its operation in the field. It was virtually recoilless after being fitted with Maurice Houdaille's rotary hydraulic shock absorber.

After the war, the American corporation that was to become Houdaille saw many other uses for the device. It bought rights to both the patent and the inventor's name. The corporation then refined the concept into the first hydraulic shock absorber suitable for automobiles. Soon these shocks became so common that Houdaille became the generic term for shock absorber. It was not unusual for a car owner to walk into a garage and ask for a new set of "Houdailles."[4]

The Houdaille division where Peo worked specialized in shock absorbers and other hydraulic equipment. He came to realize, though, that as much as he liked the challenge of making things, he enjoyed the task of running a company even more. Peo was rising in Houdaille's corporate ranks when World War II erupted, whereupon he helped convert all of Houdaille's plants into munitions factories, and became known for his managerial skills while doing so.[5]

Throughout the war, Peo prominently displayed a sign in his office that read "Get it done!" And Houdaille did. In one instance, the company organized a new plant of five thousand workers for the federal government virtually overnight. The factory, built alongside an existing Houdaille plant in Decatur, Illinois, was devoted to the manufacture of a long silver rod called a barrier. No one was quite sure why the government wanted it so urgently. It wasn't until the atomic bomb was dropped on Japan that Houdaille employees learned they had been part of the Manhattan Project.[6]

After the war Peo became restless. He was regarded as a likely successor to Charles Getler, Houdaille's chairman, but Getler showed no signs of retiring. Peo was also critical of Getler's overly cautious management and overdependence on the auto industry. The chairman was unwilling to stray far from making automobile products, and even moved company headquarters to Detroit so Houdaille could win more subcontracts. By contrast, Peo saw opportunities abounding in many manufacturing areas, and was eager to take advantage of them.[7]

In 1946, Peo resigned to set up a new company, Frontier Industries, and in less than a decade built a profitable and diversified industrial concern.[8] By 1955, however, Houdaille's board had come around to Peo's way of thinking and was anxious for him to return. Getler, by then in his seventies, was still refusing to scale down Houdaille's role as an automobile subcontractor. He had never known any other business. But the handwriting, so to speak, was on the wall.

Although subcontracted parts cost more, American auto makers had traditionally relied on subcontractors because it reduced overhead and shifted responsibility for expensive retooling. In the early 1950s, however, General Motors decided to reduce its dependence on outside manufactures. Shaving a few cents off the cost of a part added up to millions more in profits. And where the industry's mammoth went, the other auto makers had to follow, or risk losing market share. In addition, each year there were fewer and fewer auto makers. Most of the independents that had survived the depression were collapsing by the 1950s, leaving the industry in the hands of the Big

Three, namely, GM, Ford, and Chrysler. In sum, both trends meant less and less auto business for supplicants to the auto industry like Houdaille.[9]

Auto parts represented no less than three-fourths of Houdaille's sales. The very link that had made it a prosperous concern now threatened it.[10] Yet Charles Getler kept resisting, unable to bring himself to close unprofitable as well as profitable plants. He kept telling his board that "tomorrow would be better," but then some of Getler's own executives began to make their doubts known, and he lost control of the corporation. The way was paved for Peo's return and accession to the presidency in February 1955.[11]

Peo's Houdaille would continue to supply parts to the auto industry. But he intended to bring an end to the days when Houdaille's stock rose and fell simply on the basis of the kind of year Detroit was having. As Peo stated it, "certain large automobile manufacturers increasingly are integrating their own operations, thus reducing the percentage of the industry's total parts requirements purchased from independent suppliers. Houdaille intend[s] to pursue diversification in fields other than automotive equipment."[12]

Peo moved Houdaille's headquarters from Detroit to Buffalo shortly after he took over, to emphasize the new strategy of expansion into diverse industries. By 1962, Houdaille had been transformed from an $84 million-a-year supplier of auto parts into a corporation that annually sold $95 million worth of construction materials (concrete, gravel, and asphalt), industrial contracting and engineering services, lubricating machinery, hand tools, chemical feeders, and machine tools. Houdaille, in fact, was on its way to becoming a new species of corporation, what some observers were calling a conglomerate.[13]

The Houdaille that put out a feeler to the Burgs was very much Peo's creation. Yet by the fall of 1964, he no longer dominated the conglomerate because he was past sixty-five, Houdaille's mandatory retirement age. Instead, he watched a successor pursue the business strategy he had pioneered. Peo's heir was Gerald C. Saltarelli, a fifty-two-year-old executive who had been with the company since 1941. Slowly but inevitably, the company was also being recast in Saltarelli's image, if only because his grip on Houdaille was so complete. He held the titles of president, chief executive officer, and board chairman. And Houdaille was always a company that took on the attributes of its leader.

"Jerry" Saltarelli came from the tenements of New York City. That background and the Great Depression were the formative experiences of his life. "When you've lived on Mulberry Street, you get a different view of life," he would often remark. He lifted himself out of Mulberry Street through education, receiving an M.B.A. from the University of Buffalo in 1935, and a law degree three years later. Initially very liberal, if not socialist, in outlook, Saltarelli's hard-earned success began to make him increasingly conservative, wary of anything other than self-reliance and hard work.[14]

He had joined Houdaille in 1941, just as it was gearing up for war production. He said nothing about being a lawyer because Houdaille allegedly frowned on hiring them. The company only discovered that he was an attorney after Saltarelli began negotiating wartime contracts. In the late 1940s, Saltarelli became marked as an executive to watch when he brought a prolonged and bitter strike to an end. Fifteen Houdaille plants were lying idle and the UAW walkout was sixteen weeks old when the Houdaille executive in charge of the labor negotiations suffered a heart attack. Pressed into service despite his inexperience, in relatively short order Saltarelli and his UAW counterpart, a young official named Leonard Woodcock, were able to settle the strike.[15]

During the 1950s, Saltarelli argued for a "clear-eyed" view rather than Getler's sentimental attachment to the auto industry. The young executive also played a significant role in persuading the board that it was time to get Peo back. Vindicated by that success, in 1958 Saltarelli became the only senior vice president and the heir apparent.

Saltarelli was easily as dynamic and forceful a personality as his predecessor. But in certain key respects, he was quite different from Peo. He lacked Peo's understanding of industrial manufacture, an in-depth knowledge of how something was made. Instead, he brought another kind of expertise. As a lawyer and a voracious reader, Saltarelli was adept at digesting great amounts of information in a short time, and spewing out a succinct yet comprehensive summary. He also had a capacious memory for numbers.

Saltarelli actually preferred the tidiness of numbers to the disorder of manufacturing. Numbers reduced all the false starts and stops, and endless complications, to facts unencumbered by details. He considered numbers, and reports containing numbers, as the main tools he needed to keep track of Houdaille's disparate enterprises. Saltarelli was intent on, and perhaps only capable of, running Houdaille in a modern, "managerial" style. Yet his accession was far from unique. More and more, the top corporate slots in manufacturing were being handed over to men skilled in law and finance, rather than production.[16]

Saltarelli immediately recognized that the pace of diversification had to accelerate when he took over Houdaille in 1962. Peo had labored to keep Houdaille's automobile division as big as possible, but by and large it was a losing effort. The only subcontractors that were still doing well were those making sophisticated parts. Houdaille, by contrast, tended to be in the low, easily replaceable, end of the industry. "You're an iron bender," one auto company executive told Saltarelli. And nary a year went by without letters from either Ford or Chrysler, notifying Houdaille that they intended to manufacture another part in-house.[17]

But if it was evident, by the mid-1960s, that Saltarelli had to move faster, it was also clear that diversification was becoming more complicated. During the Peo years, Houdaille had been one among a relative handful of so-called conglomerates, that is, corporations that acquired existing, unrelated companies. But what Houdaille had resorted to mostly out of necessity, more and more corporations were turning to out of choice. Conglomeration was becoming a popular corporate strategy, imitated by scores of companies, many of them far richer and more aggressive than Houdaille.[18]

Conglomerates were on the rise for several reasons. One legal motive was corporations' desire to avoid antitrust problems caused by vertical or horizontal acquisitions. The Justice Department and Federal Trade Commission, which shared responsibility for antitrust investigations, were still quite active, as evidenced by their lengthy inquiries into the petroleum, telephone, and electrical industries. If a large textile manufacturer acquired the assets, say, of the biggest chain-saw company, however, then neither pesky federal agency had any legal grounds to intervene.

Supporters of conglomeration also believed that having a finger in several economic pies made corporate profits recession-proof. It would be unlikely for business to go bad simultaneously in such unrelated industries as sporting goods and helicopters. Some advocates even claimed that conglomerates were better able to manage cyclical industries because losses in one division could be offset with profits from another.

Another substantial incentive to conglomeration was the tax code. Mergers and acquisitions consummated through stock swaps were tax-free. "Full utilization" of the tax laws, as it was euphemistically called, also made some acquisitions look good even when there was little else to recommend them. Similarly, a relaxed regulatory environment in the 1960s contributed to the conglomerate frenzy. Corporations could finance takeovers through issuing convertible debentures or other "relatively imaginative securities" instead of borrowing money, or handing over cash or stock.[19]

All these legal and economic reasons, although perhaps self-serving, contributed to the proliferation of conglomerates. But there was another, unquantifiable motive that played a role. That was the human element. The relentless drive to build corporate empires for their own sake was probably as important a motive as any.[20]

Although some conglomerates, like Houdaille, were originally defensive in nature, they were outnumbered by those that existed because executives at ITT, Gulf & Western, Litton Industries, and Textron wanted to acquire greater economic power. Empire building had long been a feature of the economy; American culture venerated bigness, especially the corporation that was a dominant force in a fast-expanding industry. In the 1960s, though, there were few opportunities to build big the customary way. Few sectors of the manufacturing economy could satisfy empire-minded executives. Put another way, not many companies were in the enviable position of IBM, and conglomeration appeared to be the best, if not only, path toward a stronger or impregnable economic position.[21]

There were almost as many conglomerate strategies as there were motives for conglomeration. Some conglomerates, like Litton Industries, only acquired firms that fit into an overall, albeit diffuse, scheme. Others, like Textron, were comfortable taking over firms that had no discernible relationship with the given businesses. The more cautious conglomerates would not consider acquiring any company that lacked good executive talent or was awash in red ink. Others, in marked contrast, relished buying companies that were clearly stagnant. Modern, professional managers, after all, could manage anything.[22]

Charles "Tex" Thornton, one of the more flamboyant practitioners of conglomeration, exemplified the freewheeling atmosphere that prevailed in the mid-1960s. Thornton was the mastermind behind the Litton conglomerate, which reportedly considered up to fifty acquisitions a year. When asked about his seemingly haphazard pattern of takeovers, Thornton bluntly replied, "We are in the business of opportunity."[23] To the breed exemplified by Thornton, a potential acquisition was "not primarily a product, a technology, a market nor a consumer, but a balance sheet and an income statement."[24]

For Houdaille, all of this meant that Saltarelli's restructuring task was going to be considerably more difficult than Peo's. Like his predecessor, Saltarelli wanted sound, well-managed companies that fit under the rubric of industrial products. To that end, he carefully maintained a loose-leaf notebook, about the size of a telephone directory, on potential acquisitions. But the conglomerate mania tended to bid up the price of acquisitions, making it harder to find good values.[25] And because Saltarelli took a slow and steady approach, more than once Houdaille was outbid or the company it wanted was gone before an offer could be extended.

Houdaille was also penalized in a sense because Saltarelli looked askance at the kind of financial manipulations many other "conglomerateurs" engaged in. James Ling, the force behind the conglomerate Ling-Temco-Vought (LTV), was one of the more notorious manipulators of stocks and securities. Stock prices were generally high during the 1960s, and especially so for conglomerates. This valuation facilitated conglomerate takeovers. But for executives like Ling, the price was never high enough.

Ling was particularly adept at using imaginative bookkeeping methods to maximize earnings, thereby boosting the price of LTV stock and his power to acquire other companies. Adding fuel to the fire, Wall Street validated Ling's methods by assigning a high price-to-earnings ratio to LTV stock, which served to boost his takeover power even more. By contrast, because Saltarelli eschewed such tactics, and because Wall Street looked upon Houdaille's auto parts dependency with disfavor, its price-to-earnings ratio, or so-called multiple, was low.

This discrepancy created a disadvantage for Houdaille in the acquisition marketplace. If an LTV and Houdaille both offered $1 million worth of their stock in exchange for a company, the fact that LTV's multiple was twelve to fifteen times its earnings, while Houdaille's was only seven or eight, made LTV stock considerably more attractive than Houdaille's if the shares were held rather than sold. Assuming both stocks increased earnings by the same amount after a merger, it could be almost twice as profitable to merge with LTV as with Houdaille.[26]

Not only was Saltarelli unwilling to engage in dubious tactics, he was also adverse to incurring old-fashioned debt to finance acquisitions. Saltarelli knew his attitude was anachronistic; he knew Houdaille could grow faster and bigger if he were willing to borrow from banks or insurance companies, issue convertible debentures, or employ "funny money" techniques. But he could not shake his fear of debt, which had been induced by the 1930s depression. Houdaille would buy other companies for cash or by using its own stock, or not at all.[27]

As if all these impediments weren't enough, there was one more factor that hindered Houdaille's drive to diversify. Of all the kinds of businesses listed in Saltarelli's fat notebook, there was one industry that seemed especially suitable and largely untapped. That was machine tools. Houdaille already owned one machine tool builder, a Buffalo-based company called Strippit that Peo had picked up in 1956 for about $3 million.[28] It had proved to be one of Peo's best acquisitions, and whetted Saltarelli's interest in machine tools. Even if the industry was relatively small and destined to remain so, its centrality to all manufacturing was beyond dispute.

Ownership in the machine tool industry had not exactly been stagnant throughout the 1950s and early 1960s. But compared to other sectors of the manufacturing economy, the industry was still insular, homogenous, and conservative. Few companies engaged in anything other than tool building, and very few machine tool companies were owned by a larger, diversified company.[29] Stubborn, individualistic entrepreneurs dominated the industry, often the second and third generation descendants of the original founders. When not family-owned, then machine tool companies were almost always closely held corporations.[30] And regardless of ownership, because of the industry's cyclical nature, every reputable tool builder was conservatively managed.

These characteristics made the companies attractive to Saltarelli and Houdaille. Unfortunately, they fascinated many other conglomerates as well. Machine tool builders appeared ripe for picking and that they were tightly held made them that much easier to acquire. Their conservative management, reflected in a low asset-to-debt ratio, merely increased their attractiveness to debt-laden conglomerates. Above all, the advent of NC technology made the industry look futuristic as well as fundamental. Electronics and defense-based conglomerates in particular began to consider machine tools a natural extension of their own interests.[31]

Outsiders' enthusiasm over the industry was heightened because of the exuberance within. The promise, in the early 1960s, of a sustained boom had been fulfilled beyond most builders' dreams. Some observers believed President Kennedy's 1962 tax law changes, which included a 7 percent investment tax credit and accelerated depreciation schedules, provided the stimulus for manufacturers' capital spending, and machine tool demand. The new tax rules made it easier for a company to justify the purchase of a new machine.[32]

In truth, however, demand was too broad and deep to single out the tax factor as the sole cause. Shipments were exceeding $1 billion by 1964, and every estimate showed that sales would remain that high indefinitely. Among some experienced builders, who might have been expected to know better, there was even a feeling that the machine tool "millennium" had arrived. The bane of their existence, the business cycle, had finally been conquered.[33]

To conglomerates on the outside looking in, there seemed to be no wiser investment than a machine tool company. Even if the optimists proved to be wrong and the industry remained cyclic, weren't conglomerates precisely the kind of corporate organization best suited to riding out any future downturns? Several of the largest and most aggressive conglomerates, including Litton Industries, Bendix, Gulf & Western, Textron, White Consolidated, Colt Industries, and Teledyne, began combing the machine tool industry, looking for acquisitions.

Despite the competition, Saltarelli decided the machine tool industry still represented one of the best avenues for Houdaille's diversification in the mid-1960s. It would not take much more than a handful of machine tool subsidiaries to make Houdaille a major player in the industry. The same could not be said for many other lines of business. In addition, after being labeled an iron bender, there was nothing that Saltarelli wanted more than to move Houdaille into the front ranks of a technologically sophisticated industry. He knew the stock market would look more favorably on his conglomerate if he could legitimately invoke the magic words *electronics, silicon, computers,* or *controls* in the annual report.

Expansion into the industry, moreover, promised to be relatively easy in financial terms. Houdaille's own resources would be more than ample for the task. Perhaps Saltarelli could even turn around, to his advantage, the fact that Houdaille was a prosaic, rather than glamorous, conglomerate. Machine tool builders, after all, were a rather conservative lot. Maybe they would find Saltarelli preferable to such ostentatious conglomerateurs as Litton's Thornton, or Gulf & Western's Charles Bludhorn. Houdaille would offer the very best price it could afford, and make any other adjustments that seemed reasonable. That ought to be sufficient for Houdaille to attract its fair share of the machine tool industry, Saltarelli calculated.

Saltarelli designated one executive to identify and study prospective acquisitions. He began attending every machine tool show and diligently scouring every trade publication. He also investigated the machine tools Houdaille used in its own plants to see if they provided any clues about promising, but relatively obscure companies. By mid-1964, he had developed a catalog of a dozen or so prospects.

One of the builders was a company located in Lake City, Minnesota. The Di-Acro Corporation was a modest firm in a relatively unsophisticated branch of the machine tool industry, but it usually turned a tidy profit. Di-Acro produced metalworking equipment for shearing, bending, and rolling sheet-metal, and it sold these "metal-forming" machines to sheet-metal shops, laboratories, and vocational schools.[34]

Another company on the list looked even more promising, a concern by the name of Burgmaster. Saltarelli was not pleased when he saw where it was located. Gardena, California, was far removed from the heart of the machine tool industry. Nor did he like the thought of a subsidiary so distant from Houdaille's Buffalo headquarters. But one fact about this company could not be ignored. Its sales were 50 percent higher than the average for a machine tool builder of its size.[35]

Saltarelli resolved to find out more about both companies. He was particularly intrigued by the latter.

It was part of Saltarelli's intense, cautious style to go over thoroughly and personally anything of importance. Though he could delegate responsibility, he never fully relinquished it. After one of his executives flagged Burgmaster in the summer of 1964, Saltarelli began to look into the company himself. The more he looked, the more convinced he became that his executive had uncovered a gem, precisely the kind of machine tool company he wanted to acquire.

Burgmaster seemed to share many of the characteristics that had made Strippit, Houdaille's first machine tool acquisition, so profitable. The similarities between the two were striking, albeit not unusual for the machine tool industry. Both companies had been founded by machinist-entrepreneurs with a better idea. Just as Fred Burg started Burgmaster by inventing the Tool-flex, George Wales, the founder of Strippit, launched his enterprise in the 1930s by developing an improved die for punching holes in sheet metal. Conventional dies often caused warping or other distortions in the metal as they were withdrawn. Wales's innovation was to wrap a spring mechanism around the die, which evenly pushed it back out.

He called this invention a "Strippit," and it immediately became an industry standard. Eventually Wales also began to build his own punching presses. Strippit was a small, though state-of-the-art concern when Houdaille acquired it in 1956. With access to Houdaille's resources, the advent of NC technology, and its patent, Strippit then blossomed into one of the premier manufacturers of punch presses and tooling.

To Saltarelli, Burgmaster resembled Strippit. And the more he thought about the company, the more enamored Saltarelli became with the idea of acquiring it. In particular, he was captivated by Burgmaster's swollen backlog of orders. If the company had a modern factory instead of an overcrowded, antiquated plant on Figueroa, it would undoubtedly achieve dramatic gains in sales and profits.

The only obstacle, Saltarelli realized, would be persuading the Burgs to sell. By now, Saltarelli was familiar with the peculiar difficulty of wresting an enterprise away from its entrepreneur. "It was hard for such men to give up a company they had founded," he recalled. "Often it had started as a hole-in-the-wall, a single man with an idea. The company was part of them." But experience had also taught Saltarelli another lesson about entrepreneurs. Sometimes they were willing to part with their company once it got to be a certain size. Saltarelli was willing to bet that the Burgs and Burgmaster had reached that point.[36]

Saltarelli began his quest by contacting Burgmaster's investment banker, Shearson, Hammill. The initial word was not encouraging. Shearson told Houdaille that Ex-Cell-O, one of the top machine tool builders in the country, was also courting the Burgs. But Saltarelli asked to meet with them anyway in the fall of 1964.

When he did, he found Fred Burg to be just the kind of entrepreneur he had expected. The old man's pride in the company was fierce. He was Burgmaster. And nothing seemed firmer than Burg's desire to keep the company in the family. True, he was a minority stockholder by then, but it was patently clear that without Fred Burg's consent the company would not be sold. Saltarelli was nothing if not indefatigable though, and both sides agreed to continue discussions.

The Burgs' inclination before that first meeting was to keep Burgmaster independent. But, as Saltarelli suspected, and indeed hoped, the strain of the company's extraordinary growth was beginning to exact a toll. As the stakes rose higher and decisions became more difficult to undo, there was concern about what would happen the day Fred Burg was no longer part of the company. Although his step had hardly slowed, he was now sixty-eight years old. In some ways his absence could be compensated for. But in one respect, it was difficult to imagine how Burgmaster would continue to function without him. What would happen when he was no longer around as ballast and the final arbiter?

It was also an open question whether the generation after Joe Burg and Norm Ginsburg wanted to be machine tool builders. Their sons worked at Burgmaster during school vacations, often helping to compile the annual parts inventory. But among the heirs, only Paul Ginsburg exhibited more than a passing interest in the business.

Such considerations aside, the most salient reason why the Burgs began to rethink their opposition to a takeover was economic. It was late 1964, less than two years after the second major expansion of the Figueroa plant, and Burgmaster was once again hamstrung because it lacked sufficient capacity. Of course the Burgs had lived through half a dozen expansions before, and were confident of surviving another. Nevertheless, the stakes were higher than ever. Here was the opening Saltarelli needed to sway the Burgs.

While negotiations with Houdaille continued into 1965, the Burgs went ahead with a plan for expansion. Regardless of whether the takeover talks bore fruit, something had to be done to relieve congestion at the Figueroa plant. In the spring of 1965, after months of searching, Burgmaster purchased eleven acres seven miles south of its Figueroa factory, at a cost of $400,000. The idea was to construct a fifty-thousand-square-foot assembly plant at this site, and use the Figueroa plant for machining only.[37]

Everyone recognized it was not the optimum solution, for Burgmaster would be split into two facilities, miles apart. But despite Burgmaster's nearly unblemished record of growth, the Burgs were wary of extending themselves any further. Fred Burg was much too old a hand to believe rosy predictions about an end to the machine tool industry's chronic cycles. Burgmaster had gone through several recessions, and the fact that they often coincided with past expansions was a running, if somewhat painful, joke.

Another factor that dictated prudence was the coincidental need to develop the 20T machining center. If the Burgs had been given a choice between expansion and bringing out an entirely new kind of machining center, that would have been one thing. But Burgmaster had to do both, and at precisely the same time. Then too, it was becoming clear by 1965 that the birth of the 20T was going to be far from painless. The new machine was proving exceedingly difficult to manufacture, primarily because it was hard to accurately machine twenty holes to the required tolerance in a critical casting. This also persuaded the Burgs to keep the expansion as modest as possible.

Saltarelli was aware of these circumstances, and decided to turn them to Houdaille's advantage. At every meeting between Houdaille executives and the Burgs, the former emphasized that Burgmaster's potential warranted an entirely new state-of-the-art factory. This was presented as Houdaille's best advice, made without prejudice. Naturally, the conglomerate wanted nothing more than for Burgmaster to join its corporate family. But even if Burgmaster remained independent, its next expansion ought to be done right. Although true enough, behind this advice lay a shrewd calculation. If Houdaille could persuade the Burgs to take the eminently justifiable but bigger risk, Burgmaster was more likely to fall into its lap.

The strategy began to work. The need for a plant such as Houdaille advocated was manifest. The old man knew it, and wanted something that would testify in concrete and machines that Burgmaster was the largest tool builder west of the Mississippi. Bolstered by Houdaille's support and confidence, the Burgs scuttled plans for adding only an assembly plant. They began thinking in terms of an entirely new factory, and Saltarelli sent out some Houdaille engineers to help them with the plans, no strings attached.

Gradually, almost imperceptibly, the Burgs began to think, well, if a fitting price and the proper guarantees and conditions could be assured, perhaps a merger was desirable. Saltarelli's commitment to the machine tool industry, after all, seemed impressive. And the Buffalo conglomerate had enough resources to finance both a major plant expansion and the development of a whole new generation of Burgmasters. As Ginsburg would later recall, "From a financial end, we began to think of a merger because every expansion [had] put three families in jeopardy."[38] Just as Saltarelli had hoped, the Burgs' desire to expand the "right way" was edging them toward a deal.

Meanwhile, the Burgs learned more about Houdaille, its executives, and the companies in its machine tool group. They visited the Strippit division along with other subsidiaries located in Buffalo, and found that Houdaille's style seemed to mesh with their own. When they talked to entrepreneurs who had sold out to Houdaille, they learned something else of importance. The new management seemed to treat the founding owners and holdover employees with respect.[39]

By this time, too, the Burgs had developed considerable regard for Jerry Saltarelli. Although some of the Houdaille executive vice presidents seemed distant, Saltarelli impressed the Burgs as a dynamic and engaging chief executive. As long as Houdaille was under his control they had little doubt that it would continue to prosper. That was important, because if the deal went through, the Burgs' fortunes would no longer be tied to a company they controlled. Houdaille would be the steward of everything they had worked to build.

In the spring of 1965, after about eight months, and scores of meetings, negotiations between Houdaille and Burgmaster "got down to nuts and bolts," Norm Ginsburg recalled. Houdaille made a bid that seemed acceptable, and the Burgs turned to John Shad, the investment banker who had guided the transformation of Burg Tool into Burgmaster. He was still a member of their board. Fred Burg telephoned Shad in New York and told him that they had agreed to sell Burgmaster to Houdaille through a tax-free exchange of common shares. Burgmaster shareholders would receive a handsome premium over the amount the stock was then commanding on the American Stock Exchange. But the Burgs had only tentatively accepted Houdaille's offer—it was subject to Shad's review. The old man asked Shad to meet that evening with Saltarelli, who was already on a plane headed for New York.[40]

Shad roughed out the arithmetic, and although it was an attractive offer, he decided it could be improved. Shad was familiar with one of the practices that some conglomerates, notably Litton, had pioneered to increase their acquisition power. It was a tactic whereby the buyer exchanged new, preferred stock, instead of common stock, for the common stock of the seller. The preferred stock would be convertible, that is, it could be exchanged for common stock at any time. So in essence it was no different. But there were certain advantages to this approach, and Shad decided to make a case for it to Saltarelli that evening.

Shad told him that as the deal now stood, the proposed exchange of common shares would dilute Houdaille's earnings per share, thus lowering its market value after the takeover. But if Houdaille offered the Burgs a convertible preferred stock instead, Houdaille's earnings per common share would not fall. In fact, with Burgmaster's profits figured in, Houdaille's earnings per share would increase, and the market value of its stock would rise correspondingly.[41]

The advantages that would accrue to Houdaille seemed obvious. But why should the Burgs be interested in structuring the deal this way? Shad explained that if Houdaille agreed to a preferred-for-common swap, the conglomerate would be expected to pay Burgmaster shareholders more, by increasing the market value of the new convertible preferred shares. Something on the scale of a million dollars would be fair to both parties, Shad suggested.[42]

Saltarelli was not one to incur any added risks. But there were none. A preferred-for-common swap simply took advantage of how the stock market calculated value and the rules of the game. He promptly notified the Burgs that Houdaille would agree to offer a higher price, based on the arrangement outlined by Shad. On June 7, 1965, Houdaille and Burgmaster issued a statement announcing that both companies' boards had approved a merger in principle. Houdaille would redeem all of Burgmaster's 494,810 common shares in exchange for 340,000 shares of Houdaille preferred stock. Put another way, each Burgmaster share would be worth .68713 share of the preferred stock, which in turn would be convertible at any time into .56 share of Houdaille common stock. The par value of the preferred stock was $8.5 million, meaning that Burgmaster stockholders would receive a premium of more than $2.2 million above market value for their shares.[43]

The terms of the deal appeared to be set. But about a month later, Joe Burg decided that a higher price was in order. By late June, new sales and earnings figures had become available for the six months prior to May 1. The numbers were much higher than anyone at Burgmaster had anticipated. Earnings per share were up 40 percent, from forty-three cents to sixty cents. Burg persuaded his father and brother-in-law that they should be willing to see the deal fall through unless Houdaille upped the ante.[44]

There was another motive at work here as well. All along, Joe Burg had been the most recalcitrant about selling out. Norm Ginsburg had been the first to become enthusiastic about the idea. (Afterward Saltarelli often remarked that if it hadn't been for Ginsburg, "Houdaille would never have gotten Burgmaster.") Then the old man was persuaded that it was time to sell, although he hated to part with his enterprise, his lifeblood. Finally, Joe Burg was reconciled to the idea. But he still wasn't enthusiastic.[45]

Nothing short of an unreasonable demand, however, was going to dissuade Saltarelli at this point. Of course, Houdaille would not have to reach into its own pockets for the entire increase sought by the Burgs. Greater earnings by Burgmaster meant the price of Houdaille's common stock would also be that much higher after the takeover. Saltarelli's new offer came in at $9.35 million. It met the Burgs' demand, and there was nothing left to do but accept.

In late October 1965, Burgmaster and Houdaille shareholders officially approved the acquisition. Other than the transfer of ownership, the public announcement made it sound as if nothing was going to change. Houdaille stated that "Burgmaster would continue to operate under present management, personnel and policies [but] as a Houdaille division."[46]

Burgmaster would never be the same.

5

THE HOUDAILLE WAY (1966–1967)

When the takeover by Houdaille was announced in mid-1965, several key, longtime employees came to the Burgs. They were worried about the future. They wondered how things would change, whether the takeover meant they should look for another job. In every instance the Burgs gave assurances that things would not change, and if they did, only for the better.

The Burgs' confidence was contagious. Most employees became "upbeat and enthusiastic," recalled Bob French, a longtime design engineer. "People felt that now Burgmaster would become a big-time outfit, and that everybody would do well as the company expanded."[1] There were few, if any, doubters.

Houdaille did indeed have big plans for Burgmaster. It also anticipated big results. The conglomerate had been attracted to Burgmaster for a number of reasons, but the major one was its "growth potential." In the five years from 1958 to 1962, Burgmaster's sales had doubled; then, in a four-year period, from 1962 to 1965, sales had doubled again. Now Houdaille expected Burgmaster's sales to double for a third time, and in no more than three years.[2]

A new plant in Gardena, on 139th Street and Broadway, was the first and most important step in Houdaille's grand design. Work on it began well before the takeover was officially consummated in November 1965. By late 1966, the relocation of Burgmaster was scheduled to be complete.

For Burgmaster, it would mean being able to breathe again. The new factory, to be built at a cost of $1.6 million, would have about 176,000 square feet of manufacturing and office space, making it two and a half times larger than the Figueroa plant.[3] At last there would be ample room for receiving parts, assembling machines, and shipping them. The engineering department would no longer be cramped for space, and the machine shop's appetite for electric power easily sated. And for once, there would be enough parking spaces for everyone.

Much time and thought had also been devoted to making the new plant state-of-the-art. Ceilings in the area reserved for manufacture would be a minimum of thirty-two feet high; the low ceilings at Figueroa were a never-ending headache. There would be five separate manufacturing bays, each one sixty feet wide. This meant that an entire row of machinists would no longer have to stop work whenever a large casting was being moved, as was often the case on Figueroa. To the relief of every machinist and foreman, each bay was also to be fitted with a minimum of one, and sometimes four, traveling overhead cranes, with capacities ranging from three to twenty tons.[4] Moving large workpieces throughout the shop floor would now be like sliding down a greased pole.

All this was only the beginning. In order to double Burgmaster's 1965 sales of $9.6 million (an all-time high) to $20 million by 1968, more than a new plant was needed. Burgmaster would also require large capital investments in equipment, and the company's organizational structure would have to be totally revamped.[5]

Burgmaster's acute need was for more machine tools to build its machine tool. It did not take a sage to realize that a major production problem was the lack of lathes, millers, drills, and grinders. From 1964 to 1965, written orders had increased 90 percent, from $8.4 million to $16 million. Yet shipments had risen only 18 percent, leaving the company with a $10.5 million backlog by early 1966, the largest in Burgmaster's history. Most customers had to wait twelve to fifteen months before they could get their hands on a Burgmaster.[6]

Whenever possible, Burgmaster had tried to ameliorate its backlog by relying on outside machine shops, or "jobbers." As a result, the percentage of machining farmed out was very high. Houdaille calculated that Burgmaster supplied just over 7 percent of the labor involved in an average machine, and a major portion of that was assembly work. Naturally, the company could never hope (or want) to fabricate many of the components that went into a Burgmaster, such as the motors or the single most costly item, the numerical control. But many more parts could be machined in-house. Houdaille estimated that capital outlays of $750,000 in 1966, $800,000 in 1967, and $1 million in 1968 would be sufficient to buy the eighteen or so machine tools necessary to do the job.[7] By way of contrast, the amount Houdaille intended to spend in 1966 alone was almost as much as the Burgs ordinarily spent in three years.

In the past Norm Ginsburg felt compelled to buy a used machine if he could find it, rather than order a brand new one. And if Burgmaster had no recourse to buying a new machine, Ginsburg made sure that he didn't buy anything beyond the minimum necessary. But now Burgmaster had the luxury of picking up the telephone and ordering a machine with all the trimmings. No one enjoyed this luxury more than Joe Burg. It meshed with his own nature. Indeed, he, Ginsburg, and the old man now seemed to have the best of all possible worlds. They had access to the resources of an attentive parent corporation and their titles inside Burgmaster were unchanged. Joe

Burg remained as president, Ginsburg was executive vice president, and Fred Burg prowled the factory as a high-paid consultant. There was no more friction between Houdaille and Burgmaster management than there traditionally had been among the Burgs themselves, and perhaps even less.

Yet the family could not help noticing a degree of condescension from some top Houdaille executives in the months after the takeover. There was much criticism of the "status quo," how "unthinkable" and "disastrous" it would be if Burgmaster narrow-mindedly stuck to the path that had gotten the company where it was. As one Houdaille report awkwardly put it, "Industrial history is rich in companies formerly leaders in their respective fields who were lured by good profits with relatively little risk only to discover that failure to meet the demands of the market had forced them into a precarious position."[8] Burgmaster had never failed before to "meet the demands of the market." Its very success had proceeded from a keen appreciation of the market and constant technological innovation. If the Burgs had been a bit too hesitant about expansion, it was a caution born of a healthy respect for the vagaries of the machine tool business and their own limited resources. They were hardly adverse to risk, and Burgmaster's history was ample proof.

Such slights undoubtedly stemmed from Houdaille executives' pride in being part of a much older and larger corporation. Another source was their sense that they, and kindred conglomerates, represented the business organization of the present and future, come to rescue an industry that had been too stodgy for its own good, despite its current success. Houdaille paid some homage to the industry's chronic cycles of growth and recession: "The machine tool market is enjoying a wave of prosperity and will no doubt respond to market fluctuations in the future." But just below this acknowledgment was a confidence bordering on conceit. Houdaille believed two factors, the advent of computer controls and its own modern management, somehow changed the industry's ground rules. "The future of the machine tool market should not be judged solely by today's high demands," one Houdaille report read, "but neither should it be judged solely by past performance." Houdaille would somehow defy the busts and exploit the booms. Everyone thought we could "frustrate the cyclical nature of the business," said a Houdaille executive years later.[9]

By early 1966, this conceit had revealed itself in a singular way. The Burgs were not so naïve as to think that major decisions could be undertaken without Houdaille's advice and consent. They knew that with the sale, they had ceded ultimate control of their enterprise. But what surprised them was the kind and degree of oversight that Houdaille wanted to exercise, even within the confines of the factory. The upper echelons acted as though "we didn't know how to do anything," recalled Norm Ginsburg.[10]

The Burgs valued Houdaille's advice when it came to matters in which they had little experience or knowledge. Their reliance on Houdaille's engineering and construction expertise while the new factory was going up was proof of that. But now, decisions that they were fully (and perhaps better) qualified to make, and had always settled among themselves, had to be submitted to distant Buffalo for approval. "You could run it—not as you saw fit—but to fit [Houdaille's] corporate structure," said Joe Burg.[11] And the principal means by which Houdaille gained decision-making power was its requirement that Joe Burg write a comprehensive monthly report, teeming with numbers, on Burgmaster's operations.

If the Burgs were unprepared for this development, and a bit dismayed, Saltarelli had been waiting for the problem to arise. He knew, after the courtship and marriage, that the honeymoon with a new acquisition seldom lasted more than a few months. The smart, able entrepreneurs who started such companies often found it hard to adjust to Houdaille's ways. Sometimes Houdaille even bought companies in which the most rudimentary management tools, like account books, were missing. "Their accounting would be almost zilch," Saltarelli said. "They would have all the figures in the top of their heads."[12] Such instances were the exception, however, and certainly did not apply to the Burgmaster-Houdaille equation. The problem was getting Burgmaster to do monthly, and much more extensively, what it used to do quarterly, and leisurely.

A Houdaille monthly report was forty to fifty pages long, only some of which were routine, and covered every imaginable aspect of the company. "You can't run something without reports," Saltarelli was fond of remarking.[13] None of the Burgs disagreed, exactly. But they nevertheless found it difficult to gear the company to Saltarelli's thirst for numbers and reports. To write the monthly report, Joe Burg in turn had to have reports from the head of every department in the company. More important, the culture of reporting, Houdaille-style, seemed to be turning Burgmaster upside down.

Prior to the 1965 takeover, budgets and quotas, insofar as they existed, were flexible guides. Burgmaster shipped as many machines out each month as it possibly could, not because a monthly forecast called for twelve machines to be shipped out. "When it looked like we could easily meet a schedule we had set for ourselves," Bob French recalled, "Joe Burg thought nothing of moving up the deadline a week earlier."[14] Again, if a piece of equipment was needed—and if Norm Ginsburg agreed—then Burgmaster bought it, regardless of whether it had been in the budget or not. Such a system worked because the Burgs knew their business from the bottom up. And it gave the company the flexibility to make things happen in a hurry. Numbers were used at Burgmaster, but as a measure of performance and a guide. They had never been an all-consuming purpose.[15]

Houdaille's system could not have been more different. The conglomerate's lifeblood was reports, forecasts, and budgets, or what has been called managing by the numbers. Ultimately, of course, the emphasis on numbers could be traced to the very top. It was inextricably bound up with Jerry Saltarelli's personality, capabilities, and perception of his role as CEO.

Saltarelli was a man who found it very difficult to let any aspect of the company slip from his grasp. No Houdaille division shifted a department head without his personal involvement or active approval. He hated vacations, and would drive his wife crazy on the rare occasion when they took one. He "didn't trust anyone to run Houdaille" in his absence.[16]

Saltarelli's emphasis on control had been apparent from the day he became president of Houdaille in 1962. When he took over, there were so many vice presidents around that they were literally "tripping over one another." Saltarelli believed Houdaille could not afford to have a vice president in charge of each group in the conglomerate. Where there was a vice president, a whole retinue followed. So he devised a new structure: within each group, the president of one of the subsidiaries (usually the largest) donned a second hat and became the head of that entire group. Thus the president of the Strippit division doubled as vice president in charge of Houdaille's machine tool group.[17]

Naturally, this meant paying these executives higher salaries and bonuses, but it reduced the overhead for headquarters dramatically. Thereafter Houdaille always featured a lean executive staff, almost skeletonlike compared to the size and diversity of the conglomerate. The tightness of his corporate ship was a source of great pride to Saltarelli. But most important, eliminating an entire layer of executives enhanced his control.

Once he gained control, reports and numbers made it possible for Saltarelli to retain control. The emphasis on numbers flowed naturally. Not only were they an obvious means, they were Saltarelli's great skill. He knew he was not a production man, and that he had to rely on his division presidents and plant managers for that expertise. Instead, his formidable strength was his ability to absorb numbers and make strategic decisions based on them.

And so Saltarelli made sure that Houdaille's structure yielded the numbers he needed to do his job. He insisted on monthly reports from the vice president in charge of each Houdaille group, and monthly reports from the president of every division within each group. He read them all. Division presidents were reminded of that quite often, whenever their latest report came back with a "What do you mean?" or "Elaborate!" scrawled in the margin.[18]

If a subsidiary's shipments were higher last quarter than the current quarter, the lagging performance showed in the numbers, and Saltarelli would promptly want to know why. As for the remedy, that was left to the executives in charge, at least initially. In this sense, Saltarelli's Houdaille was decentralized—as long as the numbers pointed the right way. If they did not for too long a time, then his recourse was to fire and hire until he found someone who could get the numbers right.

There was nothing mysterious about this. Saltarelli was always frank about the nature and purpose of Houdaille's management structure. "Being a lawyer by training," he said, "you don't really know about machines and industrial operations like someone who was an engineer. So you have to construct an organization to fit you."[19]

Nevertheless, the Burgs were having a hard time making Burgmaster fit. For one, they were slow to comprehend the seriousness of the game. The cardinal sin was not meeting a forecast. Falling short in sales or shipments carried obvious implications. Exceeding a forecast, though, was not much better. It raised eyebrows about the accuracy of the initial prediction. Essentially, any substantial deviation or discrepancy in forecasts from one month to the next quickly elicited a telephone call or visitor from Buffalo. Similarly, if a piece of equipment was needed but had not been budgeted for, the purchase had to be delayed until the next cycle. It was difficult to adjust to the fact that headquarters deemed no task more important than the writing of reports, and adhering to them.

Gradually, as the Burgs became more steeped in the culture of reporting, they learned that other Houdaille executives viewed the reports more as a vehicle for telling headquarters what they thought it wanted to hear, rather than as a monthly occasion for candor. One could not, of course, doctor facts and figures. On the contrary, the emphasis was on making sure that the numbers met all of Buffalo's expectations.

The real source of the Burgs' problem, however, was that they were completely unused to running their enterprise this way. Before the takeover they readily offered a gross estimate about future shipments and sales. Indeed, they had become much more aware of numbers and the bottom line since 1961, when the enterprise became a publicly traded corporation. But even after that transformation, numbers remained a measure rather than a dictator.

The machine tool business had so many vagaries, so many things that could go wrong, that the Burgs had always operated on a radically different principle. They had devoted themselves to keeping Burgmaster ahead and solving problems rather than fulfilling prophecies. In due course, the numbers would take care of themselves. Now it was as if Burgmaster's purpose were being defined in a new way: it existed in order to file reports laden with numbers and gain the approval of Buffalo.

Despite these difficulties, the Burgs kept their uneasiness to themselves. Because they still commanded the loyalty of nearly every employee, the Burgs believed that revealing their own disappointment would foster division, and make it harder to smooth out rough spots in the transition. If the Burgs decided to be circumspect in front of longtime employees, however, the reverse was not true. Many employees were quite outspoken, among themselves and with the Burgs directly, about changes they saw—changes that went to the very heart of how Burgmaster conducted its business.

Employees in the machine shop were the first to speak up about the company changing course. At first, the hands-on approach that had characterized Burgmaster management since its earliest days seemed unchanged. The

Figueroa plant was so cramped that it was hard for white-collar managers not to be on the shop floor. But shortly after Burgmaster began moving into the new factory on Broadway midway through 1966, longtime employees began to notice something. The managers brought in by Houdaille were rarely to be found on the shop floor, and they certainly weren't going to do anything that would get their hands dirty. To the workers, it looked as if they preferred their spartan, but air-conditioned offices to knowing what was going on in the noisy, dirty, and hot (during the summer) factory. A distinction between white- and blue-collar workers that had never existed before became evident.

It wasn't that the Houdaille men believed they knew everything they needed to know about Burgmaster's operations. "The Houdaille guys, they wanted to know," recalls Ginsburg. "And we did everything we could to get them embedded, to do the best job that they could."[20] But what they had to learn, managers figured, they could learn from the Burgs and Burgmaster management. The average machinist had nothing to teach them. The Burgs' contrasting attitude toward the blue-collar work force was dismissed as an unnecessary and unbecoming relic, though understandable given their own years in the machine shop. Furthermore, it gave workers the wrong idea. In a Houdaille division, everyone knew their proper place.

In a way, this attitude alone was sufficient to begin the alienation of the workers. The situation was exacerbated, however, by a second factor. Houdaille's method for gaining more productivity from the rank and file also differed from that of the Burgs. Talking at workers was as much a part of the Houdaille way as not listening to them.

Formerly, productivity had been a natural consequence of the machinists' pride and the respect they were accorded by management. No one knew better than the Burgs themselves which workers were the most productive, and they suitably rewarded them. Houdaille replaced these tenets with posted slogans urging the workers on, productivity studies, and memos of the month. None of it was particularly harmful. But in the breach that was widening between workers and managers because of deeds, words of encouragement rang hollow and were privately ridiculed by a work force that was rather abruptly turning cynical.

One of the first persons to notice the grumbling was "Big Ben" Bezdziecki, a longtime employee. Because of his height—he was more than six foot three—Bezdziecki was tagged Big Ben from almost the moment he began working at Burgmaster in 1959. He was also a devotee of the way the Burgs ran their company, and for good reason. The Burgs had developed nearly all their managerial talent from within the company, and like many others, Bezdziecki had benefited. He rose to white-collar status after starting out as a machinist with nothing more than a high school education. By 1965, when Houdaille took over, Bezdziecki was general foreman of the machine shop, one of the most demanding positions in the entire factory.[21]

Initially, and especially after hearing the Burgs' assurances, Bezdziecki was enthusiastic about the takeover. He looked forward to managing in the Burgs' style, with simultaneous access to Houdaille's relatively deep pockets. But earlier than most, Bezdziecki heard the workers' complaints. "Before the takeover, I had never heard guys complain about the company," he recalled. "Now it became the goddamn company this, the goddamn company that. A lot of harmony was lost."[22] Then, shortly after his machinists began muttering, Bezdziecki found his own reasons to be vexed.

If nothing else, Burgmaster had always been a place where everyone knew their own role, and took a catholic view toward their work. No one stood on ceremony or worried about titles. The emphasis had been on getting the job done efficiently. "When Norm [Ginsburg] was in charge of manufacturing, if he was going to spend a nickel," recalled Bezdziecki, "we were going to make a quarter. That rubbed off, and the basic thought was to be as efficient as we could while making a quality product."[23]

Suddenly it wasn't that way anymore. Houdaille had insisted upon a wholesale reorganization of Burgmaster, and by early 1966, there were many new boxes on Burgmaster's organization chart. All of them were filled with white-collar personnel, many of whom were unfamiliar with anything except their own narrow role—and sometimes they were not even certain about that. Some jurisdictions seemed to overlap; other times, vital tasks that had been handled efficiently now fell between the boxes. Houdaille had touted reorganization as the vital third link, along with new plant and equipment, in its grand design for Burgmaster. But for foremen like Bezdziecki, the reorganization meant an elaborate "control" bureaucracy that seemed to create more problems than it solved.[24]

For many years prior to Houdaille's arrival, there had always been an easily achieved, informal accord between the assembly department and machine shop about which parts needed to be made and when. It was especially important to get agreement on big castings, such as columns and bases. Shipment of a machine could be delayed by weeks if the basic parts were not ready on time. Ginsburg, and all the responsible foremen, would sit down once every few weeks, more often if necessary, and within thirty minutes hammer out a schedule so that the appropriate times would be uppermost in everyone's mind.

Under Houdaille's reorganization, this task was ostensibly turned over to a greatly expanded production control department. From that point on, the assembly and machine shop foremen were only supposed to worry about meeting the schedule, not drawing it up. Accordingly, the informal arrangement between the two departments ended and the respective foremen were informed that any scheduling problems were to be aired at a weekly meeting of all department heads.

The people Houdaille brought in to staff production control, unfortunately, knew little about machining and even less about Burgmaster. They had neither an instinct for the lead time the machine shop needed to produce different parts nor an intrinsic grasp of which parts, in which order, enabled the assembly department to go about its work. Soon it was not uncommon for the machine shop to be tied up producing twice as many slides as were necessary while the assembly department was begging for finished tables. Meanwhile, whenever the problem was raised at the weekly departmental meeting, the session ended before anything this complicated and specific could be resolved. It took months of confusion before the machine shop and assembly foremen secured permission to resume separate meetings.[25]

Under Houdaille's management, "you learned to live with" such squandering of time and money, said Bezdziecki. The problems created by production control were no anomaly. Several Houdaille initiatives took functions that had been subsumed under the rubric and authority of manufacturing, separated them out, and staffed them with white-collar employees experienced in neither the industry nor the product. The snafus that resulted only made Burgmaster's already heavy backlog worse.

Appalled by the inefficiency and waste of resources he saw all around him, Bezdziecki's dedication quickly turned to resignation. "Just leave my people alone" became his new motto, so that at least the box he was responsible for could get its work done. "Six months after the takeover, I went to see Norm [Ginsburg]," recalled Bezdziecki. "I said if this is indicative of how big manufacturing businesses are run in the United States, I didn't understand how we as a country had gotten as far as we had."[26]

By mid-1966, corporate headquarters also recognized that the transition was not going smoothly. But Houdaille had a different diagnosis of the problem. Headquarters believed that the problem was Burgmaster's tendency to cling to the "Hey, Joe" school of production rather than adopt Houdaille's modern methods.

To be sure, there was some inertia and some resistance among longtime Burgmaster employees. Still, most employees recognized that many changes had to be made to secure Burgmaster's role as a big-time tool builder. The company had to become more orchestrated, controlled, and sophisticated. The problem, from their point of view, was that many of Houdaille's pet theories did not work in practice. The changes it demanded were not organic. There was too little appreciation of how Burgmaster did work, in Houdaille's rush to make it work better.

During the rocky transition, many longtime employees were apt to recall another occasion when Burgmaster went through growing pains. About eleven years before, in 1955, burgeoning sales had revealed many deficiencies in the way Burgmaster manufactured its machines. The company was scarcely more predictable in its manufacturing procedures than a job shop, and quality was too irregular. Fred Burg hired an experienced shop foreman, Jack Manders, to supervise a thorough overhaul of the machine shop. Manders was a hard-bitten individual and extremely difficult to work for. But his expertise was unquestioned, and the logic behind every change he instigated was there for all to see.[27]

Employees recalled this episode to prove to themselves, if no one else, that they were not adverse to new ways of doing things. Many of them quietly appealed to the old man, Joe Burg, and Norm Ginsburg. Didn't Houdaille realize what was going on? Granted, changes were necessary, but Houdaille could not possibly want to unleash such confusion, to cause Burgmaster to lose some of the qualities that had made it successful. Sometimes, privately, the Burgs would agree. In particular, they expressed disenchantment with Houdaille's "adversarial mentality" toward blue-collar employees.[28] More often, they simply responded, "that's the way it is when you get big," and offered to try to remedy the specific gripe.[29]

The Burgs felt powerless to do more. They had been prepared for more bureaucracy now that Burgmaster was employing up to 425 people. They also realized that it would be unlikely for Burgmaster to obtain, in its expanded state, the same quality people they had previously depended on. Nevertheless, they had not been prepared for the assault on their values. It was discouraging to watch the erosion of principles they had constantly sought to instill.

The forces pulling at their enterprise were not new, of course. In one form or another, they had always been present, and it had taken all the Burgs' energies to keep every employee and every department in harness. They had succeeded in keeping their company's attention riveted to "the object, the function, the program, the task, the need," mainly because everyone shared certain values. But these were being displaced by Houdaille's tenets, and there was "immense attention [paid] to the role, procedure, prestige, and profit."[30] Managerialism was displacing entrepreneurialism at Burgmaster.

The attitude of many employees to these developments, and especially to the new bureaucracy, was summed up in a dry joke that began to circulate throughout the plant not long after the takeover. It was written on a single sheet of paper and carried the title "It's This Way."

> Two Burgmaster employees were standing together in the hallway.
> First Burgmaster employee asked the other, "Is your name Mr. Saltarelli?"
> "No."
> "Are you a member of the Board?"
> "No."
> "Were you hired by Houdaille, Buffalo?"
> "No."
> "Do any of your relatives work for Houdaille?"
> "No."
> "In that case, get the hell off my foot!"

As 1967 began, Burgmaster looked from the outside like a company that had everything going for it. The move into the spacious new factory on Broadway was complete, and the benefits from Houdaille's capital investment in equipment were beginning to be felt. Burgmaster went to two full shifts in the machine shop, although it was exceedingly difficult to find good machinists. The aerospace industry in Southern California was booming because of the Vietnam War.

Another positive sign was that orders for the 20T seemed to be picking up. *American Machinist,* the industry's trade machine, had devoted a cover story to the 20T, the machining center that was supposed to keep Burgmaster at the leading edge. By early 1967, more than a dozen were on order, many of them slated for Ford Motor's Aerospace division in Irvine, California. Ford intended to put the machine to work making the "Shillelagh" missile.[31]

Burgmaster's reputation, moreover, transcended national boundaries. In 1967, a thaw in the cold war was leading to a marked increase in cultural and economic exchanges with the Soviet Union. A Soviet delegation of twelve machinery and computer experts was invited to tour American industry, in anticipation that certain trade restrictions might be lifted. One of the companies the Soviets asked to visit was Burgmaster, even though (or perhaps because) the company's NC turret drills could not be exported to the Soviet Union.[32]

The Soviet delegation, which included Anatoly Gromyko, son of the Soviet foreign minister, arrived at Burgmaster just before New Year's Day 1967. They seemed to be impressed by the state-of-the-art factory, and it was not hard to understand why. The Soviets' machine tool industry lagged far behind its American counterpart; most Soviet machines were copies of now-obsolete American tools delivered under Lend-Lease arrangements during the world war. The relative backwardness of Soviet industry became embarrassingly clear when Nicolai Sergeyev, the Soviet vice minister for machine tools and instrumentation, asked Joe Burg, via a translator, if the delegation could also see Burgmaster's "second plant." He did not believe that Burgmaster could manufacture so many NC machines with a work force of just 425.[33]

Burgmaster's capitalist owners, however, were not as impressed with the company as were the socialist observers. Houdaille was far from satisfied with Burgmaster's performance by early 1967, little more than a year after the takeover. In corporate parlance, Burgmaster's "planned-for progress [had] not been fully realized."[34] Worse, Saltarelli's goal of doubling the company's shipments by 1968 appeared to be in serious jeopardy, which meant that Houdaille would not reap the expected rewards from its investment. The biggest problem was still the backlog. But by now, Saltarelli had decided who the culprit was: Joe Burg, and his emphasis on sales.

Saltarelli had realized, soon after first meeting Burg, that he was not exactly cast in the Houdaille mold. It wasn't simply that he was "more of the salesman" than the kind of man Saltarelli liked to recruit.[35] Instead, his most prominent traits tended to be the exact opposite of those Saltarelli deemed desirable. The Houdaille ethic was to be austere; Burg leaned toward flamboyance. When Burg purchased the Beverly Hills home of Spike Jones, an ostentatious band leader, it was considered a most un-Houdaille-like thing to do, and became a source of considerable executive gossip.[36]

A Houdaille executive was well advised to favor a no-nonsense, calculated approach to business. The more ways he could find to improve Houdaille's bottom line, the more likely he was to rise in Saltarelli's esteem. This approach was far removed from Burg's easygoing, expansive view of business in general, and his paternal attitude toward Burgmaster in particular. To Saltarelli, Burg was quick to promise improvement but never able to deliver. To Burg, Houdaille had a "cop's mentality."[37] The contrast in styles was obvious, and a clash was inevitable.

Still, Saltarelli was prepared to try a number of things before taking the ultimate step. He decided to put more Houdaille loyalists into company ranks. Perhaps the production logjam could be improved by reducing the number and influence of employees whose first allegiance was to the Burgs. For he believed that Burgmaster's main problem was that it clung to outmoded methods.

But if anything, the reshuffling and new personnel made matters worse. Longtime Burgmaster managers, already skeptical about the effects of the takeover, became anxious and confused. Rumors swept the factory. The Burgs' pretakeover promise—that everyone would benefit from the association with Houdaille—was all but forgotten. People worried about losing their jobs outright to handpicked Houdaille men, or having their authority curtailed as a prelude to being forced out.

The crisis in confidence reached such a point that in early February 1967, Joe Burg issued a three-page open letter in an attempt to dispel the rumors.

> I have been listening to various people at the factory discuss their feelings on BURGMASTER and its problems....
>
> ... I feel that there is a feeling that since BURGMASTER'S merger into Houdaille's group of companies that this has become an impersonal type of operation—and this is far from the truth; that many of the jobs will be rotated automatically because the Corporation Headquarters people want to move the BURGMASTER people out and replace them with Houdaille people, and this is certainly far from the truth....
>
> ... the feeling that jobs are in jeopardy—this is far from the truth *except where a job is not being handled as it should.* I assure you that if you do your job, you are in no danger of being replaced, you are in danger of being advanced, of getting better pay, getting more responsibility, getting a chance to grow.... We have our troubles with production, we are making changes—bringing in people from Headquarters to help us and we

call on Headquarters because the people are available and save us the time of searching in the open field. This division has the option of hiring whatever personnel it desires, from whatever sources it desires. . . . I wish to dispel the thought that these people are being forced on the division in order for a take-over of personnel to take place—this is far from the truth.[38]

The letter soothed employees' worst fears, but Burgmaster's production bottlenecks remained. By the spring of 1967, Saltarelli's anxiety had risen to a point where he decided a drastic step was necessary. He told the Burgs that in order to relieve the backlog, he wanted to transfer production of Burgmaster's small tools to Powermatic, a Houdaille division located in McMinnville, Tennessee.

Houdaille had acquired the thirty-nine-year-old Powermatic in May 1966 as part of its expansion into the machine tool industry. Although Houdaille touted it as such, Powermatic was not a builder of precision machine tools. The closest it came to manufacturing a sophisticated tool was its drill press, which was about as complicated as the ones Sears, Roebuck sold in its retail stores to weekend hobbyists. For the most part, Powermatic was a manufacturer of simple band saws, sanders, and grinders, suitable for use in trade schools and vocational classes.[39]

Saltarelli's plan sparked the first open disagreement between Houdaille and the Burgs. His idea was not without merit, the Burgs had to agree. Burgmaster had its hands full with the large backlog. In addition, the cost of labor in McMinnville was far less; the Powermatic plant did not even have a union. And it would be more lucrative for Houdaille if Burgmaster's skilled and expensive work force was devoted exclusively to building NC and other precision machines.[40]

Nevertheless, the Burgs were loathe to give up any part of their business. The small, manual turret drills at issue usually accounted for less than 10 percent of Burgmaster's total shipments in any given year. Nonetheless, they were a highly profitable segment. Since 1960, sales of small tools had actually increased more than any other category, including NC. Burgmaster was capable of cranking out fifty or sixty of these machines per month with hardly any effort.[41] Even if Powermatic had cheaper labor and its own foundry, the Burgs cautioned, its work force might not be able to reach Burgmaster's level of efficiency.

The Burgs argued, moreover, that they had not sold their enterprise to see it dismembered. But Saltarelli would not budge. If there was going to be talk of broken promises, he was going to raise a few that Burgmaster had not kept. When faced with Houdaille's strict dollar-and-cents argument, the Burgs' position seemed almost sentimental and absurd.

Tensions subsided after Saltarelli's decision became final. By the summer of 1967, the only problem preoccupying Joe Burg and Norm Ginsburg was the backlog. Since January 1966 it had nearly tripled in size, to $30 million, and Burgmaster was shipping at most about $900,000 worth of machines every month.[42] Typically, the two men were of two minds over how to whittle it down. Ginsburg was convinced that immediate gains could be made if Burgmaster cut way back on sales of specials, machines tailored to a customer's specifications. They bogged down both the engineering department and the machine shop. Burgmaster stood to make more profit, Ginsburg maintained, by selling standard machines subject to fewer modifications. Added volume would more than make up for the loss of special sales.

Ginsburg had strong support from the machine and assembly departments for his position. But Joe Burg still dominated sales, as he had since the early days of the company, and was as reluctant as ever to lose a customer. As one Houdaille executive graphically put it, "if they could have gotten a machine tool to pucker, then Burgmaster would have designed one to come down and kiss your ass." But Saltarelli, for one, was no longer willing to tolerate the emphasis on sales when the backlog was "big enough to choke a horse."[43] The opening he needed to replace Joe Burg appeared during the summer, when once again one of Joe's optimistic forecasts proved to be way off the mark.

Like the other family members, however, Burg still had three years to go on his five-year contract with Houdaille. Moreover, there was a stipulation in it that prevented Houdaille from transferring him outside Los Angeles without his agreement. Saltarelli therefore "promoted" him to a new position. Burg became the Los Angeles–based vice president in charge of international marketing for all of Houdaille's machine tool products. It seemed a perfect way to employ his talents, as well as get him out of Burgmaster.

Saltarelli's first choice to replace Burg was Norm Ginsburg. His cautious and more conservative nature appealed to Saltarelli, and he pressed Ginsburg hard to take the job. But Ginsburg believed that by doing so he would rupture the family. It would seem as if his honest disagreement with Joe had been calculated to gain him the presidency. He told Saltarelli he would stay on at Burgmaster and help the new president in every way he could, but no, he would not take the job.

The machine tool industry was notable for companies that passed from father to son for generations. Yet by the fall of 1967, just two years after the takeover, a Burg was no longer in charge of the enterprise. The old man was devastated. As for Joe Burg, he never set foot inside Burgmaster again.

6

UNDER NEW MANAGEMENT (1968)

In 1968, several months after Saltarelli squeezed out Joe Burg, Houdaille ran a large advertisement in *The Wall Street Journal*. The ad invoked all the buzzwords, like *electronics*, *controls*, and *computers*, that were making conglomerates the stars of the stock exchange. Indeed, the ad was a paean to the conglomerate phenomenon. That was not surprising, since Houdaille's advertising agency also handled the accounts for ITT and Litton Industries.[1] The ad read:

Bavooom
Blast rock loose
Construction boom
Profit for Houdaille
Big in construction
Construction materials
Big in machine tools
Very sophisticated
Computer controlled
Big in industrial products
Many kinds
Very diversified
Big in automobile products
Shiny bumpers
Big in processing industries
Reliable pumps
That's Who-dye
The multi-company company
Nineteen companies in all
1968 sales up again
Forecast over $200 million
Bavooom
Another sound of growth[2]

The advertisement was not just bluster. Houdaille had shed its dowdy image, and emerged as an attractive entry in the crowded field of conglomerates vying for Wall Street's favors, such as a high price-to-earnings ratio. In the six years since Saltarelli's ascendancy to CEO, Houdaille had posted impressive gains. From 1963 to 1968, its sales, earnings per share, and dividends all doubled as Saltarelli steadily acquired the assets, sales, and earnings of eight smaller companies. Over the same period, the price of Houdaille common stock increased almost fivefold.[3]

Even if Houdaille's performance justified some bragging, in all likelihood Jerry Saltarelli would have ridiculed such an ad five years earlier as a waste of money. By 1968, however, Wall Street's enthusiasm for conglomerates was at a fever pitch, and there was a very important purpose to be served by extolling Houdaille's virtues publicly.

Historically, because of its pedestrian image, Houdaille stock had always traded at a disadvantage. It usually sold for well below ten times earnings, and rarely moved up or down more than a few points in a calendar year. In turn, this meant that the number of stockholders in the company was comparatively small, and trading rather light in volume. There was almost no speculative buying and selling.

That was acceptable in the days when Houdaille was content to be an auto subcontractor. But now that it had become a glamorous conglomerate in a bull market, the reverse was true. Broader trading was in Houdaille's interest, because it was likely to drive up the price of Houdaille shares. So Saltarelli sought, in light of the conglomerate's extraordinary gains in sales and earnings, to "make a market" for the new Houdaille.

The advertisement was only one facet of a larger scheme, one geared to making Houdaille as familiar to investors as it had been to car owners thirty years before. And no one labored as tirelessly as Saltarelli to make Houdaille more visible in the late 1960s. In his absorption with selling Houdaille, running it, divesting certain subsidiaries, and buying new companies, Saltarelli practically "lived on an airplane."[4]

He met regularly with brokers and large investors to spread the good news about Houdaille's performance as measured against the stock exchange as a whole. Saltarelli had plenty to boast about. By 1968, the price of Houdaille common stock had increased by 261 percent since 1963 while the Dow Jones rose by only 39 percent. Saltarelli also expanded his company's quarterly reports so that stockholders could follow Houdaille's fortunes more closely. He even instituted special mailings to notify stockholders of items of particular interest, such as the acquisition of another company.[5] To top the effort off, in 1968 Saltarelli had the board of directors declare a two-for-one split in common stock to increase trading. It was the second split in two years.

More was at stake than merely a higher stock price, however. In fact, it was merely the means to a far more important end. The underlying purpose of Saltarelli's campaign was to bolster Houdaille's diversification strategy. Because to a high degree, the price of Houdaille stock dictated both the pace and quality of diversification.

Taking over companies for stock enabled Houdaille to acquire larger and more promising companies than it could buy for cash. Then too, there was the matter of Saltarelli's own conservatism. He imposed strict limits on Houdaille's takeover tactics, still viewing with distrust the dubious methods employed by some conglomerates to fuel their expansion. Almost by default, the price of Houdaille stock was virtually the only variable left, aside from generating cash for takeovers from the company's own profits.

There was one more critical factor that caused Saltarelli to become a pitchman for Houdaille stock in the late 1960s. That was the Wall Street mania for conglomeration itself. By 1968, a corporate strategy had become a corporate feeding frenzy. Saltarelli's aggressive pursuit of a higher price for Houdaille stock was not only the means to further diversification. In a way, it had become almost as urgent as the original goal itself.

The U.S. economy had experienced a similar wave of merger activity twice before, once around the turn of the century, when many large (and some notorious) monopolies were formed, and then again in the 1920s.[6] But the merger mania that now seized the corporate world, peaking in 1968, easily absorbed more corporate assets than either the 1901 or 1920 wave, and was of an altogether different kind. In the late 1960s, takeovers were not "mergers for monopoly" but mergers for the sake of conglomeration. Not only small and medium-sized concerns were absorbed. Companies with hundreds of millions of dollars in sales, revenues, and assets were being gobbled up by the likes of Gulf & Western, ITT, and LTV, which seemed to grow overnight into billion-dollar companies.

For Houdaille, moreover, it was not simply that there were many more conglomerates jostling for Wall Street's attention. The competition was more acute than that: machine tools, the industry Houdaille had chosen as its preferred avenue for diversification, was also the favorite of many other conglomerates. The vast majority of machine tools had always been built by small, privately held companies. But no longer. Conglomerates were penetrating the industry in a big way.

In 1965, there had been three significant conglomerate takeovers: Houdaille bought Burgmaster, the Bendix Corporation acquired Besley-Welles, and White Consolidated Industries bought Leland Gifford. Still, that seemed a relatively small number, and the machine tool industry was comparatively unaffected, given a record 2,125 mergers in U.S. industry as a whole in 1965.[7]

Then came the deluge. In 1966, there were twenty-two machine tool mergers or acquisitions, involving several of the biggest names within the industry. To be sure, many of the major transactions occurred between tool builders only, and raised few eyebrows, such as the merger between Giddings & Lewis and Gisholt. Mergers and takeovers, after all, were among the industry's hoariest traditions. But the growing percentage and size of outsiders in the industry was novel. So too was the expectant air that gripped the entire industry. As one observer noted, "everybody wants to buy—nobody wants to sell."[8]

In the next year, 1967, mergers involving machine tool firms occurred at an even faster rate; more important, the pattern of outside takeovers dominated. "Previously," noted the trade journal *American Machinist,* "most of the mergers tended to reduce the number of firms and bring complementary lines of machines into a combined company." But lately, "more of the mergers have resulted in the acquisition of machine tool firms by large, diversified companies that have not previously been in the machine tool business." Each month saw another conglomerate proclaiming its desire to enter or expand its holdings, or another actual takeover. Many conglomerate takeovers left behind one or more frustrated machine tool builders who were unwilling to bid as much as the conglomerate.[9]

The motives behind many of these takeovers were often parallel to the ones that prompted the Burgmaster-Houdaille deal. Builders believed they needed access to the deep pockets of a large conglomerate because research and development costs were rising so high. In turn, conglomerates were attracted to the industry first, because it was available, and second, because it was doing well. Machine tool builders were enjoying perhaps their longest sustained boom in history.[10] The war in Vietnam, of course, was instrumental in fueling demand. By some estimates, 50 percent of all production was devoted to war and war-related industries.

The boom explained why conglomerates, on the prowl for acquisitions, looked to the machine tool industry. Yet ultimately, the notion that machine tools were an attractive investment fell short as a full explanation of the industry's transformation. The notion still failed to explain why conglomeration itself had reached such a fever pitch.

Some students of management, such as UCLA professor Neil Jacoby, claimed that "superior management" was the driving force behind conglomeration. According to this school of thought, assets were being removed from the "inefficient control of old-fashioned managers" and placed in the hands of supermanagers who could put them to more efficient use.[11] Such explanations were less than compelling. Even if conglomerateurs, schooled in "superior management," were spreading the gospel, why were so many corporations disposed to adopting the strategy? In truth, there was a new, powerful factor at work, acting in concert with the older motives of empire-building, antitrust avoidance, and exploitation of tax loopholes. It was the creeping inflation and instability in the American economy as a whole.

The nagging balance-of-payments deficits and gold outflows of the early 1960s had been kept under control, but never reversed. These chronic symptoms pointed to a profound and fundamental malady: *Pax Americana* was insolvent. The United States could not simultaneously provide for its citizens at home *and* bankroll all the responsibilities it had assumed overseas. The combination, in a liberal economic order, was causing a huge imbalance in the world economy. And proof came in the form of a dwindling U.S. gold supply.

The Kennedy administration had resorted to a policy of "ad-hocery," expedient steps that sought to limit or mitigate the outflows. But a land war in Asia accelerated the imbalance, especially after President Johnson belatedly moved to raise the taxes necessary to pay for it. Even when he did, however, the more fundamental insolvency persisted. U.S. government officials subsequently devised ever more ingenious ways to defend the dollar's value, but they were only postponing the day of reckoning. They could not avoid it, short of a fundamental shift in American priorities.[12]

Until the mid-1960s, most American businessmen ignored the international economic indicators. Prosperity reigned at home—the productive capacity of the U.S. economy tripled during the 1960s—and there seemed little reason to worry about empty warnings.[13] But any effort to insulate the domestic economy from the international consequences of insolvency was doomed, as U.S. businessmen found when a novel phenomenon began to appear: inflation. By 1966, the consumer price index was increasing at an annual rate of 5.4 percent. The Federal Reserve soon put the brakes on, sending corporate borrowing costs to 7 percent, a postwar high. But record interest rates did not wring out inflation. By 1969, the rate of inflation was the same as it had been three years earlier, and there was no doubt that an inflationary psychology gripped the economy.[14]

For manufacturers, inflation eroded profits and bedeviled efforts to make plans of any kind. As the cost of raw materials grew, manufacturers had to charge more for their products. That led workers to demand higher wages to keep up with inflation, which in turn forced up manufacturers' costs. No manufacturing sector was exempt from the wage-price spiral, which helped reduce the rate of profit for all nonfinancial corporations by 18 percent during the late 1960s, the first step in a long-term decline.[15]

Conglomeration was a popular corporate answer to the twin problems of inflation and eroding profits. Holding onto the dollars generated by corporate profits was foolish when the dollars promised to buy less tomorrow than they could purchase today. Corporations needed to acquire real, productive assets. Since investment in familiar lines of business often could not be justified, especially as interest rates rose, and antitrust laws prohibited the acquisition of competitors, corporations frantically embraced the conglomerate strategy. To an unprecedented degree, takeovers and mergers began to rival investment and expansion as a percentage of overall business activity.[16]

Few manufacturing sectors felt the impact of conglomeration more than machine tools. Five of the fifteen most acquisitive conglomerates during the late 1960s—U.S. Industries, Textron, Teledyne, Litton, and Gulf & Western— became major players in the machine tool industry, the last three all in the same year, 1968.[17] Gulf & Western, once an obscure car bumper company not unlike Houdaille, actually catapulted itself into the industry's front ranks within the space of three weeks. In January 1968, G&W announced the acquisition of two tool builders: Universal American (the fourteenth largest with $200 million in sales) and E.W. Bliss (the eighteenth largest with $158 million). In all likelihood, G&W executives celebrated the occasion by lighting a Dutch Master cigar, because along with the tool companies, Gulf & Western also disclosed that it was absorbing the Consolidated Cigar Corporation, with $175 million in sales.[18]

Many other large but less volatile conglomerates entered the industry as well, such as Lear Siegler, Bendix, Wickes Corporation, Colt Industries, Reynolds Metals, and White Consolidated Industries. Put another way, as recently as 1966, *American Machinist's* annual ranking of the top ten publicly owned builders had listed names familiar to everyone in the business. In order of sales, the leading public companies were Cincinnati Milling, Warner & Swasey, Giddings & Lewis, Kearney & Trecker, E.W. Bliss, Landis Tool, U.S. Industries (the sole conglomerate), National Acme, and Brown & Sharpe. By 1968, half of the top ten tool makers were divisions of conglomerates, namely, Textron, Colt Industries, White Consolidated, Bendix, and Houdaille.[19]

As he watched eight of the twenty-four largest machine tool builders disappear into conglomerates, Anderson Ashburn, the editor of *American Machinist*, was moved to remark in an editorial:

> During the Korean War a general concerned with food supply told a delegation firmly that the country's need was not for machine tools, it was for pots and pans. Historically the machine tool industry has contained many stubborn, individualistic entrepreneurs with a zealot's belief in the importance of their product. It kept some of them going when common sense said stop. We expect many of the new managements that have entered machine tool production by acquisition will bring new operating skills. We hope they will also bring boards of directors who do not confuse the importance of these new divisions with pots and pans.[20]

If some dilettantes had entered the industry, however, Houdaille was not among them. Saltarelli's conglomerate could not afford the luxury of acquiring assets and then divesting them a few years later. Houdaille was in the machine tool industry with both feet, and for the duration.

Houdaille was the tenth-largest builder by 1968 after acquiring six companies in three years. Following the purchase of Di-Acro and Burgmaster in 1965, and Powermatic a year later, Houdaille had added three companies to its machine tool group in 1967: the Cleveland-based Trabon Engineering Corporation, a maker of lubrication systems; the U.S. Burke Machine Tool Company of Cincinnati, a manufacturer of milling machines; and the Universal Engineering Company of Michigan, a leading builder of special tools. Altogether,

Houdaille's machine tool group now consisted of seven divisions, with Strippit as the anchor, and accounted for 22 percent of the conglomerate's total sales of $203.5 million.[21]

Although Saltarelli had succeeded in putting Houdaille in the front ranks of the tool industry, the intense competition from other conglomerates exacted a toll. Houdaille not only had to work hard to assemble its machine tool group but also had to cope with some divisions that were not of the highest technological caliber. By any measure, Strippit and Burgmaster were leaders in their respective segments of the industry, and Universal Engineering and Trabon only slightly less so. The three remaining components, however, Di-Acro, Powermatic, and U.S. Burke, all manufactured relatively unsophisticated tools that were sold primarily to vocational and training schools. Saltarelli would have preferred to find another Burgmaster or two. But such companies were increasingly hard to come by.

At Burgmaster, the full impact of conglomerate ownership was felt after a new president arrived in August 1967 to succeed Joe Burg.[22] In retrospect, Burg's two-year tenure was little more than a difficult interregnum. Despite Houdaille's inclination to keep Burgmaster's top management intact, the clash of cultures virtually dictated that sooner or later, Saltarelli would feel compelled to install a Houdaille man at Burgmaster's helm.

For the first few weeks after Joe left, all the Burgs were "in a state of shock," recalled Norm Ginsburg. Fred Burg had seldom missed a day at the factory following the takeover. But now his appearances became less frequent. "It had been a blow to the old man that they wanted Joe out," said Ginsburg.[23] When the old man did visit, he was noticeably subdued, exhibiting little of the demanding curiosity that had always been one of his characteristics.

Still, on occasion Burg would vigorously put forward his strong views. "You're moving too slowly," he told Burgmaster's new president, Tom Norton, at the annual Christmas party in December 1967. He thought that there were too few innovations coming out of Burgmaster.[24] But with his son's departure went much of the influence the old man exercised. He began turning his energies toward perfecting an idea for a clock that could tell the correct time in any zone. He was still inventing.

Joe Burg stopped coming to the factory altogether. He concentrated on setting up an international sales office for Houdaille at a somewhat unusual address in Los Angeles. Sunset Boulevard was more likely to house movie producers than machine tool salesmen. But the site was close to Burg's Beverly Hills home, and he was more or less at liberty to locate his office wherever he wanted.

That left Norm Ginsburg, from the all-powerful triumvirate that once ruled Burgmaster. Only he remained closely involved in the company's affairs, his title and duties unchanged since the takeover. He had briefly considered leaving Burgmaster on the heels of Joe's departure. There were many things about Houdaille's corporate culture that he found disagreeable, such as keeping up the fiction that Joe left Burgmaster because "he had become interested in other things," which was how Saltarelli put it.[25]

Ginsburg realized, however, that if he departed it would be tantamount to declaring the takeover a failure in some important respects. He wasn't prepared to do that yet, if only because he had been an early and strong advocate of the Burgmaster-Houdaille partnership. He decided to work harder than ever, to get Houdaille personnel "embedded" in Burgmaster. If the next president was willing to learn, Ginsburg was anxious to teach.

To Ginsburg's relief, he took an immediate liking to the new president of Burgmaster, Tom Norton. Many of the Houdaille executives under Saltarelli had been a poor match for the Burgs, but Norton seemed to be different. He put on no airs, and was even affable. Rumors and conjecture about what Houdaille might do with its disappointing subsidiary had been building for months, and Joe's departure hardly dissipated the tension. Norton set a tone that quickly eased the atmosphere inside Burgmaster.

Nevertheless, Norton was a Houdaille man. A Chicago native, he had been with the conglomerate for most of his working life. After earning a diploma in industrial engineering, he joined Houdaille in 1947, at the age of twenty-five. He spent the next ten years supervising production methods at various plants and evaluating the need for capital expenditures. After a stint as a production control manager at Strippit, in 1959 he became president of Houdaille's bumper plant in Oshawa, Ontario, which served the Canadian auto industry. He was there for eight years, so long that he almost "became a Canuck."[26]

Norton and his family were happy in Canada, and he did not want to move to California. But Saltarelli, forceful and persuasive as always, wanted him to take the job at Burgmaster. Saltarelli recognized that Norton knew next to nothing about Burgmaster's line of business; auto bumpers had more in common with bathtubs than machine tools. Nevertheless, he believed that Norton was the man to undo Burgmaster's bottlenecks because of his background in production methods and control. Just as important, Norton swore by the conglomerate's system of mandatory monthly reports. Norton viewed them, not as a burden imposed by headquarters, but as a necessary chore that benefited him above anyone else. Reports were ultimately the only way to know "what the hell was going on" underneath him, Norton believed. They "kept a [division] president on his toes and his nose to the fire—and everyone else's as well."[27]

In fact, Norton exemplified the kind of attitude that Saltarelli sought to engender in his division presidents. As Norton saw it, Houdaille's "decentralized" system "brought out the best in people." Every division president "got just enough rope," so that he had the *feeling* he could go out and hang himself. But the reports sent to Buffalo ensured that "if someone was going off base, they would know it soon enough" and take up the slack. "It made entrepreneurs, really, of division presidents," recalled Norton.[28]

When Burgmaster employees got their initial look at Norton, he impressed them as a likable person. But to a man, they could not help noticing that for the first time, the head of Burgmaster was someone with almost no knowledge of machine tools. To Norton, his inexperience was not an overwhelming obstacle. Even if Burgmaster machined metal while Oshawa only bent it, he believed that "85 percent of all management practices are common to all businesses."[29] Moreover, he was frank about his need to learn the remaining 15 percent, and eager to do so.

His candor disarmed many employees who were predisposed to skepticism. Most important, it won Norton an early and critical ally at Burgmaster, Norm Ginsburg. Ginsburg promptly realized that here was a Houdaille executive with whom he could work. Norton did not seem at all threatened by Ginsburg's expertise, or the loyalty accorded Ginsburg by "all his henchmen" in the machine shop and assembly departments.[30] Then too, the more Norton learned about the business, the more he seemed to share Ginsburg's views about the steps necessary to whittle down Burgmaster's huge backlog. After years of struggling with Joe about sales versus production, Ginsburg could not help feeling some relief that the debate was tilting his way. Once again, he became optimistic about the takeover.

Norton liked Ginsburg too. Norm labored as if Burgmaster were still family-owned, by putting in long hours and placing heavy demands on the managers brought in by Houdaille. A few even quietly complained to Norton about Ginsburg's expectations. "Norm was a type that could get ulcers—and he could give them too," recalled Norton. But more often than not, the new president of Burgmaster found himself in agreement with the Burg family holdover. "He called a spade a spade, and liked to argue and discuss things. But I didn't mind one damn bit," Norton said. Most of the time "we did things his way, and it turned out to be the best way."[31]

Saltarelli had hoped the two men would hit it off. Working together, they might be able to provide exactly the right mix. Ginsburg's intimate, production-oriented knowledge, and Norton's familiarity with the Houdaille way, would finally enable Burgmaster to meet the goals set for it two years earlier. His optimism rose too.

But if the notion of a turnaround prevailed at the highest levels, Tom Norton's arrival in late 1967 did not herald a renaissance. The truth was that no matter how hard he tried, Norm Ginsburg was only one man. He could not be everywhere at once; he had to choose the spots where he thought he could make the greatest impact. He could encourage Tom Norton to join him on the shop floor twice a day, to lend a semblance of the Burgs' hands-on management. But he could not ride herd on every Houdaille manager ten hours a day. The result, at least from the blue-collar point of view, was that Ginsburg's efforts were overpowered by Houdaille-style management. No one, not even he, could stop its entrenchment.

Nothing typified Burgmaster more during the Norton years than Houdaille's elaborate scheme to improve productivity and control costs. This drive actually preceded Norton's arrival by several months, but went into full gear during his presidency. Buffalo headquarters was convinced, beyond any doubt, that serious production inefficiencies were responsible for the choking backlog. Before the deficiencies could be corrected, however, they had to be identified. And for Houdaille, that meant the entire production process had to be quantified.

This was not a small task. The sheer number and complexity of parts that went into each machine meant that such an effort would take from three to four years to implement fully. But the eventual reward promised to justify the effort. Ultimately, Burgmaster would ostensibly be able to calculate with pinpoint accuracy how much it actually cost to make one of its machines. Management, at long last, would have a computer printout telling where bottlenecks existed and where production costs were excessive. If some Burgmaster employees thought it odd that Houdaille needed a printout to know exactly what was going on, they kept such heretical thoughts to themselves.

Houdaille's plan had three steps. During the first step, the machining process for every part Burgmaster manufactured was to be systematically broken down, and then painstakingly reassembled. A new department, manufacturing engineering, would compile operation sheets that described how to machine every workpiece more efficiently. Next, another new department, tool engineering, would see to it that every machinist could do his job in the manner prescribed by the manufacturing engineering department. This meant ordering or designing all the jigs, templates, and other special tooling deemed necessary for the machine shop to work at peak efficiency.

Although both steps were critical, they were also mere preludes to the third, and to Houdaille, the most important step: time studies. Once the most efficient machining procedures were theoretically in place, white-collar personnel, armed with stop watches, would observe blue-collar machinists. The studies would quantify "floor-to-floor" time, or how much time it took a machinist to finish a certain part, from the moment he picked it up to the moment he set it down.[32]

To a detached observer, Houdaille's goal seemed a reasonable one and its methods eminently sound. Burgmaster had comparatively little in the way of figures and statistics about its production costs. Even with the 20T, the machine Burgmaster was banking on to keep it at the leading edge, the Burgs had relied on what Houdaille regarded as an incredibly crude judgment. When he was calculating how to beat the competition, the old man figured out the machine's basic cost by taking its estimated weight in pounds, and multiplying it by a factor of three.

There was far more sense to this method than first appeared. Decades of experience had taught Fred Burg many things, and one was that the per pound measure was a relative constant, and guaranteed a healthy profit, if a machine tool builder operated efficiently. "All the fancy cost analyses never came out closer" than the old man's estimates, recalled Bob French, a design engineer. Whenever the price of a new machine was divided by the number of pounds, "damned if the old man wasn't on the button."[33]

No one expected a big conglomerate to adhere to such a seat-of-the-pants approach. What was disconcerting, however, was that in the course of transforming Burgmaster, Houdaille was violating cardinal precepts, such as efficiency, that had made Burgmaster such a success in the first place. Nowhere was this more evident than in how the plan to quantify production was carried out, as opposed to how it worked in theory.

The manufacturing and tool engineering departments were supposed to make the machinists as efficient as possible. Instead, they frequently saddled Burgmaster with hundreds of thousands of dollars worth of useless tooling. In 1968, when Burgmaster bought a mammoth Ingersoll milling machine capable of machining workpieces thirty-two feet long, the two departments recommended the purchase of special tooling worth $50,000. But the skilled and highly paid machinist who operated the $460,000 big Ingersoll, as it was called, soon found that about 80 percent of the tooling was unusable for his purposes. He would have advised against buying it, but no one had bothered to ask his opinion.[34]

Such profligacy was rife, and in stark contrast to the days when the Burgs were in control. When they contemplated buying a new machine or tooling, they often asked the opinion of the machinist who would be using it. They were quite capable of figuring out for themselves what to buy, but often the machinist could lend a special insight. And even if he couldn't, the process of consulting him on the expenditure of thousands of dollars gave him a vested interest in the outcome.

In an atmosphere of such waste, Burgmaster's machinists heartily resented the time studies. To the rank and file, the stopwatches were not so much a way to gauge Burgmaster's true costs as they were a means to discipline a supposedly recalcitrant work force. Management seemed to be claiming that the underlying reason for Burgmaster's disappointing performance was indolence in the machine shop. The machinists took offense at being singled out when to them the paramount problem was that management no longer knew what it was doing.

The workers' response to the time studies was anything but cooperative. Some machinists delighted in confounding their timekeepers. The first time under the stopwatch, a machinist would follow the operation sheet as if it were a religious text, taking ten hours to complete a single workpiece. The next day, he would machine the same workpiece in eight hours. The white-collar timekeeper would be mystified by the variation. It looked to him like the machinist was working all the time in both instances.

The secret, of course, was in the setup. A dedicated, experienced machinist could minimize machining time by devising the most efficient setup. Such tricks of the trade were what made skilled machinists valuable, and were beyond the ken of most engineers. But the atmosphere inside Burgmaster was no longer conducive to bringing out a worker's best. With the company wasting money left and right, why should the machinists be the only ones expected to work at peak efficiency?

Widespread ignorance in the management ranks, or at the very least inexperience, was the fundamental reason why so many Houdaille initiatives, no matter how sensible they seemed on paper, generated tremendous waste in practice and, ultimately, bred cynicism. Burgmaster was no longer a hierarchy based on knowledge and ability, but one built on allegiance to the corporate way of doing things. The Burgs, of course, had had their favorites too, and there was plenty of politicking when they ran the company. But nothing like this. "When the Burgs owned it," recalled Bob French, "results mattered more than words. But under Houdaille, words mattered more. And a good excuse mattered most."[35]

Of course, not all the personnel hired or imported by Houdaille were ill prepared for the work. The new plant manager, for example, Gene Dobmeier, had thirty years of experience as a machinist, tool-and-die maker, and foreman back East before coming to Burgmaster from Strippit in 1966. He emerged as one of the most powerful figures inside the revamped Burgmaster, ranking behind only Tom Norton and Norm Ginsburg. With the title of plant manager, Dobmeier was in charge of manufacturing, tooling, manufacturing engineering, time studies, and assembly.[36]

But if Dobmeier's central role indicated that Houdaille was not oblivious to the peculiar needs of a machine tool company, he also exemplified a primary reason why Burgmaster was now so troubled. Dobmeier was the quintessential Houdaille manager, a man who went by the corporate book and expected everyone else to do the same. Most important, in Dobmeier's Burgmaster, wisdom went only from the top down. Gone were the days when communication between management and labor was a two-way street.

By 1968 a subtle distrust permeated the atmosphere at Burgmaster. Management and labor were less like partners in an enterprise, and more like adversaries. Management presumed that machinists disliked their work, and would avoid it if at all possible. To the extent that they could be made to work, the blue-collar work force had to be controlled or coerced. Seen in this light, the time-study effort was, as much as anything, an effort to transfer skills, and thus control, from the hands of machinists to management.[37] Even something as innocuous as an annual Christmas dinner that brought white- and blue-collar employees together—a company tradition since the days of Burg Tool—was brusquely discarded in 1968. Houdaille explained that it cost too much, and that no other Houdaille plant invited blue-collar workers to such an affair. Thereafter, workers were treated to a separate buffet luncheon on the last workday before Christmas.[38]

The transformation of Burgmaster by 1968 would have lasting repercussions on the company's fortunes. Yet as profound as the changes were, at the same time they were so subtle, and happened so gradually, that they passed almost without comment. On occasion, a longtime employee would go up to the old man during one of his visits and pour out his views about what was going wrong. "They would ask him to talk to [Jim] Skinner [a Houdaille vice president] or the big fellow, Saltarelli," recalls Joe Burg. "They would say yes, yes, yes" to whatever concerns the old man raised, but nothing ever changed.[39]

In all likelihood, one reason such complaints were dismissed was that they sounded vague and "soft" in comparison to the "hard" problems dogging Burgmaster. One of the most acute during the Norton presidency was the future of the 20T, the machine that was to assure Burgmaster's leadership in the coming era of machining centers. Fred Burg's last contribution to machine tool design was turning into Burgmaster's first major mistake, and a costly one.

Every new machine had its problems, but the 20T seemed to have more than its share from the outset. It was exceedingly difficult to build, especially the drum, which required twenty holes spaced equidistant from one another. It was hard for even the best workers to machine so many dimensions that were critically related to each other. Burgmaster tried everything to overcome this difficulty, even devising a special machine tool dedicated solely to the task of making the spindle holes in the drum. That helped a little. It wasn't until reports started to trickle in from the field that the fate of the 20T became sealed.

About two dozen 20T machines had been sold, to customers as diverse as Ford Aerospace, Kenworthy, and Caterpillar. Based on their experience, the machine's congenital defect became obvious: the drum, complete with twenty spindles, was of such a great mass that it could not perform within the required tolerances. After a few months of use, the drum would no longer index (rotate and stop) to the next position accurately. Sometimes, if the machine was rotating from one position to another halfway around, the drum would gain enough momentum to shear the gears and pins that were supposed to stop rotation. The sound of breaking steel could be heard above the din of any factory. But far more often, even if it was moving from one position to the adjacent one, the 20T just did not hit the next spindle exactly right. It was chronically a little bit off.[40]

This was especially ironic, of course. Although his engineers expressed serious reservations from the beginning, Fred Burg had insisted upon his unique design because he was convinced that tool-changing machining centers (like the Milwaukee-Matic) would not prove durable or accurate over the long run. In the past his persistence had paid handsome dividends, so once again "the boys let him go ahead and do it," recalled Ed Merk, the head of sales.[41] But this time the old man was wrong. The 20T had been advertised as "Big, Fast, Rigid, Accurate," but only the first claim proved unequivocally true.[42]

After briefly experimenting with a smaller version, the "12T," Burgmaster finally admitted defeat in mid-1968. Inevitably, the failure eroded what remained of the old man's stature with the new management. At age seventy-two, he was still finding it hard to let go of Burgmaster entirely. He would come to the factory, sometimes just to visit, sometimes to corral a few workers into helping him assemble a "Zonemaster," which was the name he had given to his time-zone clock. "One had to love him," recalled Tom Norton, but "by that time, he was a pain in the ass really. [At first] out of respect for the old goat, he was invited to management meetings. Then he would start reminiscing about something fifteen or twenty years ago, taking up people's time."[43] Soon the old man was no longer asked to attend. No one wanted to hear about how he did things, or how fast Burgmaster used to move.

The old man sensed he was being "treated as a worn-out piece of equipment," recalled Joe Burg. "He felt superfluous."[44] To symbolize his disgruntlement over Houdaille's management of Burgmaster and pique over his own treatment, he sold all of his preferred Houdaille stock. His visits to the factory became rare. Genuine retirement from his beloved trade was traumatic, although orders for his Zonemaster clocks, including some from prestigious hotels, kept Burg somewhat busy. But he became so depressed that he blamed his son or son-in-law for the decision to sell Burgmaster, even though his vote had been the decisive one.[45]

Apart from the effect of its failure on the old man, the 20T was a costly blunder for Burgmaster. In addition to the money spent on research and development, Burgmaster had lost something even more precious: time. It had spent five years trying to make the machine work, time that would have otherwise been spent on developing a tool-changing machining center. There was absolutely no doubt that such tools were going to play a large role in manufacturing, as evidenced by the number of builders introducing tool changers, and the number of patent suits Kearney & Trecker had filed to protect its one-third market share.[46]

For Tom Norton, Burgmaster's president, the only problem more pressing than the failure to develop a machining center was Burgmaster's still-overwhelming backlog. In mid-1968, he adopted a new strategy to deal with the backlog, one that Ed Merk, Burgmaster's head salesman, had been urging for more than a year. Merk wanted to develop a bargain-basement version of the NC turret drill. His idea was to mass-produce a standard machine, with limited options, which he was convinced would sell by the dozens if it could be brought in at a sufficiently low price.[47]

Norm Ginsburg enthusiastically favored the concept. It would mean building many machines for which there were no firm orders, but the idea appealed to his manufacturing bias. For years, he had "been a voice in the wilderness," urging more sales of standard or previously engineered products.[48] If Burgmaster built fifty nearly identical machines, it could spread out its overhead costs, reduce production bottlenecks, and operate at peak efficiency.

The idea had the added benefit of tiding Burgmaster over until it could develop its own tool changer. The proliferation of machining centers meant Burgmaster faced increasing competition at the high end of its market. The difference in price between other builders' tool changers and a top-of-the-line Burgmaster turret drill was decreasing rapidly. If Burgmaster could mass-produce a turret drill at a price no tool changer could match, it could tout its product as a "budget" machining center and thereby retain a substantial part of the market.

The "Econocenter" was born. The initial production run was fifty machines, but a confident Norton ordered the purchase of one hundred identical NC systems from Westinghouse. Such a large purchase was practically unheard of in the industry, but its size enabled Burgmaster to pay about $5,000 for each control; ordered in smaller lots, they cost anywhere from $9,000 to $20,000. Such economies of scale brought the price of the Econocenter down to about $36,000, about 45 percent less than a normal turret drill.

In a few months, all fifty Econocenters were sold. For less than the price of one machining center, a manufacturer could have two Econocenters, and many customers in fact bought two, lined them up nose to nose, and had one machinist operate both. Burgmaster changed its advertising from "World's largest builder of turret drilling machines" to "World's largest builder of turret drilling centers."

Norton and Ginsburg thought they finally had Burgmaster moving. In little more than a year, the $30 million backlog was halved, and they were shipping about eighteen NC machines a month by mid-1968, twice as many as the year before. Moreover, Burgmaster was doing something extraordinary— building machines, including Econocenters, for stock.[49] Given Burgmaster's chronic inability to deliver promptly, that seemed like a shrewd move to Norton. In fact, his timing could not have been worse.

Norton was hardly the only machine tool executive slow to recognize that the boom of the 1960s was fast coming to an end. Few builders were prepared for the inevitable downturn. But by the fall of 1968, it was evident the bust had come. Six years of uninterrupted growth came to a halt that year, the victim of decreasing capital investment because of inflation and rising interest rates in the macroeconomy. Overall, machine tool shipments fell 17 percent in 1969 from their 1967 peak of $7.3 billion.[50]

To the conglomerates, the bust came as a rude shock so soon after their machine tool bidding wars. The recession hit nearly every tool builder, including Houdaille. Total sales of its machine tool group in 1969 took a sharp drop.[51] Nearly all the divisions contributed to the decline, but in Saltarelli's eyes, Burgmaster's performance was the most disturbing, probably because his expectations had been so high. "We were the bad guys" in the whole machine tool group, recalled Bob French.[52]

For years Saltarelli had seen Burgmaster choked by a backlog, losing orders because it could not deliver. Its reputation and credibility had become so bad that machine tool distributors, thinking ahead, had put in orders for machines to be delivered in twelve months even though they lacked a firm buyer for them. Suddenly those phantom orders were being canceled, without any penalty. And Norton had not foreseen the problem. Worst of all, he had committed the cardinal sin, much like Joe Burg; a Houdaille division president was measured by his ability to make forecasts, and Norton had erred.[53]

Saltarelli decided he needed someone better versed in the vagaries of the industry. So in late 1968, for the second time in little more than a year, he journeyed to Los Angeles to replace the president of Burgmaster. The meeting was held in the Century Hotel in Beverly Hills. While he met with Norton to break the news, in an adjoining room Houdaille vice president Jim Skinner told Norm Ginsburg about the decision to move Norton back to Buffalo.[54]

Ginsburg took the news almost as hard as Norton. He believed Norton was being made the "fall guy" for events that were largely beyond his control. He did not consider Norton responsible for all of Burgmaster's ills; indeed, he blamed Buffalo for some of them. Norton had erred, but Burgmaster had not done anything irreversible. Houdaille had to accept that it was in a cyclical industry, and had to roll with the busts, and exploit the booms. Ginsburg also could not help considering Saltarelli's decision something of a comment on his own management. Norton had been an eager student, and perhaps it was not an exaggeration to say that he ran Burgmaster more or less as Ginsburg would have.

What rankled Ginsburg more than anything, however, was how Houdaille handled Norton's firing. It summed up, in one incident, everything in Houdaille's corporate culture he had come to detest. As Saltarelli gave Norton the news, Skinner, widely regarded as the corporate hatchet man, told Ginsburg that Norton had requested a transfer back East because his wife did not like Los Angeles. That was a lie. The Ginsburgs and the Nortons had become close friends, and Ginsburg knew that the Nortons "loved" California. Sometimes, on the spur of the moment, the two couples flew up to San Francisco just to have dinner.[55]

If Saltarelli was dissatisfied with Norton's performance, so be it, thought Ginsburg. That's the chairman's prerogative. But he could no longer work for a corporation that seemed incapable of dealing honestly with its own executives. Although there were other personal considerations that prompted Ginsburg to decide that he had had enough, the treatment of Tom Norton finally confirmed Norm's feelings. The last of the trio who founded Burgmaster left in January 1969.

7

CUTTING EDGE LOST (1969–1970)

The new Burgmaster president, Allan Folger, was not so much a Houdaille man as a machine tool man.

He had spent most of his working life in the tool industry, but had been with the conglomerate only three years, since 1966. Folger had a degree in mechanical engineering from the University of Cincinnati, and had worked at Cincinnati Milacron—the GM of the machine tool industry—before acquiring an M.B.A. from the University of Chicago. He was employed as a consulting engineer in Phoenix in the mid-1960s when a close friend, who was the head of a large machine tool dealership, told him about executive openings in Houdaille's expanding machine tool group.

Folger moved to Buffalo in 1966 and was president of Strippit when Saltarelli asked him to swap jobs with Tom Norton. "Burgmaster is not generating a sufficient return on its assets," Saltarelli told Folger.[1]

The CEO was proud that Houdaille was among the most profitable tool builders when profits were measured as a percentage of equity.[2] His machine tool group averaged a 14 to 16 percent return on investment. Burgmaster's contribution, though, was about 8 to 10 percent. To be sure, Norton had done better than the 3.75 percent figure that stigmatized Joe Burg's last year as president. But overall, Burgmaster remained a drag on the entire group.[3]

Saltarelli did not have to add why this displeased him so. Wall Street regarded the profits-equity measure as the best indicator of corporate performance, far better than net income, and it figured prominently in Wall Street's calculation of Houdaille's price-to-earnings ratio. That figure, in turn, was the key to Saltarelli's ongoing efforts to boost the price of Houdaille stock, and further conglomeration.

Folger had gotten to know his predecessor slightly during group meetings, and like everyone else, thought Tom Norton was personable and intelligent. Although Folger did not blame him for Burgmaster's problems, neither did he subscribe to Saltarelli's credo that "a good man in one product is good in any."[4] Folger believed that the head of a state-of-the-art machine tool company needed to have experience, if only because the industry defied easy analysis and Buffalo put such a premium on meeting forecasts. The more attuned a division president was to the industry's vicissitudes, the better.

But Norton, and many other Houdaille executives, were taken aback when Saltarelli handpicked Folger. "I was surprised that he got the Burgmaster job," recalled Norton. "They needed someone strong in manufacturing and engineering. Allan did not have the broadest background."[5] That was true. For all his years in machine tools, Folger's experience had been mostly limited to one segment, marketing. He was unusually adept at figures, but had risen to the top of Strippit without the customary seasoning that Saltarelli preferred to give his division presidents. Houdaille executives ordinarily came up steadily through the ranks, spending a year or so in various departments, until they were distinctly comfortable with every aspect of a company's operations, from labor relations to accounting.

But Saltarelli had come to the conclusion that Burgmaster's foremost problem was marketing. He was determined to bring Burgmaster up to a level of financial performance commensurate with the money Houdaille had poured into the company. And in a period of slumping sales, it seemed sensible to rely on a man of Folger's expertise. He was confident that Gene Dobmeier, the plant manager, would prevent bottlenecks from developing if and when there was a surge in orders.

For this reason, Folger's Burgmaster was quite different from that of its predecessors. In place of the once-thoroughly integrated operation stood a company with clear separations of responsibility and power. Burgmaster's president was only in nominal control of the entire operation. Saltarelli's implicit intention was that Folger let Dobmeier run the entire manufacturing end of the business without interference. The two men therefore came to an understanding. Folger's job was to provide the numbers that kept Buffalo at bay, if not happy, and Dobmeier's was to make sure that his production backed up Folger's numbers. Dobmeier would run Burgmaster in reality, Folger in appearance.

The arrangement suited both men for different reasons. For Dobmeier, it was compensation for the fact that he was unlikely to rise any higher in the Houdaille hierarchy. He lacked a college degree, and Saltarelli firmly believed in higher education for all his top executives. Tom Norton had been one of the exceptions to the rule, and some had referred to him as the "Mustang" president because of it.[6] But Dobmeier, despite Saltarelli's high regard for his abilities, was not going to become another Norton.

The situation also satisfied Folger because it relieved him of immediate responsibility for almost everything but Burgmaster's numbers. Folger was not particularly comfortable dealing with people, regardless of whether they were peers or subordinates. To nearly everyone who worked with him, he seemed fair but remote, almost to the point of being cold. Employees were paid to do a job, and he expected them to do it without being coddled or praised, although at times criticism was in order. His predecessor, Tom Norton, had tried to keep up the appearance of the Burgs' hands-on involvement by touring the shop floor at least once a day, often with his shirt-sleeves rolled up. Folger did not. He was rarely seen outside the executive offices, and many longtime employees soon dubbed him the "invisible man." He thought of himself as a financial man, and was "only into one thing,"recalled Ed Merk. "Making forecasts."[7]

By mid-1969, a few months after taking office, Folger had developed a comprehensive view of Burgmaster's prospects and problems. One reason for optimism was the company's up-to-date plant—a fact driven home to Burgmaster employees whenever they attended a machine tool show back East and took time to visit other builders. Houdaille had carried through on its plan to invest in Burgmaster, and by the time Folger arrived it boasted one of the most modern factories in the industry. Of Burgmaster's forty or so major machine tools, Houdaille had financed the purchase of twenty-one, which meant that the bulk of productive equipment was less than five years old, although few tools were of the NC variety.[8]

Retaining the skilled labor needed to operate the machines, however, was a growing problem. Perhaps two dozen machinists, all of whom had been with Burgmaster for ten years or more, were so ensconced that they were unlikely to leave no matter what the outside inducements. But that mix of loyalty and inertia was rare. To most of the blue-collar work force, Burgmaster was just another place to work now. Though still not quite as impersonal as some of the big aerospace plants in Southern California, it no longer offered the intangible benefits that had once made it such a satisfying machine shop. Often Burgmaster found that if it did manage to find and hire two skilled machinists one month, the next month it was robbed of three by the aerospace industry. Worse, Burgmaster had come to function as a "farm system" for the aerospace industry.[9]

The siphoning-off of machinists was not unique to Burgmaster or the result of its unusual location. It was an industrywide problem, made all the more acute by the Vietnam War, which drafted many young men who otherwise would have become apprentices. Initially, the U.S. government had been slow to respond to the industry's wartime problems—refusing at one point to include machine tool production on the Department of Commerce "List of Currently Essential Activities."[10] But congressional lobbying by the industry trade association, the NMTBA, prompted the Labor Department to significantly expand and streamline its job-training program for machinists.[11]

Burgmaster was one of the earliest and most enthusiastic participants in the joint NMTBA-Labor Department program. But the results were less than gratifying. With the government subsidizing their wages, Burgmaster would hire fifteen or so apprentices, and give them on-the-job training as a supplement to the after-hours schooling also paid for by the government. But once the trainees became productive, they invariably left for higher aerospace wages. McDonnell-Douglas and Lockheed "were stealing [Burgmaster] blind" in the late 1960s, with often chaotic results.[12] For the time being, the downturn mitigated the labor problem considerably. But Folger knew he had to keep it uppermost in his mind if his forecasts were going to be accurate once the pace of orders picked up.

Accuracy was crucial, because it was not going to be easy to placate Saltarelli. In the four years since the takeover, Burgmaster had become a sore subject with him. To begin with, the rather conservative CEO "never liked California—in fact he hated it," recalled Folger. "He wasn't kidding when he said that nothing but a bunch of nuts lived out here."[13] That, plus the fact that his semiannual visits always had to include a lecture to Burgmaster employees about their shortcomings, was probably more than enough to ensure Saltarelli's displeasure with the state.

The chairman of Houdaille preferred to expend his energies on making new acquisitions, rather than scolding old ones. Even the cautious and conservative Saltarelli had finally succumbed to the indiscriminate conglomerate fever. In early 1969, for example, Houdaille found itself making a $31 million bid for a beer brewery. Although the transaction was abruptly called off the day before it was scheduled to be approved by Genesee Brewing and Houdaille stockholders, it revealed the pressures and risks Saltarelli labored under. The ongoing struggle for what was perceived to be corporate survival made underperformers like Burgmaster all the more vexing.[14]

Nor did longtime Burgmaster employees enjoy being the "bad guys" of the machine tool group. To workers as well as supervisors, the kind of attention this brought, often in the form of visitors from Buffalo, was a source of bemusement and an occasion for sarcasm. It often summed up Houdaille's topsy-turvy values. In the old days, an employee was measured by one standard—how well he did his work—and the Burgs didn't tolerate anyone who didn't do his job well. Now, among other things, neatness, as defined by Saltarelli, seemed the paramount value.

It got to the point where employees could predict well in advance a visit from Saltarelli or another top-level executive from Buffalo. A few days before the official announcement, painters would apply a new coat of bright yellow paint on the safety lines in the factory. Like clockwork, a memo about the impending visit would soon follow, with a simultaneous reminder to employees to police their work areas and remove "side-burns, moustaches and other psychedelic love charms," all items that Saltarelli found offensive. "To those few who maintain their desk and work area in an acceptable, orderly fashion, congratulations! And please ignore this memo," wrote Alf Celinder, the chief engineer, shortly before one of Saltarelli's visits in August 1969. "To the remainder, however, this memo constitutes instructions to clear up and establish semblance of order today."[15]

Folger's chief problem, though, was not a disgruntled, and sometimes undermanned, work force, or even the pressure from corporate headquarters.

Rather, his first order of business was to get into the manufacture of NC machining centers—and fast. In the nine years since Kearney & Trecker first introduced the concept, the market for machining centers had grown to more than $100 million annually, and half a dozen tool builders had entered the sweepstakes, including Cincinnati Milacron, Giddings & Lewis, and Monarch.[16] By contrast, following the abortive 20T, the only move Burgmaster had been able to make was to introduce the Econocenter line.

The days were long gone when Burgmaster manufactured a unique product, so far above what competitors could offer that Burgmaster defied the cycles affecting other tool builders. Over time, Folger believed, sales of Burgmaster's bread-and-butter turret drills, whether called Econocenters or not, would be limited. Burgmaster had to do more than come up with a marketing ploy on the industry buzzword *center* if it was to successfully adapt to a changing market. In other words, it had to have a tool changer.

Shortly after Folger assumed the presidency, Houdaille decided that Burgmaster could not afford to wait the minimum two years that it would take to build an indigenous tool changer from scratch. So a two-track strategy was devised. Burgmaster would continue to research and develop its own line of tool changers as rapidly as possible. But while it played catch-up, it would sell, for the first time, another manufacturer's machining center. "We wanted to get into machining centers and believed that the fastest way was to acquire [another's] center," Folger recalled.[17]

That center was the Hughes Aircraft Company's "MT-3," widely considered a Cadillac of machining centers.[18] The MT-3 was a horizontal machining center, that is, the spindle approached the workpiece from the side, as opposed to the vertical movement of a Burgmaster. This in itself was nothing unusual, but the machine had a number of extraordinary features, namely, three spindles and two tool changers. On the left side, two spindles were arrayed in the shape of a Y. While spindle A was machining, spindle B would get ready for the next cut by selecting the appropriate tool from a carrousel of thirty. This feature alone made the MT-3, from chip to chip, faster than any other automatic tool changer on the market. It took the left-sided spindles approximately four seconds to go from milling a slot with one cutting tool to drilling a hole with another.[19]

There was more. On the right side of the machine stood spindle C. It had fourteen tools at its disposal, giving the MT-3 a total of forty-four. This modular construction, moreover, made the Hughes machine actually two machines in one package, either of which could be sold as a separate unit. In any configuration, though, the MT-3 was extremely rigid and accurate, capable of milling as well as all drilling operations. Further, it was built to the highest engineering and manufacturing standards, more like a fine Swiss watch than a machine tool.

Yet the machine, for all its engineering accomplishments, had a checkered history. Hughes Aircraft Company was primarily a manufacturer of electronic controls for the aerospace industry, and ordinarily not in the business of making machine tools. But back in the mid-1950s, it had become fascinated by automatic tool changers, and their potential for cutting production costs.[20] Eventually, in 1956, it struck a deal with Kearny & Trecker of Wisconsin, the fourth-largest American tool builder. K&T would supply the tool changer, and Hughes would design and manufacture the NC device for it.[21]

One month after the agreement was signed, Wallace E. Brainard, the top Hughes engineer involved in the project, left Hughes to work on the machine prototype with Kearney & Trecker. By 1958, he had filed several patent claims, which together formed the basis for K&T's innovative Milwaukee-Matic design. But subsequently, K&T became dissatisfied with the electronic control Hughes developed, their partnership soured, and the development agreement fell apart. K&T turned to Bendix for the NC device it needed, and Hughes Aircraft, despite its inexperience, developed the MT-3. Hughes proceeded as if the fruits of Brainard's work, including one all-important claim known as the Brainard patent, were not exclusively Kearney & Trecker's to exploit. K&T, not surprisingly, believed otherwise.[22]

Then, around 1959, Hughes actually approached Burgmaster to see if it was interested in manufacturing the MT-3, according to some accounts. The Burgs, swamped with orders for the turret drills, declined the offer.[23] With the dollar in a strong position compared to the mark, and West Germany one of the few countries capable of manufacturing such a sophisticated tool, Hughes cut a deal with a German builder, Burkhardt & Weber, for overseas production. During the early 1960s, of course, many American tool builders were establishing subsidiaries or making coproduction agreements with European builders. But Hughes differed in that it did not really exist as an American manufacturer. The MT-3 was built in Reutlingen, after which it was disassembled, shipped to the United States, reassembled with motors and wiring supplied by Hughes, and then sold on the U.S. market. It thus qualified as a machine tool "made in the United States," and was not subject to the tariff on imported machine tools.

Kearney & Trecker's Milwaukee-Matic became a rousing commercial success, but the Hughes entry fared less well. Its NC system, as K&T had warned, was relatively difficult to operate. Many potential customers were also leery of Hughes Aircraft as a machine tool builder or even importer. Hughes was never able to capture more than a minuscule fraction of a booming market. By the late 1960s, only three dozen of its machining centers were in operation in the entire United States.[24]

Despite this lukewarm success, Hughes was not actively trying to unload the MT-3 when Houdaille initiated serious discussions about the machine in 1969, shortly after Folger took office. The new Burgmaster president was enthusiastic about the idea, mostly on the grounds that any entry in the machining center market was better than none. But there were several dissenters, including Ed Merk, the head of sales, and some of Burgmaster's own engineers.

Merk was concerned about what he considered the machine's outdated design, and had the usual qualms about the Hughes control.[25] But the engineers' reservations were particularly revealing.

Everyone recognized that the MT-3 was indeed an impressive accomplishment. Yet a few engineers thought Hughes, because of its inexperience, had gone overboard, that the machine was in fact overdesigned. One such critic was Bob French, a design engineer who had learned his trade from Fred Burg. He knew that engineers, if left too much on their own, had a tendency to design "jewels and monuments" rather than good, but inexpensive machines that simply worked as advertised and sold for a profit. He believed that the MT-3 fell squarely into this category. "It was the most overdesigned machine I had ever seen," recalled French. "Anyone can design a complicated machine. Simple designs that work are the most difficult."[26]

The final decision to buy the MT-3 or not was Saltarelli's. Nothing of such import occurred without his express approval. He was aware of the criticisms leveled by Burgmaster employees, and took them seriously. Some objections were easily overcome. It would be easy enough, for instance, to marry GE or Bendix controls to the machine in place of the awkward Hughes control. Meanwhile, to those who pointed out that only a relative handful of the machines had been sold, he suggested that Hughes's marketing inexperience had been responsible. It was harder, though, for Saltarelli to rebut critics of the machine's fundamental design. Ultimately, the element that persuaded him to go ahead was not so much the machine itself but another integral part of the deal, namely, Hughes's right to the technology incorporated in the MT-3.

Superior engineering was the reason why Kearney & Trecker had cornered more than one-third of the $100 million market for machining centers. Saltarelli believed that acquiring much of the same technology, via Hughes, would enable Burgmaster to make up for lost time. Houdaille was buying not simply a machine but designs that would accelerate engineering and production of Burgmaster's own tool changers.

It seemed to be a shrewd way to acquire technology that Kearney & Trecker was going to great lengths to deny others. Not content with simple domination of the market, K&T had sought ironclad protection through vigorous application of patent laws. Historically, continuous innovation, not lawsuits, had been the hallmark of success in the industry. Now Kearney & Trecker was writing a new page in the industry's history, one that was arousing bitter controversy among tool builders in the late 1960s.[27] As one competitor put it, the Wisconsin builder was attempting to assert exclusive rights over "not only every tool changing system now in use, but also every tool changing system that might be conceived in the future."[28] K&T brought patent suits against two of its biggest competitors in machining centers: Cincinnati Milacron in 1965 and Giddings & Lewis in 1966. Kearney & Trecker undoubtedly considered Hughes to be guilty of similar infringement, but presumably, since sales of the MT-3 were so inconsequential, it never bothered to file suit against its erstwhile partner.

Saltarelli knew there was a risk involved. If Houdaille, a machine tool builder of some consequence, bought the MT-3 and exploited its patents, Kearney & Trecker might well file a third suit. But as part of the sale, Hughes agreed to indemnify Houdaille against patent infringement claims. With this insurance, Saltarelli decided the potential gains to Burgmaster outweighed the risks. In August 1969, Houdaille paid about $4 million for the rights to "manufacture" the MT-3 in the United States, six unsold machines, and all of Hughes's associated patent rights. In addition, Burgmaster hired about a score of Hughes employees, ranging from engineers to MT-3 repairmen.[29]

One important feature of the MT-3 did not change, despite the change in ownership. Although Burgmaster had an up-to-date plant, Houdaille decided to continue the production arrangement with Burkhardt & Weber. "We thought of manufacturing it in Gardena," Folger recalled, "but an analysis showed we could not compete."[30] That was true, given the overall economic climate in the United States. With both inflation and interest rates at postwar highs, it seemed far more prudent to keep the Germans responsible for bringing in the machine at a certain price. Burkhardt & Weber was not operating in such an uncertain environment.

In other respects, however, the purchase ushered in many changes, both in the machine and at Burgmaster. To give the MT-3 a fresh start, Folger promptly renamed it the "Dualcenter," and took the necessary steps to offer GE or Bendix NC systems as an option.[31] Simultaneously, the engineering department began adapting the Hughes technology to Burgmaster's own line of tool changers on the drawing board.

Engineering was moving full speed ahead when Houdaille and Burgmaster received disturbing news in November 1969. A Wisconsin federal judge had finally reached a verdict in one of Kearney & Trecker's two patent suits, after three years of legal maneuvering and arguments. He ruled against Giddings & Lewis, validating Kearney & Trecker's claim that its patents had been infringed. The amount of damages involved was not immediately clear; the thirty-page decision instructed Kearney & Trecker to develop an estimate and submit its figure to the court.[32]

But from Burgmaster's perspective, the news was deeply unsettling. If Burgmaster went ahead and used the technology, Kearney & Trecker would surely initiate another lawsuit. Even assuming the best outcome—an eventual court ruling in Houdaille's favor—a court test would delay for years Burgmaster's own tool changer. But if Burgmaster desisted from using the technology, it would also take years to perfect a reliable design that skirted the Kearney & Trecker patents, and the purpose behind the purchase of the Dualcenter would be largely negated. Either way, Burgmaster stood to lose time, the one thing it could least afford.

To make matters worse, by January 1970, the end of Folger's first year as president, it was clear that the recession in the machine tool industry was not going to be short-lived. New orders continued to drop, and everyone predicted a 15 percent decline in sales through 1970. That meant massive layoffs, perhaps as much as half of Burgmaster's work force of about four hundred employees.

The recession on top of the patent problems were two reasons why Jerry Saltarelli was beginning to sour on the whole machine tool industry. But they were far from the only reasons.

Another was Houdaille's costly and unsuccessful attempt to manufacture its own electronic controls. Back in the mid-1960s, when Houdaille's enthusiasm for machine tools knew no bounds, Saltarelli figured that it would be logical for the conglomerate to enter the highly competitive market for NC systems. The Strippit and Burgmaster divisions were buying more and more of the devices and the market was expanding and lucrative. Saltarelli spent millions to set up and staff a Houdaille electronics division. And for a while, the investment looked as if it were going to produce large rewards. In 1968, at the Philadelphia Tool Show, Strippit exhibited the first NC machine tool to be linked directly to a full-fledged computer. This significant technological advance was eventually dubbed computer-numerical control, or CNC.[33]

Within a decade, the more versatile CNC would almost eclipse NC as the preferred means of electronic control. A machinist operating a CNC tool could program the machine by himself, whereas an NC tool was limited to reading coded instructions.[34] Yet Houdaille, despite its considerable investment and early lead, was never able to capitalize on the next generation of controls. It quickly lost the technological edge to much larger companies like General Electric. One reason was that the quality of Houdaille's controls left something to be desired. Burgmaster, which initially ordered one hundred Houdaille controls, ended up using them on only three or four of its machines. The controls "simply didn't work," recalled Bob French, a Burgmaster design engineer.[35]

The ill-fated venture into controls, moreover, had not been Houdaille's only costly mistake during these years. The machine tool group was also witness to another debacle, namely, the attempt to shift production of Burgmaster's small tools from Gardena, California, to McMinnville, Tennessee.

In 1967, Saltarelli had overcome the Burgs' opposition to the shift by pointing to hard economic facts. Burgmaster was operating at capacity but could not fill all its orders; in addition, its bench and table models were being manufactured by high-paid workers whose skills could be more profitably employed reducing the backlog of NC machines. Saltarelli wanted to transfer the production of the O, 1D, and 2 models to Houdaille's Powermatic division in Tennessee, which had lower wages, no union, and its own foundry. Inevitably, the dominant force within Houdaille prevailed.[36]

Little more than two years later, it was obvious Saltarelli had forced a costly mistake. First, Powermatic became a union shop. Suddenly the wage advantage Tennessee enjoyed was substantially reduced.[37] Yet the real reason why the shift was disastrous only became evident in succeeding months. Despite all its calculations, Houdaille had never figured in one unquantifiable factor: the skill of Powermatic's work force. It was as if Houdaille had believed its own advertising, that Powermatic was a maker of sophisticated machines. In truth, the Tennessee company only had experience manufacturing rudimentary tools, and the workers on which Powermatic had to rely were insufficiently skilled. Although they were small in size, the O, 1D, and 2 models were still precision machines, costing up to $10,000. The turret mechanisms, in particular, required the skilled labor of highly trained machinists.

No matter how many trips Burgmaster employees made to McMinnville, the turret drills Powermatic turned out quickly became notorious for abysmal workmanship. Burgmaster had transferred all the special tooling necessary to manufacture the small machines effortlessly, but it made no difference. When two parts didn't fit at Powermatic, workers thought nothing of forcing them together until they did. "We hammer it to fit," they would forthrightly explain when asked how they assembled a turret. On occasion, they even welded recalcitrant parts together. Burgmaster employees, returning from a trip to Tennessee, took to calling Powermatic's workers "barefoot machinists" because they had been hired right out of the fields.[38]

Potential customers promptly learned not to pay any attention to the nameplate on what looked like a standard Burgmaster turret drill. What mattered was where the machines had been manufactured. If it said anywhere on the machine "Burgmaster manufactured by Powermatic," the tool was to be avoided at all costs. Machine tool distributors began to ship machines back to Powermatic because they were not salable. "I don't know how many millions were lost," recalled Gene Dobmeier, Burgmaster's plant manager and a frequent visitor to Tennessee. "It was a bad, costly venture."[39]

With these reverses fresh in mind, in addition to the machine tool recession, Saltarelli decided that some tough business decisions were in order in 1970. He was impatient with the idea of waiting for the market to recover, and thought there had to be something the machine tool group could do to boost its profitability. He considered many alternatives before settling on two, and both decisions affected Burgmaster directly.

First, Saltarelli decided to reshuffle manufacturing responsibilities within the machine tool group. He closed down production at Houdaille's most recent machine tool acquisition, Kaufman Tool & Engineering. The Chicago-based company had been purchased for cash just a few months before, in October 1969. Saltarelli figured that Houdaille's assets would be more efficiently employed if Kaufman's operations were transferred to the Di-Acro division in Minnesota.

In addition, as part of the reshuffle, Saltarelli decided to move Burgmaster's small tools back to Burgmaster. In a way, the shift was more of a rescue mission than a reshuffle, an attempt to salvage an entire line of machines that had always been a small but reliable source of profit. The bottom had dropped out of the market for the tools, though not because of the recession. Powermatic had ruined their reputation. Burgmaster was going to be saddled with hundreds of thousands of dollars' worth of Powermatic's junk, much of which would have to be scrapped. It was going to be hard to restore a lost reputation.[40]

Although not exactly cosmetic, neither of these redeployments promised to bring the machine tool group out of its doldrums. The motive was simply to become more efficient and maximize profits, to eke the last dollar out of the machine tool group at a difficult time. Saltarelli's second major decision, however, carried more potential for boosting profits. In June 1970 after lengthy negotiations during which Houdaille was represented by Joe Burg, Saltarelli agreed to sell some of Houdaille's technological edge to a company in Japan, the Yamazaki Machinery Works in Nagoya.

The agreement between Houdaille and Yamazaki was far from the only one signed that year between a major American and major Japanese tool builder. In 1970, more than half a dozen of the top U.S. builders reached similar licensing or coproduction arrangements: Kearney & Trecker forged a link with Toshiba Machine, Warner & Swasey with Murata Machinery, and Norton Company with Mitsubishi.[41] All these joint ventures were formed because Japanese builders wanted to produce technologically advanced American machines. Equally important, they were possible because Japan was gradually becoming more integrated into the world economy. Rising exports had persuaded the Japanese government to relax its stiff controls on capital in the late 1960s, and inaugurate the so-called five liberalizations of their economy. Scores of joint American-Japanese ventures followed, in many manufacturing realms besides machine tools, including automobiles and semiconductors.[42]

The deals with the Japanese were unlike the foreign agreements American tool builders had commonly made during the late 1950s and early 1960s. Those were mostly one-sided affairs, whereby U.S. companies set up wholly owned subsidiaries or dealer networks abroad. The arrangements with the Japanese, were more like partnerships, in large part because the Japanese government, even as it liberalized controls over foreign capital and investment, had no intention of handing over a basic industry to American builders. Acting through its Ministry of International Trade and Industry (MITI), the government insisted on foreign equity controls that permitted joint ventures but virtually prohibited wholly owned U.S. subsidiaries.[43]

Houdaille, like many other builders, shared its most advanced technology in return for access to Japan's market. But Japanese builders would soon prove to be more than just eager students and junior partners.

8

THE RISE OF YAMAZAKI (1945–1970)

The key element for industrialization is neither capital nor laws and regulation, because both are dead in themselves. . . . The spirit sets both in motion. . . . If we assign weights to these three factors with respect to their effectiveness, the spirit should be assigned five parts, laws and regulations four, and capital no more than one part.

—From a Japanese *Report on Manufactures*, 1884[1]

No company, of course, knew better than Burgmaster that Japan had been striving for years to establish a state-of-the-art machine tool industry. That had been evident as early as 1961, when Burgmaster discovered a Japanese builder making a flawless replica of its O model. Burgmaster also knew how interested the Japanese government was in the machine tool industry. After a Japanese court found that Chukyo Electric had violated Burgmaster's patent, the government's Ministry of International Trade and Industry pressed the Burgs to license the very company that was guilty of infringement.

In many ways, though, Burgmaster's new partner, Yamazaki Machinery Works, was a renegade among Japanese tool builders. It often chafed at, and frequently ignored, the measures MITI tried to impose on Japanese industry. At the same time, Yamazaki exhibited crucial features responsible for the growing strength of the Japanese tool industry. Yamazaki's origins were classical, and its drive and ambition were second to none.

In the world of machine tools, if Tokyo was the equivalent of Cincinnati, then Nagoya, the home of Yamazaki, was Japan's Milwaukee. The city gave rise to many metalworking entrepreneurs, including one Sadakichi Yamazaki, who founded a small company to make pots and pans in 1919. Like Fred Burg, Yamazaki was mechanically inventive, and soon he turned to a much more demanding pursuit—manufacturing machinery to produce Japan's ubiquitous tatami mats. In 1926, Yamazaki Tekko (metalworking) progressed to the manufacture of woodcutting machines, and two years later reached the pinnacle of the metalworking trade: Yamazaki crafted a machine tool for its own factory. Soon the company became renowned locally for its lathes.[2]

As Japan mobilized for war during the 1930s, Yamazaki Machinery played a role in building up the country's arsenal, and reducing Japan's acute dependence on American machine tools. Like many other builders, Yamazaki Machinery eventually became directly engaged in war production, making parts for the Nakajima Aircraft Factory, which produced the Zero fighter. But like much of Japan's manufacturing capacity, by 1945 Yamazaki was reduced to rubble by U.S. bombers.[3]

The end of the war inaugurated a Darwinian struggle to rebuild and survive. Initially, U.S. occupation authorities prohibited all production because machine tools were seen as the heart of Japan's war machine. Half of Japan's tool factories were designated as war reparations, to be shipped to the empire's former colonies in China, Korea, and the Philippines.[4] Sadakichi Yamazaki returned to the manufacture of pots and pans. Within a year, though, political considerations caused an about-face in American policy. The success of Mao Tse-tung's forces in China persuaded the Truman administration to concentrate on building Japan into a bulwark against communism. Yet this was small consolation to Japanese tool builders. Short of not producing at all, their situation could not have been worse.[5]

American authorities now flooded the Japanese market with machines that had been seized for reparations or for their war potential. The overcapacity that naturally follows any war became an indigestible glut, and the weeding-out process in the late 1940s was nothing short of brutal. Some Japanese builders took up the manufacture of spinning, weaving, and printing machinery. The ones with the best reputations, like Yamazaki, were slightly more fortunate. He managed to survive by opening a shop in 1947 to repair and sell used machine tools. By now Yamazaki's eldest son, Teriyuki, had returned from university to join his father, and eventually the two younger sons, Yoshihiko and Tsunehiko, would also enter the family business. But its future seemed bleak and uncertain.

Yamazaki Machinery, like other Japanese builders, dearly wanted to get back to producing its own machines. But in addition to the glut, it was hindered by Japan's technological backwardness. The first U.S. delegation to inspect tool factories in Tokyo, Nagoya, and Osaka in late 1945 had expressed amazement at the country's machine tool stock. It had been effrontery for Japan to go to war against the Allies with such hopelessly obsolete tools. No wonder its wartime output had been so woefully inadequate, and its military had suffered chronic shortages of matériel.[6]

But after the war, tool builders anxious to modernize were caught in a bind. As Japan's recovery gathered steam, especially after the outbreak of the Korean civil war, tool consumers wanted the most modern European or American machines available, not an antiquated Japanese model. Imports flooded the domestic market, and Japanese builders lost the profits they needed to modernize. The glut of war-era machines, moreover, also depressed demand. In sum, Japanese builders lost sales because they produced outmoded machines, and could not modernize because of lost sales.[7]

In 1951, with the industry at its nadir, forty of the largest builders organized a *gyōkai*, or industry council, the equivalent of a trade association in the United States. Such groups were becoming popular in postwar Japan, and like its counterparts, the Japan Machine Tool Builders' Association existed primarily to goad the government bureaucracy into constructive action. The JMTBA was also intended to be a forum for exchanging information. Both goals seemed reasonable, but for the time being scores of companies like Yamazaki Machinery preferred to stay outside the JMTBA. They worried about being dominated in an organization run by the largest builders, their arch rivals. The independents were so numerous that they were designated within the industry as *ao-to-sidah*, a corruption of the English *outsider*.[8]

The year after the JMTBA came into existence, the Japanese government regained sovereignty. Tool builders saw that as unadulterated good news. For a century, the Japanese had seen themselves as engaged in a desperate struggle to catch up with the industrialized West. In large part, that meant catching up with the "progress of machinery in foreign countries," the true source of wealth and might.[9] Seemingly, "mother machines" had to be the foundation for a modern industrial economy, and the JMTBA expected highly preferential treatment from the government. But tool builders were destined for a rude awakening. At least initially, industrial recovery would come at their expense.

In every modern sense, postwar Japan was disadvantaged, a defeated, crowded island, singularly unendowed with natural resources. But where others saw national humiliation and permanent inferiority in 1952, Shigeru Yoshida, Japan's prime minister, saw a solution to Japan's economic backwardness. Yoshida suggested that "just as the United States was once a colony of Great Britain but is now the stronger of the two, if Japan becomes a colony of the United States it will also eventually become the stronger."[10] He believed that if Japan freely enjoyed the fruits of American hegemony without shouldering its burdens, it would hasten Japan's economic growth. Then Japan could husband its capital for productive investment, and the spirit and industry of the Japanese people, the country's sole genuine asset, could be devoted to catching up with the West.

Still, it was not easy to envision how Japan would achieve industrial parity, much less supremacy. To attain a Western standard of living, Japan would have to import vast quantities of food and other raw materials. To pay for these imports, Japan would have to export manufactured goods of high value that could successfully compete on world markets, which meant that its goods had to be competitive in the biggest and most important market of all, the United States. Only the United States, basking in the glow of the world's most productive economy, could afford to absorb, much less pay for, the volume of goods Japan had to generate.[11]

Yet in the early 1950s, it was also painfully obvious that what little Japan could manufacture was largely unsuited for export to America. Most observers shared the view of John Foster Dulles, Eisenhower's secretary of state. Dulles frankly told Prime Minister Yoshida in 1954 that "Japan should not expect to find a big U.S. market because the Japanese don't make the things we want. Japan must find markets elsewhere for the goods they export."[12] That was Dulles's relatively polite way of saying that Japanese engineering and production methods were inferior, and its goods notoriously shoddy.

Japanese government and industry knew where they wanted to go, but the problem was how to get there. The thought of a state directed or managed economy was out of the question. Instead, the Japanese conceived of an arrangement whereby the government, primarily MITI, tried to serve as an overall architect, while highly competitive private enterprise erected the industrial structure.

Over the next two decades, the government role assumed many guises, and several other ministries besides MITI were intimately involved. But essentially, the government's direct role always boiled down to one of three tasks: ensuring an economic climate conducive to manufacturing investment; protecting critical industries from being swamped by foreign competitors; and encouraging technological advancement. All three were critical if Japan was going to become one of the world's most efficient manufacturers of quality goods. Still, the tasks traditionally reserved for governments, such as public education, easily rivaled in importance any of the direct aid ministered by MITI.

Significantly, Japan's strategy explicitly rejected both foreign capital and foreign direct investment. These alternatives were considered inappropriate because both ceded undue influence over Japan's economic destiny to outsiders. The only foreign contribution Japan wanted was access to the best technology, so that its engineers could learn and leapfrog simultaneously. By necessity, a capacity to absorb foreign technology had long been a Japanese strong suit. Japan's technological isolation during World War II, moreover, had taught engineers and machinists to rely on their own ingenuity. Now these two threads could be woven together, and they promised to be a powerful force for modernization.[13]

Given the pivotal role of machine tools, and the broad outlines of what would later be called industrial policy, when the JMTBA first petitioned the government in 1952, it had every reason to think its demands would be looked upon most favorably. The JMTBA advocated a traditional position. It wanted MITI to protect domestic producers by slapping high tariffs on imported tools. The Korean War had nearly restored Japan's manufacturing output to its pre–World War II level. But Japanese builders were being left out of the boom because imports were largely satisfying the rise in domestic demand.[14]

Of course, MITI was not unsympathetic to the plight of a critical industry. The ministry promptly agreed to set up a licensing system aimed at keeping imports to an absolute minimum.[15] But to the JMTBA's dismay, MITI was not prepared to go much further. Its demand ran contrary to the ministry's prime objective: to foster efficiency and economies of scale in Japanese industry, so that eventually it would be a world-class competitor.

Tariff barriers would help domestic builders but the overall cost to the economy would be too high, MITI decreed. Modernization of dozens of other industries that used machine tools—not to mention the tool industry itself—would be seriously delayed. Consumers of machine tools had their own *gyōkai* that lobbied MITI heavily, and they vigorously opposed such tariffs. Ultimately, heavy-handed import substitution was dismissed as incompatible with the early stage of Japan's recovery.

Unwilling to accede to the JMTBA's tariff demand, MITI tried to help the industry in other ways. A March 1952 law provided for a 50 percent write-off for thirty-two classes of domestically produced machinery. Yet the consumers' *gyōkai* again quickly proved they were stronger than the JMTBA. They argued against a policy limited to domestic machines, and within a few months manufacturers won a 50 percent write-off on the purchase of imported machines. For the JMTBA, it was like adding insult to injury. Not only had it failed to win tariffs, but the final result of its first appeal to government was a regime that actually subsidized imports.[16]

It was small consolation when MITI undertook other steps to bolster the sagging industry. MITI arranged visits to American and European manufacturers, and encouraged builders to attend international tool exhibitions. The ministry also underwrote the Agency of Industrial Science and Technology (AIST), an institute that made the latest technical developments available to all Japanese industries. Later AIST established its own laboratories, one of which, the Mechanical Engineering Laboratory, issued research papers available to all builders on an equal basis.[17]

MITI also helped by devising a scheme to raise promotional funds for the JMTBA from bicycle and motorcycle races. Beginning in 1954, a portion of all race track bets was used to promote the machinery industry as a whole. Machinery encompassed a broad range of industries, of course, so only a small portion went directly to the JMTBA. But anything that promoted machinery was helpful to tool builders. The bulk of the racing proceeds went to an organization called the Japan Society for the Promotion of Machine Industry (JSPMI), which functioned as a super-*gyōkai*. It brought the JMTBA together with other machinery *gyōkai* and sought to harmonize relations among all the machinery trade associations.[18]

Such measures, however, did little to alleviate the immediate and bitter predicament of Japanese builders. The economy was growing, but imported tools, and sometimes old ones, were building the new Japan. MITI so routinely issued import licenses that from 1950 to 1955 the value of imports rose from 29 to 57 percent of domestic production.[19]

In 1955, the JMTBA embarked on another effort to protect the home market. But this time, it made sure to act in concert with other machinery makers and users, and the final result was more to its liking. In 1956, the Japanese Diet passed a law tailored to the demands of the machinery sector, called the Temporary Measures Law for the Promotion of the Machinery Industry. The law, which was to be in effect for five years, was ambitious in scope but typically brief for an industrial policy measure. It was left to MITI to supply the details and implement the goals.[20]

By the next year, 1957, MITI was ready with its blueprint. The Basic Rationalization Plan was as lengthy as the authorizing legislation was short. It set scores of goals to be achieved by 1960, ranging from gross production and investment, down to such details as increasing the rotational speed of Japanese lathes by a certain amount. But the protectionist steps taken in concert with the Basic Rationalization Plan were surely as important as MITI's investment and technical targets. MITI kept intact its licensing system, and, in addition, finally acceded to the JMTBA's longstanding demand for tariffs on imported machines. Machine tools that had a domestic equivalent were slapped with a 25 percent tariff.[21]

The JMTBA had won substantial favors from the government after a decade of hardship. Yet the Basic Rationalization Plan was the subject of intense dispute within the industry as a whole, more than 60 percent of which was still outside the JMTBA. Tariffs heartened "outsiders" like Yamazaki Machinery, but they tended to regard other elements of the plan as evidence of too close an affinity between MITI and the largest tool builders. A portion of MITI's plan advocated "rationalization" of the machine tool industry. It urged builders to "specialize by type of machine," and MITI was given authority to enforce production quotas and guide technological development if necessary.[22] To the "outsiders," such provisions suggested a hidden agenda: protection of the market shares enjoyed by the biggest producers and their dominance in certain lines.

MITI shared these JMTBA goals for several reasons. For one, the ministry was captive to the information and analysis supplied by the JMTBA. Therefore, its own plans tended to reflect the biases and interests of an association dominated by the biggest builders.[23] Like any would-be oligopolists, these builders preferred to fix prices or limit output rather than engage in price-cutting competition.[24] MITI operated in a political and institutional environment, moreover, that encouraged the ministry to think in terms of oligopolies, or production cartels, in several manufacturing sectors, not just machine tools. The relationship between the ruling Liberal Democratic Party and the ministry was almost incestuous, and since the LDP and big business interests were virtually synonymous, that reinforced MITI's tendency to think in terms of big producers.

MITI developed an elaborate economic theory about why cartels were desirable. Use of new technology invariably increased productivity, MITI argued, which often exceeded market demand. If unrestrained competition resulted, it might siphon off the profits and energies necessary to finance the next round of technological advancement. Thus price-fixing or output-limiting agreements were obviously preferable to ruinous competition.[25]

MITI also favored cartels for the same reasons that any bureaucracy would. It naturally sought to bring more order to a fractious and fragmented industry, filled with stubborn and independent entrepreneurs. Lastly, the ministry reflected the pervasive Japanese world view in the postwar era: as an industrial underdog, Japan could not afford to waste scant resources. To compete in the world market for manufactures, MITI imagined that harmful duplication resulting from competition had to be eradicated. MITI emphasized cutting expenses and increasing efficiency—anything, in other words, to get the economies of scale that would allow Japanese builders to compete with Americans.[26]

Yamazaki Machinery, however, resolved to help itself to the largess available under the Basic Plan, while ignoring the parts of MITI's program that it did not like. Sadakichi Yamazaki would not even borrow money from a bank to expand his business. He was not about to let the government or a trade association tell him what to build and how to do it. Yamazaki Machinery availed itself of a $140,000 MITI grant to purchase and study six advanced, foreign machine tools during the life of the Basic Plan. And of course, Yamazaki Machinery benefited from the protective tariff and government-supported information efforts to modernize machine tool production. But otherwise, Yamazaki paid more attention to its own ambitions than MITI's during the late 1950s. Meanwhile, MITI funneled most development subsidies to big tool makers like Makino or Ikegai, or the machine tool subsidiaries of giant companies like Hitachi, Toshiba, and Fujitsu, thinking that it would do these companies the most good.[27]

Yamazaki's foremost ambition, naturally, was to thrive solely on the basis of new production, rather than repair old machines or study foreign ones. Finally, after remodeling hundreds of machines, the moment Sadakichi Yamazaki had been anticipating for more than a decade arrived in 1958. Yamazaki Machinery was ready to unveil its own precision lathe. It met with immediate success, proof that all the years of preparation had been worthwhile and the MITI grant well spent. Virtually overnight, the Yamazaki plant burgeoned in size to one hundred workers to fill its pile of orders.[28]

Yamazaki's hard-earned reward was duplicated by dozens of tool builders large and small from 1957 to 1960, the period of the Basic Plan. All had spent years studying and mimicking the best machines produced by American and European builders. Sometimes this was done under license, but often the Japanese simply engaged in "reverse engineering," that is, a Japanese builder would buy a foreign machine, dismantle it, measure all the parts, draw up blueprints, and then attempt to build an indigenous version. That was precisely what Chukyo Electric did with Burgmaster's O model about this time. Of course, not many builders brazenly attempted to manufacture foreign designs without a license after successful reverse engineering. But nearly all of them learned how to improve their own machines this way.[29]

As domestic builders began to manufacture machines that began to approach the quality of the better imports, Japanese consumers found less reason to look abroad. The U.S. trade publication *American Machinist* was one of the first to take note of Japan's rapid rise to machine tool respectability. After visiting the 1959 Tokyo International Trade Fair, *AM* wrote, "Japanese machines for the first time appear to merit recognition and to be competitive with machines of the most advanced industrial nations."[30] Although the value of imports was still high, Japanese builders no longer complained incessantly about them. They had more orders than they could fill from the railroad, electric, and, above all, automobile industries.[31]

By 1960, Japanese production had reached $150 million worth of tools annually, up from $10 million just five years before. Imports hovered at about $55 million, or more than one-third of domestic production.[32] The machine tool revival, like much else about Japan's booming economy, seemed just short of miraculous. But no less eye-opening was that MITI's three-year-old Basic Rationalization Plan had turned out to be a poor yardstick and woeful prognosticator for the industry. None of the bureaucracy's rational targets for 1960 had proven even remotely accurate.

Under the Basic Plan, MITI had sought a 20 percent reduction in the cost of producing most machine tools. Yet instead of falling, unit costs had risen 121 percent by 1960. And despite the abject failure to reach that target, total production had grown by a whopping 225 percent, far in excess of MITI's goal. Similarly, the Basic Plan had called for about $167 million worth of new capital investment, from both public and private sources. In fact, total investment had reached $492 million by 1960, almost three times the amount projected by MITI.[33]

MITI's wildly inaccurate goals suggested that its plans were no match for the traditional forces that had always determined the machine tool industry's fate: overall cyclic demand; the availability of capital; and innovation on the shop floor and inside the engineering department of each and every builder. To be sure, by getting many economic fundamentals right, Japan's government had fostered the industry's recovery. In addition, MITI's efforts to encourage modernization paid handsome dividends, the publicly financed Japan Development Bank modestly supplemented private investment, and protective tariffs tilted Japanese consumers more quickly toward domestic machines. But MITI was quite incapable of guiding the industry to preordained targets.

Perhaps nothing better illustrated MITI's limitations in the 1950s, including its lack of prescience, than the manner in which it responded to the most important machine tool advance in fifty years, namely, numerical control. Given its mission, MITI ought to have pounced on the American development almost immediately. But that was far from what happened.

After MIT demonstrated the first NC machine in 1952, three years passed before anyone in Japan attempted to investigate machine tool automation. Eventually, in 1955, two institutions wholly independent of MITI, the Tokyo Institute of Technology and Tokyo University, launched separate researches into NC, or what the Japanese preferred to call "mechatronics." MITI did not enter the picture until mid-1956, when its Mechanical Engineering Laboratory began examining machine automation. Even then, it was at a relaxed pace. The MEL investigation was scheduled to last three years before resulting in a workable NC prototype.[34]

NC, in fact, arrived in Japan because of a commitment made in haste by Tsunezo Makino, president of Makino Milling Machine and JMTBA chairman. In 1955, he visited India as part of a business delegation trying to stir up interest in Japanese exports. A high-ranking Indian official asked Makino how long it would be before Japan could produce an NC tool, rightly regarded as the cutting edge of machine tool technology. Makino was deeply embarrassed to admit that Japan had not yet produced a single NC machine. But he rashly told the Indian official to come to the Osaka trade fair in 1958. There he would be able to see for himself what Japan could do, Makino boasted.[35]

Returning to Japan, Makino visited the appropriate MITI offices, seeking funds available under the Basic Rationalization Plan. He was turned away. MITI experts believed NC was still too unpredictable a technology, and that Japanese research and development should be devoted to more attainable goals. Undaunted, Makino turned to a young Fujitsu engineer, Dr. Seiuemon Inaba, who had begun to explore mechatronics in his laboratory just a few months earlier. Inaba immediately agreed to collaborate with Makino, who was desperate to make good on his boast.[36]

Nine months later, on Christmas Day 1956, Inaba announced that he had succeeded in using NC to move a simple punch press imported from the United States. Inaba had used as his bible a report on MIT's original 1952 accomplishment written up by a Japanese professor at the University of California. Despite their late start, the Inaba-Makino venture had beaten MITI's laboratory schedule by a full two years. And true to his word, Makino was able to display a prototype NC milling machine at the 1958 Osaka fair. Several other Japanese builders rapidly followed Makino's lead, and many lathes and milling machines on display at the 1959 Tokyo fair were numerically controlled. With virtually no MITI funding, Inaba's small laboratory would become FANUC (Fujitsu Automatic Numerical Control), and virtually synonymous with NC systems.[37]

Just as Japanese builders were starting to feel that they too were a firm part of their country's budding economic miracle, domestic tool orders suddenly leveled off in 1960. Overall demand for tools was not falling. Indeed, Japan's GNP was continuing to grow at the astounding rate of about 10 percent annually. The problem was that foreign builders had not exactly been standing still while domestic builders played catch-up. American builders, employing NC technology, were making rapid strides in productivity. Japanese builders who attended the Chicago tool exposition in 1960 were excited, but also sobered, by what they saw. American technology seemed almost as far ahead as ever.[38]

Japanese consumers of machine tools abruptly switched their allegiance back to imported tools. German and American imports skyrocketed over the next two years as Japanese manufacturers became especially keen to acquire NC tools. In industry circles the period from 1960 to 1962 became known as the first import boom, although in fact it was the third one since 1945. Meanwhile, domestic production went into a long slump that would not end until the mid-1960s.[39]

The 1960 recession caused the largest builders to quickly revive a moribund idea, the goal of rationalizing the industry. They feared cutthroat competition over a shrinking pie. In November 1960, all JMTBA members pledged not to "expand into fields for which they had no actual production." Internal distrust within the JMTBA, however, was second only to the competition between gyōkai and outsider builders, and both combined to make the agreement virtually worthless.[40] Coincidentally, and fortunately from the big builders' point of view, MITI's Basic Plan was scheduled to expire by 1961. That meant an opportunity to persuade the ministry to insert more stringent rationalization measures into its next blueprint for the machine tool industry.

MITI's 1961 Basic Recovery Plan also drew its authorization from the Japanese Diet's 1956 Temporary Measures Law. The failure of MITI's elite bureaucrats to make accurate forecasts the first time did not dissuade them from trying again. MITI once more set targets for everything from gross production levels down to specific technical achievements. Again, there was talk about rationalizing the industry.

And again, independent-minded builders like Yamazaki simply ignored the plan developed by MITI. When the ministry didn't restate the obvious, such as the need to find foreign markets for Japanese tools, with all due respect its plan amounted to little more than bureaucratic ideals concocted in a rarefied atmosphere. In the postwar era, the Japanese began to use a special term to describe MITI bureaucrats who resigned from the ministry to enter private industry. They dubbed the process amakudari, or "the descent from heaven," and it was often used to illustrate the esteemed rank of the bureaucrats. MITI's poor record of prognostication, however, suggests a double meaning, at least as far as the machine tool industry was concerned.

Quite apart from the bureaucracy, Yamazaki Machinery had its own ideas on how to grow and advance technologically. In 1961, the same year MITI unveiled a new five-year plan, Sadakichi Yamazaki retired after thirty-four years in the trade, and handed a debt-free company over to his three sons. The eldest, Teriyuki, became president; Yoshihiko and Tsunehiko Yamazaki became vice presidents. The brothers immediately put into motion ideas they had been harboring for several years.

One of the first was to join the tool builders' *gyōkai* in 1961.[41] Although they shared their father's fierce independence and his suspicion of the JMTBA, the brothers were confident about holding their own within the association. If it attempted to take measures inimical to Yamazaki's interests, the brothers intended to ignore the *gyōkai*, just as they had disregarded MITI whenever it suited them. Besides, they felt they had something to gain by joining an association dominated by the bigger companies. Their ambitions included making Yamazaki one of those big builders.

The brothers' next step was to put Yamazaki Machinery into heavy debt so that it could afford to build an entirely new plant, equipped with modern tools. Yamazaki could not hope to build lathes that were competitive unless the company itself employed the newest tools, they reasoned. It seemed a brash move by a small company that was still only the same size as Burgmaster, employing about 250 workers. The first import boom showed no signs of letting up. But Teriyuki Yamazaki, who had worked in the machine shop since he was a boy, was nothing if not supremely confident.[42]

Within a few months, the Yamazaki brothers began to wonder whether their father was wiser than they had realized. His lifelong refusal to go into debt seemed more prudent by the day. Domestic demand remained stagnant, and foreign builders, newly attracted to the booming manufacturing economy in Japan, were offering very attractive credit terms that few Japanese builders could match. With a large debt to service, the brothers became desperate. For a time, they even peddled Yamazaki lathes as if they were vacuum cleaners. The brothers took turns packing one or two lathes in a truck and driving around the country—anything to find a buyer.[43] But sales were so hard to come by that the brothers decided the domestic market was not the solution to their plight.

MITI's 1961 plan had called upon the machine tool industry to think about exports as a way to build profits, trim overcapacity, and stabilize cyclic demand. To this end, another trade association was formed, the Japan Machine Tool Trade Association, funded in part by proceeds from bicycle and motorcycle races in Japan.

Out of necessity, the Yamazaki brothers came to a similar conclusion about exports, but the pace of MITI's export drive was far too leisurely for them. None of the brothers had ever been abroad. But with typical confidence, they were convinced, after years of working on and tearing apart foreign machines, that Yamazaki Machinery was ready to export not only to less-developed countries but also to the most lucrative arena of all, the U.S. market.[44]

In the spring of 1962, Yamazaki shipped two lathes to Chicago, where they attracted the interest of Morey Machinery, a trading company. After many discussions, Simon Morey finally laid a proposition on the table. He wanted to buy two hundred lathes at $2,500 each from Yamazaki, and sell them in the American market for $5,000 a lathe.

Yamazaki was taken aback. Morey's purchase price was 30 percent less than what the same lathe sold for in Japan; moreover, Morey was demanding that modifications be made in order to sell the lathes in the United States. Yamazaki would not even have the benefit of establishing its trade name in America, because Morey insisted on marketing the lathe under his own brand name, Hercules Ajax.[45]

But Yamazaki was in no position to say no. Debt, plus the prospect of hard dollars and work for its skilled machinists, persuaded it to accept the terms. Then too, there was more than a little prestige attached to being the first builder to sell in such quantity to the U.S. market. In the fall of 1962, the first thirty lathes were ready for Morey's inspection. The brothers received a "bitter blow" when Morey rejected the lathes as unsatisfactory. Even at $5,000, they would not sell in the U.S. market, Morey said, because their quality was poor. The brothers worried that perhaps they were being taken advantage of, but they had little choice other than to bow to Morey's demands.[46]

A few months later, in the spring of 1963, an elite Yamazaki team visited nearly every major lathe manufacturer in America, Europe, and the Soviet Union. They saw that Morey, far from taking advantage of them, was right. Quality had to be improved for Yamazaki to be internationally competitive. The techniques of American, German, and Czechoslovakian manufacturers enabled Yamazaki to bring up its own standards and lower its costs. The next production run passed Morey's inspection.[47]

The Yamazaki machines began to arrive just as the U.S. tool economy was moving into high gear and a long sustained boom. As domestic backlogs built up, U.S. consumers became more willing to consider untested foreign machines. Sales of the first two hundred lathes exceeded expectations, and soon Morey wanted more. By the beginning of 1964, Yamazaki's production was up to 120 machines per month because of the brothers' "full-scale" export program to Southeast Asia and the United States.[48]

In their drive to export, the brothers pioneered the business culture by which Japanese machine tool builders would become known in the United States. Its hallmarks were ambition, pride, a willingness to learn, perseverance and, above all, competitiveness. These characteristics were in abundant display in the Japanese home market, where tool builders engaged in a paramilitary struggle for market share, the factor that invariably defined the accolade of "number-one" firm. Yet domestic competition was marked by a tacit agreement not to encroach upon other builders' strengths. Abroad, there were fewer agreements. Japanese companies were national representatives in a world contest for economic primacy. In the minds of the Yamazaki brothers, for one, the indelible picture of their father, reduced to making pots and pans in 1947, was etched.[49]

Yamazaki's success at cracking open the U.S. market was not emulated by many Japanese builders during the early 1960s. Japanese machines were invariably low priced, but U.S. consumers were wary. The foreign tools did not appear capable of withstanding the kind of abuse most American machine shops were used to inflicting. Parts and service were also cause for concern. If the Japanese tool was more likely to break down, who was going to fix it? Most shops wanted their tools fixed yesterday, and none of the Japanese builders could afford to set up expensive service networks when sales were meager. Japanese builders often found themselves allied with less reputable distributors, or even with used tool dealers.[50]

Consequently, in the early 1960s most Japanese builders thought in terms of recapturing their home market from imports. MITI helped by establishing an $89 million fund that enabled domestic builders to offer easy, competitive credit terms.[51] Simultaneously, a number of builders sought licenses to produce domestic versions of advanced foreign machines, including some NC technology. The first technological licensing boom occurred during the years 1961 to 1964, when twenty-nine foreign builders, including several from the United States, sold their technology to the Japanese.[52] These agreements gave Japanese builders not only all the blueprints but also the right to visit the home plant to learn production techniques.

MITI, which had to approve all licensing agreements, was quite willing to use its veto power if it thought it would help a Japanese company extract better terms. Acquisition of foreign technology, though, was hardly MITI's brainchild. It simply made indisputable sense. As one Japanese businessman explained, "It is worth paying a good price for [American technology] . . . the American government subsidizes American corporations to do research; we do not need to repeat that research; all we [need] do is buy it."[53]

Although selling licenses was not as profitable as selling machines, U.S. builders were willing to part with their technology. For one, American predominance seemed assured as far as anyone cared to predict. But Japan's industrial protectionism also played an important role. Several American builders contemplated erecting joint or wholly owned subsidiaries in Japan, similar to those they had established in Europe. That was not possible though, because a Law on Foreign Capital rigidly controlled investment in Japan by foreign companies.[54] When it passed in 1950, the law was a reasonable response to Japan's precarious economic situation. By the early 1960s, however, economic fears were losing their basis in fact. Still, Japan's desire to retain absolute control over its industrial economy, in order to catch up to the West, prevented early liberalization of the strictures on investment. Foreign technology was welcome, but not foreign participation in domestic production.[55]

Consequently, U.S. builders saw little choice but to sell their technology. If they did not, they knew that eventually Japanese builders would get the technology through reverse engineering. Or the Japanese could turn around and obtain a license for similar technology from a European builder. As always, the nature of machine tool technology was such that it simply could not be hoarded. If the Japanese were going to get it anyway, American builders might as well be the ones to profit.[56]

The first licensing boom cut deeply into foreign sales to Japan. In 1963, imports abruptly fell 50 percent from the level reached the year before, and by 1965 fell 50 percent again.[57] But American builders scarcely noticed the shrinkage of their market share in Japan. Partly because of the Vietnam War, their home market was in the midst of its best decade in history, and U.S. consumers were begging for machine tools. Builders were swamped by the domestic backlog, and lost sales to Japan were simply shrugged off.

For their part, while Japanese builders had reclaimed the home market, they still had little cause for celebration. Domestic demand was so sluggish and competition so fierce during the mid-1960s that a flood of bankruptcies swept through the industry. More than a dozen *gyōkai* firms and many more independents went under by 1965. MITI declared the machine tool industry one of the "sick men" of the Japanese economy.[58]

It wasn't supposed to be that way in 1965, the end of MITI's five-year Basic Recovery Plan. MITI's first plan had failed to foresee the boom of the late 1950s. This time, MITI's 1961 estimates of where the industry would be in 1965 were just as wrong—albeit in the opposite direction. Production volume was just 52 percent of MITI's forecast; investment, 53 percent. It was not hard to figure out why MITI had proven so wildly inaccurate. Besides uncritical acceptance of JMTBA figures, several of its forecasts had been based on nothing more sophisticated than extrapolations of the trends prevailing in 1960–1961.[59]

To MITI, the state of the industry was all the more alarming because of simultaneous pressure on Japan to liberalize its economy. After more than a decade of unprecedented economic growth, Japan was gradually taking its place as a full member of the international organizations that bound capitalist nations together, such as the International Monetary Fund. Along with the benefits of membership, however, came certain economic responsibilities. Many of these directly contradicted MITI's cherished powers, such as its control of foreign exchange and restrictions on foreign investment.[60]

The prospect riveted MITI. As one observer wrote, "the very thought of capital liberalization struck terror into the hearts of MITI officials and Japanese industrial leaders."[61] Just as Western Europe was perceived to be dominated by U.S. multinationals, MITI feared that Japan's industries would be overrun by the Americans. Direct U.S. foreign investment would either displace indigenous manufacturers with foreign subsidiaries, or gobble up debt-ridden Japanese companies. Either way, Japan's century-long struggle to build an indigenous world-class industrial base would be irrevocably compromised.

MITI believed that each key manufacturing sector had to be strengthened, and "excessive competition" curtailed, if Japanese firms were going to survive the inevitable capital onslaught. And that could only be accomplished by reducing, through mergers, the number of domestic companies in the steel, electric power, chemical, machinery, and automobile industries.[62]

In this sense, the 1965 recession in the machine tool industry and the need for a new five-year plan were made to order for MITI. When the JMTBA came to the ministry and asked for special measures in the new plan that would stimulate orders, MITI responded with a demand of its own. It announced that no stimulative measures, such as tax write-offs, would be forthcoming unless the *gyōkai* took steps to consolidate the number of firms in the industry.[63]

With many aggressive, former outsiders like Yamazaki Machinery now in its ranks, the JMTBA was not inclined to follow such guidance. Japanese builders were also worried about foreign competition. But each builder was so intent on being one of the survivors that collaboration with longtime domestic rivals was unimaginable. "They told us to form into larger companies," recalled one machine tool company president. "We told them 'the hell with that' and refused."[64]

In late 1965, MITI issued its third blueprint for the industry, entitled the Basic Promotional Plan for 1966–1971. It contained a compromise over the rationalization issue. In return for certain measures, the JMTBA agreed to divide its member builders into groups, ostensibly to facilitate joint research and production, and coordinate sales and marketing. Superficially, it looked like a victory for the ministry—a prelude to widespread consolidation in the industry. In truth it would demonstrate the tool builders' independence.

Yamazaki joined its *gurupu*, the "standard group," in March 1966, and by midyear ten such groups had been formed. Instead of bringing together builders who produced similar machines, however, the JMTBA craftily arranged the groups so that they united builders who did not compete. Moreover, insofar as builders participated in the groups, it was only to the extent consistent with their individual interests. Yamazaki was a case in point, for nothing was going to dampen the brothers' ambitions. The same year Yamazaki joined the standard group, it opened its very own technical development center for NC systems.[65]

Yamazaki's growth during the mid-1960s, at a time when most other tool makers considered themselves fortunate not to shrink, was attracting considerable notice among Japanese builders. Without so much as a licensing agreement, Yamazaki had raised its technology to such a level that it was becoming known in the U.S. market for its standard, low-priced engine lathes.[66] Many other Japanese builders, courtesy of licensing agreements, were also at or near Yamazaki's level of skill. They began asking themselves why they too could not penetrate the U.S. market. Perhaps they had given up too easily after the disappointing response in the early 1960s.

U.S. builders first began to take note of increased imports in 1965—

precisely when MITI was attempting to coerce Japanese builders into mergers. Historically, U.S. consumers imported tools from Germany whenever American counterparts were unavailable, and German builders still commanded the lion's share of U.S. imports, almost a full third. But suddenly more and more consumers began to view favorably machines from another source—Japan. "Our builders cannot yet match the highly sophisticated versatility of many American machines," conceded Yutaka Imai, the director of the Japan Machine Tool Trade Association, at a Cleveland trade show in 1965. "So we must concentrate for now on standard types that will produce at least as efficiently as yours, cost less, and be deliverable within 45 days."[67]

Japanese tool exports increased 140 percent in 1965, from $2 million in 1964 to $4.8 million. The next year, they jumped to $17.3 million, and in 1967, to $26.2 million. Altogether, from 1964 to 1967 Japanese exports to the United States rose 1,210 percent.[68] One anecdote cited in The Wall Street Journal exemplified why more and more customers were buying Japanese instead of American. A Pennsylvania company sorely needed a cylindrical grinder, but was told that delivery of a $50,000 American machine would take at least a year. So the company decided to order from a distributor of Japanese tools. Within weeks, it had two Japanese grinders in operation for almost the same price.[69]

U.S. builders took some consolation in the fact that so many Japanese tools were copies of foreign technology. This created the widespread perception that the Japanese could only mimic, not invent, and therefore American builders could always remain two or three steps ahead. Perhaps the low end of the U.S. market, that is, non-NC tools, were destined to belong to imports. But those profits were unexciting because they depended on volume rather than margin. And there was no way U.S. builders could compete given significantly lower Japanese labor costs. In the late 1960s, a Japanese machinist, by some estimates, earned only one-sixth of the $3.90 average hourly wage paid to his American counterpart.[70]

But contrary to the skeptics, as Japanese imports kept increasing, so did their sophistication. After winning a substantial share of the market for standard lathes, Japanese builders established a strong position in higher-precision turret lathes. Then, to the astonishment of the Americans, by 1968 the Japanese began exporting, of all things, NC tools to America. The shock among U.S. builders was palpable. Heretofore, NC production had been their exclusive domain.[71]

Once again, Yamazaki Machinery led the way. It had been one of the first Japanese firms to commit itself in a big way to NC, and by 1968 Yamazaki was producing a reliable NC lathe. Most significant, the Yamazaki brothers decided to sever their tie to Morey Machinery and do their own marketing and service. For one reason, they were no longer satisfied to see the Hercules Ajax brand name on all their lathes. That was near blasphemy to a builder as proud and as enterprising as Yamazaki. That year the brothers opened a wholly owned U.S. subsidiary, the Yamazaki Machinery Corporation, on Long Island, New York.[72]

Some U.S. builders thought it was a little early to panic over such developments. All told, imports were still no more than 10 percent of domestic consumption. Once U.S. backlogs were whittled down and demand in Germany and Japan increased, "we will see an end to this rapid rise in machine-tool imports and probably a dropoff," averred James C. Hodge, president of Warner & Swasey, one of the largest tool builders.[73]

But such views were a decided minority within the NMTBA, the American builders' *gyōkai*. Most took seriously the admonition in the *American Machinist* that "the Japanese are a competitor now."[74] Japanese exports to the United States in 1967 had totaled $24 million, twice the amount of U.S. exports to Japan. The NMTBA decided to express its deep concern over imports to the government, and ask for protection. It suggested a schedule of selective tariffs, spread out over a fifteen-year period, to ensure that imports would not exceed 10 percent of consumption in any of the major machine tool categories.[75] The NMTBA also sent a trade mission to Japan to see the situation at first hand.

The NMTBA mission wanted to investigate Japanese barriers to U.S. exports and direct investment. MITI had a ready rebuttal for the first complaint: Why should Japanese consumers exhibit more patience than U.S. consumers over the long American backlogs? The Japanese pointed out that they had imported more than $48 million worth of machine tools in 1967. Most of them were European because they couldn't get American tools. Lack of service networks was also cited as a reason for lagging U.S. exports. Still, the American delegation complained that its exports were hampered because MITI had to approve every expenditure of foreign exchange—a source of bureaucratic power dating back to the 1950s, and one that MITI was extremely reluctant to give up.

The discussions took a turn for the worse when the subject became direct investment. MITI officials voiced a familiar refrain: for all its accomplishments, Japan was "still a half-developed nation . . . trying to build itself up to a fully developed country." The Americans then pointed out the benefits of unlimited foreign investment. Even 100 percent foreign-owned subsidiaries were no threat to Japanese national interests, the NMTBA mission argued. As in the United States, "the government . . . really controls the actions of private industry."[76] The flatness of that assertion must have brought a smile to MITI bureaucrats, given their difficulty with the unruly JMTBA. Nor would it have been widely accepted back home.

Predictably, MITI suggested that licensing rather than direct investment was preferred. The U.S. delegation countered that "licensing agreements were not advantageous to American manufacturers, and that it was doubtful MITI could hope to get any licensing agreements in the future from American firms." If anything, joint ventures would be the answer. The "most unsatisfactory" meeting, from the Americans' point of view, ended without any concessions from MITI.[77]

It was not hard to see why MITI, the guardian of Japan's desire to catch up with the West, politely but firmly turned aside American protests. By 1968, the long slump in domestic demand had finally ended, and Japan was once again in the midst of a machine tool boom. The chief spur was the Japanese automobile industry, which would experience a twentyfold increase in production by the end of the decade. [78] But along with increased demand, a second import boom was in the making in Japan. In 1968, imported tools would amount to nearly 19 percent of domestic consumption (nearly twice the level in the United States), and Japan would export only 11 percent of its production (while the United States was exporting 13 percent). Moreover, Japan was still only the third-largest exporter to the United States, behind Germany and Britain.[79] True, Japanese trade in machine tools could not be labeled free. But to MITI, fixated on Japan's underdog status, the American complaints seemed out of proportion to the injury, and Japan unfairly singled out.

Success at home and abroad buoyed Japanese builders in the late 1960s, but not the chronically pessimistic MITI. The ministry still believed that excessive competition would lead to chaos and make Japanese builders vulnerable to foreign domination. But its fervent wish for production cartels had gone unfulfilled. The boom sounded the death knell for consolidation, and the *gurupu* deteriorated into social gatherings.[80]

To make matters worse, from MITI's perspective, in the late 1960s the American machine tool industry was undergoing the very rationalization that MITI so devoutly espoused. MITI watched as the American machine tool industry was largely taken over by powerful conglomerates. The American machine tool industry was the largest and most advanced in the world, the recipient of generous R&D subsidies courtesy of the Pentagon, now bolstered by the capital from corporate giants. How could Japanese builders withstand this juggernaut, once their market was pried open? To MITI, the Japanese industry—never more prosperous—was blissfully ignoring a crisis.

Almost frantically, MITI embarked on a final effort in 1968 to stop wasteful competition. Although the five-year plan formulated in 1965 still had three years to run, the ministry decided to put forth a supplemental program, the Basic Promotional Plan for the Metal Cutting Machine Tool Manufacturing Industry. Its centerpiece was the so-called 5–20 rule, which would rationalize the Japanese machine tool industry by apportioning market shares. If a builder had less than 5 percent of the market for any of his tools, he was to cease production of the tool. In addition, any line that represented less than 20 percent of a builder's production was to be discontinued.[81] MITI was intent on using its waning, but still considerable influence, to have the rule accepted. It almost had the ring of a wartime measure.

Yet once again, MITI was outflanked by the JMTBA. The trade association inserted so many escape clauses that the measure, highly restrictive on its face, became virtually toothless. The 5–20 rule was modified so that it only applied to twelve types of rudimentary tools, like ordinary lathes, grinders, and milling machines. New machines, machines developed in joint ventures with foreign builders, and, most important, all NC machines were totally exempt. JMTBA members were more than willing to make this gesture because they knew NC represented the future. The machines covered by the rule were anachronisms, part of a market that was bound to shrink.[82]

As meaningless as the rule was, to MITI bureaucrats the 1968 agreement did not come a moment too soon. That same year MITI finally lost its grip on the powers to which it had so tightly clung. The Diet revised the restrictive statutes of the 1950s, and now joint ventures between Japanese and foreign companies were automatically approved so long as they were on a fifty-fifty basis. MITI also lost its veto power over licensing agreements.[83] As a result, there was a rush of American builders seeking to invest in or link up with Japanese builders.

Many of the deals struck were joint ventures, since American builders were eager to benefit from Japan's inexpensive but skilled work force. A surprising number, however, given the NMTBA's complaints a year earlier, were licensing agreements. Japanese builders would later label this period, 1969 to the early 1970s, the second technological licensing boom. Japanese builders negotiated twelve licenses, nine of them with American firms, all of which covered state-of-the-art NC technology.[84]

One of those deals was between Yamazaki Machinery and Houdaille Industries, specifically, its Burgmaster and Strippit divisions. By some accounts, Yamazaki made the first approach. The brothers' ambition to make their company the largest privately held builder in Japan was not likely to succeed if they only manufactured lathes. They knew they had to expand into other machine tool lines, and NC machining centers, as everyone recognized, were the tools of the future. So they approached Houdaille.

The negotiations lasted about eight months. During that time, it became clear to Houdaille's president, Jerry Saltarelli, that he was negotiating with one of the most dynamic, if not aggressive, tool builders in Japan. But if Saltarelli gave any thought to where that might lead, he was more likely to take comfort in the idea rather than worry about it. In the end, Houdaille stood to profit handsomely, without risk or the expenditure of a single penny. And licensing, of course, was the way to go rather than exports because "getting access to that market was so damn remote—it would never happen."[85]

Strippit and Burgmaster negotiated separate agreements with the Japanese tool builder. In the case of Burgmaster, Yamazaki agreed to pay a one-time fixed royalty of $190,000 for the rights to manufacture and sell nearly the entire Burgmaster line for a period of ten years, in a "licensed territory" that encompassed all of East Asia. In addition, Yamazaki was obligated to pay another periodic royalty of $750,000 over the life of the agreement, bringing its face value to just under $1 million.[86]

In all likelihood, however, the deal was going to be worth far more than that to Houdaille. The $750,000 royalty payment was a minimum. The contract stipulated that Burgmaster was to receive a 4 percent royalty on every Dualcenter Yamazaki sold, and a 5 percent royalty on all other machines covered by the agreement—including the automatic tool changers that were still on Burgmaster's drawing boards. The average royalty payment worked out to around $4,400 per machine; that meant as soon as Yamazaki sold annually more than an extremely modest number of machines, about fourteen, it would owe Burgmaster more than the minimum payment. It was not unreasonable to expect Yamazaki's aggressive sales force to boost Burgmaster's gross profits by at least $375,000 annually, or almost 10 percent.[87]

Gone were the days when Fred Burg aggressively went after promising markets, and never, but never, parted with his latest technology.

9

STAGNATION (1971–1978)

By the fall of 1970, after nearly two years on the job, Allan Folger was comfortably ensconced as Burgmaster's president. He was unlike any other president Burgmaster had ever had. In contrast to the very visible Burgs, and even Tom Norton, Houdaille's first successor to the Burgs, Folger was reserved and rather aloof. Employees saw Folger so little they joked about it. If there was a faint aroma of cigar smoke in the hall near Folger's office, he was at Burgmaster. Otherwise, it was impossible to tell.[1]

Still, Folger commanded respect, if only because he was so adept at keeping corporate headquarters at bay. Three presidents in almost as many years had been unsettling to many Burgmaster employees, and the signals coming from headquarters seemed mixed until Folger arrived. Houdaille talked about goals—efficiency, productivity, and innovation— that were familiar to everyone. But if employees tried to pursue these aims in the Burgs' manner, it became evident that Houdaille was merely paying lip service. What seemed to matter most to headquarters was the bottom line, as reflected in the monthly reports.

Folger finally clarified the uncertainty inside Burgmaster. First, he gave headquarters what it desired, and then, he let Burgmaster employees know unequivocally what he expected of them. Jerry Saltarelli wanted, above all, flawless monthly reports that never missed a forecast, and Folger's financial acumen allowed him to succeed where both Joe Burg and Tom Norton had fallen short. In turn, Folger let everyone at Burgmaster know that there was only one cardinal sin, and that was screwing up a forecast. Once everyone understood that the bottom line was indeed the bottom line, things settled down.

Burgmaster, five years after the takeover, had finally arrived at a semblance of managerial equilibrium. But if stability had been reestablished internally, it was also clear that Burgmaster was headed for more turbulent times than ever.

The most immediate problem was the deepening slump in the machine

129

tool industry as a whole. The downturn, which seemed to be no more than a pause when it began in 1968, was turning into a steep recession. Houdaille's net sales from its machine tool group in 1970 had fallen to $39 million, and were heading still lower, to $31 million in 1971.[2] Nevertheless, Folger knew that cyclical downturns were part of the industry, and just how to handle one. The time-honored way was to reduce the work force in one motion to a core group of the best machinists and engineers. In this way the heart of the enterprise would be guaranteed work, and Burgmaster would not lose its most productive employees because of uncertainty over layoffs. Deliveries might be delayed, and orders canceled, but this was the best way to guarantee Burgmaster's long-term health.

There was a second and equally troublesome economic problem, however. That was inflation. A persistent, nagging inflation seemed to be embedded in the U.S. economy by 1970. Moreover, it was a tendency soon to be exacerbated by the first round, in 1970–1971, of a new phenomenon: steep and sudden increases in the price of crude oil.

Inflation put all manufacturing industries in a bind.[3] But for Burgmaster, in particular, it carried a hidden consequence. The baleful influence of inflation, combined with Houdaille's emphasis on short-term profits, caused Burgmaster to abandon prematurely the very business strategy it needed to embrace in the early 1970s. And by doing so, it committed a colossal blunder.

The concept at stake was the Econocenter, Burgmaster's attempt to lower costs and put its NC turret drilling machines within the reach of small job and production shops. These consumers constituted a large and largely untapped market. They wanted to move into NC tools, but could not afford the expensive and overly elaborate NC machines manufactured by American builders primarily for the aerospace market.[4]

The Econocenter tried to solve these problems, and reach that market. Burgmaster engineers redesigned several major castings and came up with a turret drill that was easier and therefore less expensive to manufacture. The strategy also entailed producing the Econocenters in large batches of fifty or more. Such large production runs drastically reduced per unit costs, and made the NC machine affordable to small shops.[5] In addition, the machine featured a standard, simplified NC device that made it less intimidating to operate for first-time NC operators.

Following their introduction in mid-1968, the Econocenters had become an instant success. They were priced so low as to be competitive with single-spindle NC drills of comparable capacity, and Burgmaster ran several competitors (Pratt & Whitney and Brown & Sharpe) virtually out of the market. With the downturn, however, the market for the budget NC machines began to erode. Still, inflation proved to be their greatest nemesis. Corporate headquarters, still struggling to diversify, preferred short-term, in-hand profits rather than market share. Houdaille insisted that Burgmaster pass along all the costs steadily added by inflation. In the market Burgmaster was trying to reach, which was sensitive to price, the consequence was lost sales.

A vicious circle then resulted, as Ed Merk, Burgmaster's head of sales, recalled. Each price increase reduced the market for the mass-produced NC machines, necessitating shorter and shorter production runs. Houdaille then insisted on raising prices still higher to reflect the added costs incurred from shorter runs. That shrunk the market still more. By 1971, the original strategy behind the Econocenter concept almost completely disappeared. Burgmaster returned to its normal mix of custom-built and standard models, a combination that resulted in chronic production bottlenecks.

On top of these economic and production problems, in December 1970 Burgmaster suddenly found itself facing a legal assault on its technology. The issue was not Burgmaster's indigenous engineering achievements. No builder could possibly challenge Burgmaster's turret drills. Rather, the lawsuit concerned the Dualcenter patents, which Burgmaster had acquired from Hughes Aircraft in order to leapfrog into production of tool-changing machining centers.

When Burgmaster bought the Dualcenter from Hughes in August 1969, everyone knew that another builder, Kearney & Trecker, claimed exclusive rights to the patents. Moreover, Kearney & Trecker had already proven, in two pending suits against Cincinnati Milacron and Giddings & Lewis, its determination to litigate at the slightest hint of patent infringement. Nevertheless, the need for Burgmaster to get into tool changers without delay overruled whatever reservations Houdaille had about getting into a legal thicket. Burgmaster urgently needed unrestricted access to proven technology.

In November 1969, three months after Burgmaster and Hughes signed their deal, a federal court issued an initial ruling in favor of Kearney & Trecker in its lawsuit against Giddings & Lewis. Stunned by this adverse development, Burgmaster considered trying to find a way around the patents, but that defeated the main purpose of buying the Dualcenter from Hughes. Other builders, with far better engineering departments than Burgmaster's, had been trying to do exactly that for years, with mixed results. The key patents for a tool-changing kind of machining center, unlike most machine tool patents, were difficult to skirt.

Burgmaster decided to plunge ahead, despite the specter of a lawsuit. And for a while, the risk seemed to be paying off. Perhaps Kearney & Trecker recognized that its former partner Hughes, which helped develop the first Milwaukee-Matic in the late 1950s, shared a right to the patents, and was free to assign them to another builder. By late 1970, with nary a word from Kearney & Trecker, Burgmaster was ready to unveil its own vertical, thirty-piece tool changer based on the patents. Then came word that Kearney & Trecker was filing suit against Houdaille in a Chicago federal court.

Kearney & Trecker asked the court to enjoin Houdaille from infringing on its patents, and for treble damages. Houdaille, in its May 1971 rebuttal, asked the district court to throw out Kearney & Trecker's claim and simultaneously filed a lawsuit of its own. Houdaille wanted treble antitrust damages levied against Kearney & Trecker for attempting to restrain trade. Hughes Aircraft, which had indemnified Houdaille against any patent infringement claims, also joined the legal fray. And to muddy the legal waters even more, it became obvious that many of the claims and counterclaims were identical to those raised in Kearney & Trecker's lawsuit against Giddings & Lewis. The initial ruling in that case was being appealed by Giddings & Lewis, and movement in the Houdaille case was inextricably bound up with that lawsuit.

As frustrating as the patent dispute was, it nevertheless was just one more sign that the Dualcenter deal seemed to be cursed. Another sign, of course, was the Dualcenter itself, which Burgmaster imported from Germany, and planned to market as its top-of-the-line machining center. But that August, Burgmaster's marketing strategy for the Dualcenter received a blow from which it would never recover. President Nixon was forced to let the dollar collapse.

The breakdown in the international monetary system had been building for at least a decade. Some realignment of the postwar system was inevitable, given the growing strength of the Japanese and West European economies vis-à-vis the United States. Nonetheless, the insolvent U.S. economy was the acute reason why the system was breaking down. The United States was flooding the world with unwanted and inflated dollars, which caused periodic bouts of panic on foreign exchange markets. The crisis was not only financial, however. It also featured an unprecedented U.S. trade deficit. An overvalued dollar encouraged imports and discouraged exports, and in 1971 the United States was heading for a $2.3 billion trade deficit—its first since 1893.

Presidents Kennedy and Johnson both had had to grapple with the fundamental insolvency, and had tried several ploys to stave off the economic crisis as long as possible. Nixon was no more disposed than his predecessors to address the root discrepancy between America's economic means and its politico-military aims. The only genuine difference, in fact, was that time ran out during Nixon's watch—in August 1971 to be precise.

To most Americans, the international details of Nixon's New Economic Policy seemed arcane and remote compared to its domestic component. His plan to reduce inflation and restore U.S. industrial competitiveness included a ninety-day freeze on all wages and prices. But next to that component, the factor that loomed largest for Burgmaster was Nixon's simultaneous decision to sever the dollar from fixed exchange rates. This de facto devaluation meant the same number of dollars suddenly bought fewer deutsche marks in August than in July. That augured poorly for Burgmaster's top-of-the-line, German-built Dualcenter.

The machine that Allan Folger likened to a Swiss watch was now more expensive than ever. Under the new regimen of floating exchange rates, the price of the Dualcenter promptly rose by almost 15 percent, and there was nothing Burgmaster could do about it, since it was committed to manufacturing the Dualcenter in West Germany. The ostensible Cadillac of the market now became a certified white elephant, a machine whose capabilities did not justify spending almost a quarter of a million dollars. For much less than that amount, a customer could buy a tool changer whose performance was only marginally less.

By 1972, Burgmaster's losses from the deal with Hughes totaled approximately $1 million.[6] The red ink occurred at a time when Houdaille's machine tool group was barely netting $2 million a year in profits.[7] The longtime Burgmaster employees who had always been skeptical about the Dualcenter were vindicated. They had argued, from the start, that the machine was overdesigned, an engineering dream but a marketing nightmare. But Houdaille executives had questioned their motives. The conglomerate suspected that wounded pride, rather than an objective commercial judgment, was at the root of their skepticism. So the employees had been overruled.

About this time, conglomerates akin to Houdaille were coming under fire for an unwillingness to invest in their acquisitions. In Houdaille's case that was clearly not quite accurate. Yet, insofar as Burgmaster was concerned, there was something deficient about Houdaille management. Taken together, the abandonment of the Econocenter and the Dualcenter debacle vividly illustrated Houdaille's corporate culture. In the former, Houdaille compelled Burgmaster to abort a promising strategy, even though knowledgeable Burgmaster employees were convinced it could work. In the latter, the conglomerate rammed an overdesigned machine down Burgmaster's throat, despite the better judgment of Burgmaster employees. Houdaille put a premium on expediency and instant, imported prestige, rather than patience, indigenous effort, and even some sacrifice of profit margins, if that's what it took to build a market. The real problem was not that Houdaille didn't invest, but that Houdaille didn't invest wisely.

Not surprisingly, Jerry Saltarelli's enthusiasm for the machine tool industry was ebbing dramatically by the early 1970s, compared to his enthusiasm of the 1960s. The industry's overall depressed state did not recommend it, of course. In dollars adjusted for inflation, shipments were at their lowest level since 1959.[8]

Intellectually, Saltarelli had known from the outset that the machine tool industry was cyclical. But like many other conglomerate CEOs, he had taken refuge in the conceit that modern management could somehow frustrate these cycles, and smooth out the bottom line so that it tended in only one direction—up. He was not prepared to see profits from the machine tool group plummet. Nor was he pleased with net returns on investment that were scarcely higher than bank interest rates.[9]

Saltarelli's disenchantment with the industry went even deeper than that, however. Building machine tools or their components was far more complicated than Houdaille had anticipated. Again and again, major investments of money, time, and energy did not yield the expected returns. Many ostensibly shrewd moves turned out wrong. The field, in fact, was littered with Houdaille's costly mistakes, of which the Dualcenter was but one. There was Houdaille's ill-fated and expensive venture into the manufacture of NC systems. The decision to shift production of Burgmaster's small tools to the Powermatic division had also been a disaster. Not only were millions of dollars lost, Burgmaster was finding it almost impossible to resuscitate sales because of the notorious reputation Powermatic had attached to these machines.

Saltarelli's disillusionment was not just a passing thought. It had tangible consequences, because the conglomerate still needed to diversify away from automotive products. Houdaille closed down its Detroit automotive parts division in 1974 and further shrinkage was inevitable.[10] The machine tool recession in the early 1970s meant many builders could be bought for a song, relative to the prices they were commanding during the late 1960s. Yet Saltarelli was in no mood to expand Houdaille's exposure after being singed, not once, but many times by the vagaries of machine tools.

He found a new favorite category that was much less taxing and more reliably profitable. Industrial products, especially pump manufacturers, became the object of Saltarelli's attentions, especially after the 1968 acquisition of Viking Pump proved a resounding success. In 1972, Houdaille bought Warren Pumps, a deal that reflected Saltarelli's determination to concentrate on companies that fit under the industrial products rubric, and build them into Houdaille's most important group. Machine tools were no longer exalted in Houdaille's annual reports.

The machine tool industry lost its luster for other conglomerates besides Houdaille in the early 1970s. Many large corporations that had lusted after builders just a few years earlier were now soured on the industry. The merger and takeover frenzy that gripped conglomerates and builders alike dissipated.[11] A new trend emerged, whereby some of the smaller conglomerates began divesting themselves of acquisitions. As the *American Machinist* observed in early 1973,

> A process that we might term deglomeration—the unwinding of some of the unlikelier corporate matings that took place in the synergistic sixties—has been developing. . . . At the heart of the original acquisition binge was the theory that skilled management in one place would prove to be skilled management in another. People forgot that, for many companies, skilled management is based on thoroughly and painfully acquired understanding of the engineering, manufacturing, and marketing of a particular product line—knowledge that could be less useful or even wrong when applied to some other product line.[12]

But the big conglomerates—the Textrons, the Teledynes, the Houdailles—showed no evidence of cutting and running. Sure, their enthusiasm had waned. But they were in machine tools to stay. At least for now.

The upturn that was inevitable began sometime in 1972, gained momentum in 1973, and by 1974, Burgmaster seemed as busy as ever. The impetus behind the surge in demand was the energy crisis. The automobile industry wanted to manufacture fuel-saving cars, and airplane builders a new generation of commercial jetliners. To do so efficiently these industries needed new tools.

Like most American builders, Burgmaster was determined to try and make up for the profits lost during the three-year slump from 1969 to 1972. That was standard industry practice: exploit the booms to the hilt, and endure the busts. But there was something different about the economic context of this boom. Despite Nixon's vow to cure inflation and put the U.S. economy on a steady footing, the fundamental imbalance had not been altered. So rather than marking an end to the inflation, Nixon's policies simply removed barriers to it. The U.S. economy became more addicted to inflation after 1971 than before.[13]

The uncertain value of the U.S. dollar drove Houdaille to emphasize short-term profits and the bottom line more than ever. This was entirely natural, given a climate where the only thing predictable about labor and matériel costs was that they were going up. Allan Folger's mastery of numbers made him virtually irreplaceable in such treacherous times. His ability to accurately gauge costs and consistently meet forecasts gained Folger the staunch admiration of Saltarelli. Consequently, the CEO allowed Burgmaster more latitude than any other division in Houdaille's machine tool group, and probably as much as any in the entire conglomerate.

After the long drought, a lengthy backlog of orders was most welcome. Burgmaster embraced its old habit of soliciting and taking as many orders as possible; custom orders or standard models—it did not matter. The strategy of mass-produced NC tools was totally defunct, a victim of inflation and Houdaille's insistence on maximum profits. The name Econocenter survived, but only as a marketing gimmick. Almost every Burgmaster model, from basic six-spindle turret drills on up, carried the label. Chronic production bottlenecks reappeared with a vengeance, and put Burgmaster through the wringer at the end of each month, as everyone raced to meet Folger's numbers. "The gyrations they'd go through," recalled Ed Merk, shaking his head. At the end of the month "there would be trucks lined up until midnight" just so Burgmaster could make its forecasts.[14]

Bottlenecks or not, to outside observers Burgmaster was a model builder. During the height of the 1974 boom, *American Machinist* ran a two-page spread on how Burgmaster was coping with the industrywide surge. It cited "creative planning" and a willingness to invest in up-to-date tools as the main reasons why Burgmaster was able to handle a threefold increase in its workload with ease.[15] And in many respects, the article was accurate. Burgmaster's plant, after all, was barely ten years old, and most of its tools the same age or even younger. It was one of the more modern machine tool facilities in the country.

Indeed, Burgmaster was a major reason why Houdaille's machine tool group began posting respectable numbers once again. Houdaille, which had sunk to eighteenth place in the 1971 industry rankings published by *American Machinist*, stormed back into the top ten during the mid-1970s. Sales rose to $65 million by 1974, more than double the 1971 figure, and Houdaille grossed $8.6 million in profits from its machine tool operations, a fourfold increase since 1971.[16]

But appearances aside, Burgmaster was in fact stagnating. If sales and profit figures were adjusted for inflation, a considerably different picture emerged. Burgmaster's balance sheet had improved since the nadir reached in 1971, but the upward trend was much flatter in inflation-adjusted dollars.[17] In an effort to boost sagging profits among manufacturers, the Nixon and Ford administrations had made depreciation rates considerably more generous.[18] The bottom line was becoming more dependent on sharp accountants, not just top manufacturing foremen.

In any case, what was happening inside Burgmaster itself was far more significant than any passing figures. Burgmaster's future, as always, rested on its shop floor and engineering department. Here stagnation was evident. Burgmaster could not seem to find solutions to two chronic problems. The first was production bottlenecks on the shop floor. The second was the engineering department's inability to come up with a new generation of machining centers that were just as reliable as Burgmaster's old turret drills.

After abandoning the Econocenter strategy in the early 1970s, Burgmaster had reverted to turning out parts in relatively small lot sizes. The typical run of major pieces was two to five, which increased manufacturing costs exponentially. But when the record inflation of 1973–1974 hit, Folger and plant manager Gene Dobmeier decided that another assault on the problem was needed. The department heads mapped out a new production strategy. Eventually they agreed to revamp Burgmaster's entire line of machines, in order to reduce the number of parts and increase the number of shared parts. That would permit larger production runs, which in turn would lower costs and ease bottlenecks.[19]

Folger had another aim in mind as well. Jerry Saltarelli often complained, when times were good, about orders that Burgmaster lost because of its lengthy backlogs. Folger figured that a greater number of shared parts would enable Burgmaster to build up an inventory of standard, basic parts, like tables, columns, and bases. Even when there was a surge in demand, Burgmaster's backlog would be a maximum of four to six months. There was a risk involved in stockpiling, though. Saltarelli disliked nothing more than higher costs and higher inventory taxes, and stockpiling parts meant increases in both. Folger bargained that more sales over the long run would offset higher costs.

Just as this strategy began to be implemented in early 1975, the machine tool industry went into another slump, its second of the decade. Houdaille did not look favorably on building parts for nonexistent orders, and once again Burgmaster shied away from making parts in large lot sizes. Although Folger had achieved greater commonality, Burgmaster was still dogged by production bottlenecks and higher manufacturing costs.[20]

Next to the situation on the shop floor, Burgmaster's most critical shortcoming was the long delay in marketing a full-fledged, reliable, and competitive tool changer. It had taken nearly three years, until October 1973, to settle the patent infringement suit between Houdaille and Kearney & Trecker. The first break in the case occurred in October 1971, when the favorable judgment in Kearney & Trecker's suit against Giddings & Lewis was reversed on appeal. That doomed K&T's case against Houdaille. Even so, it dragged on for two more years before both Kearney & Trecker and Houdaille dropped all claims, and retreated from the court without a victor being declared.[21]

By then, the damage was done. The net effect of the whole affair was to stall Burgmaster's entry into machining centers. For a long time the engineering department found itself torn between skirting the patents and using them to perfect Burgmaster's own machining centers. The patent dispute stymied the marketing department for a long time too. It did not know what kind of machine to boast about, much less the price of Burgmaster's entry into the market.

It took until late 1975, or six full years after the Dualcenter deal, before Burgmaster could market with any confidence a line of vertical and horizontal tool changers—"VTCs" and "HTCs." The engineering problems that plagued these models were not unprecedented for new machines, but they came when Burgmaster could least afford delays. Initially, the holder that gripped the tool on the vertical model had the nasty habit of failing. It took eighteen months for Richard Polacek, Burgmaster's chief engineer at the time, to come up with a reliable mechanism that avoided unnecessary patent problems. Meanwhile, the horizontal tool changer had chronic trouble with oil leaks around its spindle.

Eventually, trial-and-error engineering solved these problems, as well as others, but at a high price. By some estimates, the first tool changers, which sold for $150,000, cost twice that amount to build.[22] All told, it would be years before Burgmaster truly realized profits on its tool changers. The company's bread-and-butter product during the mid-1970s continued to be turret drilling machines, virtually unchanged from the models manufactured while the Burgs were still in command. Burgmaster had managed to push out all of its competitors and had this market niche to itself.[23] Thus success, such as it was during the mid-1970s, derived more from past efforts than from a continuing ability to innovate. Burgmaster's technological edge had vanished forever.

Although many of Burgmaster's problems were practical matters, they were exacerbated by the fact that the company no longer had a work force that was as dedicated and motivated as the one that had labored for the Burgs. Alienation or lack of pride, or both, had first become apparent in the ranks of the blue-collar employees following the 1965 takeover. Over the next several years, Houdaille's corporate culture seeped into every department, affecting employees of senior rank and responsibility. By the mid-1970s, the transformation in management-labor relations wrought by the takeover was complete.

In turn, this disaffection led to another phenomenon at Burgmaster during the 1970s: a small but steady exodus of the company's oldest and most valuable employees. Although the immediate cause was usually a dispute over a raise or a promotion, senior employees who quit were invariably dissatisfied with Houdaille's way of managing Burgmaster. They could not help comparing Houdaille's management to that of the Burgs, and in their view, the former had turned Burgmaster upside down. Burgmaster no longer was a flexible, innovative builder. Instead, it was a company with a top-heavy bureaucracy, obsessed with procedure and prestige rather than function and need. Burgmaster's product was not served by Houdaille's management system. Rather, the product seemed geared to serving the system.

From the perspective of the older employees, the good part about Allan Folger, Burgmaster's president, was that he kept corporate headquarters at arm's length. But the other half was that he did not really care to hear about anything unless it was germane to his forecasts. He was wholly content to rely on the monthly reports and figures submitted by each department. These passed on only the good news, not the bad. But Folger didn't care if a "bunch of smoke was being blown up [his] rear end," as one longtime employee put it.[24] Like an aging Latin dictator, Folger was remarkably ill informed about what was going on inside his realm.

Absent Folger's strong direction, centrifugal forces kept pulling apart Burgmaster, until it was no longer a tightly knit operation, but a collection of separate, seemingly unaccountable little fiefdoms. Employees and even entire departments were afraid to take risks and ran away from responsibility. "Don't rock the boat" was almost a bylaw. Still, not even Folger's worst critics blamed him entirely for this state of affairs. Everyone recognized that he had his hands full doing what Saltarelli deemed most important. They therefore directed their frustration, not at Folger, but at the Houdaille way.

It was Houdaille's corporate culture that fostered an atmosphere where people were afraid to do anything controversial, for fear of losing prestige. It was Houdaille that emphasized obedience to authority and procedure, and by doing so stifled initiative. "I got along a lot better in the organization when I started doing less," recalled Bob French, a longtime design engineer. He watched the engineering department turn from a fast, contentious, and innovative team into a sluggish, intimidated bureaucracy, more hospitable to clerks than engineers. This was a complete reversal from the environment cultivated by the Burgs. Under them, results mattered more than hierarchy, and certainly more than words.

Houdaille was well aware of the rumblings from some malcontents. As Burgmaster faltered, in fact, the conglomerate tended to blame the holdovers from the Burg era. They were labeled negative thinkers, men who had not adapted to Houdaille's modern techniques. Upper management could not help noticing that many of the same critics did not have college degrees. They had risen to senior positions under the Burgs based on their skills and dedication, not because of a piece of paper. This lack of credentials supplied Houdaille with a reasonable pretext for closing off the careers of the critics, for, as everyone knew, Saltarelli placed a great deal of emphasis on college credentials for all his top managers.[25]

Big Ben Bezdziecki was not the first longtime, valued employee to leave Burgmaster in the 1970s. That distinction probably belonged to Alf Celinder, the Burgs' chief engineer for many years, who left in February 1970. But Bezdziecki, as much as anyone, exemplified the clash between Burgmaster's old, outspoken guard and Houdaille.

Bezdziecki had started working at Burgmaster in 1959, as a machinist on the second shift, and had risen to become general foreman of the machine shop by the time of the Houdaille takeover in 1965. "Working for the Burgs was a once-in-a-lifetime proposition," he often said. "I would have died in that place. They would have had to shovel me out. Everyone knew what they were building and what they were doing. You were always appreciated."[26]

Like other department heads after the takeover, Big Ben learned to protect his enclave in Burgmaster from what he thought were useless and arbitrary management edicts. But unlike many supervisors, he was also frank and persistent in his criticisms of upper management. Perhaps this attitude was related to his sheer height. Bezdziecki stood more than six foot three, and no one intimidated him.

Eventually he paid a price for his outspokenness. Corporate subterfuge, not candor, was the Houdaille way. In early 1974, Bezdziecki was quietly told that he should not expect to rise any higher in the Burgmaster hierarchy, despite his unquestioned ability and experience. The reason cited was that he lacked a college education. He quit that May.[27]

Burgmaster could ill afford to lose Bezdziecki and others like him who left in the mid-1970s. The cost of this exodus would become apparent sooner than anyone imagined.

Throughout the early 1970s, Burgmaster played host to what seemed to be an endless stream of visitors from its Japanese partner, Yamazaki Machinery.

Every three or four months, a group of Yamazaki foremen, engineers, and executives came to Gardena, and Burgmaster would show them everything: new models on the drawing boards (the horizontal and vertical tool changers); the venerable turret drills being made to customer specifications; marketing strategies; in sum, anything and everything the Japanese cared to learn, including Burgmaster's most intimate trade secrets. They took countless pictures of every facet of Burgmaster's operations, and on more than one occasion, Burgmaster personnel took their Yamazaki counterparts to the field, so they could meet customers and see Burgmasters in operation.

Only a handful of longtime employees expressed any reservations. They recalled that it was a Japanese builder, after all, who blatantly copied Burgmaster's O machine in the early 1960s. And they wondered about opening up Burgmaster to any builder in a manner and to a degree that would have been unimaginable just a few years before. "Yamazaki scared the death out of me," recalled Bob French, a design engineer. "These guys were organized. They used to swarm all over, asking questions up the kazoo, of me and other people who were doing the work. I used to say watch out—these guys are going to bury us in ten years."[28]

But the fears of Bob French were dismissed out of hand. He was a Burgmaster holdover and a "negative thinker" who seldom thought well of anything Houdaille did. It's a new age, French was told. Burgmaster has to internationalize. The Japanese can mimic anything, but they will always be behind.

Yamazaki was proud of its link with Burgmaster. In its domestic advertising brochures, it underscored its relationship with the historic and innovative American builder.

> The best selling NC machines in the world have finally arrived in Japan, and they are in your hands!
>
> Approximately 30 years ago, the founding president of Burgmaster Corporation, Mr. Burg, first installed turret heads in ball bearings, and this invention has become the model of all turret-type machining centers in the world today. After countless research and large volumes of production, coupled with advancements in NC technology, the current model of the Econocenter has finally arrived. . . .
>
> Not only did Yamazaki introduce this excellent machine tool to our country, it also incorporated technological excellence from the Burgmaster Corporation, which made possible the domestic production of this machining center.[29]

But at some point in the early 1970s, the Yamazaki brothers' pride in this link gave way to ambition. After minutely studying Burgmaster for several years, Yamazaki decided it could do better than its tutor. The Japanese realized that Burgmaster's elaborate designs could be simplified and improved. Versatility would not be compromised and reliability would increase. At the same time, the cost of Burgmaster's vertical tool changer could be reduced by as much as one-third by large-scale production of the NC machine with NC tools rather than manufacturing it in small lots.[30]

Yamazaki said nothing about the plan to market its own tool changer. But Burgmaster got a hint about the extent of its partner's ambitions when Yamazaki became the first Japanese builder to open a tool plant in the United

States in 1974. The supremely confident Yamazaki brothers were intent on competing with American lathe builders on their home turf. They planned to produce about fifteen lathes a month at their new factory, which they located in Florence, Kentucky—just across the river from Cincinnati, the heart of the American tool industry.

By this time, Yamazaki was the largest privately held builder in Japan, its volume as big as or greater than any of the "Big 5" Japanese builders (Hitachi Seiki, Toshiba, Toyoda, Okuma, and Ikegai).[31] As evidenced by its Florence plant, it was also ahead of its fellow Japanese builders in its willingness to take risks. More significant than Yamazaki's lead, however, was that many other Japanese builders were not far behind.

Aided by the tremendous surge in Japanese auto production and FANUC's rapid strides in NC systems, Japanese builders were fast chipping away at U.S. engineering superiority.[32] American builders who attended the Seventh International Machine Tool Fair in Osaka in 1974 saw a number of innovative machines on display comparable to any built in the United States. State-of-the-art pallet systems, which allowed a machine to cut away on one workpiece while its operator loaded another, were demonstrated in abundance. No one doubted that the Japanese had arrived.

But it was not just a matter of technological prowess. The Japanese were also bringing to market machine tools that were less complex, more reliable, and considerably less expensive than American equivalents. The majority of Japanese NC tools had been developed for a highly commercial and competitive market, namely, auto parts subcontractors. Japanese auto makers typically relied on hundreds of these small subcontractors to produce needed parts, and demanded just-in-time delivery. This meant subcontractors had to have flexible, low-cost NC machines—and Japanese builders made them. The contrast between these economical tools and American NC machines, developed primarily at the behest of the U.S. aerospace industry, was stark.[33] American machines demonstrated a technical virtuosity that only a relative few could afford. Japanese tools appealed to a much larger market.

In September 1976, two years after the Osaka fair, Chicago hosted its biennial machine tool extravaganza. Some Burgmaster employees decided to drop by the Yamazaki booth, and promptly became speechless at what they saw. Yamazaki was handing out handsome, color brochures advertising its new "V-15" machining center. It was listed at $89,000, which meant that it could probably be bought for $70,000. That was 50 percent less than Burgmaster's "VTC-30," not to mention that the V-15 seemed obviously derived from it.

Only now did the full meaning of the assocation with Yamazaki finally dawn on Burgmaster. In essence, Houdaille had given Yamazaki carte blanche to do to Burgmaster what Fred Burg used to do on his own during the 1950s and 1960s—imitate good ideas and beat the competition by simply doing them better. When they had taken their Yamazaki counterparts to visit

Burgmaster customers, for example, they had undoubtedly prodded Yamazaki into realizing how vast and untapped the U.S. market for economical machining centers truly was.

When Houdaille complained vehemently to Yamazaki, the Japanese staunchly denied violating the licensing agreement or infringing on Burgmaster's patents. The Yamazaki brothers insisted that the V-15 was an improvement on Burgmaster's design, and that nothing in the licensing agreement prevented Yamazaki from marketing its own tool changer in the United States.

After months of useless negotiation, in April 1977, Houdaille filed a complaint against Yamazaki with the International Trade Commission in Washington. It asked the ITC to forbid Yamazaki from selling the V-15 in the United States on the grounds that it violated Burgmaster's patent rights, and represented unfair use of Burgmaster's trademark, trade secrets, and know-how. The ITC quickly agreed that under Section 337 of the Tariff Act of 1930 ("Unfair Practices in Import Trade") an investigation was in order.

Yamazaki responded by initiating arbitration hearings in Japan, as provided for under the terms of the licensing agreement with Houdaille. Over the next several months both sides engaged in extensive legal skirmishing, filing a total of fifty pre-hearing motions in order to obtain one advantage or another. Most of Houdaille's motions pertained to the nature and extent of the discovery proceedings. Houdaille wanted the right to depose Teriyuki Yamazaki and other top executives, examine all relevant documents and drawings, inspect Yamazaki's manufacturing plant and procedures, and delve into any other aspects of Yamazaki's operations in Japan that it deemed pertinent. In a sense, Houdaille wanted to exercise many of the same privileges accorded Yamazaki under their licensing agreement, and more.

Yamazaki was adamantly opposed to such a process, and used every tactic to limit, frustrate, and otherwise delay Houdaille's fishing expedition. Before Houdaille turned to the ITC for relief, Yamazaki had turned over a few V-15 drawings in an effort to prove that the machine was qualitatively distinct from any marketed by Burgmaster. Houdaille turned around and used the drawings to buttress its case against Yamazaki. The Japanese builder thereafter resolved to block an unlimited investigation into its affairs, if only to protect *its* trade secrets from Houdaille.

The two sides wrangled and fought over the discovery issue almost the entire summer of 1977. The ITC tended to side with Yamazaki on many of the procedural questions, including the issue of whether or not Teriyuki Yamazaki had to submit to a deposition (eventually he did respond in writing to some questions). Even so, the Japanese government intervened directly on behalf of Yamazaki just as Houdaille's lawyer was about to embark on an extensive investigation of the builder. The Japanese Foreign Ministry abruptly cancelled his visa, and refused to issue another one unless he agreed to rely solely on documents presented voluntarily by Yamazaki, and desisted from taking any depositions. Faced with this formidable obstacle, the American lawyers for Houdaille and Yamazaki negotiated a more limited discovery agreement that involved bringing relevant documents over from Japan, and deposing Yamazaki executives in the United States.[34]

Finally, in November 1977 the ITC hearing began. Five days of hearings suggested that Houdaille's case was not quite as straightforward as it had alleged. The ITC staff, which conducted an independent investigation, tended to believe that Houdaille had no grounds for claiming patent infringement, although Yamazaki had clearly used proprietary information gleaned from Burgmaster. The staff also believed there was no grounds for Houdaille's claim that Yamazaki had unfairly used the Burgmaster trademark. In sum, although the ITC did not say so in as many words, if Houdaille wanted to guard its know-how and withhold secrets from a potential competitor, it should never have licensed Yamazaki.

During a one-week recess in the hearings, Houdaille and Yamazaki decided to settle the matter privately by abrogating their agreement. Yamazaki also agreed to return every drawing ever received from Burgmaster, and desist from using the Burgmaster trademark in any way. For its part, Houdaille agreed to allow Yamazaki access to certain patent rights, and dropped all claims against Yamazaki.

Houdaille also received some money as part of the settlement. The sum was not made public at the time, but eventually it came out that Houdaille received about $835,000.

What Yamazaki did was "pretty damn shady," recalled Allan Folger, and "left a bad taste in our mouth."[35]

Yet Burgmaster's president also knew, long before the final settlement, that the whole dispute was irrelevant. Suppose Burgmaster had never opened itself up to Yamazaki—or even better, that Yamazaki did not even exist—the problem for Burgmaster was absolutely unchanged. Japanese builders were entering the U.S. market in large numbers in the late 1970s. One builder more or less was of no consequence whatsoever.

In 1978, a striking 78 percent increase in imports occurred. Foreign machine tools now supplied 22 percent of total U.S. consumption, compared to just 10 percent five years earlier, and Japan was rapidly supplanting West Germany as the number-one supplier of tools to the U.S. market.[36] Everyone knew what that meant. German machines competed for a relatively expensive, specialized, and small segment of the market. Japanese machines competed for the rest of it.

Some American builders were not yet ready to sound an alarm. The second bust of the 1970s had lasted just two years, from 1975 to 1976, and demand for new tools was brisk. The automobile industry led the way, but manufacturers of aircraft, farm implements, and oil well rigs were right behind. Growing backlogs for U.S. builders suggested that there were enough orders for everyone, including foreign builders. The Detroit-based Snyder Corporation even prophesied that the steadily declining value of the dollar and the rapidly rising labor and matériel costs in foreign countries would make machine tool imports "a factor of less significance in the future."[37]

But many other American builders were not as sanguine. They were stunned by how low Japanese machine tools were priced, and a few decided it was not too early to raise a warning cry. "I believe the Japanese are the major competitors now and they are out to do to us in machine tools what they have done in autos, cameras, steel, TV, motorcycles, and other fields, " a TRW executive told *Industry Week*.[38] At the urging of its members, the National Machine Tool Builders' Association swung into action. In late 1977, the NMTBA began to investigate the Japanese tool industry to see if it could collect any evidence of "dumping" by Japanese builders. Try as it might, the NMTBA could not find any.[39]

MITI, however, clearly heard the underlying complaint. The ministry quickly reacted to the murmurs emanating from U.S. builders and a warning from the Carter administration about dumping. In March 1978, MITI called in the JMTBA and other trade associations, and declared that it was imperative for them to form an export cartel. Its purpose would be to establish minimum prices for every class of machine tool exported to the United States. Japanese builders initially balked at the paper work involved, but MITI was adamant. It knew that charges of dumping would be forthcoming unless positive, documentary evidence to the contrary was available.[40]

Insofar as Burgmaster was concerned, Japanese inroads were still superficial as late as 1977. Imports of machining centers accounted for only 10 percent of U.S. consumption. The market was still dominated by domestic builders, and after almost a decade of effort, Burgmaster had finally managed to carve out a small, profitable niche for its vertical and horizontal tool changers. They occupied the middle range of the market in price and technology, a cut below the models offered by Cincinnati Milacron and Kearney & Trecker. In addition, of course, Burgmaster still had the not-inconsiderable market for turret drills all to itself.

But no one was deluded by the momentary calm, least of all Ed Merk, Burgmaster's vice president for marketing. "Remember what I say," he warned. "The Japanese are going to kill us."[41] In every sales report, Merk raised the specter of Japanese competition. He not only saw Japanese builders making rapid strides in terms of technology, reliability, delivery, and service; as a salesman, Merk was an eyewitness to the lengths to which the Japanese were going to attract buyers. To consumers who had never bought anything but an American machine tool, all kinds of lures were being offered, from local golf club memberships to all-expenses-paid trips to Japan.[42]

It was not lost on anyone at Burgmaster that at least one element in Japan's success was strikingly familiar. Japanese builders' standardized production of NC machines using NC machines smacked of Burgmaster's

Econocenter strategy, abandoned in the early 1970s. Yet Allan Folger knew that Houdaille would not countenance a revival of this approach, nor was he particularly eager to embrace it. The Japanese strategy required a different corporate mind-set, one that was geared to fighting for market share, rather than extracting short-term profits. And given economic stagflation, Houdaille was not about to switch to a strategy that was more difficult to forecast. Making forecasts was already hard enough.[43]

At Houdaille's Fort Lauderdale headquarters, the last thing Jerry Saltarelli wanted or needed to hear in 1977 was that his machine tool group was facing stiff foreign competition. (Saltarelli had moved the conglomerate from Buffalo, New York, because Florida had no state income tax.) Business had almost never been as tough. Stagflation in the economy sapped some vitality from each of Houdaille's four groups: machine tools, industrial products, automotive products, and construction materials. The last one was especially hard hit, and Saltarelli soon decided to get Houdaille out of construction materials entirely.[44] By contrast, the industrial products group, now Houdaille's most important and profitable segment, was doing well. But even there, Saltarelli had headaches. Most of them stemmed from Fort Worth Steel, which Houdaille had purchased for about $18 million in late 1976. Within months, Saltarelli was regretting the acquisition.

The automotive products group gave Saltarelli no respite either. Houdaille's West Virginia bumper plant, the last remnant of its once-thriving auto business, was in danger of closing. Market forces had already reduced production from a high of 2.7 million units per year to only 80,000 units annually, all of which went to one customer, American Motors.[45] In addition, at the urging of insurance companies, the federal government seemed intent on establishing auto safety standards that threatened to close down the market for steel bumpers entirely. The government was toying with the idea of bumpers that could withstand collisions at speeds up to five miles an hour. That was a virtual mandate for aluminum, instead of steel bumpers, given that the government also wanted auto makers to build lighter, more fuel-efficient cars.

To Saltarelli, the whole controversy underscored the urgency of further diversification. But finding new companies to acquire took time. Meanwhile, he devoted himself to improving the performance of his industrial products and machine tool groups, especially given the specter of foreign competition in the latter.

His schedule of almost constant travel over the years had turned Saltarelli into an inveterate reader, especially of management books. He became intrigued by a new concept in manufacturing called material requirements planning (MRP). Several corporate executives who had joined the MRP crusade were willing to swear by it. Gradually, Saltarelli became convinced that MRP was just what his conglomerate needed. It would impose more efficient production systems upon several Houdaille divisions, not least of all Burgmaster, with its chronic bottlenecks.

MRP essentially turned control of the shop floor over to a computer. In Burgmaster's case, the first step would be to feed into the computer a master schedule of all the machines to be built over the next several months. After thousands of calculations, the computer would transform the schedule into a precise breakdown of every step in the manufacturing process. The computer would say how many castings were needed, when they had to be ordered, and determine the size of each production run. At least theoretically, the computer could even specify the day, if not the shift, during which production of certain parts had to begin.

In exchange for turning the shop over to a computer, MRP promised to deliver sizable benefits. It would reduce inventories, increase productivity, improve control of engineering changes, and virtually eliminate "hot" orders, that is, parts that had to be expedited through the production process. Some manufacturers, like Black & Decker, a maker of hand tools, and Steelcase, an office furniture manufacturer, reported getting these kinds of results from MRP.

Yet Allan Folger, Burgmaster's president, did not share Saltarelli's enthusiasm for MRP. He knew there was a difference between making file cabinets and machine tools. The former were low-technology goods with at most several dozen parts. Machine tools had thousands of parts, many of which had to be manufactured to extremely close tolerances. What MRP proposed to accomplish at Burgmaster sounded great, but Folger was skeptical about its ability to accommodate an extremely complicated task. MRP would lock the machine shop into a strict production schedule, ignoring the possibility that a machinist might be out sick for a few days; a critical machine could break down, for hours, days, or weeks; a casting might have to be sent back to the foundry; machined parts could fail inspection. There were simply too many variables to account for.

But Oliver Wight, the management guru behind MRP, persuaded Saltarelli it could be done. Saltarelli did not seek Folger's advice on the matter. He merely asked him when MRP would be in effect at Burgmaster. And so, over a period of several years in the late 1970s, Burgmaster spent hundreds of thousands of dollars and uncounted hours on adjusting to MRP. Naturally, a few new bosses had to be added to Burgmaster's white-collar organization chart to serve the new system. And expensive management consultants had to repeatedly explain and resolve problems.

Burgmaster's employees soon came to rue the day they ever heard the initials MRP. For one, it drowned everyone in a flood of paper work. Since the printouts were no better than the information fed into the computer, every single item that affected the production schedule or product had to be documented, for entry into the computer. MRP turned everyone—foremen, engineers, and machinists— into clerks while taking them away from necessary duties.

Worse, MRP did not work, no matter how hard everyone tried. As Folger

had feared, there were simply too many variables and too much lead time between the initial master schedule and final assembly.[46] Despite updates and
changes, delays in production had a way of cascading in the MRP program, so
that what was correct in the January computer printout was misleading by
February and grossly inaccurate by March. MRP's promise of an exact association between what was needed and what was produced was never realized.

Whenever Burgmaster followed MRP to the letter, the assembly department ended up with excess parts of one kind and one or two parts short of
another. Consequently, in order to make forecasts—which not even MRP was
allowed to violate—the machine shop was compelled to expedite production
on more parts than ever. And expedited parts meant production "splits." Instead of machining the same fifteen parts in a row, a lathe operator would have
to stop after seven, change his setup, and make the one or two parts the
assembly department needed desperately. Then he had to change his setup
again to resume work on the remaining eight parts.

The increase in manufacturing costs that resulted was astronomical.
Machine shop foremen literally begged Folger to release them from MRP,
which ran directly contrary to their own instincts and experience. But his
hands were tied. "We kept cutting our own throat month to month," recalled
one employee.[47]

Perhaps, a few years earlier, Burgmaster employees might have shrugged
off the whole program as Saltarelli's folly. But the episode was unnerving
because it coincided with the Japanese challenge to Burgmaster and greater
pressure from corporate headquarters to maintain sales and profits. It was an
absurdity. Just as Burgmaster had to muster all its resources to cope with
mounting foreign competition, Houdaille imposed a paper monster and
manufacturing nightmare on its hapless division.

Allan Folger, though forced to swallow MRP, had his own ideas about
what Burgmaster needed to do. During the late 1970s, he tried to implement
them as best he could. Befitting his marketing background, he decided that a
patriotic appeal might help Burgmaster retain its market share. As a result, the
"Powerhawk" model line was born. All of Burgmaster's brochures and advertisements were redrafted to feature a stylized eagle in flight, along with the
slogan "Powerhawk: American Made for American Needs." But the Burgmaster machining centers underneath the ad campaign were unchanged. It was
akin to putting an "old broad in a new dress."[48] Cosmetic gimmicks did not
win Burgmaster any more customers or even keep old ones.

With considerable fanfare, Folger also announced a cost-reduction program in mid-1978. To be sure, given double-digit inflation, such an initiative
was wholly reasonable. Yet as much as anything, the program illustrated just
how far Burgmaster had traveled since the days when economy was embedded in its purpose. Now a special task force had to be assembled to do what
used to come naturally, and bring together a company whose departments
worked at cross-purposes. The memo outlining the program revealed a per-

vasive lack of accountability at Burgmaster that not even a dozen task forces could cure.

> We have given minimal effort to the cost versus profit picture over the past few years, possibly due to the feeling that individual job responsibilities are the first order of importance.
> Operating with the high cost picture and maximum selling prices, leave only one avenue open, and that is to establish a cost reduction program. . . .
> Of course it must be recognized and thoroughly understood at the outset that the adoption of a formal cost reduction program by no means indicates that what has, or has not been done in the past, is to be held up for criticism. We do not normally know the circumstances under which such decisions were made and, therefore, no one will ever be called upon to justify or defend his past actions.[49]

By 1979, despite operating in the black, Burgmaster was a troubled company. Everything that could go wrong during the decade had gone wrong. Its once-sizable technological lead had evaporated, and worse, Burgmaster was falling behind. A tough foreign competitor had been given an inadvertent boost, although the real problem was not just one competitor from Japan. Burgmaster was also suffering from the loss of many talented and devoted personnel. Big Ben Bezdziecki no longer ran the machine shop; Bob French no longer designed economical new machines in engineering. Both men, each in his own way, had been just as responsible as the Burgs for the rise of Burgmaster. And each had left Burgmaster out of anger and frustration.

By this time too, Burgmaster was severely hampered by a chronic shortage of top-level machinists. It hired kids fresh out of high school, or Asian and Latin American immigrants, and trained them for a year or so. Then, invariably, the workers with the best aptitude for machining would quit to take jobs with McDonnell-Douglas or another defense contractor.

Burgmaster was always left with the least motivated and most uneducated machinists, including many high school graduates who could barely add and subtract. The scrap rate in the machine shop soared. To old-timers, it seemed like Burgmaster spoiled as many castings in one month now as it used to make.

A new cry became popular in the machine shop whenever a new piece of useless, but heavy, scrap iron was produced.

Use it for an anchor!

10
BUYOUT (1979–1980)

> You have to love the machine tool business to be successful in it.
> Even to stay alive in it, as a matter of fact.
> —Francis Trecker, chairman of Kearney & Trecker, 1972[1]

So long as Jerry Saltarelli was chief of Houdaille, there was no question about who was in charge. His persona dominated the company at a time when corporate managers elsewhere seemed to be increasingly bland.

Well known in business circles as one of the top industrial CEOs in America, Saltarelli was liked by bankers because they knew he never took great risks and always paid his debts. Further, Saltarelli's adherence to conservative accounting techniques and his willingness to invest in up-to-date machinery when there was money to be made reputedly endeared him to investors. His salary and benefits, which totaled $945,600 in 1978, seemed prudent compensation in a company that some Wall Street analysts hailed as "one of the best-managed industrial companies in the United States."[2] If an investor was looking for flash, the word on the Street was that Saltarelli's Houdaille was not the stock to buy. But it always paid a dividend.

Saltarelli also prided himself on the lean corporate staff at Houdaille's Fort Lauderdale headquarters. He had pared it down from a high of about sixty executives in 1971 to no more than forty by 1978.[3] This contributed to his reputation for knowing what was going on inside every Houdaille division. Of course, the extent of his knowledge depended on the paper trail from each division to corporate headquarters. But it was clear that he read the monthly reports as if they were valentines.

Saltarelli was so dominant at Houdaille that when he reached sixty-five, the mandatory age of retirement, in 1977, he continued in office with nary an objection. Inevitably, however, he had to begin thinking about how to yield control of the company that had been his life's work. Passing the baton was not going to be a simple matter, for a number of reasons.

149

The foremost problem, from Saltarelli's point of view, was his own stake in Houdaille, combined with his unwillingness to trust the conglomerate to anyone else. A significant portion of his assets was tied up in Houdaille stock. He owned outright or would have the option to buy 130,000 shares by 1979, which meant that about $2 million of his own money was invested in Houdaille.[4] And Saltarelli was the kind of CEO who could not stand to take a vacation and let a trusted vice president run his conglomerate for three weeks, let alone without him.

An obvious alternative was a merger between Houdaille and a larger corporation. But Saltarelli did not consider that a wholly satisfactory solution either. After the transaction he still might be stuck holding a large block of stock in a concern beyond his control. As important, Saltarelli, not to mention the rest of Houdaille management, preferred to see Houdaille continue as an independent entity. Several vice presidents were aching for the chance to run the conglomerate, and Saltarelli wanted to accommodate at least one of his loyal lieutenants. Only he wanted to get his money out too.

In the winter of 1977–1978, Houdaille common stock was selling for about $14.50 a share, well below the conglomerate's book value of about $20 per share. A depressed stock price was a familiar problem for Houdaille, now that the glory days of the conglomerates were long gone. Houdaille's lines of business were either mature or cyclical, and although they were a dependable source of profits, the conglomerate's overall return on assets was lackluster. Houdaille was not an anomaly in industrial America. The profitability of U.S. manufacturers as a whole had been steadily declining since the mid-1960s. Alternating periods of low economic growth (stagnation) and uncertain prices (inflation), and sometimes both together (stagflation), had exacted a heavy toll on industrial enterprises.[5] And as profits eroded, so did capital investment and productivity.

About this time, that Saltarelli was going to be sixty-six years old in March—well past "normal" retirement—became widely known on Wall Street. So did his dilemma. Both were sufficient to touch off the Wall Street rumor factory and speculation in February 1978. The more speculators looked, the more they liked what they saw. In particular, Houdaille's relatively debt-free and cash-rich condition aroused great interest, because it made it an attractive takeover candidate. The conglomerate had a nominal debt of perhaps $25 million, but almost $60 million in cash.[6] In a sense, Saltarelli's Houdaille was becoming a victim of its own "solid but unglamorous" reputation.

In February there was some heavy trading and sudden upward movement in Houdaille stock. By March it was trading at $18, and in April the shares reached $22. Trading leveled off in May, but in June and July the stock price shot up again, until it was near $28 per common share. According to the rumors, Houdaille's possible suitors included U.S. aerospace companies and a West German manufacturer aiming to establish itself in the United States. A

Buffalo, New York, newspaper also reported that the Eaton Corporation, a one-time neighbor of Houdaille's, might be interested in taking over the conglomerate that had fled south.[7]

Houdaille learned that two separate buyers had acquired large blocks of stock, on the order of 2 to 3 percent each. But their intentions were unclear. The Securities and Exchange Commission reported receiving no notice that more than 5 percent of Houdaille's shares had been purchased with a takeover in mind. It seemed that speculation, and little more, was driving up the price of Houdaille. Reportedly, so-called hedge funds were particularly active. The funds were usually small partnerships of wealthy and sophisticated investors willing to take a high risk. Hedge funds were buying up Houdaille stock "like it was going out of style."[8]

None of this pleased Saltarelli, and the prospect of an unfriendly takeover frankly disturbed him. "I was concerned about unfriendly rumors," he later recalled. "Houdaille was part of me."[9] Given the depressed market, he worried that Houdaille might be acquired for a relative pittance if it were a hostile takeover. He might profit to some degree, but his company would be swallowed up, his assets might be tied to a concern he had no control over, and he would be abandoning his subordinates to an uncertain fate. Perhaps the only thing worse would be to leave Houdaille, and his stock, in the hands of the executives he had supposedly groomed.

Wall Streeters sympathetic to Saltarelli advised him to make quick acquisitions if he wanted to keep Houdaille independent. Putting lots of stock in friendly hands through mutually agreeable mergers would promptly make Houdaille less attractive. But small, well-managed industrial concerns, as Saltarelli knew all too well, were not easy to find, and once they were found, took time to court. Saltarelli could not see making "dumb deals" just to protect Houdaille's independence, especially when his own interests stood to suffer as well.[10]

At this point Saltarelli decided to seek advice from Goldman, Sachs, a prominent investment banking house. After considering the choices, the bankers suggested that the best alternative was for Houdaille to actively seek a purchaser rather than risk a hostile takeover. The conglomerate seemed destined for some kind of merger one way or another; an attractive price and other favorable terms were more likely if Houdaille instigated the deal. Saltarelli, albeit reluctantly, concurred. He instructed Goldman, Sachs to begin exploratory talks with several other companies.[11]

Throughout the summer of 1978, the speculation in Houdaille common shares continued. In August, after the stock rose $2.38 in one day, to close at $32.75 a share, the New York Stock Exchange asked Houdaille to clarify its situation publicly. The stock had doubled in price since February, and although sales and earnings were strong, they were nothing extraordinary or unexpected. Houdaille announced that it was "exploring the possibility of merger with a limited number of companies," but wasn't engaged in any active negotiations, nor had it received any proposals.[12] Its stock promptly went down $10 per share.

When there seemed to be no good solutions, Saltarelli received a phone call from an investment banking firm by the name of Kohlberg, Kravis, Roberts & Co. They told Saltarelli and one of his vice presidents, Phillip A. O'Reilly, that there was one way that Houdaille might have its cake and eat it too. Saltarelli could liquidate his stake in Houdaille, but at the same time the conglomerate could avoid a takeover and remain independent. Moreover, there would be frosting on the cake for the rest of Houdaille management—an opportunity to reap large profits in just a few years. Saltarelli and O'Reilly thought they had heard it all, but when Kohlberg, Kravis said "leveraged buyout," they had to admit they did not know what the investment bankers were talking about. "We asked them to come down [to Florida] and see us," O'Reilly recalled.[13]

Kohlberg, Kravis, Roberts or KKR as it was known in investment circles, was not one of the fabled banking houses on Wall Street. It was only about two years old. The senior partner was Jerome Kohlberg, Jr., a fifty-three-year-old native New Yorker with a distinguished business pedigree. Kohlberg, a graduate of Swarthmore College, held an M.B.A. from the Harvard Business School and a law degree from Columbia University. After practicing law for five years, he joined Bear, Stearns in the mid-1950s, eventually becoming head of its investment banking department. It was there, at Bear, Stearns, that Kohlberg first learned about leveraged buyouts in 1965, or "bootstraps" as they were then called.

A bootstrap, stripped to its essence, raised cash based on a company's assets and its ability to service a debt through its cash flow.[14] As a method of business financing, bootstraps were few and far between in the mid-1960s. They were considered appropriate only in certain situations—most often, when the owner of a relatively small, private company was in trouble financially or wanted to sell out to a buyer who lacked the necessary cash.

In 1965, the head of a company called I. Stern, which produced precious metal alloys, came to Kohlberg seeking advice. H. James Stern, the owner, was then seventy-two years old and wanted to put his business affairs in order, by either selling the company altogether or going public. But he was torn between the two choices. Like Saltarelli, Stern wanted his money out but did not want to hand over the company to other owners. "I suggested he could have his cake and eat it too," recalled Kohlberg later. He arranged a bootstrap for $13.8 million, which kept the old management in place as part owners but simultaneously enabled Stern to cash in. Over the next two years, the new entity, Stern Metals, did well enough to pay off its creditors (the Paul Revere Insurance Company), and the other part owners (including Bear, Stearns) were able to cash in through public offerings of stock. The partners with Bear, Stearns realized a $17.50 gain on stock initially valued at $2.50. Kohlberg himself made a profit of $175,000 on the deal in a little less than two years.[15]

Clearly, thought Kohlberg, he was onto something. He knew he "wasn't inventing the wheel because other people were doing [similar] deals."[16] But Kohlberg had devised an innovation that nobody had thought of before. He had refined the financial engineering by adding a role for management as owners after the bootstrap. Incumbent managers, in other words, could raise enough cash to purchase the company they were running. Almost inadvertently, Kohlberg had greatly expanded the useful financial universe of bootstraps, or leveraged buyouts (LBO) as some preferred to call the financing scheme. In time, this innovation would become the most important impetus behind the growth of buyouts. Nor would it be Kohlberg's last novel twist.

In 1966, Kohlberg arranged three more leveraged buyouts, and in 1969, he did another. In the fourth transaction he was assisted by two twenty-nine-year-old investment bankers who had recently joined Bear, Stearns. Henry Kravis and George Roberts, who were first cousins, not only shared Kohlberg's passion for tennis but also relished, like Kohlberg, the financial engineering required to pull off an LBO. In 1971, after much searching, the trio found another good candidate for a buyout, Cobblers, a Los Angeles shoe company. It was the most ambitious LBO yet attempted by Messrs. Kohlberg, Kravis, and Roberts. It was also the first one to flop badly. Six months after the LBO was consummated, the shoe company's chief executive committed suicide. Kohlberg searched frantically for someone to run the business, but could not retain anyone with the same acumen. Ultimately, the company had to be sold off in pieces to satisfy its creditors. The equity holders, including Kohlberg, suffered a $400,000 loss.[17]

The failure did not deter the Bear, Stearns trio from pursuing more LBOs. It simply underscored one of the cardinal principles that had to be observed. An LBO promised rewards that were generous to everyone involved, to say the least. But it put a company on a steep, slippery slope where the slightest misstep could be fatal. Anything that disturbed the carefully calculated flow of cash through the company threatened the entire, delicately balanced LBO mechanism. It wasn't enough to retain pre-LBO management. The managers also had to be strong enough to withstand the strain.

In 1972, Kohlberg, Kravis, and Roberts pulled off another LBO, even bigger than the failed shoe venture. They engineered a $38 million buyout of the Vapor Corporation, a manufacturer of industrial valves and pumps. The company was part of the Singer Company conglomerate, and like many Singer subsidiaries, Vapor, which had thrived prior to its acquisition, was now struggling. Because of the apparent risk, the interest on the debt incurred by the LBO was high, as much as 9.5 percent. But Vapor's management was able to service it. Six years later, Vapor's shares, valued at $2.80 at the time of the buyout, sold for $33 when the company was acquired in 1978 by another conglomerate, the Brunswick Corporation.[18]

The Vapor buyout was another milestone. By taking a subsidiary of a publicly traded corporation and transforming it into a private company, Kohlberg, Kravis, and Roberts had pushed the limits of LBO financial engineering further than ever before. It could not help occurring to Kohlberg and his associates that the opportunities for such transactions were virtually unlimited. The conglomeration of American industry in the 1960s had proven to be a dubious blessing, as hundreds of corporate marriages fell short of expectations. Stagflation made industrial life harder for all corporations, but conglomerates seemed to make matters considerably worse by sapping managers' morale. The emphasis in the mid-1970s was on divestiture, and "back to basics" corporate restructuring. Conglomerates were heeding the advice of analysts who urged them to dump poorly performing divisions in businesses that headquarters knew nothing about.[19]

Kohlberg and his associates believed that dozens of these "underperforming" subsidiaries could return to profitability if their managers were freed from the shackles of conglomeration. Besides freedom, an LBO gave knowledgeable executives an incentive to trim costs and become more efficient. After an LBO they were equity partners in the business, working as much for themselves as for anyone else.

In the mid-1970s, Kohlberg, Kravis, and Roberts faced a similar decision of their own. Their innovative LBOs were generating far more income than the pursuits of the other Bear, Stearns partners, and that fact had begun to grate. They could continue to pursue LBOs from the relative security of Bear, Stearns and underwrite its less profitable aspects. Or, they could strike out on their own, and keep all the proceeds.

They decided on the latter course, and in May 1976, Kohlberg, Kravis, Roberts & Co. opened for business, the first investment banking "boutique." Rather than offer the entire range of corporate financing techniques, KKR intended to specialize in only one: leveraged buyouts. At the time, the corporate establishment was not exactly crowding KKR's office, eager to do such deals. But the founding KKR partners firmly believed that the "deconglomeration" of America translated into unbounded opportunity. There were any number of "swollen, unfocused" corporations around.[20]

Next to their affinity for LBOs, the new KKR partners unanimously agreed about one other aspect of their affairs. Although investment bankers are discreet by nature, KKR was intent on a lower-than-low profile, to the point of keeping the firm shrouded in a Garbo-like secrecy. When possible, openings in the firm would be filled by persons related to the partners; Kohlberg's son and Roberts's brother-in-law joined KKR in this manner. Over the years, even as the firm gained prominence, KKR made a habit of rejecting requests for interviews from the business press. On the rare occasion an interview was granted, KKR would never receive a journalist without having its public relations counsel vet the request or chaperone the interview.[21]

Aside from their passion for LBOs, secrecy, and tennis, however, the founding partners were a disparate group. Kohlberg, the pillar of the firm, was well known and liked on Wall Street, his caution and reserve legendary. He had a bookish air, and his rimless glasses made him appear almost prim and constricted, like a Victorian accountant. Kohlberg was once described as "impenetrable as a two-foot-thick vault door" by *Fortune*. Yet he was also considered a low-key, genial man, and his political views were quite liberal. He was apt to support Senate Democrats such as Carl Levin, Tom Harkin, Gary Hart, and Jim Hunt in his effort to unseat Jesse Helms.[22]

If Kohlberg supplied the ballast, then Henry Kravis and George Roberts furnished KKR's cutting edge. They were the activists, the partners who located candidates for LBOs, stitched up the financing, and recruited participants for the equity and debt pools. They were both short, wiry, and intense men, with Kravis considered the more volatile of the two, sometimes to the point of being abrasive. Kravis's father was a well-known Oklahoma petroleum engineer whose clients included the Kennedy family and Chase Bank. Like Kohlberg, he had gone to the best schools, earning a B.A. from Claremont College and an M.B.A. from Columbia University. Unlike Kohlberg, though, Kravis's political views were catholic, although not in the sense of being liberal. He tended to invest in political candidates of many different stances, ranging from Bill Bradley to Phil Gramm. But the large bulk of his contributions were reserved for the Republican National Committee, to which Henry Kravis gave $10,000 on more than one occasion.[23]

In its first full year of business, KKR engineered three buyouts worth a total of $154 million. It was a promising beginning, although KKR would not know the full extent of its gains or losses from the deals until the companies went public again. Then, as "general manager," KKR would be entitled to 20 percent of any capital gains realized by the equity partners. In the meantime, however, the buyouts themselves were a lucrative source of revenue. In addition to the standard, one-time, 1 percent fee KKR charged for putting a deal together, KKR also received annual fees, ranging from $150,000 to $300,000, for acting as an investment adviser and management consultant to the reconstituted companies. Lastly, KKR always obtained the majority share of seats on the board of a leveraged company, and thus received substantial directors' fees.[24]

The second year of KKR's independence, 1978, began inauspiciously, with no buyouts at all. KKR and other investment banking boutiques intent on spreading the LBO religion faced a considerable corporate and financial bias against leveraged buyouts. Many corporate executives assumed that if their company could be bought partly on the basis of its cash flow, then the price being offered was too low. Some bankers from the old school also looked askance at the whole idea. To lend someone their equity and then expect them to earn their way out of it, as one banker put it, was "contrary to all banking principles."[25]

A few skeptics, moreover, disputed the notion that a buyout improved management's motivation to perform. They likened it instead to a Faustian bargain: the promise of spectacular returns balanced against the loss of the entire enterprise. Buyouts were always structured so that the greatest risk fell on management. "If the business fails, we want them to have lost everything before we start losing," observed one buyout specialist.[26] In this sense, management participation was one part incentive and one part fear—golden handcuffs, some Wall Street wags labeled it.

But the profits from buyouts past outweighed the objections of skeptics. The only genuine obstacle KKR faced was that it took time to find good candidates for LBOs. Generally, KKR believed that there were five conditions for a successful buyout:

- the company had to have a long-established, predictable cash flow, sufficient to service the debt;
- it was best if the company had usable, but fully depreciated fixed assets—plants, property, and equipment—which would cost significantly more to replace than their book value;
- the company had to operate in mature markets where technological upheavals were unlikely, thus minimizing the need for capital investment;
- the company had to be relatively debt-free prior to the buyout; and
- the company had to have strong management, all or most of which had to stay on to ensure continuity.

The first four factors could vary depending on the numbers involved. Indeed, the four conditions could be reduced to a single sentence: A candidate for an LBO had to be a "mature, stable, asset-rich company with low capital needs," or what was referred to in some financial circles as a cash cow.[27] But KKR regarded the fifth factor as absolutely indispensable, which was why good prospects took time and effort to locate. Management participation, according to Kohlberg, was the heart of a buyout. "It makes for tremendous motivation. It puts everybody on the same side of the table. That is their incentive, and we as investors really require that."[28]

Like many others on Wall Street in 1978, the KKR partners could not help noticing the rampant speculation in Houdaille stock. Initially, the wild gyrations persuaded KKR that Houdaille's dilemma was someone else's problem. Certainly, the delicate structure of an LBO could not be erected in the midst of a bidding war over Houdaille. Apart from that, the sheer size of the conglomerate seemed to rule out a buyout. No one had ever attempted to leverage a concern worth more than $100 million.[29] To even think it was possible bespoke a certain audacity.

Yet once KKR realized that Houdaille was halfhearted about even a friendly merger, the partners began researching the company and playing around with numbers. The more they learned, the more interested they became. Yes, the numbers involved were unprecedented. Depending on the exact price, a Houdaille LBO would be three times larger than any other buyout ever consummated. But Houdaille fit KKR's own profile almost perfectly, down to the fact that many of its manufactures occupied market niches that seemed to protect the conglomerate from unbridled competition.

Through Goldman, Sachs, Houdaille's investment banker, KKR approached Saltarelli in the late summer of 1978. KKR mentioned a price for Houdaille that came out to somewhere in the high $30s per share, perhaps as much as $40. Saltarelli wondered if he were dreaming. He had never expected to hear such an offer in his life.[30] Once he heard the rest of the offer, however, Houdaille's CEO became skeptical. Any scheme that involved debt instinctively provoked his disdain. He could not imagine managing the conglomerate with such a debt to service. Saltarelli was even more mystified by KKR's claim that Houdaille could not only survive but thrive in spite of the heavy burden. Nevertheless, he was willing to hear KKR explain, in chapter and verse, how Houdaille could have its cake and eat it too.

KKR did just that during a lengthy meeting in Fort Lauderdale. The investment bankers began by hastily explaining that they agreed with Saltarelli: so long as a leveraged company had to service its high-interest debt, it operated at extreme risk. An LBO was predicated on a steady, if not expanding, market for a company's products. In a stagnant or down market a leveraged company could quickly go bankrupt. From experience, KKR knew that after a company was leveraged, the loans had to be retired quickly.

There was a second reason for paying off the debt rapidly. For until then, as KKR explained, the "pot of gold" that theoretically lay at the end of every buyout was unattainable. A private, leveraged company could go public and claim the pot of gold only after its debt-to-equity ratio had returned to acceptable proportions. This was the precise juncture, of course, where KKR, holdover management, and other equity partners reaped their huge reward—as much as twenty times their original investment.

Saltarelli was quick to appreciate this kind of thinking, but he was still mystified by one thing. How was Houdaille going to generate all the profits necessary to pay off the high-interest debts so quickly? Here the key phrase to remember, KKR told Saltarelli, was managing for cash flow.

As CEO of a company publicly traded on the stock market, it was only natural for Saltarelli to think in terms of net profits, returns on investment, and other measurements featured in quarterly and annual reports. But a buyout meant Houdaille would have to reorient its corporate mind-set and think more broadly, in terms of cash flow. That would be the secret to removing the shadow of debt over a leveraged Houdaille.

Not that profits ceased to be important, KKR assured Saltarelli. Profits would remain a key element in generating cash flow, so Houdaille still had to be in the black as much as possible. But there was another, more accurate way to think about Houdaille's situation after the buyout. It was here that KKR introduced Saltarelli to the third partner in the proposed deal: Uncle Sam.[31]

Stripped of all the complicating factors, Uncle Sam's contribution was at the core of an LBO. KKR could offer an unheard-of price for Houdaille stock, leverage the company to the hilt, and then cash in on the pot of gold all because of Uncle Sam's generosity when it came to the depreciation of capital assets and interest write-offs. The new, private Houdaille would hire an appraiser to revalue all assets to their present cost level. Partly because of a decade of inflation, but primarily because the appraiser would be in Houdaille's hip pocket, the assets could be marked up to artificially high values.

Even assets that were not being used at all could be assigned a new value. Houdaille would then redepreciate the capital assets according to the federal tax laws. If a leveraged Houdaille remained sufficiently profitable, the annual value of the depreciation allowance, together with the tax write-off for interest payments, would effectively shield Houdaille from the 48 percent corporate tax rate for years. By the time a tax liability was unavoidable, it would be time to make Houdaille a publicly traded corporation once again. In essence, much of the cash Houdaille would need to service its massive debt would be generated courtesy of a silent but consenting partner, Uncle Sam.

The depreciation allowance, KKR told Saltarelli, was why a leveraged Houdaille would have to manage with cash flow uppermost in mind, rather than profit. If, for argument's sake, the value of the depreciation allowance during the first year after the buyout was $15 million, then Houdaille's job would be, above all, to see that its cash flow took full advantage of the allowance. Deft management of all Houdaille assets and accurate forecasts of cash flow would be absolutely essential.[32]

KKR did not attempt to make this sound easy. The managers of a leveraged Houdaille would have to be financially astute and psychologically prepared to handle the pressure, which would not abate until the last debt was repaid. A bad year, even a bad quarter, could put Houdaille into a tailspin. No doubt it would tax their management skills to the utmost, the investment bankers confided to the assembled Houdaille executives. But other companies had proved that it could be done. If Houdaille executives could do it too, they would enjoy a financial windfall at the end of the buyout—not to mention the immediate profits they would enjoy from the $40 per share buyout.

The Houdaille executives had two other major concerns. They wanted to know if there would be sufficient funds for capital investment and further acquisitions. For many corporations, the bloom was off the conglomerate rose. But for Houdaille, which had diversified out of necessity, it was still considered an integral business strategy. KKR assured the executives that if they managed the cash flow properly, there would be ample funds for investment and diversification while the debt was being serviced.[33]

The last issue that had to be discussed was corporate power and authority after the buyout. KKR would control a majority of seats on the reconstituted board of Houdaille directors. But the investment bankers hastened to reassure Saltarelli and the others that it had no intention of running a leveraged Houdaille. At most, KKR would function as informed and interested directors, willing when necessary to share their knowledge about how to manage for cash flow. Otherwise, KKR had no intention of interfering. Indeed, as Jerome Kohlberg emphasized at every opportunity, giving capable managers a free rein and an equity stake was the heart of any leveraged buyout.

The first of many lengthy meetings between KKR and Houdaille executives ended on that note. During the next few months, KKR and prospective partners in the deal visited Houdaille subsidiaries, including Burgmaster, to make sure everything was as it was reported to be. Meanwhile, Saltarelli pored over the proposal with Goldman, Sachs and other tax and corporate finance experts. Try as he might, he could find no inherent flaw in the proposal. An inquiry showed that KKR was everything that it claimed to be: an investment banking boutique that was considered the premier expert on LBOs. Saltarelli was impressed in particular by Kohlberg, a man whose word was clearly as good as his bond. He found no instance where KKR broke its promise and interfered with management after a buyout.[34]

KKR's proposal seemed better than any other conceivable solution. Saltarelli could make a clean and extremely lucrative break from the conglomerate, clearing almost $5 million from the buyout. At the same time, Houdaille would not be swallowed up, and Saltarelli's successors stood to profit from the buyout and even more from the pot of gold. What shareholder would dare bring a suit, charging that $40 per common share was too little? Saltarelli was far from the only person who never expected to see Houdaille stock command such a price. In every way, the buyout appeared to live up to the billing attached to such deals by some financial wags. They called it the "Kiss which turns the Frog into a Handsome Prince."[35]

In late October 1978, after several weeks of arduous negotiations, both parties were ready to state their intentions publicly. Houdaille announced that Kohlberg, Kravis, and Roberts planned to form a group of investors that would buy the conglomerate for $347.7 million in cash, or $40 per common share. The announcement stunned Wall Street. Although it was hardly news that Houdaille was going to be sold, no one had considered it a candidate for a leveraged buyout. The implications were profound. If KKR could pull it off—and that was still a big if—then there were virtually no limits on how large a buyout could be. Believers outnumbered the skeptics though. After the announcement, Houdaille common closed at $32 on October 25, up $11.25 a share.[36]

While Wall Street held its collective breath, Henry Kravis and George Roberts struggled to stitch together KKR's most ambitious piece of financial engineering. It was not an easy task. After more than two months passed without any apparent progress, rumors began flying that KKR was having unanticipated problems. In January, the New York Stock Exchange delayed trading in Houdaille stock, and KKR was compelled to issue a rare public statement. Major insurance companies and banks have given KKR "indications of interest" in providing "more than half" of the needed financing, Henry Kravis told *The Wall Street Journal*. "We hope to close this deal in the first quarter" of 1979.[37] By now, for Kravis and Roberts, engineering the Houdaille buyout was much more than just a big deal. It was a point of honor. Everyone on Wall Street was looking, waiting to see whether they could pull it off.

Two months later, arbitrageurs began to panic because the deal seemed no closer to being consummated. The stock fell $3 on March 2, a Friday, as speculators began to sell short. "Kohlberg Kravis is obviously negotiating oral commitments on financing that could involve anywhere from two cents to $50 million," one arbitrageur complained. "We just don't like the quality of information they've put out on this." On Monday morning, the New York Stock Exchange suspended trading in Houdaille stock once again until the situation could be clarified.[38]

Houdaille subsequently announced that "oral or written commitments" had been obtained for all the necessary financing, and in principle the deal was set. That was more than enough to renew the market's confidence, and the stock shot up $5 a share the moment the NYSE reopened trading.[39] By April 1979, everything was signed up, and KKR could afford to breathe a little easier. The final package totaled $355 million, about $8 million more than

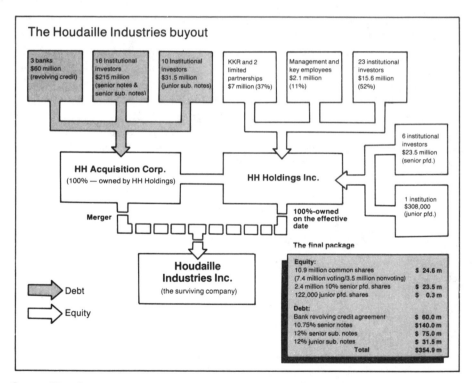

Source: "Funds Galore for LBO Prospects," *Euromoney* (Special Supplement), December 1986, p. 13.

originally announced. As the details gradually became known, Wall Street was astonished by their intricacy. "Highly creative" is perhaps the highest encomium in the investment banking trade, but that hardly seemed to do justice to KKR's elaborate financial engineering.[40]

The $355 million leveraged buyout used two, specially created holding companies, and involved a staggering array of instruments and participants, including three banks (Continental Illinois, Manufacturers Hanover, and Bankers Trust), insurance companies (Prudential), and state pension funds (Oregon Investment Council). Several of the investors were involved at multiple levels of the package. The deal was a master stroke of financial engineering, and Wall Street recognized immediately that the rules were no longer the same. As one investment banker later recalled, "The public documents on that deal were grabbed up by every firm on Wall Street. [KKR] showed everybody what could really be done. We all said, 'Holy mackerel, look at this!'"[41]

In early May 1979, after fifty years as a publicly traded corporation, Houdaille Industries passed into the hands of a select group of investors. The switch from managerial to financial capitalism would be Houdaille's and Burgmaster's last transformation.

To most Houdaille employees, the complexities and implications of the leveraged buyout were difficult to fathom. It was far easier to associate the buyout with the dramatic change in personnel that resulted. Nothing seemed more fundamental than the fact that Houdaille and Jerry Saltarelli were no longer synonymous, for the first time in seventeen years.

Not that KKR wanted Saltarelli to leave. Jerome Kohlberg repeatedly asked Saltarelli to stay on. The CEO's energies were undiminished, even at the age of sixty-seven. But financially speaking, there was no reason to stay. Besides the stock windfall that was already his, Saltarelli was entitled to a lump sum retirement payment of more than $1 million and supplemental compensation of $94,500 annually for the rest of his life. That made him more than willing to leave the headache of running a debt-laden Houdaille to someone else. At the risk of being labeled anachronistic, he knew himself well enough to know one thing: he was not constitutionally disposed to running a leveraged company.[42]

The passing of the baton occurred in late May, three weeks after the buyout documents were executed in the New York offices of Skadden, Arps, Slate, Meagher & Flom, the law firm that served as KKR's legal counsel. The first of Saltarelli's three posts—chairman of the board—was handed to Jerome Kohlberg, KKR's senior partner. Altogether, that gave KKR three of the five seats on the board, since Henry Kravis and George Roberts also became Houdaille directors. That left two of Saltarelli's titles vacant, namely, president and chief executive officer. At his recommendation, the posts went to Phillip O'Reilly, long his most energetic lieutenant.[43]

The accession of the fifty-two-year-old O'Reilly came as no surprise to anyone familiar with Houdaille's executive politics. From almost the moment

O'Reilly joined the conglomerate in 1960, it was apparent that he was destined to rise through the company's ranks. He had a B.A. in mechanical engineering from Purdue, but even more impressive was his willingness to work long and hard. O'Reilly was willing to sacrifice anything and everything for Houdaille, even if it meant being on the road thirty days a month.[44]

O'Reilly was not as smooth and polished as other possible heirs apparent. But what he lacked in this regard was more than made up for by his physical presence. He was a huge man, about two hundred pounds and more than six feet tall. He resembled nothing more than an ex-football lineman, which in fact he was. Although a knee injury ended his playing career in college, he never forgot what it took to push aside opposing linemen and win in football. In business, he was apt to rely on the same skills when faced with an obstacle.

In 1976, O'Reilly was all but anointed Saltarelli's heir when he became one of two executive vice presidents and a member of the board of directors. Of course, until KKR came along it was not certain there would be an independent Houdaille for O'Reilly to run, so he strongly favored the LBO as a solution to Houdaille's problem. Then too, like other executives with large blocks of stock, O'Reilly profited handsomely from the buyout itself. It made him a millionaire.[45]

On the day that he assumed the Houdaille presidency, O'Reilly told the *New York Times* that he was eager to take up the reins. "We're looking forward to working with KKR," he said. "Their experience in finance coupled with our experience in manufacturing and marketing will make a very complementary group." He also indicated that Houdaille retained its appetite for growth through acquisition, but for the time being, that aim would have to be set aside in deference to a more pressing concern. "We're highly leveraged right now, so our first goal is to pay off some of the debt."[46]

In fact, the pressure from the debt would be unrelenting, and prompt far-reaching changes in Houdaille's corporate goals. Insofar as Burgmaster was concerned, Houdaille's entire philosophy would shift, from one that depended on manufacturing for profits, to one that stressed accounting. Something akin to what happened to Burgmaster when it was taken over by Houdaille would now happen to Houdaille. The shift in ownership would transform the conglomerate.

One of the first changes was the emergence of the Fort Lauderdale headquarters as the third tier in what had always been a two-tier corporate structure. The executives at the very top, meaning O'Reilly and all the others wearing golden handcuffs, were inclined to peer down and view division managers as impediments as much as colleagues. Division presidents had been given the opportunity to purchase equity in the "new" Houdaille. But the response of many had been lukewarm, and some were no longer fully loyal associates in a joint enterprise. Headquarters became distant, removed, and impersonal. Perhaps the withdrawal was entirely natural, given that they bore the psychological brunt of the debt burden.

One division president who quickly sensed the changes was Burgmaster's president, Allan Folger. When the leveraged buyout occurred in 1979, his first thought was to wonder, "How is Houdaille going to service all that debt?" The machine tool industry was in the midst of a boom, but he had been around long enough to know that a bust would surely follow. He had always exercised his rights to buy Houdaille stock when it was traded on the NYSE. But now he refused to invest in a leveraged Houdaille. It would take about five years before the conglomerate could go public again, and claim the pot of gold. Folger thought the likelihood of a cyclical downturn in Houdaille's machine tool group during that time was too high.[47]

Initially, Folger tended to attribute the change in Houdaille's corporate culture to the personnel shift at the very top. Not only Saltarelli but several other senior executives decided to leave on the occasion of Houdaille's transformation. Folger had liked working under the Saltarelli regime, and was less than enamored with O'Reilly. Saltarelli had always taken a friendly interest in the families of his top executives, and "that atmosphere disappeared," recalled Folger. Within a few months after the May 1979 buyout, however, Folger came to realize that the changes being wrought transcended even something as fundamental as O'Reilly's accession.[48]

"After the buyout, Houdaille per se changed," Folger later recalled. "It seemed to lose its equilibrium." Financial expertise became the single most valued resource, and understandably so. "Accounting hires grew faster than manufacturing hires" because managing for cash flow "to service the debt became the whole end," said Folger. Corporate headquarters now demanded so many extensive financial reports that even Folger, with his capacity for numbers, came to believe that it interfered with attempts to improve Burgmaster's product and defend its market.[49]

Folger deemed such efforts crucial, even though Burgmaster was enjoying a boom not seen since the mid-1960s. The 1978–1979 increase in oil prices, the second largest jump in less than a decade, had pushed U.S. auto makers into making massive capital investments. They were spending billions of dollars to improve one of their most backward manufacturing areas, the machining of auto parts. New, computerized machine tools were needed to manufacture the new energy-saving engines, transmissions, and power trains for the cars of the 1980s. Hot on the heels of auto makers were the commercial aerospace and oil field machinery industries. The former needed to build a new generation of fuel-efficient models. The upturn in the latter, meanwhile, reflected a worldwide increase in oil and gas drilling, now that many idle fields promised to be profitable because of higher prices.[50]

Yet there was a black lining in the silver cloud. Burgmaster, along with virtually every other American builder, had happily taken orders until its backlog was a year and growing longer. That was the standard way the industry operated: survive the busts and take full advantage of the booms. But this time the industry's customers were not being so cooperative. Small and medium-sized customers began cancelling orders delayed by lengthy back-logs, because now they had a genuine alternative. They could buy a standar-dized, Japanese NC machine that no longer represented much, if any, of a technological compromise. Better still, it cost less than its American equiv-alent, and the Japanese were gaining an enviable reputation for their after-sales service. Most important, a Japanese machining center could be delivered within weeks rather than months. "Delivery was where they cut us to rib-bons," recalled Ed Merk, Burgmaster's head of sales. In 1978, imports con-stituted more than 20 percent of American consumption and exceeded U.S. exports for the first time in modern history.[51]

Folger wanted to improve Burgmaster's competitive stance while overall demand was still high, and before Japanese builders became competitors for a declining number of orders. There had been very little capital investment in plant or new machines during the stagflation of the 1970s. Burgmaster was shipping about $40 million annually, but only three new NC machines had been added to the machine shop since 1971, and the plant was virtually un-changed from when it opened in 1966.[52] There was fifty-three thousand square feet of unused land on the north side of the factory, and Folger wanted to modernize and expand the machine shop by building a third manufactur-ing aisle on the site. Although it would not be easy to find the additional machinists needed, expansion would presumably ease Burgmaster's chronic production bottlenecks and make it easier to meet Japanese delivery times.

Folger hired an architect to draw up the necessary plans, confident that he carried sufficient authority to push the idea through. After more than ten years at Burgmaster, he had more than the usual amount of independence accorded a Houdaille division president. His record of forecasts was almost un-blemished, and he could point to a steady, mostly upward graph of shipments and profits. Of course, if these were adjusted for inflation, Burgmaster was not quite as successful as it seemed. But few manufacturers had done much better in the difficult business climate of the 1970s.

Folger's planned expansion indicated that he was having difficulty adjust-ing to the new culture at Houdaille. With his aptitude for numbers, he had been quick to comprehend the mechanics of managing for cash flow. But it was hard to shake the habit of managing Burgmaster as if setting production goals and meeting them were still paramount. He underestimated, in fact, the extent to which the rules had changed. In particular, the idea of major capital expenditures ran counter to the whole concept of an LBO. The idea was to delay such investments while milking Houdaille of whatever cash it generated to service the debt, and bring the company one step closer to the pot of gold.

In retrospect, the firing of Allan Folger in March 1980, less than a year after the buyout, was inevitable. There was an inexorable logic at work, one that almost guaranteed that he would be a casualty in the post-Saltarelli, leveraged era. First, his personal relationship with Phil O'Reilly, as well as with Kenneth Slawson, the head of Houdaille's machine tool group, was un-easy at best. Added to the personal frictions was a growing sense inside headquarters that Folger just didn't measure up anymore. He was "too content."[53] The new ethic was to cut costs mercilessly, not invent new expenses.

Early in 1980, Folger promoted a friend with no particular experience to a comfortable, do-nothing job in the front office. Given all the new white-collar employees, Folger did not consider it inappropriate, or beyond his authority to do so. Once O'Reilly heard about it, however, he seized this opportunity to accomplish what he had been aching to do: put someone entirely obligated to him in charge of Burgmaster.

One Burgmaster employee who recalls the firing of Folger likened it to an execution by a Mafia hit squad:

> Unannounced, those guys flew into town and booked rooms at a downtown hotel. Monday morning, they called the office, and asked [for Folger]. "How are you doing, Al? Why don't you come down to the St. Bonaventure."
>
> Early that afternoon [I] got paged to come to Folger's office. Phil O'Reilly was sitting there, along with Slawson and another man in a blue suit. One by one, [Burgmaster] employees walked in. To each, O'Reilly said, "Al decided to take early retirement."[54]

The third blue-suited man sitting in Folger's office that March 31 was Burgmaster's new president, George Delaney. A Houdaille executive since 1967, Delaney was coming to Burgmaster from the Powermatic division in Tennessee. He also carried the dubious distinction of knowing less about manufacturing, not to mention machine tools, than any of his predecessors. Delaney's credentials consisted of a B.S. in business administration from the University of Buffalo and expertise in computer data processing. After joining Houdaille to oversee its computer operations, Delaney decided what he really wanted to do was run his own division. When an opening as Powermatic's marketing director appeared in 1970, he lobbied for the chance to get into line management. Two years later he became Powermatic's vice president in charge of manufacturing, and in 1973 Saltarelli promoted him to the presidency.[55]

In a way, Delaney's inexperience was of little consequence. His job was more an exercise in accounting than production. All that really mattered was keeping costs as low as possible, and seeing to it that Burgmaster generated enough cash to take the full measure of its depreciation allowance. As far as Delaney was concerned, Burgmaster's machines were primarily a commodity that had to be shipped out the door as fast as possible.

Obviously, someone in the plant hierarchy had to have in-depth knowledge of the product. Phil O'Reilly and Ken Slawson knew that Delaney could not run Burgmaster without a strong right hand. Fortunately, from their point of view, the decision to install Delaney coincided with another shift in Burgmaster's top ranks.

Charlie Deischter, one of the more popular managers at Burgmaster since the heyday of the Burgs, had quit as plant manager in early 1980, about a month before Folger was fired. Anxious to avoid a prolonged disruption at Burgmaster while Houdaille was highly leveraged, O'Reilly and Slawson tried to coax Gene Dobmeier out of retirement. Dobmeier, of course, had been responsible for all manufacturing at Burgmaster during most of Folger's presidency. From 1969 until 1976, while Folger concentrated on his forecasts, Dobmeier exercised unquestioned authority over the machine shop and assembly departments. He was the one man, O'Reilly thought, who could pick up where Deischter left off without missing a beat. There were few Houdaille men whose corporate loyalty exceeded Dobmeier's, and if they needed him that much, he was ready to come out of retirement. He agreed to become the vice president for manufacturing and train a successor to Deischter.[56] Then three weeks after Dobmeier resumed work, Folger was fired, and Dobmeier's return took on even greater significance.

George Delaney was glad to have Dobmeier aboard. Delaney was aware of his own limitations and the insecurity that permeated Burgmaster in the wake of Folger's abrupt dismissal. Folger had been aloof, but he had had the respect of nearly everyone who worked under him, and after more than a decade, everyone knew what was expected. In this sense, O'Reilly and Slawson were correct in viewing Folger's Burgmaster as too complacent. And if one of their aims was to shake up the division, they surely accomplished that. The manner in which Burgmaster was decapitated shocked nearly everyone.

To put everyone at ease and acquire a knowledge of the product, Delaney made a point of being visible and inquisitive during his first weeks on the job. He earnestly sought the opinions and advice of the most experienced employees, including men such as Ed Merk, the vice president for marketing who had been with Burgmaster since 1958. Delaney acknowledged that he was going to have to rely on their knowledge and skills. He even tried to talk to many of the blue-collar workers, shaking their hands, trying to remember first names. His openness immediately eased a tense and uncertain situation.[57]

Delaney's first task was to take a hard look at Folger's plans for expansion, which were explained and justified in a one-and-a-half-inch-thick report. Burgmaster was employing about four hundred workers, the highest number since the late 1960s, and its backlog of orders was almost fourteen months. In an effort to get as many machines as possible out the door, the machine shop was working almost two full shifts, and there was talk about adding a third shift in assembly.[58]

Years afterward, Delaney recalled that he began to question the need for expansion because "it did not appear [we] were fully utilizing the facilities and resources [we] had."[59] But the strongest vote against expansion came from Dobmeier. New orders were beginning to weaken by mid-1980 as interest rates rose to unprecedented levels—nearly 18 percent. Dobmeier smelled the beginnings of a downturn, and was not hesitant to say so. He also sensed that this was precisely what O'Reilly wanted to hear, that Burgmaster could do as well or even better with less. That was the end of expansion, although Burgmaster installed several of its own machining centers inside the plant in an attempt to whittle down the backlog.

Management's plan to do more with less, however, hit a sharp snag in June. That month the contract with the Steelworkers Union expired, and blue-collar employees were intent on recouping the earning power they had lost to inflation over the past three years. Burgmaster machinists eyed the company's healthy backlog of unfilled orders and decided that it was a good time to strike.

A walkout that had ended just a few weeks earlier at Houdaille's Strippit division was a harbinger of what was to come. "The union there caved in," recalled Ed Rubenstein, the union negotiator for Burgmaster workers. "And Houdaille was feeling pretty cocky."[60] There was no way Houdaille was going to meet rank-and-file demands for real pay increases in 1980—not with the entire conglomerate operating on a razor's edge. Houdaille offered a 24 percent wage increase, take it or leave it. That sounded high, except that the workers had seen their real earnings decrease by 12 percent since 1979; Houdaille's offer amounted to nothing more than a cost-of-living increase.

The strike lasted three full weeks, making it the longest and most bitter labor dispute in Burgmaster's history. Midway through the walkout, Rubenstein sensed that the union was going to lose and asked Houdaille to sweeten its offer, if only by a few cents an hour. "You have to let striking workers save face. You can't ask them to go back with nothing," said Rubenstein. But even a token increase was rejected. The final settlement was the same as Houdaille's original offer, down to the penny.[61]

By August 1980, about a month after the strike ended, it was clear that Gene Dobmeier's prediction about a downturn had been right on the mark. New orders continued to fall rapidly, and Delaney came under increasing pressure to find new ways to trim costs and generate cash. That month, Burgmaster also made some personnel changes that would have a lasting effect on its fortunes. In quick succession, Delaney hired Bill Bystrom as controller, Paul Campbell as controls manager, and Richard Parks as factory manager and Dobmeier's heir apparent.

Longtime Burgmaster employees had seen Houdaille managers come and go, and many reorganizations since 1965. But what was striking, and unprecedented, was the amount of power now concentrated in the hands of the new controller and, to a lesser degree, Campbell and Parks. The only fact more astonishing was their thorough ignorance about how to run a machine tool company. Soon the trio of Bystrom, Campbell, and Parks became known throughout Burgmaster as Delaney's "fair-haired boys," or the "whiz kids."

As orders fell, Delaney quickly retreated to the front office after his early attempt at recreating a sense of common purpose. The pressure from corporate headquarters was increasing by the week, and what it required of him did not mesh with his earlier vision. He had enough problems of his own, and was not interested in coping with any others.

This alone ended the period of good will that Delaney had inaugurated. But the factor that cost Delaney even more respect was his inexplicable reliance on the whiz kids. Delaney appeared to not know his own mind. He would not make a major decision without consulting Bystrom privately, and he seemed unduly swayed by Campbell and Parks despite their inexperience. Meanwhile, the advice of old hands like Ed Merk was treated indifferently. To the disgust of almost every employee who still had a lingering loyalty to Burgmaster, or even Houdaille, Delaney appeared to listen only to a small clique of people who "brown-nosed him," as some employees indelicately put it.[62]

Nothing illustrated this more than Gene Dobmeier's experience. The ultimate Houdaille loyalist, Dobmeier had always followed corporate policy even when he privately thought it was unwise. He seldom if ever made waves; it was Houdaille, right or wrong. He thought he was doing his old employer a great favor by returning to Burgmaster to oversee all manufacturing operations. Yet finally, even Dobmeier lost faith. Houdaille, not to mention Burgmaster, was no longer the company he once knew and was passionately loyal to.

MRP had much to do with undermining Dobmeier's lingering loyalty. Despite its problems, material requirements planning was still in force at Burgmaster. Insofar as possible, Dobmeier tried to accommodate himself to the computerized schedule. But it was far too crude a system for a product as sophisticated as machine tools, and Dobmeier knew it. The assembly department would panic because MRP had failed to schedule a sufficient number of parts. One or two machines could not be assembled because a single part was missing. Meanwhile, in the machine shop, machinists would stand idle, with little more to do than sweep the floor, because MRP said they had nothing to do. Even worse than having to hastily produce the missing part was that per unit costs skyrocketed because of such production splits. Dobmeier took to calling Burgmaster the "house of splits."[63]

One encounter in particular persuaded Dobmeier to call it quits in January 1981. One day he was walking down an aisle and saw a large, unmachined base sitting near the giant Ingersoll milling machine. He did a little checking, and quickly realized that the milling machinist had to start working on the base immediately, otherwise havoc would ensue in the assembly department. Later that day, during a top-level meeting, he raised a question about when the base was scheduled to go into production. One of the whiz kids said, in effect, that "we are several days away from M[anufacturing]-day on that base." Dobmeier replied, "I don't care what MRP says. We have to get it into production." Finally, Delaney stepped in—and sided with the whiz kid. "You could see Dobmeier lose interest then," recalled one of the participants at the meeting.[64] Dobmeier could not believe that Delaney would give greater weight to the views of a novice than to his vice president for manufacturing.

About this time, one of the machine shop foremen posed a question during a routine management meeting. He had been with Burgmaster for twenty-five years, and he was stumped. All his experience, and some rough calculations, told him that Burgmaster had to be losing money. There was no way for the company to prosper given the scrap that was being produced by inexperienced machinists, and given the splits caused by MRP. One executive smiled, and reassured him. "We are making more money than ever."[65]

That was true. Even though new orders were dropping alarmingly, Burgmaster still had a substantial backlog to work off. And because of the redepreciation of Burgmaster's capital assets and interest write-offs, all the cash Burgmaster generated was tax-free. But these were "profits" without production.

11
TURNING TO WASHINGTON
(1981–1982)

For most of the Houdaille conglomerate, the first two years after the 1979 leveraged buyout passed without undue changes. There was restructuring, but that probably would have been undertaken anyway. In 1980, Houdaille won its battle in Washington against the aluminum bumper interests, and forced a reduction in bumper collision standards. But it was an empty victory, because plastic bumpers arrived and steel bumpers became obsolete anyway, forcing Houdaille to close down its remaining bumper plants. In addition, the leveraged conglomerate liquidated the balance of its construction materials and contracting group.[1]

But a new acquisition more than compensated for these closures. In 1981, Houdaille acquired John Crane Packing, the world's biggest maker of mechanical seals, which are used to secure and prevent leaks around rotating parts. Crane made seals for everything from submarine propeller shafts to auto water pumps, and enjoyed tremendous market shares: more than 40 percent of the domestic market and 30 percent of the global market for mechanical seals. The new division immediately became Houdaille's biggest revenue producer, and greatly enhanced the conglomerate's standing as a manufacturer of industrial products. Phil O'Reilly, Houdaille's CEO, was justifiably ecstatic over his business coup. John Crane outclassed any of Houdaille's previous acquisitions.[2]

But if the future looked bright for industrial products, the same could not be said for the machine tools group. The first problem was the 1981–1982 recession, not only in the machine tool economy but also in the U.S. economy as a whole. After nearly a decade of stagflation, a new chairman of the Federal Reserve, Paul Volcker, had decided to wring inflation out of the U.S. economy no matter what the cost, and put the economy on a sounder footing. But meanwhile, a price for years of mismanagement had to be paid, and it was all the higher because it had been postponed. Unemployment and interest rates shot up to record postwar highs as the economy fell into its worst recession in fifty years.[3]

Inexorably, the recession worked its will on the machine tool industry. Because machine tool orders are a leading indicator of capital investment, builders were among the first to feel the brunt, and depth, of the recession. By 1981, net new orders were down 52 percent from their 1979 level.[4]

Then there was the problem of Houdaille's debt. Nothing like this recession had been expected when Houdaille underwent its leveraged buyout in 1979. Indeed, the LBO had been predicated on an expanding, if not slightly inflationary, economy. The beauty of an LBO was that it depended more on cash flow than real profits to pay off the junk bonds. But if the machine tool group wasn't contributing to the cash flow—and one-fourth of Houdaille's business was still machine tools—the full value of the all-important depreciation allowance could not be tapped. Servicing the LBO debt would therefore threaten the entire conglomerate.[5]

To make matters still worse, Houdaille's machine tool group was simultaneously faced with strenuous competition. Japanese imports were continuing to penetrate a once-captive domestic market. Imports now accounted for 26 percent of U.S. consumption, an all-time high, and showed every indication of going higher. Japan accounted for about 40 percent of all imports.[6]

The recession, moreover, gave a cruel twist to the competition from overseas: one of the byproducts of the recession was an artificial increase in the value of the dollar over other currencies. Since the Japanese yen was probably undervalued to begin with, the net effect was to give every Japanese builder a very comfortable cushion. He could sell at a price virtually no American builder could afford and make a handsome profit. Houdaille, like many other U.S. tool builders, began to suffer a tremendous loss of market share, not just a cyclical decline. Japanese builders increased their share of the machining center market (Burgmaster's) and punching machine market (Strippit's) from about 4 percent in 1976 to 60 percent and 46 percent, respectively, by 1982.[7]

Houdaille's machine tool group, and therefore Houdaille itself, was caught in a triple bind of debt, recession, and competition. The conglomerate could not erase its debt, or single-handedly stimulate demand for machine tools. But Phil O'Reilly believed that the last problem, foreign competition, might be amenable to a cure in Washington. He would hardly be the first manufacturer to contest Japanese imports, and he realized it was not going to be easy. His earlier experience with Washington—when Houdaille challenged the Transportation Department over automobile bumper standards—involved only domestic interests. Taking on "Japan, Inc.," and the powerful, well-organized Japanese lobby in Washington promised to be a more formidable challenge. But O'Reilly was nothing if not combative, and far from adverse to politics as they are played in Washington. In fact, he had rather enjoyed his earlier exposure to the capital, the strategy meetings, the meals, and the hobnobbing with lobbyists, lawyers, and politicians.

O'Reilly knew he would have no problem proving the extent of Japanese inroads. Nor did he worry much about proving that the Japanese were engaged in unfair trade practices. To him, the extent of their penetration was prima facie evidence; there "had to be an explanation."[8] Before he made his petition for redress to Washington, however, what he really needed was a handle on the problem. Previous experience had taught him that one key to success was an easily understandable remedy, something that he could point to and say, "This will solve my problem."

He had tried for years to persuade officials in the executive branch and Congress to use the investment tax credit to bolster U.S. manufacturing. The ITC, as it was called, was a tax break very dear to the heart of U.S. business. The credits allowed businesses to deduct from their federal taxes 10 percent of the amount invested each year in capital goods, such as machine tools. O'Reilly had lobbied Washington to apply the ITC on a sliding scale, making it dependent on a capital good's domestic content. A business that bought a machine made in the United States would be entitled to the full 10 percent credit. A product made entirely abroad would get no credit at all.[9] But he had never gotten very far with his idea because it violated U.S. obligations under the General Agreement on Tariffs and Trade (GATT), which prohibited using taxes as a means to discriminate against foreign manufactures.

The thought nevertheless occurred to him: perhaps an easy way to reclaim the domestic market would be to deny the ITC to Japanese machine tools specifically. O'Reilly roughly calculated that Japanese builders would have to lower their prices by 15.2 percent should their machines become ineligible for the tax credit. Although that would do nothing to improve Houdaille's machine tools, O'Reilly believed Japanese builders could not cut their prices that much and still remain profitable. They would lose orders, Burgmaster's and Strippit's cash flow would be somewhat restored, and Houdaille would gain much needed breathing room.[10]

In mid-1981, O'Reilly described his idea to James Mack, public affairs director of the National Machine Tool Builders' Association (NMTBA). Mack told O'Reilly that he vaguely recalled an obscure statute that gave the president discretion over investment tax credits. Mack couldn't recall exactly what its terms were, because the law he had in mind was at least a decade old. But he seemed to think that a statute disqualified foreign goods from the ITC under certain conditions. O'Reilly, excited by the possibility that his remedy was already embodied in law, turned to the NMTBA's legal counsel, Covington & Burling. The Washington firm had advised the NMTBA for decades on antitrust, regulatory, and trade matters.[11]

If any firm was going to be able to win a respite from Japanese imports, it was Covington & Burling. It was the largest, one of the oldest, and certainly one of the most prestigious firms in Washington. One-third of its lawyers were Harvard Law School graduates. It had just moved to strategically placed new offices on Pennsylvania Avenue, midway between the White House and the Capitol. More than five floors of the thirteen-story building were devoted to housing 219 Covington & Burling attorneys. The offices included the largest private law library in Washington, as well as a twelfth-floor roof garden and dining room.[12]

Insofar as Covington's politics went, it was generally known as a Democratic firm. Several Carter administration officials had come from (and returned to) Covington's ranks, so its ties to the Reagan administration were few. But its lawyers were skilled in ways that transcend anything as narrow as party affiliation. In fact, in terms of corporate clientele it was indistinguishable from a typical Republican firm. Covington was counsel to several blue-chip corporations, including AT&T, Du Pont, IBM, Exxon, Textron, and several large pharmaceutical concerns. From O'Reilly's point of view, though, what mattered was that Covington had but one client who was a Japanese manufacturer, namely, Honda.[13]

Instead of asking for the lead attorney on the NMTBA account, O'Reilly submitted his research question to Dick Copaken, the Covington partner who had proven so effective during Houdaille's bumper struggle two years earlier. O'Reilly, besides admiring Copaken's work, had enjoyed working with him. Copaken was not austere or condescending like some Washington lawyers. He was approachable, even gregarious, almost cherubic in appearance. Under that engaging demeanor, however, was a shrewd advocate. If anyone could find a way to resuscitate Houdaille's machine tool group in Washington, it was likely to be Copaken. He was hard working and imaginative, with a finely honed political sense—and bold enough not to shy away from an idea because it had never been done before. Above all, Copaken knew that politics do not end once a law is written. They also influence the interpretation of laws.

The thirty-nine-year-old Copaken had not acquired his skills and characteristics out of thin air. The son of two Kansas City lawyers, Copaken had graduated summa cum laude from Harvard College in the early 1960s, while indulging his bent for art by drawing editorial cartoons for *The Harvard Crimson*. After graduating from Harvard Law in 1966, where he "made law review" in lawyers' parlance, he won a coveted year-long White House fellowship. That was his first peek at how Washington politics, in addition to legal analysis and imagination, shape the law. Working in the Johnson administration taught him about congressional lobbying and negotiating, and deepened his appreciation for how the media could be manipulated.[14]

Copaken joined Covington & Burling as an associate in 1967 but quickly became bored by a seemingly endless procession of bank mergers and airline route cases. Eager to make his mark, and gain a full partnership, he latched onto a *pro bono publico* (for the public good) case that Covington agreed to take on in 1970. The firm budgeted ten days for what seemed a worthy, but lost cause. Copaken ended up working on the case almost exclusively for the next five years.[15]

The issue pitted Puerto Rico against the U.S. Navy, and before it was over, Copaken became renowned for his tenacity, zealotry, media sense, and sheer *chutzpah*. The mayor of Culebra, a tiny Puerto Rican island, wanted to stop the

U.S. Navy from expanding its gunnery operations on the island, which had been used as a target for almost seventy years. Copaken immediately realized that the fulcrum needed to stop the navy was political, not merely legal. He began to furnish information to the media that showed the navy to be reckless and mendacious. He wrote letters to every conceivable public figure who might help, including Billy Graham and the Pope. He persisted even when senior Covington partners grumbled about the amount of *pro bono* time an associate was putting into the case.

In 1975, President Ford signed an order that ended the navy's control over Culebra. Meanwhile, Copaken's political ally in Puerto Rico defeated the incumbent governor, enabling Covington & Burling to charge for Copaken's services. (Eventually Puerto Rico would shift all of its legal work to Covington.) For his efforts, Copaken was rewarded with a full partnership.[16]

There was no doubt that Copaken's tenacity, combined with an acrobatic legal imagination, made him a lawyer to be reckoned with. That's why O'Reilly turned to him in mid-1981. Copaken's counsel was not going to be inexpensive: in legal circles, he was considered a "heavy hitter," that is, a lawyer who (then) commanded upward of $180 per hour in addition to expenses.

There was also a risk involved in retaining the Covington & Burling lawyer. Copaken's "leave-no-stone-unturned approach" had also proven, on occasion, to be extraordinarily costly even by heavy-hitter standards. One colleague had taken to calling Copaken's schemes "Rube Goldberg scenarios." But if O'Reilly had reservations about Copaken's tendency to be obsessive, his final decision was that Houdaille did not have much choice. The stakes could not be higher, and as Copaken himself liked to say when questioned about the expense of his novel tactics, "It could be very costly to approach these things in a traditional way and lose them."[17]

After a little research, Copaken found the provision that James Mack had vaguely recalled in the Revenue Act of 1971. The legislation's innocuous title did little justice to its historical significance. The law had been passed just as the Bretton Woods system collapsed, the victim of insolvency in the United States, and the growing economic might of Japan and West Germany. That August, President Nixon took a series of drastic economic measures aimed at stopping inflation and redressing the U.S. balance-of-trade deficit. The most telling was his decision to allow a de facto devaluation of the dollar. To further stem imports, however, Nixon also imposed a 10 percent surcharge on foreign goods. Meanwhile, the Congress included what was called the Buy America provision in the 1971 Revenue Act. The provision, Section 103, denied the investment tax credit to foreign goods as long as the import surcharge was in force. The idea was to prevent Nixon's surcharge on imports from being undercut by the ITC. Otherwise the effort to enhance the competitive position of U.S. manufactured goods would be pointless.[18]

Originally, proponents of Section 103 wanted the suspension of the ITC on foreign goods to lapse whenever the surcharge did.[19] But with scarcely any debate, at the last minute the Senate rewrote the language and gave the president authority to extend the sanction against foreign goods. The purpose, ostensibly, was to give U.S. negotiators leverage in future trade talks with countries like Japan. Under the new language that became law, Section 103 gave the president power to suspend the tax credit on goods from countries that engaged in practices that "substantially burden, discriminate against or unjustifiably restrict United States commerce."[20]

After he read Section 103 and its legislative history, and once his imagination began working, Copaken could hardly contain his excitement or believe his luck. A vaguer "unfair trade" clause was hard to imagine.[21] Better still, he had unearthed what he chose to interpret as a potent, unused weapon. Many experienced Washington lawyers had been vainly poring over the trade laws for years, trying to find novel ways to impose quotas or other restrictions on behalf of battered American manufacturers. But no one had ever tried to invoke this all-but-forgotten provision, nor had the executive branch even bothered to craft the necessary regulations. Section 103 was that rare bird in Washington: power unencumbered by precedent.[22]

Copaken immediately realized what this vacuum signified. "This meant that we were free to craft our approach to the Administration in any way we determined would best serve the interest" of Houdaille.[23] That was no small advantage given all the obstacles trade disputes traditionally must overcome. Of course, there were still many problems left. Copaken's proposed remedy, for example, ran smack up against U.S. obligations under the General Agreement on Tariffs and Trade. Even if Japan could be "proven guilty" somehow, using the ITC as a sanction was prohibited. But if O'Reilly had any doubts about his counsel's legal research, they were quickly put to rest by Copaken. Nor did he have to do much convincing. The idea was exactly what O'Reilly had in mind.

Once both men decided to proceed, the first problem—as well as opportunity—was how to influence procedure. Copaken realized that as soon as he threw any petition for redress "over the transom at the White House," the administration would have to decide where to route the petition for proper "staffing." Given the nature of bureaucracies, the "lead agency" would exercise tremendous power and control. The petition could be dead on arrival if it landed in the wrong hands. If the State Department became the lead agency, for example, the petition would surely falter. State was always "more keen to represent the interests of foreign nations in trade disputes than those of the United States," Copaken thought. Fortunately, State's track record was so well known that it was not likely to be designated.[24]

The Treasury Department presented an even greater threat. Treasury would not be good for Houdaille either, Copaken thought, because it traditionally took a "dim and jaded view" of domestic interests under foreign attack. But, since the petition involved a tax issue, Treasury was in a strong position to assert jurisdiction. The Commerce Department was the ideal venue. But it was so distrusted by State and Treasury—it always, and uncritically, supported U.S. industry—that if Copaken pushed for Commerce he just might provoke Treasury into asserting itself. Copaken decided that discretion was the better part of valor. Better to settle for a more neutral agency than go for broke and end up with Treasury.[25]

The most promising possibility, Copaken thought, might be the Office of the U.S. Trade Representative (USTR), a tiny, but cabinet-level agency. USTR was one of the smallest autonomous units in the federal government, with only 113 employees. It was also a young agency, born in 1962, after Congress became concerned about America's declining share of world trade and the tendency of State and Treasury to disregard domestic interests. Congress gave USTR the one power that ensured bureaucratic survival: it reported directly to the president. Soon the agency won a reputation as a "can-do" bureaucracy, because it moved with a flexibility that cumbersome, naysaying behemoths could only dream about. Over the years, USTR also won high marks as an impartial judge of competing foreign and domestic interests, and not as a predictable advocate of either. If Copaken selected USTR, it would be an appropriate choice: an agency that is an anomaly in government handling an anomalous petition.[26]

President Reagan's top appointee at USTR was William Brock, a Tennessee Republican, former senator, and one-time head of the Republican National Committee. Brock had wanted the top post at the Commerce Department, but his credentials as a staunch Reaganite were less than stellar, so he was offered USTR instead. The small agency was still a place where his congressional experience would prove valuable. And Brock would be responsible for setting policy on the most divisive issue in the Republican party, namely, international trade.[27]

True Reaganites spurned the Republicans' traditional advocacy of free trade. In the early days of the 1980 campaign, Ronald Reagan constantly charged that free trade, as espoused by such groups as the Trilateral Commission, undermined the American economy. After he became the nominee, however, the more liberal wing of the party forced Reagan to modify his public stance. Free trade was now identified as a desirable and ultimate goal. Nevertheless, strong protectionist impulses remained just below the rhetoric. As the Reagan administration took office, many of its top officials, including Brock, were prepared to take whatever steps were necessary to protect key U.S. industries from foreign competition.[28]

The Reagan administration's attitude toward protectionism augured well for Houdaille's chances. Still, Copaken wanted to make sure that USTR would look upon his plan with sufficient fervor to warrant its selection as the lead agency. He decided that a discreet meeting with an agency official was in order, so that he and O'Reilly could informally broach their idea.

Like his boss William Brock, David Macdonald, the deputy U.S. Trade Representative, wanted the United States to be much tougher with the

Japanese on trade. The 1981 U.S. deficit was heading toward a new high of $18 billion. The problem was how to stem Japanese imports without violating international norms. As soon as he heard Copaken's scheme, Macdonald recognized a promising approach. By letting a private party press an unprecedented complaint, the Reagan administration could reap whatever advantages accrued from the petition, all the while maintaining to the Japanese that the U.S. government was detached from the grievance. Macdonald wasn't prepared to judge the merits of Houdaille's case, but the penetration of the U.S. market by Japanese tool imports was beyond question. It seemed well worth trying.[29]

The coincidence of interests between Houdaille and the USTR was manifest, and Copaken and O'Reilly came away thoroughly encouraged. As Copaken later said, USTR "had been looking for the proverbial two-by-four with which to command Japan's attention as well as that of the EEC. Some in [that] office thought Section 103 of the Revenue Act of 1971 might be just the club they needed."[30]

Copaken had found his "honest broker." But if a proper reception for the petition was critical, Copaken also recognized that it was only half the task. In addition, he had to amass a persuasive evidentiary tale. He was savvy enough to realize, of course, that, "Presidents do not decide trade cases on their merits; it is naïve to assume that they will. Because of the fanciful posturing to the contrary, however, it is a useful first step to establish a compelling case on the merits."[31]

Developing such a document for Houdaille was not going to be easy. Merely demonstrating the extent of Japanese inroads would not be compelling, or sufficient, proof. Instead, Copaken had to show how Japan, Inc., had consciously and methodically relegated U.S. builders to second-class status.

Reading a few scholarly books on Japan was a good start. Copaken soon learned, however, that even though a consensus existed on the fact of Japan's success, *how* the Japanese achieved their economic miracle was the subject of fierce and ongoing debate. Scholars like Chalmers Johnson and Ezra Vogel emphasized the role of the government, and especially MITI. Their view coincided neatly with Copaken's preferred thesis. But numerous scholars disputed the effectiveness and wisdom of MITI's guidance. No one doubted that MITI had protected and tried to rationalize Japanese industry. Yet the latter group of scholars suggested that other, relatively mundane economic elements were more instrumental than MITI in creating the Japanese export machine. One factor was a soundly managed economy that encouraged capital formation and investment, and the second was an industrious, well-managed work force.[32]

Copaken could invoke one school of thought to bolster his claim, but he was far from having a compelling case. Moreover, no one had specifically chronicled the rise of the Japanese machine tool industry and the reasons for its success. That was the task he now set for himself, in August 1981.

Copaken, aided by three Covington & Burling associates and numerous secretaries and researchers, began by conducting extensive research in Washington libraries. Then he turned to Covington & Burling's affiliate in Tokyo, the firm of Nagashima & Ohno, for extensive primary research. Nagashima happened to be an old law school classmate of Copaken's, and that was a big help.[33] For obvious reasons, Japan was a forbidding place to do research.

Combing Japanese trade publications, government documents, and legal publications going back to the 1950s, Nagashima retrieved and translated thousands of pages for Copaken's use. Even for native Japanese, the research was formidable. "We didn't have textbooks or court decisions we could rely on. We were going to the very sources," recalls Oscar Garibaldi, one of the Covington associates who worked under Copaken. Documenting the nature and extent of suspected subsidies to Japanese builders was particularly difficult. Government sources did not divulge what Copaken considered reliable figures.[34]

While he digested the translated documents himself, Copaken began traveling to Japan, often with O'Reilly. During the life of the Houdaille petition, Copaken would make more than a dozen such trips. He began by interviewing anyone remotely connected with Japanese industrial policy, machine tools, or antitrust statutes, including builders, MITI bureaucrats, U.S. embassy officers, and officials from Japan's Fair Trade Commission, the government agency charged with pursuing antitrust violations.

During interviews with Japanese officials, Copaken employed a ruse that he thought might be useful, based on previous experience. In the late 1970s, he had represented the Marshall Islands in negotiations with the Japanese over a tuna-fishing treaty and economic assistance. Copaken knew that the Japanese prepared copiously for every diplomatic or business negotiation; if he arrived in Tokyo extremely well prepared, he might induce Japanese officials to reach the wrong conclusion, that he was a "cat's paw" for the U.S. government (although in a sense he was). If so, he might be able to exploit that ambiguity and extract more information from discreet officials. He later described one trip.

> When I arrived, I had a series of meetings at MITI. They were quite surprised that we had done enormous amounts of homework, and that we were not satisfied with the superficial answers that they normally gave and which seemed to satisfy everybody else. We had all the follow-up questions that they didn't want to answer.
>
> After a day of this, and hundreds of questions we had prepared in advance, we were notified that this was all the time they could afford to spend for one private attorney representing one private company. Of course, they told us, "If it were the government of the U.S. that were asking for this information, it would be a very different situation. . . .

Essentially, what they were doing was trying to flush out into the open what they were convinced was a fact—that this was a trial balloon by the U.S. government, and not just a legitimate private party pursuing a private case. With considerable malice aforethought, I added to their discomfort by truthfully insisting to them that I was just one lawyer representing one small company. This, of course, convinced them that the opposite was the truth. It was a wonderful situation, filled with irony, where the only way to persuade them that I was actually a secret agent of the U.S. government was to flat out deny it.[35]

After "man-years" of research accomplished in nine months by a small legal army, Copaken was ready to assemble and write the petition with the aid of his associates. The final result was massive—714 pages. By any measure it was an impressive compilation. But it also made for sensational reading.

The essence of the Houdaille petition was contained in a fifteen-page introduction. It alleged that U.S. builders had lost a major share of their domestic market because "the Japanese Government instigated the formation of [a] cartel." MITI was singled out as the ringleader, responsible for nurturing Japanese builders into an "international" cartel (even though it contained only domestic companies) through a series of laws and guidances dating back to the 1950s. After "weeding out" manufacturers with small market shares, MITI pressed Japanese builders to pool their resources and jointly develop and manufacture NC machine tools. Simultaneously, the government aided and abetted this cartel by failing to enforce Japan's antimonopoly law. Lastly, the petition claimed to document that the Japanese government "backed this cartel with tax advantages, concessionary loans, research grants, and other direct and indirect subsidies." The introduction breathlessly purported to show, for the first time, how Japanese industrial policy worked, and why it was unfair to American tool builders.[36]

The petition went on to cite several milestones on Japan's road to subjugation of the American market.

- June 1956: the Diet passes an "Extraordinary Measures Law," a blueprint and the legal basis for concentrating Japanese industry. One month later the Japanese cabinet issues a formal order identifying machine tools as one of the industries targeted for promotion.
- November 1960: MITI and the machine tool industry agree to allocate production. Participating companies are exempted from Japan's antimonopoly laws.
- July 1968: MITI orders builders to stop production of certain kinds of machines if their market share for that product is "less than 5 percent" or if the product constitutes "less than 20 percent" of the company's production.
- April 1971: A "Second Extraordinary Measures Law" empowers MITI to

rationalize the machine tool industry. Builders are ordered to make NC machines at least half of their total output.
- March 1978: A government-instigated cartel is formed to regulate prices for NC machining centers and lathes exported to North America.[37]

A subsequent section in the petition was devoted to establishing the injury to Houdaille's machine tool group. Although the clear implication was that the "cartel" was intent on international primacy in a wide range of NC machine tools, the petition limited itself to the extent of Houdaille's injury and its lost market shares in machining centers (Burgmaster) and punching machines (Strippit). The proof appeared unambiguous: MITI's industrial targeting had increased Japan's exports of machining centers from 3.7 percent in 1976 to 50.1 percent in 1981, whereas U.S. manufacturers' share of the domestic market shrank from 95.1 percent to 48.7 percent. The statistics for punching machines were comparable.[38]

All told, the petition seemed to present a thorough, if not ironclad, case. An unholy alliance existed between MITI and the Japanese machine tool industry, and Houdaille's machine tool group had been among its casualties. Copaken took considerable pride in his accomplishment, but then he was not known for his modesty. In any case, he finally had completed a "compelling case on its merits."

All that remained was to make the proper arrangements so that USTR would be designated the lead agency. There was ample precedent for it to assume the role. USTR already chaired petitions filed under Section 301 of the Trade Act of 1974, the statute most industries resorted to when faced with unfair foreign competition. Copaken smoked out a key Treasury official, and persuaded him to not contest USTR jurisdiction, even though the Houdaille petition would involve a tax remedy. Both the Section 301 precedent and USTR's reputation for fairness and objectivity persuaded the Treasury official to go along with Copaken. Everything was now arranged. When the time came for Houdaille to submit its petition, Copaken and O'Reilly obtained their preferred venue simply by stating on the top of the petition, nominally addressed to the president, that it was being submitted "through the Office of the United States Trade Representative."[39] It was "thrown over the transom" on May 3, 1982.

The early and sympathetic support accorded the Houdaille petition was critical, because it could easily have been thrown back over the transom. There was ample reason to question the legal "spin" Copaken wanted to give Section 103. During House debate on the measure in 1971, Congressman Wilbur Mills, then chairman of the Ways and Means Committee, stated that the sanction would be effective against a country that "maintains burdensome nontariff restrictions against U.S. exports or engages in discriminatory actions or policies which unjustifiably restrict U.S. exports." A similar statement was made during Senate consideration. In fact, everything in the legislative history suggested that Section 103 applied only in instances where U.S. *exports* were unfairly treated. Most important, Section 103 also did not contain any language suggesting that private parties could petition the president to obtain relief.[40]

Eventually, opponents of the Houdaille petition would successfully challenge Copaken's interpretation of Section 103. But by that time, the petition would have momentum and a life of its own. The Reagan administration ought to have dismissed Copaken's legal sleight of hand at the outset. The fact that it did not was tribute to Copaken's shrewd politicking. It was also the first clue that he and O'Reilly had set in motion something much bigger than an obscure trade case.

With the petition filed, Copaken had a moment to stop and take stock of the situation. He had compiled an extraordinary evidentiary document; just as important, the petition was in USTR's safe hands. Moreover, the novelty of the remedy, the discretion allowed the president, and the sympathy of key officials were all factors working in Houdaille's favor. But this was no time to rest. As he knew from his earlier work on behalf of clients fighting an uphill battle, a lawyer must pay "the same careful attention to analyzing and marshalling politically relevant facts as one devotes to questions of law and legally relevant facts."[41]

Copaken had first learned the lesson at Harvard Law School, and tried never to forget it. The precise "words of wisdom" had been uttered by a professor during a first-year class in property law, and for many years afterward, Copaken was fond of telling the complete anecdote.

[The professor] described an especially poignant case involving a poor widow with numerous children who was about to lose her home due to the inexorable logic of some arcane peculiarity of property law. The Professor then challenged each of us to explain how we would handle her case. One traditional approach after another was put forward. Each in turn was ripped to shreds by the good professor wielding the pernicious law of property as an unyielding saber.

When we at last became convinced that our client's case was hopeless, Professor Leach sputtered: "You mean you are going to just let this poor wretched creature be thrown out on the street? That's shameless, and even worse, unnecessary. When faced with a case such as this you should march straight in to the local newspaper and tell your client's story. Fortunately, that is precisely what her attorney did and she is still living in that house today."[42]

Copaken had put this nontextbook piece of advice to good use when he battled the U.S. Navy over Puerto Rico. He intended to employ it as well against the Japanese. Media attention was vital, if only to "overcome the enormous inertia that confronts any effort to rouse the President to action" in a trade dispute.[43]

If media attention was indispensable, then novelty was indispensable as well. Copaken knew that nothing captured the media's attention faster than something new. The fact that Section 103 had never been invoked before was a good start. The petition itself also helped. It made purveyors of the Japan, Inc., theory look as though they had understated their case, and *The Wall Street Journal*, upon receiving an advance copy, ran a largely favorable story the day the petition was submitted. Still, it was not going to be easy to attract the consistent attention of the newsmakers among the media, that is, such papers as the *Journal*, *New York Times*, and *Washington Post*. The Houdaille petition, after all, was only one trade complaint among hundreds.

It was then that Copaken and O'Reilly inadvertently reaped a public relations windfall from a gambit originally intended to reduce Houdaille's mounting legal bill.

Well before the petition was ready for submission, O'Reilly had begun to feel uncomfortable about the expenses Copaken was piling up. By May 1982, more than a year had passed, Burgmaster and Strippit were worse off than ever, and all O'Reilly had to show for it was the petition—and a bill from Copaken for more than $500,000.[44]

O'Reilly decided the time had come to recoup some of Houdaille's legal expenses. The cost of documenting Japan's industrial targeting ought not to be borne by Houdaille alone, he told his counsel. "I'm not going to do this on a silver platter for everyone," O'Reilly said. He insisted on a copyright for the petition because he wanted to sell it for substantially more than its reproduction cost. Copaken thought that Houdaille's interests would be better served if it charged little more than what it cost to print the petition. Then it would be distributed as widely as possible. Nevertheless, O'Reilly insisted, and put a price tag of $1,250 on the petition.[45]

There were bound to be some buyers, even at that price. O'Reilly was determined to reach a wide audience and sent out a mass mailing to scores of American CEOs and heads of trade associations. O'Reilly assured them that Houdaille was not seeking a "new profit center" by marketing the petition. But in a pitch reminiscent of late-night TV ads, the executives were told that "if your business is suffering from the onslaught of severe and perhaps unfair Japanese competition . . . you cannot afford to delay getting this revealing information . . . if you order our complete package now, you will receive by express mail the complete 145-page petition, which sets forth the legal basis for our claim, and appendices of approximately 500 pages of reference data and sources."[46]

To Copaken's surprise and delight, O'Reilly's letter created a sensation. Trade briefs are usually so boring that the only people who read them are paid to do so. But the sheer novelty of copyrighting one, and then attaching a hefty price tag to it, created demand. Within days of its submission to USTR, the document was a Washington best seller.

Donald deKieffer, the USTR general counsel, congratulated Copaken for thinking up "the cleverest way of gaining attention for a trade case" he had ever seen. But then he told Copaken that to meet public demand, the USTR deemed it necessary to make the petition widely available. USTR intended to reproduce the petition for a nominal fee even if it meant risking a copyright suit. Not wishing to engage in a peripheral argument, Copaken then persuaded O'Reilly to allow USTR to publish the petition for about $15 a copy.

That only seemed to heighten interest in the petition even more. Knowing a bargain when they saw one, trade lawyers, lobbyists, foreign governments, and scores of businessmen ordered so many copies that it threatened to drive USTR into bankruptcy, because all the money accepted by the agency had to be remitted to the Treasury Department, but there was no mechanism to transfer an equal sum back to USTR. It had to pay for the copies out of its own budget. After several printings sold out, USTR beat a hasty retreat. All further requests for the petition were referred to Covington & Burling.[47]

Besides being a stroke of public relations genius, copyrighting the petition attracted more media attention. The merits and substance of Houdaille's petition were given scant coverage, but that was to be expected and could be rectified. The critical fact was that the petition had achieved a significant level of interest.

Media attention, however, was hardly the only pressure Copaken intended to bring to bear on the administration. Displaying his consummate understanding of how bureaucratic and trade politics are played in Washington, Copaken lost no time in plotting a scheme that would involve every conceivable Washington "player": the public, trade associations, trade unions, business groups, lobbyists, and the Congress. In effect, he intended to orchestrate a full-court press on the administration.

Copaken first focused his attention on the USTR because of its lead role. The agency had decided to follow the same procedure it used with petitions filed under Section 301 of the 1974 Trade Act. For the next three months, all interested parties would be free to submit written comments on any of the issues raised in the petition. Subsequently, USTR planned to convene an interagency task force, an ad hoc group comprising representatives from every federal agency with any conceivable interest at stake: the Departments of State, Commerce, Treasury, Defense, and Labor, the Council of Economic Advisers, the CIA, the National Security Council, even the Office of Management and Budget. After due deliberation, the task force would present its recommendation to the Trade Policy Committee, another interagency entity, but one with cabinet-level rank. In turn, the TPC would make a final recommendation to the president.[48]

Copaken was determined to let USTR know that interest in the petition was wide and deep during the period of public comment. Within a week of the petition's arrival USTR received dozens of letters, most of them from Houdaille employees, but also from employees of companies that supplied Houdaille, as well as local bankers. Blue-collar workers implored the president to "please save our jobs." A secretary to the president of Houdaille's Di-Acro division wrote,

> I am a Houdaille employee . . . I am also a widow and the mother of three children. . . . If I were to be placed on layoff, I would not be able to support my children . . . act NOW on the petition.[49]

The letter from George Delaney, Burgmaster's president, was also typical. "The Japanese have been allowed, for too long a period, to use unfair trade practices. . . . As an American citizen, and as a Houdaille employee, I urge your assistance now." Meanwhile, Richard Polacek, Burgmaster's vice president of engineering, wrote, "The Japanese are formidable competitors and I respect them for that; however, I have long suspected that it has been an unfair competition . . . support Houdaille Industries' petition."[50]

By mid-July, USTR had been inundated by a thousand personal letters from Houdaille employees and other individuals. Some of the latter made barely disguised racial attacks, with references to "Japs." All applauded the petition and supported Houdaille's suggested remedy. Letters also arrived from machine tool builders, such as Cincinnati Milacron and Brown & Sharpe, domestic machine tool distributors, the NMTBA, the Semiconductor Industry Association, the National Association of Manufacturers, the AFL-CIO, and the UAW.[51]

After receiving dozens of letters from constituents, senators and congressmen began to weigh in as well. The petition attracted an unexpectedly broad range of political support, from Howard Metzenbaum, one of the Senate's most liberal Democrats, to Jack Kemp, a leader of Republican conservatives in the House. Kemp was especially emphatic. Houdaille's Strippit division was located in his district, and his association with the company went back to the Saltarelli era. At the bottom of his letter he scribbled, "This is very important to me."[52]

Many weeks passed before USTR began to receive substantive comments opposed to the petition. The most important salvo was fired by the firm of Wender Murase & White, legal counsel to the Japan Machine Tool Builders' Association (JMTBA). Wender Murase was not exactly a legal powerhouse like Copaken's firm, Covington & Burling. Its main office, with about two dozen partners, was located on Park Avenue in New York, and the Washington branch, which handled the petition, was small, housing just four partners and a few associates.[53]

On the other hand, Wender Murase was extremely well versed in the Japanese economy and trade law. It represented more than two hundred Japanese companies in the United States.[54] The partner who would pull Wender Murase's "laboring oar" in the case was Carl Green, a forty-two-year-old graduate of Yale Law School. A more striking contrast to Copaken was hard to imagine. Whereas Copaken was flamboyant and subject to legal flights of fancy, Green was in equal parts sober and serious. Then too, whereas Copaken had acquired his expertise in Japanese industrial policy over a period of nine months, Green had spent years working on matters related to Japan, including five years as the Ford Foundation's representative in Tokyo.

The Japanese government did not appear to take the Houdaille petition very seriously at first, nor was Green inclined to. For the most part he thought the petition was "absurd" and "an exercise in fluff rather than truth-seeking." In his 132-page rebuttal, submitted to USTR in July 1982, Green attacked the Houdaille petition at every legal soft spot. He pointed out that Copaken had twisted the purpose of Section 103, which was intended as a sanction against countries that discriminated against U.S. exports; Copaken was attempting to wield it as a shield against Japanese imports. No restraints on U.S. exports to Japan had been proved, Green maintained. He also denied the existence of a Japanese cartel in any American legal sense. He closed his summary by vigorously asserting that Houdaille's proposed remedy was not "GATT-able," that is, it violated the international obligations of the United States under GATT.[55]

Green's rebuttal also presented some counterarguments. He suggested that the loss of market share suffered by U.S. builders was a self-inflicted wound, caused by insufficient investment, poor quality, oversophisticated tools, and lack of attention to customers' needs. Japanese imports, instead of being the *cause* of the problem, were the *result* of U.S. builders' inability to compete. In addition, Green asserted that any presidential decision along the lines suggested by Houdaille would seriously damage American-Japanese relations, perhaps the most important bilateral relationship in the world.[56]

With his rebuttal, Green clearly was aiming for the lawyer's equivalent of a technical knockout. He considered the Houdaille petition a jumbled, illogical set of arguments. Copaken had not resorted to the laws appropriately invoked by parties seeking relief from unfair trade practices, and Green believed he knew why. Copaken recognized that Houdaille had no case, so he took refuge in an unused law dubiously interpreted. Green fully expected the Houdaille petition to be given a perfunctory review, even by an administration that seemed inclined toward protectionism.

Copaken, of course, had quite another result in mind. Two days after Green submitted his earnest rebuttal, Copaken submitted a 250-page supplement to the Houdaille petition. In part, the purpose of the addendum was to anticipate some of Green's comments, and shore up weak spots in the original petition. Copaken copiously defended his proposed tax remedy, in particular, the question of whether or not denying tax credits was "GATT-able." Yet the supplement's major thrust was not further development of previously stated positions. Rather, the bulk of it was devoted to what Copaken liked to call new facts.

The "continual discovery and presentation of new facts," Copaken thought, served several critical functions in cases that were, above all, political. For one, there had to be a constant stream of new facts because so much hinged on keeping the media's attention. The media had an insatiable appetite for new facts, which had to be fed, lest the media become bored. Regularly introducing new facts also smoked out bureaucratic opponents within the U.S. government. Invariably, such elements couched their ideological or jurisdictional opposition in terms of factual questions. New facts tended to strip away the veneer and expose the real reason behind the opposition. Since Houdaille's fate would likely be decided by an interagency task force, Copaken thought it was imperative to expose the bureaucratic bias of each agency opposed to the petition.[57]

Not least of all, new facts were essential in cases where the chief opponent was a foreign government. Copaken knew that "most governments take so much time to clear positions that they cannot respond effectively to rapidly changing circumstances." Regularly introducing new facts puts them at a tactical disadvantage; it was especially "sublime if the new facts [were] easily understood, shock[ed] normal sensibilities, and [were] contrary to the interests of none but foreign parties that neither vote in the United States nor influence votes here."[58]

The new facts cited in Copaken's supplement were intended to achieve all these ends, and more. Copaken claimed to have uncovered something even more sensational than Japan's international machine tool cartel. Through dogged persistence, and because he was unwilling to take MITI officials at their word, Copaken claimed to have unearthed hitherto unknown facts about subsidies to Japanese manufacturers.[59] Beginning in 1954, Copaken said, the Japanese government had systematically siphoned off a portion of the proceeds from all bets placed at bicycle and motorcycle race tracks in Japan. These monies were then quietly disbursed to the machinery industry in furtherance of MITI's goals, namely, joint research and development, and the creation of anticompetitive cartels. Over the course of three decades, Copaken alleged, the government had funneled hundreds of millions of dollars to Japanese industry in this manner. In 1980 alone, the subsidy to the machinery industry totaled $104 million.[60]

As Copaken expected, his shocking discovery caused a big stir. One of the first media outlets to pick up the story was NBC Reports, the network's documentary arm. NBC was in the midst of producing an hour-long program on trade frictions between Japan and the United States, entitled "Japan versus USA: The Hi-Tech Shoot-out." Both O'Reilly and Copaken were interviewed at some length, although in the final edited version their comments were reduced to a few seconds of air time. Nevertheless, it was enough to make their point. Said Copaken, "We found that the Japanese government had instigated, encouraged and nurtured the formation of [a] machine tool cartel that has been a major spur to their penetration of the U.S. machine tool market." The documentary went on to show a bicycle race track and lines of Japanese bettors. Proceeds from such wagers helped "explain how the Japanese machine tool industry has kept its cost[s] down."[61]

The documentary was not quite as one-sided as this vignette would indicate. The program contained opposing views, including direct quotes from MITI officials denying the substance of Houdaille's charges. Nor did the program conclude on a note that was to Houdaille's liking. "It is tempting and human to put a black hat on the Japanese and claim that they're the bad guys and they don't fight fair," said NBC reporter Lloyd Dobyns. "They fight as fair as anyone else, including us, but they fight differently. . . . So if Japan's government and industry cooperate, if they are better organized and more productive, if their quality is higher and their price lower, whose fault is that?"[62]

But if he was somewhat disappointed with this exposure, Copaken was nevertheless undeterred. His charges had been aired, and not completely dismissed. If anything, on balance NBC had contributed to their credibility. Copaken believed in the old adage of Hollywood press agents: better to be mentioned in the press, even critically, than not to be mentioned at all.

It took a full month before the true facts began to catch up with Copaken's new facts. The existence of the racing subsidies to the machinery industry was, of course, true. The problem, however, was that Copaken had intentionally buried, in a footnote, a crucial distinction between the *machinery* industry and the *machine tool* industry. Machine tools were naturally part of the Japanese machinery industry, but a minuscule fraction, less than 1.5 percent. As such, they annually collected an equally minuscule percentage of the government-directed subsidy from race track betting. As Copaken noted, the total amount of that subsidy in 1980 had amounted to $104 million. What he neglected to make clear, however, was that Japanese tool builders received a total of about $600,000 from this amount. And rather than furthering an insidious cartel, the monies had been used for relatively innocuous purposes, such as translating *American Machinist* into Japanese, translating Japanese catalogs into English, German, and French, and subsidizing participation in international machine tool fairs.[63]

Rather than being "badly misled" by MITI officials, Copaken in fact had been given roughly accurate figures.[64] MITI had told Copaken that the total subsidy to the machine tool industry in 1980 amounted to 90 million yen; the exact total was closer to 107 million, or $600,000. Of course, Copaken could make the argument that Japanese builders benefited from the entire $104 million, since any increases in the machinery sector were bound to have a trickle-down effect on the machine tool industry. But such logic was inadmissible in trade cases; subsidies, in order to be tagged unfair, had to be direct and quantifiable.[65]

Carl Green, the counsel to the Japanese builders, was confident about beating back whatever new facts Copaken was prepared to publicize. But Green was also mystified by all the serious attention the petition was attracting. The case had looked "a lot like a regular trade complaint" when it was filed five months ago, in May. Since then, not only had the administration refused to dismiss the petition summarily, but the case seemed to be acquiring broad political significance. Houdaille's argument could not withstand close scrutiny, but Green was repeatedly surprised by the initial willingness of "otherwise intelligent people" to believe any far-fetched claim, such as a hidden, $100 million Japanese subsidy to a "pipsqueak industry." To Green, it was as though "allegations only had to be made about Japan to be believed." True facts had a hard time catching up with so-called new facts.[66]

The Japanese government, specifically MITI, which had all but ignored the petition, decided that such a course was no longer wise. No Japanese exports would be exempt from discriminatory treatment if MITI's efforts over the past thirty years were now going to be declared per se unfair. In mid-August, the Japanese government relayed its official response to USTR through the State Department. The charges made by Houdaille were based on "misunderstanding or misinterpretation," the diplomatic note said. It went on to say:

> While it is true that the government of Japan executed certain actions and policies to stimulate and promote the recovery of the Japanese machinery industries, including the machine tool industry, from their devastated situation after the war, not only were they legitimate and justifiable, but also similar governmental actions and policies were found in various other countries, including Europe. Furthermore, the government of Japan has been implementing its industrial policies by presenting future visions of relevant industries or issuing instructions to relevant industries, when necessary. The aim of such actions has been to promote or maintain the fair and sound development of relevant industries in accordance with the level of maturity of each industry. Neither the objective nor the effect of those actions is anticompetitive.[67]

By the fall of 1982, after more than five months, the contest between Houdaille and Japan was tied. The lawyers representing Japanese interests had the better of the legal argument. But the fact that the game was even being played showed that Copaken was ahead where it mattered most: the political arena.

12

BLAME THE JAPANESE (1982–1983)

Throughout the summer and early fall of 1982, while Dick Copaken and Carl Green were engaged in their legal jockeying, an interagency task force deliberated the merits of the Houdaille petition. All the external maneuvering, in essence, was calculated to influence the recommendation the ad hoc group would make at the cabinet level.

The Houdaille task force, as it was called, first met at USTR's request on June 22. Initially the meetings were infrequent, no more than once a month, because each participating agency had to go through its own internal debate about the big and small issues the Houdaille petition raised. The foremost concern of Treasury and State was whether Houdaille's proposed remedy was consistent with GATT obligations. The Justice Department spent a considerable amount of time mulling over whether an "international cartel" could be said to exist if all its members were from the same country. Altogether, it soon became clear that there was no chance for a decision by the Houdaille task force until after Labor Day, at the earliest.

The word *idle*, however, was not in Dick Copaken's lexicon. He wanted to use the time to bolster the petition itself with supporting documents, cultivate bureaucratic allies on the task force, and undermine opponents. He knew he had the staunch backing of USTR, although by some accounts career staff members at the agency, as opposed to superior political appointees, saw little merit in the petition. Nonetheless, USTR was firmly in Houdaille's camp. There was one other agency whose allegiance had to be assured, and that was the Commerce Department.

Commerce represented the views of big business in the government, and as such everyone expected it to support Houdaille. The secretary of commerce, Malcolm Baldrige, was a Connecticut Republican from the same wing of the party as William Brock. And like Brock, Baldrige had been drifting away from the mainstream Republican position in favor of free trade. In fact, his desire to do something about the growing U.S. trade deficit was one of the main reasons Baldrige agreed to become commerce secretary. He was far less

191

interested in Commerce's domestic duties than he was in finding ways to improve the export performance of U.S. manufacturers.

Baldrige was not exactly uncritical of the corporate establishment, however, and notably refused to shift all the blame for the trade imbalance to unfair foreign trade practices. On more than one occasion, the Yale-educated Baldrige was characteristically blunt about who was at fault for sagging U.S. productivity. He blamed American management for being "too fat, dumb and happy."

> I don't think it's labor productivity that's a problem. It's management. . . . Management hasn't been sharp enough or hungry enough or lean enough.
>
> It's overstaffed. It concentrates on one-year goals, which is costly. It's not close enough to labor to understand labor's problems. It's insulated from what goes on in the world, even from what goes on at home. It's not as innovative in working on new ideas and generating money for research as the Japanese.[1]

Despite a willingness to point his finger inward though, Baldrige disdained the arguments of pure free traders, and was determined to bring about a fundamental shift in the government's attitude toward trade. He firmly believed the United States could not sustain its economic and political primacy without a strong industrial base, especially one that excelled in the manufacture of so-called high-tech goods. That capability had to be enhanced even at the risk of adopting quasi-protectionist measures. As he would later tell the *New York Times*, "occasionally we have to insist on fair trade [regarded as a code word for protectionism] because, literally, our fair trade laws are the bedrock on which free trade stands."[2]

During the first few months of the Reagan administration, Baldrige tried to implement his trade vision by rearranging the government. He proposed folding the USTR into the Commerce Department, to create a new entity called the Department of International Trade and Industry. MITI was the obvious model for the new department that Baldrige had in mind.[3] Baldrige's idea, however, did not curry favor from other parts of the government, much less USTR, and was discarded almost as soon as it was proposed. He was forced to adopt a case-by-case approach, and measure success incrementally, rather than accomplish his goal with one broad reform.[4]

Thus, for all intents and purposes the Houdaille petition was made to order for Baldrige. Most trade disputes revolve around arcane points indecipherable to everyone except the lawyers involved. By contrast, the Houdaille petition took what Baldrige regarded as a properly broad view of the problem. It graphically illustrated how the Japanese government nurtured high-technology industries. The respite the petition promised to bring the American tool industry was significant, but that was not the main purpose to be served by backing Houdaille. To Baldrige the petition was an excellent platform from which to mount his attack for a tougher trade policy vis-à-vis Japan.

No doubt, Baldrige was also sympathetic because Houdaille's dilemma struck close to home. Prior to becoming commerce secretary, Baldrige had been president of an industrial conglomerate similar to Houdaille. Indeed, he had accomplished the same feat at Scovill that Jerry Saltarelli had performed at Houdaille. After joining Scovill in 1962, Baldrige single-handedly transformed the brass manufacturer into a diversified conglomerate that produced door chimes, corn poppers, sewing notions, and other consumer goods. Many of Baldrige's future opponents would trace his efforts on the Houdaille petition back to these roots. As David Stockman, one of those antagonists, would later write, "Mac Baldrige was a protectionist-leaning manufacturer . . . [who] had little understanding of free market doctrine and less willingness to hear about it."[5]

At this early and low-level stage, Baldrige did not participate directly in the deliberations over the Houdaille petition. But he made sure that Clyde Prestowitz took an active part. Prestowitz was a political appointee who had joined the Commerce Department in September 1981 as a deputy assistant secretary for international economic policy. The title belied his true role. Baldrige had handpicked Prestowitz to be his point man on trade disputes with the Japanese, and unlike many other political appointees, Prestowitz was superbly prepared for his task. A former journalist, State Department Foreign Service Officer, and businessman, Prestowitz had lived in Japan for many years and spoke the language fluently. At the same time, he was far from being an apologist like many American experts. In fact, Prestowitz and Baldrige saw eye to eye on the need to get tough with Japan, so much so that Prestowitz would rapidly earn a sobriquet inside the government. He would become known as the Commerce Department's, if not the administration's, leading "Jap-basher."[6]

In early September, Copaken had the first of many meetings with Prestowitz about the petition. Prestowitz made no secret of the brief that had been handed him by Baldrige. And even though Commerce was a predictable ally, Copaken was delighted. He could not have asked for a more persuasive, determined champion of Houdaille's cause. Whatever expertise Prestowitz lacked in the details of trade law was more than offset by his grasp of Japan's industrial policy and the fundamental issues at stake.

One of the first things Prestowitz asked Copaken about were his videotapes.[7] A few weeks after submitting the petition in May, Copaken had developed the habit of carrying around a small video cam-recorder whenever he made a visit to Japan. Despite his inability to speak more than a word or two of Japanese, which meant the likelihood of a misunderstanding was great, Copaken took along the camera to nearly all his appointments. His practice was to arrive unannounced at an office, such as the Bicycle Rehabilitation

Association in Tokyo or the Japan Machinery Exporters' Association, and begin asking questions with the camera running. Invariably, the Japanese were nonplussed and didn't know what to think. But they tried to answer the camera-toting foreigner as best they could.[8]

Copaken did not exactly misrepresent himself during the video ambushes, but he did not declare his precise interests either. During one of his first efforts, a May 1982 visit to the Bicycle Rehabilitation Association, a Japanese official asked, "Television?" Copaken replied, "I don't speak Japanese.... [It's] for my own edification right now ... possibly there's a good idea [here] ... a good way for the United States to earn some money." The Japanese official obligingly showed Copaken English-language documents outlining the extent of the association's activities. Included were charts and figures that showed how much bicycle racing contributed to promoting Japan's machinery industries. Afterward Copaken was so pleased by his "60 Minutes"-style coup that he commented, "all we need is another character like that fellow ... who knew just enough [English] to tell us everything we wanted to know and open up his books."[9]

While Copaken labored in the fall of 1982 to acquire enough footage for a hard-hitting video on Japan's industrial policy, Carl Green decided that it was time to borrow several pages from Copaken's game plan. Factual rebuttals were obviously not going to be enough. Belatedly, but not too late, Green recognized that the petition was as much a political issue as it was a question of trade law. He too would have to cultivate the press, seek out allies in the bureaucracy, and, when possible, bring public pressure to bear on the administration.

One of the first things Green tried to balance was the flood of favorable letters that USTR had received. He helped organize a letter-writing campaign against the petition, even though the window for public comment was ostensibly closed.[10] Dozens of letters began pouring into USTR in October, this time in opposition to the petition. American distributors of Japanese tools wrote in protest, as did many satisfied customers. Mazak, the brand name of Yamazaki's U.S. subsidiary, was one of the most effective at generating letters. Some roundly criticized not only Houdaille but the U.S. tool industry as a whole.

One distributor complained:

> The American machine tool industry has lost [its] incentive to compete with other manufacturers to produce quality machines at the lowest possible cost. The Japanese are not smarter than we Americans, they just have more ambition. I should know. I was affiliated with the American machine tool industry for 40 years and the Japanese for 7. This Republican for 44 years does not believe our government will punish people for working.

Another distributor, who sold both domestic and foreign tools, wrote:

It is also amazing to me that some of the United States builders, who are pushing this effort the most, are the very companies that had no reservations about selling their technology 10 or 15 years ago to foreign machine tool builders under licensing arrangements. The fact that these foreign builders have seized this technology and actually improved and leap-frogged the domestic builders is not the fault of the foreign companies. It is the fault of the U.S. manufacturers who have failed to keep pace.

One distributor took Houdaille, and Burgmaster specifically, to task:

> I represented the Burgmaster machining center division of Houdaille Industries from 1970 thru 1978. During that time imported machines were not much of a factor because of less than modern technology. It was very very difficult to compete with other domestic builders as Burgmaster machines were less than average in technology, quality, and they had a horrendous reputation for service and spare parts. That reputation is with them today. . . . In an average month we did more business in Burgmaster parts than my present company has done in Mazak parts in 4 years.[11]

Green also went to great lengths to get his side of the story before the press, specifically, analytical reporters and editorial writers. Although not as media oriented as Copaken, he nevertheless had some personal insight into the profession. Prior to embarking on a law career, Green had spent two years as a correspondent with the *Far Eastern Economic Review*. He saw the media's role as crucial, if only to "cast some sunlight on the proceedings and help forestall a backroom deal."[12]

Green's first break occurred in mid-October. Robert Samuelson, a columnist for the *National Journal*, a small but influential Washington magazine, wrote the first of two articles that discussed the novel petition. He alone emphasized that Houdaille's lawyers, despite churning out reams of documents, had failed to prove the existence of a cartel. The classic elements, price fixing and allocation of market share, were missing, and could not be proven. MITI's role had primarily been exhortative, and Japanese builders were fiercely competitive. Indeed, Samuelson wrote, the only price fixing that could be documented was MITI's insistence on floor prices in 1978 because of complaints from U.S. builders.[13]

This favorable coverage, in turn, helped Green finally locate his champion within the councils of government. It was William Niskanen, a member of the president's Council of Economic Advisers. The CEA generally looked askance at any measure that hampered free trade, and Niskanen, in particular, had a reputation as an outspoken critic of protectionist measures. Prior to joining the Reagan administration, Niskanen had been dismissed by Ford Motor as the company's director of economics in 1980 after he publicly criticized auto industry efforts to restrict Japanese imports.[14]

Green first met with Niskanen in October. He reiterated in painstaking detail his arguments against the Houdaille petition, and explained Copaken's sleight of hand regarding "huge" subsidies to Japan's machine tool industry. He also pointed out that it would "ill behoove" the U.S. government to punish Japan for setting up an antidumping cartel at the request of the Carter administration. Niskanen asked why Green had not distributed his information sooner. Green explained that he had sent twenty copies to USTR, fully expecting that they would be distributed to all interagency participants. Niskanen muttered an expletive. It would not be the last time such procedural irregularities cropped up. But Green came away from the meeting confident that he had "at last found a truth-seeker and a man not easily buffaloed."[15]

While both sides tried furiously to whip up support in the public, the media, and the government, the Houdaille task force continued to meet through September and October. By now it was becoming evident that resolution of the issue was not going to be an ordinary bureaucratic exercise. Task force participants were sharply divided over the merits of the petition, and even more so over the proposed remedy.

USTR, on more than one occasion, tried to circulate a short paper summarizing the issues of law and fact as presented by Houdaille, the Japanese, and all other parties to the case. The paper was not intended to demonstrate "a bias, predisposition, or recommendations for any specific decision or course of action." Once everyone in the task force agreed to the facts, USTR intended to obtain from each task force member specific recommendations for courses of action. Then USTR planned to summarize these recommendations, and with everyone's agreement, submit them to a cabinet-level group for the penultimate decision.[16]

Try as it might, however, USTR found it extraordinarily difficult to accomplish even the first step of the exercise. Neither side was willing to agree to a statement of facts. The division was so deep that to admit or deny certain facts or interpretations of facts seemed tantamount to a decision. On one side, opposed to the petition for a variety of reasons and with varying degrees of conviction, were the Departments of State, Treasury, and Justice, the Council of Economic Advisers, and the Office of Management and Budget. Since they all essentially advocated a policy of free trade, the group dubbed itself the White Hats. On the other side stood the Jap-bashers, namely, USTR and the Commerce Department, or, as they preferred to call themselves, the Realists.[17] Commerce, in particular, considered Houdaille's petition "a credible" exposé of a "MITI-directed cartel." Commerce may not get as good a chance, said one internal memo, "to send a powerful message to the Japanese that predatory competitive practices will be countered by a timely U.S. response." The remaining participants in the interagency meetings, such as the Defense,

Agriculture, and Labor departments, tended to support Houdaille, but had reservations.[18]

In mid-October a rumor started. The administration was going to announce its decision just before the November congressional elections.[19] Presumably, with the economy in a deep recession, a visible swipe at Japan's "unfair" industrial policy might save a few Republicans at the polls.

Copaken did his best to encourage stories in the media about an imminent decision, figuring that it might help break the logjam. Houdaille's legal approach was "a gem buried in the sand of time, waiting to be discovered," he told the *Los Angeles Times*. Copaken also held out Houdaille's remedy as a panacea that would bring immediate relief to the beleaguered tool industry. The Japanese market share would be reduced from 60 percent to 10 percent within two or three years if the president approved the petition, he asserted.[20]

Although Copaken was exaggerating the effects of his proposed tax remedy, he was correct in suggesting that the interagency task force was on the brink of a favorable finding. The sheer mass of Copaken's evidence had proven overwhelming, even though several of his arguments were, to put it mildly, in dispute. But just short of a positive recommendation to the president, the Houdaille juggernaut was stopped dead in its tracks by William Niskanen. At a pivotal juncture, he rallied the White Hats when it looked as though they were going to be routed.[21] Election day came and went, with nary a peep from the administration.

Phil O'Reilly, Houdaille's CEO, was crestfallen. "This [interagency] report has been promised every Friday for the last four weeks," he complained to the press.[22] After the early triumphs enjoyed by Houdaille, O'Reilly had imagined that relief was just a few months away. Now he realized that for all Copaken's ingenuity, there was one real flaw in his strategy. The novelty of the petition could work against, as well as for, Houdaille. Since Section 103 had never been intended as an avenue for relief, there was no deadline, no 90- or 180-day limit that compelled the government to reach a decision. Having taken a decidedly political route, Houdaille was at the mercy of political forces. Meanwhile, the legal bills from Covington & Burling continued to arrive. O'Reilly had no choice now but to see the petition through, no matter what the cost.

The same rumor that lifted and then dashed O'Reilly's hopes caused extreme consternation in Tokyo. The Japanese government had tried to react to the continuing controversy with relative aplomb.[23] But now the political popularity of Jap-bashing seemed unmistakable, and the fundamental nature of the attack on Japan undeniable. Despite Copaken's earlier demur, the Reagan administration *was* using the Houdaille petition as a stalking horse. The goal was to brand Japanese industrial policy unfair and illegal. If the petition succeeded, there was no telling where such a declaration would end. Other "targeted" American industries were dropping broad hints about filing similar complaints.

The Houdaille petition became the topic of headlines in Japanese newspapers, and Copaken and O'Reilly were on their way to becoming celebrities.[24] One Japanese news weekly, mindful of the prejudice that has long troubled Japanese-American relations, hired a Washington research firm to contact the people who had written to USTR in favor of the petition. The magazine wanted to explore whether the Houdaille supporters' opinions were "really based on concrete examples of unfair Japanese competition," or simply reflected "general anti-Japanese sentiment."[25]

Meanwhile, Japanese economic interests, perplexed by the seemingly inscrutable progress of the Houdaille petition, redoubled their efforts to buy access to the decision-making process in Washington. Japan was already notable for having one of the largest and best-financed foreign lobbies. The 1980 Justice Department list of every American consultant and lobbyist on Japan's payroll ran forty pages.[26] Apparently, though, more influence had to be brought to bear.

In particular, the Japan Machine Tool Builders' Association, although not dissatisfied with Carl Green, brought in a second law firm, Anderson, Hibey, Nauheim & Blair, for more advice and lobbying. The Japanese wanted the freshest talent available, which invariably meant the most expensive. The first name partner in the firm, Stanton Anderson, had been a deputy assistant secretary of state from 1973 to 1975, and was a leading Republican party fund raiser.[27] More to the point, Anderson directed the Reagan administration's "transition team" for economic affairs following the 1980 election. That gave him a good feel for who was who in the administration, as well as how and why they were there. Anderson was one of the very first Reagan insiders to exploit his connections, and the JMTBA retainer helped him emerge as the leading Washington lawyer-lobbyist for Japanese trade interests during the 1980s.[28]

As far as Copaken was concerned, the commitment of greater resources by the opposition only raised the stakes, and whetted his competitive spirit. While his client fidgeted, Copaken decided to turn up the political pressure on the administration a notch higher. Organized labor was eager to help, on the grounds that Houdaille was trying to protect domestic jobs. Other "victim" industries, such as the electronics industry, also enlisted because they ostensibly faced similar targeting by the Japanese. Throughout the fall, the USTR received additional letters from the International Association of Machinists, the National Shipbuilders' Council, the Electronic Industries Association, the Semiconductor Industry Association, the American Metal Stamping Association, the steel caucus, and individual companies ranging from Phillip Morris to Motorola. The last one even went one step further. It paid for an expensive, national advertising campaign that complained about Japan's "government-ordained, concerted targeting by selected companies that aims to dominate whole industries worldwide." Motorola's ads also called on the U.S. government to "eliminate, counter or offset" the "market-distorting effects of Japanese government and business policies."[29]

Aided by tips from his allies about the nature of the interagency deadlock, Copaken also tried to influence the internal debate by continuing to pepper the USTR with new facts. Invariably, these were couched in the most dramatic terms possible, and often labeled *"HAND DELIVERED,"* to underscore the urgency of the information. Copaken's favorite, recurring topic was the nature and extent of Japanese government subsidies to the machinery industries.[30] But the sensationalism did not end with claims that he had unearthed previously secret subsidies. In addition, Copaken repeatedly charged the Japanese government with deception. "We have ample proof that it has flat-out lied," he told the media more than once.[31]

By mid-November, in fact, the struggle over the Houdaille petition was being fought as vigorously in the press as it was inside the administration. Nearly every thrust by a journalist cultivated by Carl Green was parried by Copaken or O'Reilly, and vice versa. In a November 8 editorial, the *New York Times* chastised the Reagan administration for egging Houdaille on because it wanted to "scare the Japanese into unrelated trade concessions." "Playing games" with U.S. trade laws would only encourage other countries to do the same. The sooner the White House sent Houdaille packing, the *Times* concluded, the better.[32]

The editorial provoked an immediate and angry letter from O'Reilly. Houdaille had not lost market share because of Japan's hard work, better management, or superior technology.

> Our quarrel is not with Japanese competition. It is with cartel activities, funded with governmental subsidies, which nurtured this competition.
>
> . . . the Japanese technique has been that of the old-fashioned monopolist, funded by a national government.
>
> We can compete successfully with any machine-tool company in the world. We cannot compete with a nation that has targeted us for extinction.[33]

This rebuttal echoed comments that O'Reilly, suddenly in demand as a speaker, was making before numerous audiences. His opening line always grabbed attention: To everyone who claims that "we ought to be ashamed of ourselves for letting the Japanese beat us with their superior quality, better economics, improved technology, etc. . . . To all of that, let me say phooey." O'Reilly would then assert that Japan's "achievements in large measure have resulted from very well organized, very well implemented plans initiated by the Japanese government to target major penetration of world markets for various Japanese industry groups."[34]

If O'Reilly was flattered by all the attention, it was outweighed by his exasperation at the U.S. government. The bureaucracy was moving at a snail's pace while Houdaille remained strapped in its triple bind. If anything, the conglomerate's predicament had become worse in the sixteen months that had passed since O'Reilly first decided to turn to Washington for relief. Moreover, by late November 1982, Houdaille's legal bill was nearly $750,000, with still no end in sight.[35]

Copaken, anxious to pacify his client, now decided to deploy the video weapon he and Prestowitz had discussed several months earlier. By portraying himself as an "interested" and "impressed" lawyer who was making a videotape for a lot of "interested" people in Washington who couldn't come to Japan, Copaken had been able to gain unusual access with his camera (a Japanese Hitachi). In addition to the Bicycle Rehabilitation Association, he had taped interviews with engineers at subsidized research laboratories throughout Japan, and meetings with MITI officials. He had even had the presence of mind to obtain footage of a bicycle race in Tokyo, replete with lines of bettors—to "add color," as he put it.[36]

Copaken edited the hours of tape down to segments lasting no more than twenty-five minutes or so. Anything that could be construed as contradicting Copaken's vision of a seamless cartel was left out of the final tapes. He added voice-overs to explain what was going on to viewers and heighten the drama. "This is where it all takes place," he intoned during one segment as the videotape zeroed in on one of the government-subsidized research labs.[37]

With the help of his Commerce Department and USTR allies, Copaken held a private screening at the White House in mid-December. Every member of the interagency Houdaille task force was present. The "extraordinary images," to use Copaken's words, moved his audience like no lawyer's brief ever could. A "deeply-impressed" White House official later told *Fortune* magazine that "it was quite a little show-and-tell." Copaken brazenly asserted to his audience that there could no longer be any doubt "as to whose version of the facts was correct." Japan, for all intents and purposes, was bent on carving up the world machine tool market.[38]

Publicly, even to those who had not seen the video, Copaken claimed the same thing. The petition's "legal issues have already been settled," he told a trade publication. "The decision to grant this petition or not is essentially political."[39] If this was an overstatement, Copaken nevertheless operated as if it were true. The winner would be whichever side mustered the most political support. And that set the stage for Copaken's most ambitious political effort since the petition's submission seven months earlier.

Securing the support of key congressmen and senators, in the form of letters, was standard operating procedure for Copaken. Getting members to make telephone calls to the administration was more difficult. And getting them to hold congressional hearings and insert strongly worded statements into the *Congressional Record* took even more work, since that often meant

Copaken had to write the questions and the statements himself. He had done all this and more in the Houdaille case. For Copaken believed, "The prosecution of a major political trade case involves the orchestration of numerous actions by a number of individuals in several different institutions, many proceeding simultaneously, and all of which must be designed to work in concert."[40]

Virtually any special interest, however, can find members of Congress to act on an individual basis. A step considerably more difficult is to turn congressional pressure one notch higher by obtaining joint action. That was exactly what Copaken now had in mind. It just might be the extra push needed to get the Houdaille petition over the top.

Copaken deemed that a "Sense of the Senate" resolution would be the most desirable expression of congressional will. Subsequently William Brock, head of USTR, met with members of the Senate Finance Committee behind closed doors, and told them of the interagency deadlock. Out of that meeting came an agreement to pass a resolution before the Senate adjourned.[41] Republican senator Charles Grassley of Iowa, whose state contained several machine tool companies and a Houdaille division, introduced the Copaken-authored resolution on Wednesday, December 15, 1982. Senate Resolution 525, as it was numbered, initially carried seventeen cosponsors (six Democrats and eleven Republicans), and wholeheartedly endorsed Houdaille's allegations.

> Whereas the Government of Japan has selected the United States high-technology industry in numerically-controlled machine tools for domination through unfair trade practices; and
>
> Whereas the Petition . . . submitted by Houdaille . . . thoroughly documents continuing anticompetitive cartel policies and practices, including the financing of a machine-tool cartel with multi-billion dollar off-budget subsidies earned from bicycle- and motorcycle-race wagering, employed by the Government of Japan to further its industry-targeting goals . . .
>
> *Resolved*, That it is the sense of the Senate that the President should issue an Executive Order disqualifying Japanese-manufactured, numerically-controlled machining centers and punching machines from the United States investment tax credit.[42]

After the resolution was introduced, Copaken took full advantage of an opportunity presented by the pre-Christmas rush to adjourn. During December, the Senate often tries to cram in as much business as possible before the holidays, and consequently, the *Congressional Record* often comes out two or three days late. Copaken was off and running, lining up additional cosponsors at a "feverish pace," days before Carl Green and Stanton Anderson, the JMTBA's counsel and chief lobbyist, even knew the resolution was in the hopper.[43]

It did not prove difficult to sell the proposed resolution, especially after Copaken devised an argument to counter one of the most telling objections to the Houdaille petition. The petition had provoked vehement opposition inside the administration because it threatened to open up a Pandora's box. If Japan's industrial policy toward machine tools was declared a restraint on U.S. commerce, there would be no end to similar complaints from other high-tech industries, such as computers, robotics, and optics. Lawyers for the semiconductor industry, for one, were already hard at work assembling a "much clearer case" than the one Houdaille presented.[44]

Implicitly recognizing this weakness, Copaken deftly skirted the issue by focusing exclusively on the proposed tax remedy. It "could be the ideal surgical instrument in the president's hands to fight off cartelized trade," he told Congress and the media. "He could choose which products to penalize and from which countries."[45] Before long, Copaken had added three cosponsors to the original seventeen, and his coalition featured senators of virtually every political stripe.

Japan's highly paid lobbyists and lawyers tried frantically to chip away at the resolution's backers. A Japanese automobile company that had just opened a major plant in the Midwest contacted a senator who had cosponsored the resolution and pressured him into backpedaling. Copaken, much better versed in Capitol Hill politics than his opponents, was swift to respond to even this slight erosion. He quickly learned that the auto plant was nonunion, and brought the story of the senator's waffling to the attention of a "feisty" AFL-CIO lobbyist. Before the senator could publicly disavow the resolution, telegrams were sent from his home state "congratulating" him for staunchly backing Houdaille.[46]

The senator found himself between a rock and a hard place. He could hardly help lead the charge against Japan, given the major investment in his state and the promise of more to come. But he could not publicly repudiate the resolution either. The most he felt he could do was remove his name as a cosponsor.

Meanwhile Copaken added a few more senators to the list of cosponsors, which now totaled twenty-six. On Tuesday, December 21, as the Senate worked late into the night, the resolution came up for a voice vote. Unwittingly, the lobbyists for Japan had committed a crucial error by allowing the news of the senator's defection to leak out. The only way the resolution was going to reach the Senate floor that evening was through a suspension of the rules, which required unanimous consent. As Copaken delighted in acknowledging later, his opponents could have easily blocked passage by "using the one Senator [they] controlled to quietly express to his party leader his unwillingness to see the rules suspended."[47] Instead, the resolution passed by voice vote, with no dissent. Afterward, Republican Senator John Heinz summed up the sense of the Senate: "The resolution was aimed at making it clear that many of us in this country are not prepared to sit still and allow our industries to be decimated by unfair trade."[48]

Heinz's comment illustrated another political dividend from the Senate resolution. Not only was it a valuable measure of congressional support—now the petition could be upheld as a "moderate" solution compared to more "demonic" proposals waiting in the wings (such as a proposal to deny the investment tax credit to all imported goods).[49] Both Copaken and O'Reilly would shrewdly employ this argument time and again in the weeks ahead. To avoid congressional agitation for "onerous" new legislation that was blatantly protectionist, Houdaille argued, the president should demonstrate his willingness to abide by laws that were already on the books.[50] This position also dovetailed nicely with Copaken's insistence that Houdaille was not aiming a broadside at Japan, but placing a "surgical instrument" in the president's hands.

What had started out seven months ago as a simple duet, Copaken and O'Reilly, was now a symphony chorus, conducted by Copaken and with O'Reilly as lead baritone. There were one or two dissonant voices after the Senate resolution passed. A *New York Times* editorial, mimicking the language of the resolution, "RESOLVED that it be the sense of the *public* that the President refuse to set a dangerous precedent."[51] But otherwise, media coverage of the Senate resolution was amazingly positive, given that the facts, not to mention Houdaille's conclusions, were subject to dispute.

Even the *Times* ran a story, one day before its editorial blast appeared, that seemed to suggest that sympathy, more than criticism, was in order. In "How Competition Led Houdaille to Ask Trade Curb," the Japanese and then the overall economic recession, in that order, were assigned responsibility for Houdaille's predicament. The remaining strap of Houdaille's triple bind—the leveraged buyout—was mentioned only in passing. There was nothing about how it saddled Houdaille with a usurious debt.[52]

The press attention and political chorus conducted by Copaken were not the only sources of pressure on the administration. Objective facts were putting heat on the administration as well. The economic recession, along with Japanese imports, was wreaking havoc in the machine tool industry as a whole, not only at Houdaille. U.S. builders were mired in their deepest slump ever in the winter of 1982, with worse still to come. Adjusted for inflation, the total value of shipments was heading for its lowest level since World War II, and nearly every builder would be awash in red ink. The "strong" dollar, propelled upward by high interest rates, would enable imports to garner 34 percent of the U.S. market.[53]

The administration manifested its concern over the tool industry's crisis by doing what comes naturally to all governments—studying the problem. By December 1982, the administration had asked the Central Intelligence Agency to prepare a classified report on the Japanese machine tool industry and, in addition, had initiated two major public inquiries.[54] Under a 1981 contract with the Defense Department, the National Academy of Sciences was in the midst of a comprehensive study of the tool industry.[55] The International Trade Commission, an authoritative and quasi-judicial body, meanwhile announced an exhaustive, "competitive assessment" of the U.S. tool industry in December 1982. This inquiry was of special interest and concern to Copaken. It necessarily involved an independent evaluation of many of the questions raised in the Houdaille petition, in particular, the issue of Japanese government subsidies and attempts to cartelize the industry. But Copaken planned to have a decision in the Houdaille case long before the ITC published its report.[56]

For the most part, then, Copaken welcomed all of the additional attention. The industry's troubles and the plethora of studies tended to redound to Houdaille's political advantage because they reinforced the atmosphere of crisis. They also made the Florida conglomerate appear to be something of a bold seer. At the same time, Houdaille's counsel was deeply worried about a competitive effort at import relief, another petition that might overshadow Houdaille's.

He knew such an effort was in the works. Covington & Burling, his own law firm and longtime counsel to the National Machine Tool Builders' Association, was hard at work on a sweeping petition to restrict imports. At its national convention in December, the NMTBA announced publicly its intention to ask for protection from imports, citing Section 232, the so-called national security clause. This provision authorized the president to take whatever steps were necessary to limit imports, of any product, that threatened to impair the national security.

Copaken feared that this petition would clutter his agenda and the administration's. He wanted an up or down decision on the Houdaille petition before the complaint was lost in a din of protest from the entire machine tool industry. Although a "232" petition would be handled bureaucratically as a separate matter, Copaken recognized that it would inevitably work its way into interagency deliberations on the Houdaille case.[57]

But there was no way to persuade the NMBTA to hold off. As the trade association was quick to point out, if the Houdaille petition were granted it would presumably only rescind the tax credit for Japanese machining centers and punching machines. That left dozens of other kinds of U.S. tools unprotected. Besides, the NMTBA argued, what if the administration ended up rejecting the Houdaille petition?

There was another factor at work here too. Despite the NMTBA's public displays of support for Houdaille, many builders in the trade association were acidly critical of the petition. They knew Houdaille's case was mostly buncombe, because the NMTBA had carried out its own investigation of the Japanese tool industry in 1981. That inquiry concluded that Japan's success derived from "the willingness of management to invest heavily in its future, market its products aggressively throughout the world, work doggedly toward long-term goals, and pay an unusual amount of attention to the training and motivation of its workforce."[58]

Well aware of this criticism, Copaken had kept the NMTBA at arm's length from the outset. Houdaille notified the association that it intended to file the petition just a few days before submission, and Copaken did not coordinate his subsequent tactics with the NMTBA.[59] Now, with the association intent on asserting what it considered a legitimate defense, tensions between the NMTBA and its most outspoken member increased.

Copaken took some consolation in one fact. The "232" petition and supporting legal briefs were at least two months away from being ready for submission. By that time, he fully expected his own uphill struggle to be over. After all, he was clearly outmaneuvering his opponents so far. At least it seemed that way.

MITI felt stung by the Senate resolution once the text reached Japan. Within days, it issued its strongest protest to date. In a written statement, the ministry's top official, Sadanori Yamanaka, asserted that the Senate was lending support to a remedy that violated GATT, bilateral treaty obligations, and the free trading system.[60] The ministry decided to send a delegation to Washington to "correct misunderstandings" about the Houdaille petition. The message carried by Chikao Tsukuda, a deputy vice minister for industrial policy, was that "MITI is quite vocal, but what it has been doing is less than what it says. It is simply wrong to say that Japanese industry policy is the result of MITI actions."[61]

Simultaneously, MITI sought to appease American opinion by making a substantive concession. The ministry announced that as of January 1, 1983, the floor price of all NC machining centers and lathes exported to the United States would be increased by 10 percent. The upward revision was explained as an adjustment made necessary by the falling value of the yen relative to the dollar.[62]

The highest levels of the Japanese government were also extremely concerned about the direction the petition was taking, particularly since Prime Minister Yasuhiro Nakasone was scheduled to make his first visit to Washington in mid-January. In the past, there had been many harsh differences with the Americans over trade and investment. Now the Americans seemed bent on wresting a concession that was tantamount to demanding that Japan cease exercising a sovereign right. Industrial policy, to the Japanese, was a necessary and proper role for government, inextricably linked to sound management of their economy and the husbanding of Japan's resources. As one American scholar put it, "The problem with going after industrial policy is that it amounts to declaring Japan illegal. You can't just do that."[63]

Some Japanese critics suggested that the Houdaille petition raised the right questions, but that its locus was misplaced. In other words, it properly raised the question of industrial policy, but industrial policy, or lack of it, in the

United States was the genuine issue. Indeed, the notion of a conscious industrial policy was just beginning to be widely debated in the United States in 1982–1983. Some of the same factors that had led to the petition were prompting the industrial policy debate. And notwithstanding Copaken's astute politicking, in retrospect the coincidence between this debate and the Houdaille case was a major reason why the petition grabbed so much attention.

The year 1982 had been perhaps the most economically disastrous since the Great Depression. Imports, interest rates, and unemployment soared as thousands of workers saw their skilled jobs wiped out. A public debate began as forces usually associated with the Democratic party clamored for the party to take a stand on the economy. Soon there was a surfeit of proposals that all carried the "industrial policy" rubric. But its charm rapidly began to wear thin as the Democrats bickered over what it exactly meant. Help for "sunset" industries to modernize? Seed loans for "sunrise" industries only? It became all too apparent that to many interests, industrial policy merely signaled pork-barrel politics, a grab bag of favors for selected industries or regions. Then too, some Democrats were extremely leery of industrial policy for fear of being labeled creeping socialists.[64]

While the Democrats engaged in a desultory search for an industrial policy, the Republican party shunned the idea entirely. Its solution to the decline of the industrial economy, aside from doses of thinly disguised protectionism, was less government, as in less taxes, less antitrust enforcement, less regulation. The reason was put most succinctly by Lionel Olmer, under secretary of commerce for international trade:

> Industrial policy . . . means establishing a national planning unit with authority to pick industrial "winners" and "losers" and to divide up government favors accordingly. Such a policy would, of course, distort the critical functioning of the free market. But it would also create a bureaucratic nightmare—one destined to be controlled by political pressures rather than any kind of rational process.[65]

As one scholar noted at the time, "Any government that cannot define its role in the economy is in trouble."[66] Together, the Democratic debate and Republican critique added up to an unenlightening exchange on the proper functions of government, an abdication rather than an assertion of responsibility. But just as fundamental as this failure was the parties' unwillingness to recognize that a de facto and ad hoc industrial policy existed, whether or not it was part of the political consciousness. The government's visible hand decided how much industry had to pay for capital; the government's visible hand, more than any other institution outside the family, determined the skills and education of the American work force; and the government's visible hand acted as a tiller on the economy, steering it away from the manufacture of

goods that could be used to create greater wealth to goods whose use everyone hoped to avoid.

Given this abdication in the middle of the worst recession since the
1930s, it was inevitable that Japan, since it was not going to be a model,
became a villain. The Houdaille petition's timing in this respect was uncanny;
as one government official noted, "it seem[ed] to confirm Americans' worst
suspicions about Japan's trade practices."[67] There had to be an untoward explanation for the Japanese challenge to American superiority, and the predisposition to believe that Japan was engaged in an industrial conspiracy was
the political well from which Copaken could draw again and again. Even
during an administration that branded the Soviet Union an evil empire, more
genuine anger was reserved and directed at an ostensible ally. Japan was
perhaps the only country in the world from which congressional delegations
returned more hostile than when they left. As Senator Charles Grassley, the
chief sponsor of the Senate resolution, said, "something drastic" had to be
done to get Japan's attention, and that something was the Houdaille
petition.[68]

The dispute over Houdaille was a major question mark in American-
Japanese relations in January 1983, and one reason why these relations were
at their lowest ebb since 1945. The impending visit of Prime Minister
Nakasone was not a moment too soon. In turn, it incited both sides engaged in
the Houdaille dispute to redouble their efforts. Partisans of the petition
wanted to hand the Japanese a fait accompli. Opponents, with equal fervor,
wanted to dispense with the petition before it poisoned the waters more.[69]

Copaken was optimistic, firm in the belief that the momentum was all on
Houdaille's side. "We've nailed this case down tight," he told *The Wall Street
Journal* just days before Nakasone arrived. "We've everything in there including the smoking gun."[70] Copaken's "videotape lawyering" was reaping almost
as much attention as O'Reilly's copyright gambit back in May. Requests to see
the videos rivaled early demand for the Houdaille petition, and Copaken
reveled in his new role as film maker. *Fortune* magazine even prepared a small
article on Copaken's imaginative ploy."I'm a frustrated Fellini," Copaken told
the magazine, although his style was more aptly described as borrowed from
Mike Wallace.[71]

As for Copaken's opponent, Carl Green, he was frustrated and angry to
the same degree that Copaken was upbeat and optimistic. For one, Green had
noticed that despite his efforts to regularly monitor the official, public file on
the Houdaille case, on more than one occasion he was caught unawares by a
new fact alleged by Copaken. Sometimes he read the new allegation in the
press, other times he learned about it during a conversation with a government official. In any case, Copaken's allegations were not always inserted into
the file even when they were accepted as part of the official record. Green also
found, to his shock, that his rejoinders did not always receive the same wide

circulation that Copaken's allegations enjoyed. "Key officials had not been exposed to our briefs," recalled Green.[72]

Copaken's video antics were another source of frustration to the JMTBA's lawyer. Since they were shown in secret, they amounted to an ex parte (one-sided) communication to the government, which was irregular and unfair. The unprecedented nature of Houdaille's petition had not changed the ground rules, Green protested. He demanded that the videos, along with verbatim transcripts, be made part of the official public record if they were going to be accepted as evidence.[73]

In early January, Green's exasperation reached a new high. He was astonished by the news stories that appeared following passage of the Senate resolution in December. It became clear to Green that not only had William Brock, USTR's head, lobbied in favor of the resolution, but USTR had also aided and abetted Copaken long before the petition was even formally submitted. Any recommendation to the president from USTR "would be so tainted with bias as to be meaningless," asserted Green in a scathing letter to Brock. Green asked the USTR to terminate the entire proceeding immediately and disqualify itself from any future reconsideration of the Houdaille petition.[74]

Everything Green claimed in his January letter was true, and all the more surprising given USTR's carefully built reputation for integrity. But neither the proceeding nor USTR's involvement would come to a halt. Brock smoothed ruffled feathers, pledged to ensure due process, and then resumed the struggle to win relief for Houdaille. Unknown to either Copaken or Green, the logjam inside the government was at last showing faint signs of movement.

By January 1983, debate over the petition was no longer confined to the ad hoc Houdaille task force. At one point or another the case had been placed on the agenda of nearly every standing interagency committee with any responsibility for trade and commerce. These included two sub-cabinet groups, the Trade Policy Staff Committee and the Trade Policy Review Group, and two cabinet-level groups: the Trade Policy Committee, chaired by William Brock, and the cabinet Council on Commerce and Trade, presided over by Malcolm Baldrige. Regardless of venue, however, the order of battle on both sides remained essentially the same. The leading Jap-bashers were invariably Brock and Baldrige, or their representatives. "At most of those meetings it was Brock and Baldrige against the world," one high administration official later recalled.[75]

These deliberations were also notable for their extraordinary rancor and outbursts of temper. The petition seemed to incite internecine warfare, and more than one meeting was marked by shouting and "vituperous" language.[76] What had begun as a skirmish between White Hats and Jap-bashers had become nothing less than the main battleground in the Republicans' ongoing war between so-called free and fair trade.

After a very long and hard labor, USTR had finally managed to come up with "factual findings" that were not rejected outright by either side. Nor were they exactly embraced. The USTR document recited how the Japanese government had promoted, subsidized, and otherwise encouraged domestic builders, although its findings fell way short of what Houdaille had claimed.[77] Still, the White Hats fiercely resisted the conclusions the Jap-bashers wanted to draw from the findings. They argued that it would be no more logical for the United States to penalize Japan for its industrial policy than it would be for Japan to damn the United States for its agricultural policy.

Both sides fought tenaciously before Prime Minister Nakasone's visit in mid-January, but neither could prevail over the other.[78] Nevertheless, the pressure of that impending visit, along with spreading uneasiness over Houdaille's proposed tax remedy, were finally causing some movement in the bureaucratic stalemate.

The breakthrough of sorts occurred during a meeting of the Trade Policy Committee (TPC) on January 13, four days before Nakasone was scheduled to arrive in Washington. The seniority of the officials who attended (William Brock, Treasury Secretary Donald Regan, state and commerce under secretaries, and a justice assistant secretary) was an indication of the bureaucratic prize at stake. The meeting began on an old and frustrating note, namely, the question of government subsidies. The American tool industry had also been the beneficiary of assistance from government, the White Hats pointed out, dating back to the 1950s when the air force underwrote NC research through its Advanced Manufacturing Techniques Program (ManTech). In 1981, the Pentagon's ManTech funding was more than $150 million, much of which served as an R&D subsidy to the U.S. tool industry. Nor did ManTech represent the sum of the federal subsidy, since other Pentagon programs as well as other agencies, notably NASA, underwrote "factories of the future."[79]

The debate then moved to the cartel issue. Led as usual by William Niskanen, the White Hats vigorously asserted that the only true cartel-like action undertaken by the Japanese had occurred in 1978, when floor prices were set in response to U.S. complaints. To take action against Japan would be protectionism in the extreme. It would also hurt U.S. consumers by raising the price of Japanese machines.[80] The Jap-bashers accused their opponents of naïvete, and for a time it appeared as if this round were going to end just as inconclusively as all the others.

But then, perhaps out of sheer exhaustion, a partial consensus began to emerge. During every interagency debate, Treasury had never wavered in its adamant opposition to Houdaille's proposed tax remedy, even after Copaken deployed former Senator John Sherman Cooper to lobby in favor of it. Treasury again pointed out that at every GATT negotiation since the 1960s, the United States had argued against all efforts to use national tax laws for trade purposes. Accepting the Houdaille remedy in 1983 would be unconscionable. Gradually, even USTR had to admit to some doubts about the wisdom of denying the investment tax credit to Japanese tools. Only Commerce resolutely stuck to the position that the remedy was "GATT-able."[81]

Finally, the TPC more or less agreed to discard the notion of a favorable finding along the lines proposed by Houdaille. Aside from the GATT problem, even Commerce recognized that a Section 103 ruling would be far too limited to help the tool industry overall. Houdaille had only asked for sanctions against Japanese punching machines and machining centers. Even if O'Reilly's 15 percent solution were applied to machine tools across-the-board, it was unlikely to offer sufficient protection against Japanese imports.[82]

Yet this concession by the Jap-bashers did not mean that the White Hats had won. Far from it. Although they were willing to dispense with Copaken's fanciful legal interpretation, the Jap-bashers claimed that Houdaille could not be turned away empty-handed. Its petition proved that the Japanese government and machine tool industry had engaged in an unholy alliance. The government's failure to grant any relief now would send precisely the wrong message to Japan, the pro-Houdaille bloc argued.

A sharp discussion ensued. The TPC participants hotly debated the wisdom of other possible remedies, especially quotas, either imposed by the United States or self-imposed by Japan. Finally, everyone agreed to let USTR attempt to develop a new remedy, along with the necessary legal justification. The Jap-bashers had managed to keep the Houdaille case alive, although the White Hats made no promises.

Privately, the Commerce and USTR officials who were insisting upon relief were motivated by something more than their sympathy for Houdaille, and their concern for the plight of the tool industry. Reflecting their fundamental concern over the size and nature of the trade deficit, they yearned to keep Japan on the defensive, apparently hoping that the pressure would lead to unilateral concessions in several high-tech industries, not just machine tools. As Clyde Prestowitz wrote in an earlier memo to Lionel Olmer, under secretary of commerce,

> I am reminded of your comments about "stirring the pot." Some positive action on this petition would be a wonderful way to keep the pot stirring. It would create uncertainty on the part of the Japanese not only with regard to machine tools, but also with regard to robotics and other targeted industries. I think we both agree this would be a good thing.[83]

On January 28, the Trade Policy Committee, chaired by William Brock, met again. It was the first session in the wake of the Nakasone visit, which had come off surprisingly well. (Reagan and Nakasone would soon begin referring to each other on a first-name basis.) The 4:00 P.M. meeting was devoted to a single topic: trade frictions with Japan. In particular, the participants gathered to discuss whether to "keep the pressure on" or "to take it easy." Nakasone had promised to further liberalize Japan's economy, a move some thought would "de-fuze" trade frictions. The Houdaille petition figured prominently in the discussion.[84]

In the two weeks since the last TPC meeting, USTR had been hard at work trying to come up with a law that the Houdaille petition could be hitched onto. The agency came to believe that a presidential finding under Section 301 of the Trade Act of 1974 would be the best course of action. The statute authorized the president to impose trade sanctions against any country engaged in a policy that was "unjustifiable, unreasonable, or discriminatory and burdens or restricts United States commerce."[85] The president could pick and choose from a wide variety of sanctions, everything from an outright embargo to tariffs or quotas. Most important, the statute expressly invited private parties to petition the president, via USTR, for relief. All along, of course, Houdaille's Section 103 petition had been treated procedurally as a Section 301 petition by USTR. This meant that there would be a veneer of legality to the magical transformation the Jap-bashers were intent on performing.

There were alternatives, of course, which USTR felt compelled to include in its proposal to the TPC. The most reasonable perhaps was a finding under Section 201 of the trade law. This provision authorized the president to impose tariffs or quotas whenever an industry was being seriously injured by imports. If it invoked the statute, however, the administration would be implicitly acknowledging that the injury to U.S. tool builders had arisen from perfectly fair competition.[86]

In the USTR paper presented to the TPC on January 28, both an expedited "301" finding and a "201" investigation were listed as possible courses of action. In addition, to demonstrate the seriousness of American resolve, USTR proposed immediate, unilateral steps to restrict imports of Japanese tools pending the government's final decision. USTR also suggested simultaneous consultations with the Japanese government on the trade effects of industrial policy.[87]

The USTR proposal satisfied no one, including USTR's erstwhile ally the Commerce Department. Consultations would be naïve, Commerce argued. They would only give the Japanese an ideal excuse to stall. Moreover, Commerce was aghast at the notion of a Section 201 finding. The statute, although rarely invoked, was blatantly protectionist. The Japanese would have ample grounds for suggesting that the U.S. government was simply "trying to penalize their success." No agency, not even USTR, was more intent than Commerce on using the Houdaille case to establish a precedent, namely, that the flood of Japanese tools had resulted from unfair industrial targeting.[88]

The White Hats vigorously objected as well, but for the opposite reasons. It almost went without saying that the White Hats opposed a protectionist "201" finding. But they also argued vehemently against resorting to Section 301. Any such finding would require an acrobatic interpretation and retroactive application of the law, they argued. Section 301, the White Hats pointed out, only applied to *ongoing* violations of fair trade practices. Everyone agreed that the Japanese had ceased using, long ago, nearly all of the so-called unfair practices cited in the Houdaille petition. The use of racing proceeds and other government subsidies to the machine tool industry were virtually the only "targeting" tactics still officially condoned by the Japanese government. The White Hats maintained that Houdaille was free to initiate a countervailing duty investigation by the Commerce Department, but that was all. And everyone at the TPC meeting knew what that meant. MITI's subsidies were too negligible to justify any duties on Japanese imports.[89]

By this time, the Houdaille case had been the subject of more deliberations than any other trade issue during the Reagan presidency. It was a dubious distinction. Moreover, the bureaucratic deadlock was as bad as ever, perhaps worse. Earlier, the squabble had pivoted around the tax remedy proposed by Houdaille, and whether or not it was a proper application of trade law. Eventually a consensus was reached and a Section 103 finding was dismissed as untenable. But in the process, other issues were exposed. *Everything* was now subject to question and argument: the facts, the remedy, and the appropriate law. The Jap-bashers had already been forced to backpedal once from their original position. They were not about to abandon a Section 301 finding now, because it represented their last hope of branding Japanese industrial policy as unfair.[90] If necessary, they were prepared to take their case all the way to the president.

At this point, in early February, William Brock decided to attempt a classic bureaucratic maneuver. He was tired of being thwarted and wanted to have a decision before he left for a trip to the Far East.[91] So he decided to bring in a new player. At his behest, presidential counselor Edwin Meese, Reagan's longtime associate and chief adviser, stepped in. The Trade Policy Committee had wearily scheduled another meeting on the Houdaille petition for February 4, a Friday. The meeting was suddenly canceled, and instead, Meese agreed to convene a select group to decide the matter in his office on Thursday afternoon.[92]

When Brock and Malcolm Baldrige arrived in Meese's office, they found three other persons there in addition to the president's counselor: James Baker, the White House chief of staff; Edwin Harper, a top presidential assistant; and W. Allen Wallis, under secretary of state for economic affairs. Conspicuous by his absence was Robert (Tim) McNamar, deputy secretary of the treasury. He had represented Treasury Secretary Donald Regan at many of the cabinet-level meetings on the Houdaille petition, and, after Niskanen, was emerging as a leader of the White Hats, and certainly the most vociferous.[93]

The meeting immediately got down to business. Outmanned and lower in seniority than nearly everyone else in attendance, Allen Wallis was no match for the overwhelmingly pro-Houdaille sentiment. The ad hoc committee quickly came to a consensus. The administration had to respond in a positive way to the Houdaille petition, and protect the beleaguered U.S. tool industry. Although the exact remedy eluded the group, one specific decision was made. Meese instructed Brock, who was about to leave for Japan, to inform MITI that a finding would be made against them in the Houdaille case, most likely under Section 301.[94]

Brock did as ordered. The next week he told MITI Minister Yamanaka that a consensus had been reached on the Houdaille case "at the highest levels" of the White House. The Reagan administration intended to brand Japanese industrial policy unfair, specifically, its targeting of the machine tool industry. The nature of the remedy was still undecided; indeed, if Japan took "appropriate measures" it might render U.S. action unnecessary. The idea was to prod Japan into announcing "voluntary" restraints on exports, or perhaps even an export tax on all NC machines shipped to the United States. Such actions, since they would be self-imposed, would completely remove the legal onus from the United States. (Virtually any Section 301 finding was likely to violate American obligations under GATT.) The Japanese were shocked by Brock's message, in the wake of Nakasone's seemingly successful visit.[95]

Meanwhile, back in Washington, USTR began asking various agencies for their suggestions on quotas, tariffs, or other possible sanctions. Now that a decision favorable to Houdaille was set, the administration had to decide what it wanted and, failing any action from Tokyo, what it was prepared to do unilaterally.[96] Before all the suggestions were in, however, the Japanese blinked. Presumably they wanted to avoid, at all costs, a presidential finding that would label their industrial policy as unfair. Although it was publicly denied, MITI reportedly offered to negotiate a voluntary restraint agreement, using the 1981 VRA on Japanese automobile exports as a model.[97]

Before the administration could take up the Japanese offer, Tim McNamar complained bitterly about Meese's end run. The deputy treasury secretary had learned the full story about the Japanese "offer," namely, that it came subsequent to a secret meeting in Ed Meese's office. Officials from OMB and CEA, two other White Hats that had been kept in the dark, were also furious. The consensus that had been reached in Meese's office immediately fell apart. The White Hats wanted no part of the voluntary Japanese concession. And the Jap-bashers, firmly convinced that the president would ultimately side with them, abandoned the idea too. Why settle for half a loaf, they figured, when with Meese's powerful backing, the whole loaf and an invaluable precedent were in sight?[98] "Government-directed industrial policy and how it affects Japanese performance in the United States is more important than the openness of the Japanese markets," Commerce Under Secretary Olmer told a group of trade lawyers in February.[99]

Around this time, Copaken's Jap-bashing allies finally told him what was going on. He was not pleased to hear that his inventive "103" remedy had been consigned to the dustbin. He recognized, however, that even though he had lost that particular battle, Houdaille seemed to be winning the war. "Like Uncle Remus' Br'er Rabbit about to be tossed in the Briar Patch," Copaken later wrote, "Houdaille complained, but only half-heartedly since Section 301 conferred very broad discretion on the President." In public, Copaken tried to obscure even the meaning of the tactical defeat. He invariably suggested that his proposed remedy had been abandoned primarily because it was deemed insufficient, a penalty that Japanese tool builders could all too easily absorb.[100] Privately, he tried to assuage O'Reilly, who was practically inconsolable. More than eight months of effort and a $1 million in legal work had failed to bring Houdaille the government succor it so desperately needed.

At USTR's request, Copaken submitted an alternative proposal, now that the tax remedy had been ruled out. After citing a dozen sources on the large inventories of unsold Japanese machining centers already in the United States, the reports of price cutting by Japanese manufacturers, and the depressed U.S. demand for machine tools, the lawyer for Houdaille made an immodest proposal. "Our client believes, " Copaken wrote, "that a temporary embargo may be essential." He suggested that such a ban would probably have to last two years if it were to be a truly effective remedy.[101]

As usual, through no fault of his own, Carl Green was slow to learn about the transmogrification of the Houdaille petition. In fact, it wasn't until he read a copy of Copaken's letter proposing an embargo that Green realized the rules of the game had been changed. Of course, the Houdaille case, in procedural terms, had long ceased to resemble any trade case Green had ever heard of. Even so, he was flabbergasted when he realized the meaning of the latest turn of events. It was unprecedented for the government to accept a trade petition under one law, and then unilaterally assign it to another. He registered his "grave objections" to such "irregular and secretive proceedings," which "could not be reconciled with fundamental principles of due process." His protest went unanswered. Later he would remark ironically, "and [here] we were, telling the Japanese to make their trade policy more transparent."[102]

In March, while Copaken busily added to his paper mountain of allegations, which by now ran to almost 2,000 pages, interagency groups inside the administration, both at the cabinet and subcabinet levels, continued their struggle over the Houdaille case. No one was looking forward to the Trade Policy Committee meeting scheduled for March 10. There was little reason to believe that anyone's position, after nine months of hardening, was susceptible to change. USTR, Commerce, Defense, and Labor all supported taking action immediately, while State, Treasury, OMB, CEA, and Justice stood in opposition.[103] The Japanese had also made clear their position: they were prepared to both increase prices and limit volume if the U.S. government desisted from a "301" finding. But the Jap-bashers considered Japan's sensitivity to such a finding all the more reason to do it.[104]

Accusations and recriminations were hurled back and forth during the March 10 meeting of the principals, as the heads of the various agencies were called. The USTR and Commerce Department stoutly maintained that as a result of Meese's intervention, a cabinet-level decision in support of a "301" finding had already been made. The only issue now, the Jap-bashers claimed, was the exact remedy.[105] Just as fervently, the White Hats denied ever reaching a deal. Moreover, they claimed, despite all the sound and fury no one had yet proved that Japan had done anything illegal. The Jap-bashers countered with a curious argument. Although each of the individual Japanese actions may not have been illegal or unfair, the totality amounted to unfair trade, even if it wasn't strictly illegal. U.S. companies were being forced to compete on uneven terms with Japanese companies.[106]

The debate was so strident that it tended to obscure a significant softening in the State Department's position. State had always been among the whitest of the White Hats. But it was edging away from its absolutist position. After participating in the secret White House meeting arranged by Meese, the State Department was at a disadvantage. It could not quite disown the consequences of the high-level gathering. In addition, the State Department worried about the constancy of the U.S. government's position toward the Japanese. If the U.S. government retreated too far from the position enunciated by Brock, that would seriously injure his credibility as a trade negotiator. State began trying to stake out a middle ground, one that essentially called for further internal study of the Houdaille petition and more discussions with the Japanese over the whole question of industrial targeting. But State's quasi-defection from the White Hats did not start a stampede, nor did its compromise position satisfy the urges that motivated the Jap-bashers.[107]

If the administration was at an impasse, however, it was not operating in a void. Gathering political pressure outside the executive branch promised to bring the Houdaille matter to a head. The new Congress was ready to put political heat on the administration, and one way or another, the time for a resolution of the Houdaille case was approaching. Commerce Department officials, for one, believed that a decision could not be postponed past April because of the political consequences.[108] If nothing else, failure to dispose of the petition would become an acute political embarrassment.

Congress and particularly the Democrats applied pressure by giving interested parties a public platform on which to perform. Among "targeted" industries, Houdaille was a star witness, and congressional committees would repeatedly invite the conglomerate to state its position regarding trade issues and the idea of an industrial policy. The House Subcommittee on Trade convened one of the first such hearings on the morning of March 10—hours before the Trade Policy Committee was scheduled to discuss the Houdaille petition. Among the very first witnesses were John Latona, a Houdaille vice president, and Richard Copaken. Describing Houdaille as a "private company . . . fighting the Japanese Government," Latona proudly introduced the legal counsel who was making it all possible. "Our modern-day David," Latona said, "does not use a sling. He uses a more contemporary weapon, a video camera, and thus far . . . the results have been almost as dramatic as they were in Biblical times."[109]

As far as Copaken was concerned, everything political seemed to be pointing in the right direction. The only fly in the ointment was the NMTBA's decision to introduce its own Section 232 petition in early March. Copaken had tried to stave off the inevitable as long as he could, repeatedly pleading with the NMTBA to hold off. The administration clearly recognized that the entire industry was in distress, he argued. Now that it was heading toward a finding under Section 301, relief for all tool builders, not just Houdaille, could be just weeks away. Copaken cringed whenever he thought about the political and bureaucratic consequences of a separate petition. It was coming just as a victory for Houdaille appeared to be within his grasp.

But the NMTBA's attorneys said they were ready to go, and the association decided it could wait no longer. The law permitted the administration to spend a full year deciding whether or not machine tool imports posed a threat to national security, and no one doubted the full year would be required. The NMTBA wanted to restrict all imports to 17.5 percent of domestic consumption, by value, for five years.[110] It was going to be a difficult struggle. Despite repeated attempts, only one industry had ever succeeded in obtaining a Section 232 finding. That occurred in the late 1950s, when domestic oil producers won limits on cheap oil imports from the Middle East.

The NMTBA's determination to go ahead despite Copaken's plea was the most dramatic proof yet of the deep split within the industry. Outwardly, of course, the NMTBA still expressed support for Houdaille. Protection against imports was just too attractive a possibility to eschew, no matter how dubious the grounds. But privately, many builders felt differently.

The Wall Street Journal, in late March, was the only newspaper to pick up the story. In a long article that began on the front page, the Journal finally brought out into the open what had been inside knowledge for months. Many builders had been amazed by the serious consideration given the Houdaille petition. And frankly, they gagged whenever they heard Copaken extol the virtues of Houdaille's Burgmaster and Strippit divisions. Copaken liked to paint Houdaille as "one of the most productive and innovative manufacturers of high-technology machine tools," a company that "has consistently outperformed the U.S. machine-tool industry as a whole on the critical measure of productivity—sales dollar per employee."[111]

Houdaille's industrywide reputation was markedly different. Particularly in recent years, it had come to epitomize the "get-it-out-the-factory-door, we'll-fix-it-in-the-field" attitude. It was hardly the sole U.S. builder with that approach. But then Houdaille was the only one that had resorted to blaming the Japanese for its troubles. As one builder, who refused to be identified, told the Journal, the Houdaille petition "may be great for Houdaille and for the U.S. Senate, but it's a bunch of foolishness [and Houdaille's allegations] sanctimonious."[112]

Yet Copaken was nothing if not adroit at turning adversity into opportunity. There was only one way to turn the situation to Houdaille's advantage, now that the split in the industry was out in the open. He knew that his allies inside the government were determined to use the Houdaille petition as the vehicle to attack Japan's "unfair" industrial targeting. Their enthusiasm for the Houdaille case would not wane because of the NMTBA's petition. What he needed to do was explain that a national security finding would be protectionism pure and simple, and make no demands of Tokyo. But a "301" finding in the Houdaille case, by contrast, would at least shift the onus for American protectionism onto Japan. That was politically more appealing and more elegant.

He managed to get the gist of this across in the *Journal* article. Better still, his was the last word. "Whatever action the president takes on the Houdaille petition," Copaken said, "will send a significant signal to American industry, workers, the United States Congress, the government of Japan, our other trading partners, and above all, the American electorate."[113] In other words, Copaken was attempting to raise the political ante as high as conceivably possible.

Because of the State Department's quasi-defection, the number of ardent White Hats had been reduced in number to three: the Treasury Department, Office of Management and Budget, and Council of Economic Advisers, with Treasury carrying the most influence by far. On learning of the declining numbers, Copaken decided to take a new tack. He would meet the most potent of his enemies head-on. In mid-March, he and Phil O'Reilly arranged to speak directly with Tim McNamar, deputy secretary of the Treasury. Together they hoped to learn what it was going to take to win Treasury over.

Representatives of nearly all the interested agencies attended the March 14 meeting at the Treasury Department. O'Reilly, the physically imposing ex-football player, sat across a large table from McNamar, a welterweight jogger. McNamar convened the gathering by paying tribute to Copaken's Herculean efforts and the vast amount of information that Houdaille had provided the government. He then said what Copaken and O'Reilly came to hear. Treasury was willing to make a positive recommendation to the president, especially since Houdaille's proposed tax remedy was now a dead letter. But McNamar still had serious doubts and questions. He needed more facts. To at least one observer, McNamar sounded like Sgt. Joe Friday from the old television series "Dragnet."[114]

As McNamar peppered him with questions, O'Reilly vented all the tension that had been building up inside him for months. The one bureaucracy that had done more in the past eleven months to deny Houdaille its just relief was now asking for more facts. How can one company be expected to take on an entire foreign industry and government? O'Reilly asked, his voice sputtering. McNamar responded by upbraiding O'Reilly. Japan's penetration of the U.S. market was not de facto proof of a government-subsidized cartel, no matter how many times Houdaille repeated that allegation. The meeting abruptly ended in a shouting match.[115]

Copaken was nearly in a panic. He had hoped to switch Treasury's allegiance at almost the last moment, before the remaining White Hats, Carl

Green, and Stanton Anderson knew what hit them and had time to recover. He brought O'Reilly along because he had always proven persuasive in the past, and meeting with top officials helped keep his frustration in check. What was intended as a shrewd initiative now looked like a terrible mistake, made at the worst possible time.

Copaken's fear was premature. After a day or two, McNamar's anger receded, and he wrote O'Reilly a letter. He reiterated his willingness to back Houdaille if certain lingering questions could be answered to his satisfaction. O'Reilly blanched at the thought of what it was going to cost. But he passed the letter on to his counsel, and Copaken, with his leave-no-stone-unturned approach, promptly accepted the challenge. He wrote McNamar, and promised to be as "responsive as humanly possible" to his questions.[116]

Winning McNamar's allegiance was going to be pivotal, because the White Hats, including Treasury, simultaneously decided to launch an all-out attack on the Houdaille petition. On March 23, they submitted a so-called White Hats Paper intended to finish the Houdaille case once and for all. It challenged every premise and conclusion in the petition, including points of fact that the Jap-bashers insisted were no longer in dispute. The White Hats maintained that Japan had not violated GATT, MITI's targeting amounted to nothing more than exhortations, a cartel never existed, and government subsidies were insignificant.[117]

The USTR and Commerce Department were caught by surprise. But they quickly regrouped, and the most bitter debate in a long series of rancorous discussions followed. The meeting ended, just as the McNamar-O'Reilly session had, in a shouting match, but this time it was Treasury pitted against Commerce.[118] It was almost as if the government itself were breaking down over the Houdaille petition.

Both Brock and Baldrige searched desperately for a formula to regain the momentum that had been lost. Finally, at a subsequent meeting of the principals in early April, Baldrige came up with the idea of throwing the entire issue back to a subcabinet group. With the help of a neutral party from the White House, the subcabinet group, operating under a strict deadline, would make a last-ditch attempt to obtain everyone's agreement to the facts and reach a consensus on the appropriate remedy. The senior White House staff immediately agreed, and handed responsibility for that unhappy task to a junior presidential aide named Wendell Willkie Gunn. After eleven months, it was "back to the drawing board."[119]

With the Houdaille case inching toward resolution, Copaken decided that a last dash to Japan, to find new facts, was in order. From April 5 onward, he subjected Deputy Secretary McNamar, the one official who could be the difference, to a virtual barrage of any information he could get his hands on. Copaken "rapifaxed" his findings almost daily to McNamar, repeatedly emphasizing his willingness to "go the extra mile" to uncover "what the Government of Japan apparently views as damaging secrets."[120]

Copaken submitted more than sixty pages of documentation to McNamar during this time. The evidence included documents that ostensibly proved the tool industry's "responsiveness" to MITI's directions, as well as descriptions of new videos he planned to screen in Washington upon his return on April 11.[121] By now, of course, the Japanese were wise to Copaken's video ambushes, and they denied him physical access to research labs. So Copaken shot footage of these confrontations as well: "Even though MITI and the government of Japan are officially committed to licensing technology, we were turned away at the door when we tried to explore such a possibility for Houdaille."[122]

More than once, the irrepressible Copaken found a "smoking gun," or so he claimed to McNamar. One of the most incriminating pieces of information, Copaken asserted, was a 1963 article from the Japanese publication *Machine Tool News*. In his zeal, Copaken even suggested that

> there are some officials in Japan's Ministry of Finance who are quietly rooting for us because they view the possibility of favorable action on the Houdaille petition as providing them with an opportunity to begin dismantling Japan's vast array of subsidy programs and thereby contributing to the solution of an increasingly important national deficit problem in Japan which they have been unable to solve on their own.[123]

Japanese officials who argue for dissolving MITI do so on the grounds that Japanese industry has succeeded despite the ministry, and could do as well or better without it.

By the time Copaken returned to Washington on April 11, Wendell Gunn was putting the finishing touches on his distillation of the facts. Gunn had sifted the evidence and gone over all the arguments put forth in the preceding eleven months. He had managed to whittle down this morass to a few carefully worded pages, which he called the "Agreed Facts." On the morning of April 12, the summary was circulated to six representatives from the agencies most actively involved in the dispute: Treasury, OMB, CEA (which opposed relief), Commerce and USTR (in favor), and State (in the middle). After a marathon meeting that started at 4:00 P.M. and ended five hours later, a slightly revised version of Gunn's "Agreed Facts" emerged. It was surprisingly short, a mere three to four pages long.[124] Yet once again there was no consensus about what the facts meant, or any agreement on a course of action. Gunn's paper was so carefully drawn that it simply papered over the same old split. There was nothing left to do but send the whole matter back to the principals.

Three days later, at 4:00 P.M., the climactic cabinet-level showdown occurred. At first, the meeting went smoothly. Within fifteen minutes, all the participants agreed to the "Agreed Facts." But it was the calm before the storm. The Jap-bashers asserted that the facts allowed only one conclusion, an unfair trade finding under Section 301. Just as vehemently, the White Hats argued that such a conclusion was not warranted by the agreed facts. For the next two hours and fifteen minutes, to everyone's great weariness, the debate went back and forth, as fractious as ever. Treasury was not quite the convert Copaken had hoped to gain.[125]

In the end, the only accord the principals could reach on that Friday night was to send the dispute to the president, and let him decide. Presumably the evidence would support whatever action the president wished to take. This procedure was a last resort, reluctantly accepted, because it was not the Reagan administration's way. The administration's whole decision-making process was set up to avoid and insulate the president from conflict. President Reagan was a man of "simple beliefs, with a striking lack of intellectual depth or curiosity."[126] The president preferred ratifying cabinet decisions, not choosing between sharply different options.

The principals also agreed to isolate the president as much as possible from any last-minute, one-sided appeals. Reagan's decision, whatever it was, was bound to create controversy, and if news that a decision was imminent leaked out, a torrent of political pressure would descend on the White House. Therefore, the agreement to place the matter on his desk and the exact timing of the decision were both considered extremely sensitive and confidential.[127]

The cabinet agreed on the following plan. Over the next few days, an "options" paper would be prepared for President Reagan in time for the next cabinet meeting on Friday, April 22. To keep the matter quiet, in contrast to normal procedure, no copies of the original paper would be circulated. A White House aide would hand-carry the document to each of the cabinet officials involved. They would be allowed to read it, and initial their approval. Each department would then be allowed to make its case before the president at the meeting, but nothing more.[128]

The goal of insulating the president from last-minute lobbying collapsed within minutes after the cabinet meeting ended. As William Brock left the White House, and crossed 17th Street to enter the USTR offices, he encountered Kazuhiko Otsuka in the anteroom to his office. The Japanese diplomat, a trade specialist who was regarded as one of Japan's most affable representatives, had been assigned to follow every twist and turn in the Houdaille case. He politely buttonholed Brock and asked whether a decision had been reached. When Brock did not say yes, Otsuka deduced that there was still time to influence the White House.[129]

It was past 7:00 P.M. on a Friday night in Washington, but midmorning of the next day in Tokyo. Otsuka was able to speak almost immediately with MITI and Foreign Ministry officials, who normally work part of Saturday. The conversation led to a high-level lobbying effort over the next week via the Japanese ambassador in Washington, Yoshio Okawara. He hand-carried a letter to Secretary of State Shultz, and also telephoned Edwin Harper, a top presidential aide. In both communications, Japan's message was that a "301" finding would be akin to branding an ally an enemy. The political and economic risks of such a declaration, the Japanese averred, would be incalculable.[130]

On April 22, most of the officials assembled in the cabinet room overlooking the Rose Garden were primed to put up a stout defense of their respective positions. Only a handful of the president's top aides knew that he had already made up his mind. Shortly before the meeting began, as a courtesy to the lead agency involved in the case, Brock was informed that the president was going to reject the petition. The news stunned him, especially when he thought back to his inadvertent indiscretion.[131]

When Houdaille came up on the agenda, President Reagan declared that there was no need for a debate because he was going to reject the petition. Since the president usually just listened during the cabinet sessions and made his decisions alone afterward, it was immediately obvious to everyone that the decision had been "pre-cooked." A surprised Malcolm Baldrige replied, "Mr. President, you are being naïve." The commerce secretary then launched into a sanitized version of the Jap-bashing that had characterized so many of the previous deliberations. He warned the president that negotiations over trade with the Japanese were futile, a "naïve effort," and that sanctions were the only unambiguous response Tokyo could understand. Baldrige's comments seemed to strike a raw nerve in Reagan, who curtly cut off the commerce secretary. The president said he believed that Prime Minister Nakasone was an honorable fellow and could be dealt with. Baldrige expected his fallen banner to be picked up by Brock, but "I looked behind me to see where the troops were, and found there were none." The head of USTR was unexpectedly subdued. Later Baldrige found out why.[132]

A chastened USTR released news of the president's decision at a time calculated to attract the least possible media attention: the two-paragraph statement was held back until 9:00 P.M. on Friday, and news of it did not appear in the major newspapers until three or four days later. By some accounts, Houdaille still divided the administration even after the president had made his decision. There was a lengthy disagreement over how to word the simple press release announcing the decision.[133] Finally, everyone agreed to a statement declaring that Houdaille's *original* request for relief under Section 103 had been rejected. That left the conglomerate free to refile its complaint under applicable trade laws.

To save face—a characteristic perhaps overly attributed to the Japanese—USTR simultaneously announced that "the petition did raise questions concerning the possible effects on U.S. commerce of certain Japanese practices," and that Brock would immediately begin consultations with the Japanese government to "deal with these problems, making further action unnecessary."[134]

That gesture, of course, was no solace to Copaken and O'Reilly, who maintained to the end that their case was airtight. O'Reilly told the press he was "extremely disappointed," adding that "I think there's a lack of understanding about how pernicious industrial targeting policies of the Japanese really are."[135] He defiantly spoke about taking Houdaille's complaint else-where, to Capitol Hill or the International Trade Commission.

Privately, though, O'Reilly knew his words were empty. Above all, he was bitter about the cost of the failed petition, which ultimately totaled more than $1.5 million. Houdaille "certainly knew all along what the costs and the risks were," said Copaken. O'Reilly did not blame his counsel anyway, since Copaken's efforts were always approved in advance. Instead, he directed his anger at the Treasury Department and other bureaucracies for sucking him into a costly process.[136]

"Dick's as creative a lawyer as I've encountered anywhere," O'Reilly would later say. "We couldn't have done it without him. Whether we should have done it at all is another question."[137]

13
DEMISE (1983–1985)

If O'Reilly was bitter about losing, Copaken was deeply chagrined. In terms of media coverage and political support, Copaken had succeeded way beyond expectation. The Houdaille petition had become a celebrated case—and that made defeat all the harder to swallow.

Defeat also raised the question: Had Copaken taken his client down a primrose path? That was certainly the opinion of Houdaille's adversaries in the proceeding.[1] But it was a view also shared by most objective experts in trade law and policy. Implicitly, if not explicitly, Copaken recognized the need to "cover his ass," as one observer put it, and justify both his approach and the cost of the petition.

O'Reilly's lingering bitterness, Copaken's wish for vindication, and both men's desire for political revenge resulted in an unusual campaign by Houdaille, one that persisted long after the petition's demise. The platforms for this effort were the same ones that had proven so valuable earlier, the media and Congress. Ordinarily, neither would have paid any attention to a defunct trade case. But the Houdaille petition continued to resonate because it underscored a theme. The decline of smokestack America was a popular refrain in the press in 1983, and the notion of an industrial policy was a hot subject for debate within Congress. So O'Reilly and Copaken took every opportunity to embarrass the Reagan administration for supposedly sacrificing Houdaille on an altar of foreign interests.

Nor was this campaign a vain, meaningless exercise. The Congress was intent on a thorough overhaul of U.S. trade statutes, and its final product, a 1,000-page bill signed into law by President Reagan in August 1988, would contain what trade experts called a "Super-301" clause. The new law would define "export targeting" as unreasonable, unfair, and actionable; shift responsibility for "301" decisions away from the president and to the Office of the U.S. Trade Representative (although the president could override the USTR finding); and impose strict time limits on the decision-making process. Nearly everyone in Congress believed that Houdaille's unfortunate experience should not be repeated, and the failure of its petition was an important catalyst for these far-reaching changes.

The campaign began in late April 1983, just days after the final ruling, when Copaken began to develop and circulate a stab-in-the-back legend about the Houdaille petition. Upon hearing William Brock's noncommittal response, the Japanese government had engaged in timely lobbying in the days just before Reagan made his decision. Whether or not these messages were decisive in making up the president's mind, Copaken was intent on insinuating that they were. Copaken claimed to anyone in the media who would listen that Houdaille's petition was on the verge of being approved, only to be derailed by a last-minute plea from Prime Minister Nakasone himself. The implication Copaken sought to leave was manifest. Rather than decide the case on its merits, the Reagan administration had ruled against Houdaille because it was more worried about Nakasone's political future than the well-being of American industry.[2]

An article along these lines first appeared in the press in mid-June, almost two months after the petition was rejected. Helen Thomas, UPI's White House reporter, wrote a story clearly inspired by Copaken and the information he had been able to glean about the decisive cabinet meeting. Then, two months later, an even longer article appeared on the front page of the *Washington Post*. O'Reilly and Copaken were key sources for the *Post* story on the administration's "confused and inconsistent" trade policy. "The President succumbed to lobbying pressure from Japan," the article quoted O'Reilly. Rather one-sidedly, the article put forth the notion that a key industry had "fallen prey to subsidized foreign competition." Nothing was done about it because the Reagan administration was more concerned about upcoming parliamentary elections in Japan and Nakasone's pledge to increase military spending if his party won. The article specifically cited "two personal messages" from Nakasone that prompted Reagan to make up his mind before the cabinet meeting.[3]

The Japanese embassy subsequently sent a short letter to the *Post*, in an attempt to correct the record. Though not denying that high-level messages were sent to the administration, the embassy said that Prime Minister Nakasone had never gotten personally involved with the Houdaille matter. But, as usual, the facts never quite caught up with Houdaille's allegations.[4] Nakasone's alleged eleventh-hour attempt was widely believed to have turned the tide.

Two months later, in November 1983, O'Reilly and Copaken achieved their greatest media revenge, courtesy of the top-rated CBS program, "60 Minutes." The string of journalistic half-truths and misrepresentations in the Houdaille case, of course, was already extremely long. And to be sure, CBS had a problem reporting the story because the Japanese government and Yamazaki refused to be interviewed for the broadcast. Nevertheless, no overall portrait was more egregiously distorted than the one painted by "60 Minutes" for millions of Americans.

A good portion of the program was factual, describing Houdaille's patent suit against Yamazaki in the 1970s and Houdaille's struggle in Washington against overwhelming odds. But "60 Minutes" also broadcast a number of unsubstantiated claims, such as the simplistic assertion that "Japanese companies have been able to take over so much of the market because the Japanese government targeted this industry."[5] There was no reference to the unpredictable economic climate that made it difficult for Houdaille to invest and compete; no mention of the leveraged buyout; and no discussion about whether any of Houdaille's wounds were self-inflicted by management.

Instead, the conglomerate was depicted as a state-of-the-art manufacturer that single-handedly put Yamazaki into business as a competitor. (Actually, this was a comparatively modest claim by Houdaille. In other forums, Copaken was apt to assert that "Houdaille had put *Japan* in the machining center business.") Licensing rights were sold to Yamazaki in 1970 because that was the "only way" Houdaille could sell its machines in Japan. Unsuspecting viewers were led to believe that Japan subsidized its machine tool industry to the tune of $100 million in 1980, since, once again, the distinction between "machinery" and "machine tools" was blurred. Overall, "60 Minutes" painted a picture of a brave David (Houdaille) defeated by a cunning Goliath (Japanese government and industry), who snookered the president of the United States. "If we had done in the United States what was done in the case of the machine tool industry in Japan," said Phil O'Reilly, "every machine tool manufacturer in this country would be in jail and the key would be thrown away."[6]

The other forum where Houdaille continued to enjoy high visibility was Congress. Congressman Sam Gibbons, chairman of the House Subcommittee on Trade, typified congressional reaction. Speaking just a few days after the administration turned Houdaille down, Gibbons said,

> As I look upon some of [Japan's] industrial policy, it is a very sophisticated form of subsidy. I don't mean sinister or sneaky. They do it all open and above board and they have got a right to do it . . . but when it impacts upon our markets, then I think their right has to be subservient to our rights.
>
> Now, we haven't got a very good record of enforcing our rights . . . it appears to be improving but the constant complaint is that it takes too long, costs too much and when we get to the end of the road, like in the Houdaille case, the President decides for some other reason that we shouldn't enforce the law. That breeds nothing but cynicism. . . .
>
> That is the problem. We are undermining not only our domestic economy by not enforcing our laws, but we are undermining the whole basis of law.[7]

Sympathetic congressmen aside, Houdaille continued to strike a responsive chord on Capitol Hill for the same reason the case still reverberated in the media. From June 1983 to March 1987, Houdaille testified before six separate congressional panels, ranging from the prestigious Senate Foreign Relations Committee to the tiny House Subcommittee on Antitrust and Restraint of Trade Activities Affecting Small Business. Sometimes the subject of the hearing was the machine tool industry itself; other times the rubric was international trade, foreign targeting, or industrial policy. No matter what the subject or venue, however, Houdaille's testimony was always the same. U.S. builders faced a government directed and subsidized Japanese machine tool cartel, and Houdaille's quixotic petition had failed because of "an extraordinary, last-minute intervention" by Prime Minister Nakasone. Houdaille also castigated the Reagan administration for "hassling" Houdaille over the exact amount of the subsidy to the Japanese cartel, instead of thinking about the big picture.[8]

At a hearing before the House Small Business Committee, Houdaille introduced some of Copaken's videotapes as visual evidence of the Japanese cartel at work. At another, called by the Foreign Relations Committee, Senator Charles Percy began the session by inserting the complete transcript of the "60 Minutes" segment on Houdaille. Invariably, Jack Latona, the Houdaille vice president who testified at the hearings, ended his statement with a calculated appeal to elementary fairness. "American businesses and American workers cannot be burdened with a double standard which allows other nations to practice all of the elements of targeting while we remain 'free,'" Latona would conclude. "Houdaille is not giving up. But America must wake up."[9]

Houdaille would give up very shortly.

Although they were quite aware of the petition, Burgmaster employees were slow to connect the long, drawn-out struggle in Washington with their own jobs. Gardena was thousands of miles from the capital, and if Burgmaster employees were going to worry about anything at that distance, they were more likely to be concerned over events in East Peoria and Joliet, Illinois. Caterpillar, one of Burgmaster's most important customers, had large factories in the two midwestern towns.

By April 1983, when the Houdaille petition was rejected, Burgmaster was firmly in the grip of George Delaney and his whiz kids. To those employees who had been there long enough to remember the company's heyday under the Burgs, Burgmaster had experienced a long fall from grace. But even among employees who knew only the reign of Allan Folger there was widespread dissatisfaction. Perhaps Burgmaster under Folger had been too complacent, and never rose above a certain plateau of performance. Yet there had been a steadiness of purpose and constancy to the company. Now all that was gone, and Burgmaster seemed to be spinning out of control.

In building machine tools, everything should be geared to the needs of manufacturing and assembly, and helping these departments. They are crucial to a builder's raison d'être, and ostensibly, making machines for a profit was still Burgmaster's reason for existence. Under Delaney, however, manufacturing and assembly were geared to the needs of the front office, whose needs, in turn, were dictated by Houdaille's debt service. Burgmaster was more genuinely dedicated to generating cash flow than building machines.

Much of what Delaney ordered seemed irrational and self-defeating, if not downright stupid to Burgmaster employees. They tended to ascribe different reasons to his actions, but the simplest explanation was the most popular. Delaney was a "round peg in a square hole," a president "trying to keep control over costs, [who] overall didn't know what the hell he was doing."[10] Nor were his whiz kids equipped to run a machine tool company. As plant manager, Richard Parks, one of the three whiz kids, was more powerful than anyone else when it came to manufacturing. Yet he was and remained remarkably ignorant about what it took to build a machine tool. Talking to him about manufacturing problems was "like talking to a brick wall."[11]

Delaney was acting more rationally, though, given the circumstances, than most Burgmaster employees imagined. In truth, the irrational factor in the early 1980s was the heavy corporate debt Burgmaster, and Houdaille, had to service because of the leveraged buyout. Yet, no matter how pervasive, the blatant reality was hard to accept because it was so alien to the way Burgmaster had always operated. It was slow to dawn on most employees that Burgmaster was not being managed for the long term and not even for the short term. Rather, Burgmaster existed primarily to pay off a gamble. Investors had paid an extraordinarily high price for their stock, betting that a leveraged Houdaille could survive until the pot of gold could be claimed. They expected a generous return.

The tendency to blame people rather than circumstances for Burgmaster's tailspin was reinforced because Delaney was extremely closemouthed about the pressures being exerted upon him. He preferred to be safe inside a shell, and understandably so. That was easier than contending openly with the conflicting demands imposed by debt on the one hand and what needed to be done if Burgmaster was going to survive increased competition. He resorted to his whiz kids, not because he respected them, but because they always told him what he needed to hear. They did not raise doubts, like older Burgmaster employees, about what had to be done. They merely said it could be done.

Burgmaster was suffering from a change in its mission and a loss of identity. One act, above all, painfully symbolized the company's predicament by 1983. Delaney decided to remove the prototype of the first Burgmaster turret drill from the front office lobby. For more than thirty years, Fred Burg's prototype had been proudly displayed in every factory occupied by Burgmaster, one of the few adornments in otherwise spartan offices. It served as a constant reminder of the company's modest beginnings, the precursor to all its accomplishments. Delaney deemed it an embarrassment. He did not want to give anyone the mistaken impression that Burgmaster dwelled on its past.[12]

Before the prototype was consigned to the back lot, along with the rest of the scrap metal, one of the few longtime employees left at Burgmaster made a hurried telephone call to Norm Ginsburg. He wanted it if Burgmaster did not. It was something to save and show the grandchildren.

Delaney found it easier to dispose of some other relics from the Burg era. The company still owned a fair, albeit rapidly declining, reputation for quality, engineering, and service. Now Delaney put into motion policies that destroyed what was left of this good name. Corporate headquarters was putting enormous pressure on him, and he shifted some of it onto the assembly, engineering, and sales departments. "I thought our strategy was quite apparent," recalled Delaney. "Let's increase shipments, and let's enhance the product line."[13] He forced assembly to begin shipping machines faster, and simultaneously urged the other two departments to break new ground. The policies were calculated to improve Burgmaster's cash flow. But they also proved contradictory and disastrous.

Burgmaster's backlog by early 1983 was quite modest, only two to three months instead of the eighteen months that were common when Delaney arrived in 1980.[14] The decline, of course, was the consequence of the overall economic downturn, plus competition from Japanese builders for what new orders remained. Imports of machining centers had risen to more than 65 percent of total U.S. consumption.[15] No matter how small the backlog, however, Delaney was relentless about getting Burgmaster's machines out the door. Ostensibly, the idea was to improve Burgmaster's performance so that it could match the delivery times promised by Japanese builders. The underlying and more important truth was that Burgmaster had to have the cash.

Delaney had a new banner posted in the factory: "THE NEXT INSPECTOR IS THE CUSTOMER. HE MUST BE SATISFIED." But if ten machines were scheduled to be shipped by the thirtieth of the month, Delaney was going to show, on his monthly report to Fort Lauderdale, that ten machines had been sent out, no matter what shape they were in. It became routine for Burgmaster to ship a machine costing a hundred thousand dollars or more to a customer with a two-page list of items to be "fixed by field service."[16]

In a flicker of the time it took to establish its reputation, Burgmaster became notorious as a buyer-beware tool builder. Problems that should have been "plant corrected" had to be "field corrected." Burgmaster's repairmen bore the brunt of the anger caused by the new policy. Their job was to fix Burgmasters that needed repair after rigorous use. Under Delaney, however, they increasingly had to accept responsibility for making new machines that had been prematurely delivered work for the first time to the customer's specifications. Customers began to insist on sending their own employees to check their purchase out before they would accept delivery. Burgmaster had to *prove* the new machine performed properly and met specifications—something unheard of for a Burgmaster product.[17]

Even when new machines performed "up to spec" in the factory, out in the field Burgmasters became notorious for excessive downtime.[18] Spindles would stall for no apparent reason; metal chips would build up to excessive levels and damage the pinpoint accuracy of the giant ball screws that moved a machine's various components up and down or sideways. Oil leaks were a chronic problem. Sometimes, to satisfy Delaney's schedule, the assembly department would put new hydraulic seals on machines just so they could pass inspection, knowing full well that after three weeks or so, the leaks would recur in the field.[19] Even the best machine tools have defects and need repair, but Burgmasters seemed to have more than their share. Customers began to ask themselves, why bother with Burgmaster? More than thirty other U.S. tool builders made NC machining centers, and more than sixty different makes were available from abroad.[20]

Burgmaster machines were becoming less reliable not only because they were being shoved out the door. The other track of Delaney's two-track policy was even more to blame. The compulsion to generate cash, combined with a declining, more competitive market, prompted Delaney to mold Burgmaster into a sales-run company. Burgmaster's new motto was "promise customers anything," and the sales department, at Delaney's insistence, made lavish promises in order to sell machines—any machines—during the downturn. Purchase orders read more like poems than contracts, filled with pledges to include chip-removal systems, totally automated coolant systems, and other state-of-the-art features Burgmaster had yet to engineer.[21]

Orders were eagerly accepted for these specials, even though experience showed that these machines always took longer to build, and exceeded cost estimates in the process. "They were trying to build machines like Hughes builds satellites," recalled Pete Ives, a longtime employee. "Every machine became a tailor-made machine."[22] Each one tested the engineering, manufacturing, and assembly departments to their limits. Inevitably, unforeseen complications reduced profit margins. Nor did the specials result in models that were easily marketable to other customers.

The strategy was the exact opposite of what Japanese builders were doing with astonishing success. They did not market machining centers with all the bells and whistles offered by Burgmaster, but limited their lines to a few standard, reliable models that they constantly sought to improve. New, advanced features were added constantly, but gradually. In this sense, Japanese builders were treading much the same path followed by the Burgs in the early 1960s, when the basic strategy was to emphasize different variations on a theme. Burgmaster had not eschewed specials entirely, but superior management and the high quality of Burgmaster's work force had enabled it to meet the challenges posed by machines tailored to customer specifications. By contrast, during the 1980s, the engineering and manufacturing departments were weaker than ever. In that respect, Delaney's marketing strategy was not only radical, it was reckless. But there was no other choice, given the need to service Houdaille's debt.

It wasn't that Delaney didn't know any better or was unwilling to emulate the Japanese. Earlier, in late 1982, he had tried to borrow a leaf from them. Bridgeport Machines, a subsidiary of the Textron conglomerate, had just decided to market its machining centers directly, leaving its old distributors without a product. At their suggestion, Delaney ordered his engineers to develop a standard vertical machining center for under $80,000, several thousand dollars less than any Japanese machine on the market. The distributors told him, recalled Delaney, "We think as a group we can do a helluva lot of volume for you folks." All Burgmaster had to do was come up with a bargain-basement machining center.[23]

Within six months, the first machines were ready to go into production. Burgmaster's engineers had met or exceeded all the specifications, and at $77,500, the machine was well under the upper limit suggested by the distributors. Delaney then asked the distributors how many they wanted to order. "When we went back to the group, it was gone," recalled Delaney. Because of the slump, several distributors were unwilling to risk buying a machine without a firm customer. Others had jumped the gun, and had already signed up to represent Kitamura, a Japanese builder.[24]

Undaunted, Delaney ordered a dozen of the machines built anyway. He reasoned that "if those [dealers] felt that way, what do we have to lose?" But when the time came to find buyers, Delaney was shocked to find that the price of equivalent Japanese machines had fallen from about $80,000 to the mid-sixties. And if Burgmaster cut $2,500 off its price to come closer to a Japanese bid, the next day the prospective customer would call to say the Japanese had lowered their price by a comparable amount. There was simply no way Burgmaster could undersell its foreign competition. Panic set in, because if there was one thing Delaney knew that Burgmaster could not do, it was carry unsold machines. It ruined cash flow. The standard machines that were to bring a measure of salvation to Burgmaster were torn apart, reengineered, and rebuilt as specials.[25]

Once again, Burgmaster was a victim of economic circumstances beyond its control. Japanese builders could beat any Burgmaster price because they had an unfair advantage: the Reagan dollar. An allegedly conservative Republican administration had simultaneously cut taxes and increased military spending. One consequence of this yawning gap between economic means and ends was a rapid, upward appreciation of the dollar against the yen because the United States had to offer high interest rates to attract the foreign funds necessary to underwrite Reagan's military Keynesianism. Thus, no matter how inexpensively Burgmaster could build a machine, or how willing it was to reduce its profit margin, Japanese competitors could beat any deal. If the least expensive U.S.-built machining center sold for $85,000, the Japanese would sell theirs for about $80,000. If they had to protect market share by lowering prices another 10 percent, that posed no problem whatsoever because of the dollar's inflated value.

The Reagan administration's shortsighted management of the economy affected Burgmaster in other ways too. Not only were Japanese builders given an artificial advantage, but all foreign manufactured goods gained new markets because American products were suddenly more expensive than the competition. As Caterpillar lost out to Komatsu, both here and abroad, Burgmaster saw its own sales decline. A grossly overvalued dollar was only the latest in a long series of economic misfortunes to hit American manufacturers. Yet not even stagflation matched the swift and brutal impact an overvalued dollar had on U.S. manufacturers' market share.

Stymied in his effort to pull Burgmaster out of its doldrums through conventional means, Delaney fell back on the more radical strategy of selling machines however he could. Houdaille's ravenous appetite for cash demanded nothing less. In fact, it demanded more. Delaney was pressured to pump up cash flow through every possible means. Some of these suggestions came from Houdaille's board of directors, for Kohlberg, Kravis, and Roberts were well schooled in all the gimmicks that could be employed to boost cash flow. Other ideas were the brainstorm of Houdaille's own accountants, including Burgmaster's controller, Bill Bystrom. These measures were not quite as damaging to Burgmaster's reputation as the drive to meet monthly production quotas, and sell custom machines. But they did not enhance Burgmaster's good name either.

Prior to the leveraged buyout, Burgmaster had enormous good will among its suppliers because it always paid its bills on time. This was an invaluable commodity. Suppliers invariably accorded Burgmaster preferential treatment whenever goods or services were in short supply, or needed desperately. In many instances, the ties between Burgmaster and its vendors went back to the time when the Burgs ran the company.

The debt turned decades of good will into ill will. To generate cash, Burgmaster stopped paying its bills on time, often delaying payment for months. But the payables problem was only one of the gambits that incurred the wrath of Burgmaster's suppliers. In addition, the company routinely began asking suppliers to reschedule confirmed orders two or three times, before finally putting an order on indefinite hold. Burgmaster also began rejecting, on specious grounds, parts that it had ordered.[26]

The last straw for many suppliers came in January 1983. In a form letter, Burgmaster adopted what some called the "General Motors philosophy—give them what they want and the hell with them."[27] Burgmaster unilaterally declared that it was reducing the price on all outstanding orders because of the recession and foreign competition. "No response to this letter is necessary," wrote Burgmaster's purchasing manager, "as we will automatically reduce all invoices by 5 percent."[28]

Suppliers were astonished and outraged by Burgmaster's *chutzpah*. In many cases, these businesses had carried Burgmaster's unwanted orders in their own inventories for months. As one supplier wrote in response to the January letter,

> We understand the effects of this recession and decided to accept the losses incurred due to the continual rescheduling and product hold without complaint. And now, our past generosity is being repaid with more demands without any mention of the credits already extended.
>
> ... My relationship with Burgmaster began in 1965. ... During the last 18 years, I have worked on; designed for; re-engineered, when required; re-worked at night and Saturdays; estimated, sold and interfaced with engineers in Burgmaster's behalf. This was done in the belief that Burgmaster and Pico Metals were part of a team that represented quality and efficiency. But, I question if I am a member of the team, or indeed, if a team exists at all.
>
> ... I hope that the new grinder recently installed in your plant was manufactured in the U.S.A.[29]

The last remark was intended as sarcasm. Everyone who did any business with Burgmaster knew that the company had made few capital investments in recent years. Of these, the single biggest had been the purchase of an Italian-manufactured grinding machine for $980,000. The Favretto grinder had been ordered in 1980, before the seriousness of the downturn was fully apparent. Naturally Burgmaster had done everything in its power to cancel the order, but to no avail.[30] The reason the Italian grinder now evoked particular comment was that Burgmaster's letter to its suppliers was replete with references to the need to meet foreign competition head-on. Burgmaster's "buy American" rationale rang a bit hollow, given the Italian grinder.

The need to keep the cash flowing not only estranged Burgmaster from its suppliers but also led to policies that alienated the company from many of its dealers. Ostensibly, Burgmaster was obligated to sell spare and repair parts exclusively through its dealer network. Even if a customer called Burgmaster directly, the company was bound by an agreement to pay its dealers a fixed percentage of all the repair parts sold in their respective areas. Now Burgmaster began to sell parts "under the table." [31] In the search for cash, no agreement, legal or otherwise, no business relationship, no matter how old or trusted, was inviolate.

To the extent that George Delaney communicated with his work force during the early 1980s, he constantly uttered one refrain. Burgmaster employees had to work harder to match the Japanese. Blue-collar workers had acclimated themselves a long time ago to this kind of attention. Management demanded their best efforts but otherwise treated them indifferently. During the Delaney era, however, the same alienation became rampant among white-collar employees. Burgmaster's president confided only in his whiz kids, and shunned the rest of the white-collar work force. These employees began referring to themselves as the mushrooms, because they were always kept in the dark.[32]

Notwithstanding the poor communication, gradually the work force began to detect that the 1981–1983 bust was not just another cyclical downturn that could be ridden out. One reason for the rising uncertainty was that there seemed to be no end to the layoffs at Burgmaster. Traditionally a machine tool company intent on surviving a prolonged recession cuts its work force in one fell swoop. As a result, a core of highly skilled machinists is assured work and the company does not lose the hard-to-replace workers who are at the heart of any tool-building enterprise.

Delaney was managing this downturn differently, almost as if he were peeling an onion. Every layoff was branded the "last one." But inevitably, a few months after the "last" layoff, another group of workers would find pink slips in their pay envelopes. From a high of about 400 workers in 1980, by early 1983 the work force was down to about 120 blue- and white-collar employees. Such a contraction was not unheard of. But to lose key, skilled employees in the process was unprecedented.

If paring down the work force in this manner did not make sense historically, in the context of Houdaille's debt Delaney's actions were understandable. It didn't matter if Burgmaster lost good machinists because they lacked confidence in the company's future. The alternative—cutting the work force to the bone—was worse. It would extend delivery dates and cost Burgmaster sales and precious cash. That took precedence over managing for Burgmaster's long-term health.

This was Burgmaster's condition at the time the Houdaille petition was finally rejected in April 1983. Delaney knew that the decision "did not bode well for Burgmaster's future."[33] There was still one avenue of import relief for Burgmaster to pin its hopes on, namely, the national security petition introduced by the NMTBA in March. If approved by the Reagan administration, it would result in across-the-board quotas on machine tool imports.

After his own bitter experience, though, Phil O'Reilly knew better than to count on Washington. Even if the Reagan administration could be persuaded ultimately to slap on import quotas, there was no telling how long it would take, and Houdaille did not have the luxury of waiting. The money-losing situation at Burgmaster was replicated, to a greater or lesser degree, throughout Houdaille's machine tool group. Given the delicate debt mechanism, the group represented a potentially fatal hemorrhage that had to be staunched lest all of Houdaille be lost. There was no time to ride out the downturn, and certainly no money to invest to make Burgmaster or Strippit more competitive. The machine tool group had to be restructured, and the sooner the better.

The first major step, taken just a few months after the petition failed, was to consolidate the manufacture of similar lines. That meant shutting down the

Di-Acro division in Lake City, Minnesota, in August 1983, and shifting its production to the Strippit division. More than 250 jobs were lost as a result (in better times, Di-Acro had employed as many as 500 workers).[34]

As far as Burgmaster was concerned, O'Reilly saw only four possible destinies for Houdaille's second-largest tool company. The most desirable course would be a joint manufacturing agreement between Burgmaster and a profitable Japanese builder seeking to expand. Failing that, Burgmaster might be salvaged by turning it into an assembly point for machines produced in Korea or Taiwan. The third option was to sell Burgmaster outright to another builder, foreign or domestic. Then there was the fourth option, which no one relished, for it would be a stark admission of failure: close Burgmaster down.

If not evident before, Burgmaster's perilous situation became obvious to its blue-collar work force in June 1983. That month the contract between Burgmaster and the Steelworkers expired, and the company submitted its proposals for the next three-year contract. When they read it, blue-collar workers were jolted. For more than a year, the salaries of all white-collar employees had been frozen; now Burgmaster wanted to extend the freeze to hourly workers. In addition, management's offer contained a number of "take-backs." The proposal tossed out the workers' cost-of-living adjustment, reduced by three the number of sick days permitted, and lowered wage rates for new employees. Management even proposed to eliminate the five-minute wash-up periods allowed prior to lunch and the end of a shift.[35]

Burgmaster was foundering, there was no question of that. But the workers believed they were among the last to blame for the company's predicament, and that it was unfair to make them pay to set the company right. A few workers muttered about going out on strike for the second contract in a row. Everyone soon realized, however, that a walkout was impossible. In 1980, when times were still good, the longest strike in Burgmaster's history had cost workers three weeks' wages while failing to win any concessions from management. A strike now would almost surely end on the same note, or worse.

There was nothing to do but accept the offer and try to salvage some of the take-backs demanded by Burgmaster. After nearly three months of bargaining, a new three-year contract was signed in September 1983. The company got most of what it wanted. But whatever Burgmaster gained in dollars and cents was more than lost in intangibles, even before the ink on the contract was dry.

Skilled machinists who had been willing to stick with Burgmaster now scanned the help-wanted ads, looking for the first good opportunity to leave. Midlevel, white-collar employees also saw the handwriting on the wall. Overall, the company experienced an unprecedented velocity of turnover in personnel. From one month to the next, or so it seemed, the names of midlevel management changed, and responsibilities of blue-collar workers shifted.

There was no continuity, and confusion over who was in charge created a "who gives a damn attitude."

Yet, on a fundamental level, whatever happened inside Burgmaster now did not matter. Its future was no longer in the hands of Burgmaster's engineers, its salesmen, or its machinists. If engineering developed a number of imaginative but reliable designs; if the sales department out-hustled all its competitors; if the factory floor was more productive than ever; none of that was of consequence anymore. Instead, Burgmaster's fate depended solely on a few Houdaille executives, and the foreign companies they were negotiating with.

"If we can't beat them, we'll joint venture with them," was Houdaille's new refrain. Since President Reagan had "demonstrated a complete disregard for the [U.S. machine tool] industry," Richard Copaken explained, Houdaille had no choice but to seek out a Japanese partner. This news created a considerable stir in Japan, and also in the United States. Several publications, including *The New Republic* and *Business Week*, commented on the irony. Houdaille, an obscure corporation until it made a name for itself as Japan's most bitter critic, was now "cozying up" to its former foe, as *Business Week* put it.[36]

By early 1984, Phil O'Reilly was exploring, with typical forcefulness, the possibility of a joint venture with several Japanese tool builders. "Flexible manufacturing systems" was the new catch phrase in the machine tool industry, and O'Reilly hoped to capitalize on this trend. Such systems featured a host computer that linked several NC machines together. With the addition of shuttle tables, FMS could operate virtually unmanned, bringing completely automated "factories of the future" one step closer to realization.

O'Reilly hoped to link up with a Japanese lathe manufacturer who wanted to be a player in the growing FMS market. It was generally agreed that to be a strong entrant, a builder had to manufacture at least two complementary lines of machine tools, such as lathes and machining centers. O'Reilly envisioned a joint venture whereby Burgmaster would supply the machining center to complement a Japanese lathe. The system would be sold and serviced in the United States through Burgmaster's established network, and the Japanese builder would perform that role overseas. Stand-alone machines manufactured by both builders would also be marketed in this manner.[37]

To O'Reilly's pleasant surprise, no one was more helpful to this endeavor than MITI, the erstwhile villain of the Houdaille petition. The ministry helped Houdaille identify three Japanese builders that fit the necessary profile, namely, manufacturers with significant exports to the United States that had yet to open any kind of factory there. Moreover, MITI paved Houdaille's way by helping to arrange the first face-to-face meetings. It also let the Japanese builders know, in no uncertain terms, that it would look favorably upon a joint venture with Houdaille.[38]

When asked about the ministry's seeming turnabout, O'Reilly explained that some MITI officials "were not unsympathetic" to Houdaille's plight.[39] The implication was that a few MITI officials somehow felt guilty and wanted to make amends. Nothing could have been further from the truth. Instead, MITI wanted to ward off measures that would inhibit Japanese exports to the United States, specifically, the Section 232 petition pending before the Reagan administration. A partnership between a Japanese builder and a notorious MITI critic might persuade the administration to reject a plea for protection. "The U.S. industry needs to be rescued and to do that we think the cooperation of the Japanese machine tool industry is important," said a MITI official.[40]

By April 1984, the three possibilities for a joint venture had been winnowed down to one. To O'Reilly's delight, the last remaining Japanese hope was also the most promising. With MITI's support, Houdaille had been able to pique the interest of the Okuma Machinery Works, one of the largest machine tool builders in the world.[41] Okuma was a publicly traded corporation, so in that respect it differed from one of its archrivals in Japan, Yamazaki Machinery. But otherwise, the similarities between the two Japanese builders were striking. Houdaille's executives almost had a sense of *déjà vu*.

Like Yamazaki, Okuma had risen to prominence in a classic manner. The company was still managed by the descendants of its founder, who was one of the first to produce a lathe in Japan at the turn of the century. Takeo Okuma, the crusty seventy-five-year-old patriarch who now ran the company along with his son, Hajime, swore by the two precepts that were the quintessential mark of every successful builder. "We have two traditional management policies," Okuma once told an interviewer. "Promote high technology and maintain good labor relations."[42]

Okuma was intrigued by the notion of a joint venture with Houdaille for one reason. Okuma had a large showroom and technical headquarters on Long Island, but little else.[43] By contrast, not only Yamazaki but a dozen other Japanese builders, including Hitachi Seiki, Ikegai Iron Works, and Makino Milling Machine, were far ahead in setting up shop in the United States. Hitachi had a production plant in New York, Ikegai an assembly plant near Los Angeles, and Makino now owned a 51 percent stake in Cincinnati's LeBlond Machine Tool Company.[44]

Okuma could ignore these developments, but only at great risk. Its export ratio was high, about 30 percent of total sales, and with import restrictions looming, a U.S. plant of some kind was necessary. In addition, Okuma needed unimpeded access to the U.S. market for the long-term success of its flexible manufacturing systems. Although FMS was still in its infancy, such systems already constituted 15 percent of Okuma's sales. Okuma could probably go it alone in the United States, like Yamazaki, or "shake hands," as Takeo Okuma put it, with an American builder.[45] Either way, Okuma had to decide what kind of presence it wanted on U.S. soil, not whether one was desirable or not.

Takeo Okuma picked his English-speaking son, Hajime, to negotiate with

Houdaille. He was joined by an executive from the Mitsui trading company, which handled Okuma's exports.[46] O'Reilly, Slawson, and to a lesser extent Delaney represented Houdaille during the negotiations. From the outset of the talks in early 1984, it was clear that the two sides had very different timetables in mind with regard to the negotiations. Okuma recognized that direct investment in the U.S. market was inevitable, but was unwilling to rush into a decision. In what might be considered typical Japanese fashion, Hajime Okuma wanted to get to know his prospective partners, and the company upon which the good name of Okuma would rest. O'Reilly and Slawson were considerably less patient.

The first meeting in Japan went well enough, or so Houdaille thought. Burgmaster's plant, O'Reilly admitted, was underutilized. A joint venture would save Okuma the expense of starting up its own operations in the United States. Burgmaster had to have lathes to enter the FMS market, and Okuma excelled in lathes, although it also built a line of heavy machining centers. But O'Reilly maintained that these were not directly competitive with Burgmaster, and that the two companies were close to an ideal fit.[47]

After weeks passed without a response from Okuma to Houdaille's specific proposals, O'Reilly began to get restless. His board of directors supported fully his effort to salvage the Burgmaster division, but their patience was not endless. O'Reilly contacted Dick Copaken, who had been involved in the early discussion with MITI, and the two men discussed the situation. Both agreed that since MITI seemed to be so interested in the outcome, perhaps they could use the ministry to prod Okuma into bringing matters to a head. It seemed worth a try.[48]

Thereafter, whenever the two sides got together in Japan, Houdaille executives would invariably schedule a subsequent meeting with officials from MITI.[49] Ostensibly, Houdaille simply wanted to keep MITI apprised of the progress of the negotiations from Houdaille's point of view. But the underlying intent was to bring MITI's influence to bear on Okuma and increase Houdaille's leverage. O'Reilly also invited Copaken to some of the gatherings. The mastermind of the Houdaille petition served as a convenient reminder. If Houdaille felt it was being treated unfairly and decided to "raise a ruckus," Copaken would be at the center of it.[50]

But not even MITI could get Okuma to budge from its deliberate pace, and to O'Reilly's chagrin the spring passed without an agreement. The delay seemed interminable, yet both he and Copaken were convinced, beyond any doubt, that MITI was doing its utmost. The ministry's inability to bludgeon one company into a joint venture was nothing new to either MITI or Japanese builders, although it ran directly counter to the image fashioned by Houdaille. But O'Reilly, for one, was unwilling to recognize that something had been amiss in the Houdaille petition. At most, he would acknowledge that the "Japanese machine tool industry [is] much less under the control of MITI now that the cartel [has] been established."[51]

By this time, O'Reilly decided not to put all his Burgmaster eggs in the Japanese basket. He traveled to Europe to see if a prominent Italian builder was interested in a joint venture with Burgmaster. In like manner, George Delaney visited South Korea, hoping to find a builder of NC lathes who was interested in assembling his machines in the Burgmaster plant.[52] There was nothing unusual about any of these inquiries. The internationalization of the machine tool industry was a growing trend in the 1980s.[53] But in the struggle to survive in the global marketplace, there was a sharp delineation between successful builders and desperate builders, between those who were being pursued and those who were the supplicants. As far as Burgmaster was concerned, Houdaille belonged unequivocally in the latter camp.

While the negotiations with Okuma dragged on, George Delaney kept hoping for a break that would give Burgmaster breathing room. There was no refuge from Houdaille's punishing debt service. In fact, because of the machine tool group's poor performance, the conglomerate's total debt was increasing rather than shrinking as scheduled.[54] As for protection against Japanese imports, by the spring of 1984 the NMTBA's petition was more than a year old. But the Reagan administration appeared to be just as bitterly split over the NMTBA's national security approach as it had been over the Houdaille petition.[55]

The only ray of hope for Burgmaster was the resurgent U.S. economy. Reagan's brand of military Keynesianism had pumped enough dollars into the economy to produce a recovery after the 1982 recession. Traditionally, increases in capital spending for new plant and equipment had always been good news for the American machine tool industry. But there was something odd about this upturn. Machine tool orders gained ground, but remained anemic overall, and nowhere close to the level of new investment. Rather than share in a feast after years of famine, U.S. builders were relegated to the sidelines as foreign builders, most notably Japanese, retooled America. Imports soared to all-time highs in 1984, as much as 39 percent of total U.S. consumption.[56]

Once again, the macroeconomy was to blame, in this case, the peculiar mix of policies that constituted Reagan's recovery. Since Reagan steadfastly refused to raise taxes to pay for his military buildup, U.S. interest rates had to be kept high to ensure a steady infusion of funds from abroad. This, in turn, boosted the dollar to heights that were impressive to many, except prostrate manufacturers in the machine tool industry.

Burgmaster could no longer even count on the industry's familiar rhythms for relief. The company watched in disbelief as Caterpillar, one of its oldest and certainly most valued customers, turned to Yamazaki instead of Burgmaster for new machining centers.[57] Delaney, who had persuaded himself that something had to break Burgmaster's way, began to feel like a man waiting for a sun that was never going to come up. Even his nights were not peaceful. His dreams were filled with what seemed to be an endless procession of names: Yamazaki, Kitamura, Mori Seiki, all competitors to Burgmaster.

By now Okuma loomed not only as a saving partner but also as a savior. While he waited for the negotiations to bear fruit, Delaney struggled to keep Burgmaster afloat as best he could. The situation inside the factory by mid-1984 was almost farcical. Because it carried almost no inventory, Burgmaster never had the parts it needed. It wasn't unusual for a machine to sit half-assembled for days until a missing piece could be manufactured, at an exorbitant price.[58] The sales department's promises were costing Burgmaster hundreds of thousands of dollars in unforeseen development costs. One machining center, made to order for General Electric, was engineered to operate at such close tolerances that changes in the weather affected its performance. GE paid less than $300,000 for the state-of-the-art machine, which probably cost Burgmaster at least $750,000 to build and perhaps closer to $1 million.[59]

With no orders coming in, Houdaille headquarters virtually "beat on" Delaney to "be creative" in the search for cash.[60] At one point he decided to turn Burgmaster into a job shop. Given the huge aerospace industry in Los Angeles, there was plenty of work around. But being a jobber is an art unto itself. It takes an extremely talented work force, one that can machine extraordinarily difficult, one-of-a-kind parts with maximum efficiency and minimum waste. Castings alone, if made out of titanium or other expensive metals, can be worth thousands of dollars, and jobbers were always held responsible for spoilage.

Burgmaster no longer had anything close to the necessary talent. Moreover, its overhead costs were so high to begin with that it could not realistically compete with the best jobbers. By some estimates, an hour of a Burgmaster machinist's time cost $100 with all the overhead figured in. The best job shops asked $45 an hour. After a few expensive lessons, Delaney quickly abandoned this venture.[61]

Despite such internal perversions, to the outside world Houdaille attempted to present a business-as-usual demeanor. The standard line, for public consumption, was that the 1979 leveraged buyout had been good for Houdaille. The company "has not had any problems in servicing the debt," O'Reilly told the *New York Times* in May 1984. Houdaille's president said that if he had to do it over, he would leverage Houdaille again, without hesitation. Indeed, O'Reilly extolled the virtues of corporate life after an LBO.

> Mr. O'Reilly now manages more for cash flow than for earnings per share. "They impact on each other," he said, "but there is a subtle difference. You can look out at a longer horizon as a private company."
>
> At a public company, "fortunately or unfortunately results are measured in very short periods such as a quarter," he said. "You try to make them look improved and so forth. At a private company you don't have to be quite as conscious as that."[62]

O'Reilly's snow job may have played well publicly, but the facts and the whispered word on Wall Street contradicted him. The Houdaille buyout had turned out to be a dog, in the vernacular of the Street. More than five years had passed since the buyout, and the pot of gold promised the equity investors was nowhere in sight. The gain would not be realized until Houdaille went public, and Houdaille could not go public as long as its machine tool group was dragging down the entire conglomerate. Investors were losing patience, and KKR did not have to push O'Reilly very hard before he realized the urgency of the situation. As he later told *Industry Week,* Houdaille had to "show some returns for the shareholders."[63] Or to paraphrase Jerome Kohlberg, everyone was on the same side of the table. O'Reilly's golden handcuffs ensured that much.

O'Reilly redoubled his efforts to bring the negotiations with Okuma to a head in the summer of 1984. More meetings were held in Japan, and O'Reilly made a point of bringing Copaken along, to keep "the meetings [with Okuma] focused and MITI's interest alive."[64] From O'Reilly's perspective, the talks were like the sets of wooden dolls in which each doll opens up to reveal a smaller version of itself. Every time the two sides met, Okuma seemed intent on trimming the deal that Houdaille thought had been struck during the previous session.

From Okuma's perspective, however, the negotiations had a different cast. About this time, Okuma conducted a thorough inspection and audit of the Burgmaster plant. The Japanese were not impressed by what they found. There was certainly enough room for a state-of-the-art facility, but Burgmaster fell short of being one. Okuma personnel found deficiencies in most places they looked. In certain critical areas the Burgmaster plant was antiquated because of a lack of capital investment.[65] Perhaps the Italian-made grinder, the most expensive new machine to be installed since the late 1960s, summed up the situation best. In 1982, Burgmaster thought it was buying a bargain at $980,000, but instead it had been stuck with a lemon. The machine had a congenital, irreparable defect. To avoid spoiling nearly every workpiece machined on the grinder, Burgmaster workers had to follow special procedures that doubled normal machining times.[66]

The extent to which Okuma explored Burgmaster's name outside the factory was not clear. But if it did, Okuma undoubtedly heard from dealers and consumers alike that Burgmaster was a builder in deep trouble. By now the company's reputation was in tatters. The pressure to meet monthly production quotas was awesome, and quality control just a pretense. Burgmaster had long been accustomed to shipping most machines during the last three or four days of every month. Now, it seemed as if they were being built in three or four days too.[67]

Given Okuma's cautious and deliberate decision making, the Japanese builder, in all likelihood, also used the time to make discreet inquiries about Burgmaster's financial health, as well as Houdaille's. The huge debt by itself was probably not disconcerting. After all, it was not unusual for Japanese tool builders to operate with debt-to-equity ratios of anywhere from 150 to 560 percent.[68] But there was a crucial difference in the reasons behind the respective debts and the interest rates. Japanese builders incurred debt because they invested in R&D and up-to-date plant and equipment, and the interest on their loans was manageable. Burgmaster's burden reflected no such investment, only the conversion of equity into debt at exorbitant rates.

Despite its misgivings, Okuma found itself almost locked into an embrace with Houdaille. First and foremost, there was unremitting pressure from MITI for a deal. The NMTBA petition for import relief was still pending, and MITI continued to view a satisfactory Okuma-Houdaille arrangement as one way to relieve the pressure for protectionism. The importunings of Houdaille, meanwhile, ran a close second to MITI's attempt at coercion. No matter how many qualifications Okuma thought to introduce, Houdaille could not be dissuaded. When Okuma withdrew its lathes from any deal, Houdaille remained interested. When Okuma indicated it wasn't willing to manufacture and market any machines under a joint name, Houdaille nevertheless persisted. The Americans would simply not quit.[69]

Houdaille's determination finally won out and in November 1984 the two builders announced that a deal had been hammered out. As a first step toward a "more comprehensive relationship," Burgmaster would manufacture an Okuma-designed machining center at its plant, though many details were still vague. The model to be manufactured was not yet decided. Nor was it clear whether Burgmaster would market and service the machine through its network or Okuma's. These questions were to be resolved by the end of the year.[70]

January came and went and Houdaille was still waiting to receive a technical delegation from Japan. After several delays, it became obvious that Okuma was intent on backpedaling again. Now the Japanese builder wanted Burgmaster to produce just a few components and ship them to Japan for final assembly. "They were going to test our ability, to see if we could make these parts well enough," recalled George Delaney.[71]

Houdaille vice president John Latona went public with the discouraging news, in an attempt to pressure Okuma. Houdaille is concerned that "things are not moving forward as we had anticipated they would," Latona told a trade publication. "This was an arrangement that was important not just to the two parties but to all Japan-U.S. trade relations." But neither Latona's appeal nor a broad hint by Richard Copaken to MITI brought any results.[72]

Even if Okuma's last offer was genuine, it was too little, too late, to do Burgmaster any good. Not even the omnipotent MITI could force the Japanese builder into an accommodation it did not really want. Nor was Okuma interested in purchasing part, half, or all of Burgmaster. That meant Burgmaster's days, as O'Reilly put it, "were numbered." By early 1985, the company was losing, by some accounts, almost $1 million a month, and even that figure probably underestimated the degree to which Burgmaster was a millstone around Houdaille's neck.[73]

In the weeks immediately following the collapse of the talks with Okuma, a tight-lipped Delaney sought desperately to find a way to keep Burgmaster open. Every possibility was considered, and most were checked out. Under a strict deadline imposed by O'Reilly, Delaney made a trip to the Far East, to see if Burgmaster could undersell the Japanese by employing inexpensive labor in South Korea or China. Under the plan, Burgmaster would be reduced to a shell, fit only to assemble the machines it once built.

A Korean builder, Wachoen, politely declined Delaney's offer. Subsequently Delaney met with the China Machinery and Equipment Council, the state agency that directed that country's machine tool industry. CMEC expressed great interest in Burgmaster's old but still renowned turret drilling machines. Machining centers, however, were beyond China's capabilities.[74]

By June 1985, the fifty or so workers left at Burgmaster noticed that there were no jobs waiting for the big Ingersoll milling machines. The machines made all the bases and columns used by Burgmaster, and the rough sum of these parts invariably represented the number of machines in production. Nor was Burgmaster writing new orders. Then came the news. Not only Burgmaster, but Houdaille's entire machine tool group had been quietly put up for sale.

Even though the strangely quiet, cavernous factory said otherwise, most of the remaining employees believed that some builder, somewhere, would attempt an eleventh-hour rescue. The idea of devoting the plant to anything other than machine tool production defied belief. Some even welcomed the sale, on the grounds that if it survived, Burgmaster had nowhere else to go but up. But after three months passed without a serious buyer in sight, time ran out.

On September 24, Houdaille issued a press release from its Fort Lauderdale headquarters. The statement described a "business restructuring program" designed to lower Houdaille's debt, thereby "reducing its interest expense and enhancing its future."[75] The divestiture was a complicated one. All told, seven Houdaille divisions were split off from the conglomerate, including its entire machine tool group. Three subsidiaries (Penberthy, Powermatic, and Universal) were to be sold as a package to a private investor, three others were going to undergo leveraged buyouts (Warren Pumps, Strippit/Di-Acro, and Hydraulics), and one division was to be liquidated altogether. That was Burgmaster.

Because of Houdaille's trade petition, the conglomerate's unglamorous exit from machine tools received widespread attention in the business sections of most leading dailies. The coverage in the *Los Angeles Times* was typical, and so sympathetic that it could have been written by Houdaille itself. It was one more opportunity to blast the Reagan administration. The thrust of the *Times* coverage was that Houdaille had been forced to abandon the industry because "Japan has secretly subsidized an industry cartel, allowing its machine tool producers to unfairly gain an edge in the U.S. market." Houdaille's only genuine error, the *Times* seemed to suggest, was to mistakenly assume that the Reagan administration understood the primacy of machine tools in a modern economy. Or as O'Reilly put it graphically to another publication, "They treat[ed] us like second-class citizens with dirty fingernails. We thought we had a perfect case for keeping out imports, and we got absolutely nothing for it."[76]

At noon on October 1, Delaney called two meetings to tell employees the news they already knew. Symbolically, white- and blue-collar workers were told separately. An obviously distraught Delaney said that Houdaille management had decided to sell the Strippit/Di-Acro division to Ken Slawson, Houdaille's vice president for machine tools, through a leveraged buyout. The new entity would also own, and possibly license, manufacturing rights to Burgmaster's complete line of machining centers. But Slawson intended to shut down the Gardena factory.

Both announcements took scarcely more than one hour. Employees asked a few questions about severance pay. The response was otherwise muted.

Just short of forty years, Burgmaster was out of business.

14

WORKERS, MANAGERS, AND
ALCHEMISTS (1986–1987)

For one last day, Burgmaster hummed with the activity of machine tool builders.

On January 15, 1986, auction day, the factory was jammed with builders and machinists looking for bargains. National Industrial Services, a St. Louis–based auctioneer, was in charge of liquidating the plant. The auction began at 10:00 A.M. near the receiving dock. There two dozen display tables stood, end to end, groaning under the weight of hundreds of steel and carbide cutting wheels and every imaginable kind of drill, reamer, and tap. Many of the tools were unused, still encased in their protective, oil-soaked wrapping. It took hours to auction them all off, even at a cost of five cents on the dollar, and that was just the beginning. Everything, from office lamps, ashtrays, and company briefcases with the Burgmaster logo, to milling, turning, boring, grinding, and drilling machines, was for sale to the highest bidder.

It took an entire day and three auctioneers to walk with the crowd through the plant, which twelve years earlier had been cited in the trade press as a model industrial facility. Several factors combined to make the auction less than a rousing success, including the depression in the U.S. machine tool industry; the large number of repossessed machines on the used tool market; the cost of moving aging machines that weighed tons; and the distance of Burgmaster from the heart of the machine tool industry.

A working Dualcenter, which once represented Burgmaster's commitment to state-of-the-art machining, sold for $1,500, about what it was worth to a scrap dealer. The barely used Italian grinder, listed at $450,000, attracted no interest. Prospective buyers had learned through the grapevine that the grinder was defective, and doubled the machining time of any workpiece that was placed on it.

But for the discerning, there were a few bargains. A $76,000 Cincinnati Milacron lathe went for $20,000. A Burgmaster NC vertical machining center, worth $200,000 new, went for a fifth of its selling price. Perhaps the shrewdest purchases were made by Bill Melton, a former Burgmaster employee. Like many others, Melton had left Burgmaster during the 1970s, the decade of ex-odus, because he was dissatisfied with Houdaille's management. He opened his own job shop, which specialized in machining extremely sophisticated components for NASA, including navigational parts for the space shuttle. At the auction, Melton bought two machines for his lucrative business: a DeVlieg mill and a small, extremely precise Swiss tool suitable for making jigs and fixtures.

Melton was not the only former Burgmaster employee in attendance. In-deed, among the three hundred or so persons who came to the auction there was a reunion of sorts as more than two dozen veteran Burgmaster employees turned up. Some were long retired, others had left the company years before to seek more satisfying employment elsewhere. But all were curious, for they shared one thing in common. Burgmaster, at one time or another, had been one of the most important investments in their lives. Many had gotten their start in the trade under the Burgs.

These men were not going to show anything other than a stoic attitude, and no tears were shed. Yet they spoke with disbelief about Burgmaster's demise and debated its causes as the auctioneer's voice droned on in the back-ground. A few thought that Burgmaster should never have ventured outside the manufacture of turret drills. Others suggested that no, the problem was that Burgmaster had proven incapable of adjusting to a more demanding and competitive market. Everyone who worked under the Burgs recalled those twenty years as the company's golden age. "We could make things happen in a hurry," said Ed Merk. "We were entrepreneurs."[1] Houdaille's twenty-year stewardship, by contrast, was damned by faint praise.

They also talked about what former Burgmaster employees were doing. Soc Lenders, an electrical engineer, had formed a company that imported in-expensive machine tools. Several old Burgmaster hands worked with Lenders, including Aki Tokunaga, who used to be one of the top NC trouble-shooters at Burgmaster. Now he spent his days ironing out the kinks in foreign-built NC devices attached to imported tools. Meanwhile, someone else observed that one or two other ex-Burgmaster employees could be found at the brand-new Yamazaki technical center located on West 190th Street, not five miles from the Burgmaster plant. It was one of seven technical centers–showrooms that Yamazaki had established in the United States, in addition to its state-of-the-art factory in Kentucky.

One of the men said that he had heard that Norm Ginsburg, a few days before the auction, took his grandchildren to the Burgmaster plant. He wanted them to see what had once been the family business before it was gone. Joe Burg never came back, even after his five-year contract with Houdaille expired in 1970. And what about the "old man," Fred Burg, who was still alive at age ninety? His 1968 retirement had been traumatic for him, but freed from work for the first time since he was ten years old, Burg gradually began to look at life a little differently. He started to educate himself, reading books on philosophy, history, and psychology. Rachel Carson's *The Sea Around Us* made a deep impression, and at the age of eighty-one, Fred Burg discovered a new vocation. He became an ardent conservationist. "I don't know anything about geology or oceanography," he told a local newspaper that ran a profile about the entrepreneur-turned-environmentalist in 1977. "I'm a retired businessman. But I've got common sense. I know oceans must be treated with respect; that we can't destroy all living things; that our sources of water must remain unpolluted." To help educate people, he financed the rendering of a suboceanic model of the earth, four feet in diameter. Eventually it was put on display in the Copernicus Room of the California Museum of Science and Industry.

But now, nine years later, Fred Burg was ailing. He was physically unable to visit, one last time, the company that he started in his garage. In fact, the family was inclined not to tell him at all about Burgmaster's ignominious dissolution.

During the auction, bidders were free to wander anywhere in the plant except for two small areas cordoned off by ropes. In one area, near what used to be the assembly line, stood the last two machine tools that would be shipped from Gardena. Destined for Hardinge Bros., a Connecticut tool builder, the machines were identical, horizontal NC tool changers with shuttle tables. As was typical during the Delaney era, the machines had been sold prior to being fully designed and had undergone extensive reengineering for almost two years. Three employees were now being paid special retainers to correct the last stubborn problems. The tool holder was still leaking oil, the computer software was incomplete, and the shuttle tables were not performing up to specifications.[2]

Several yards away, there was another area cordoned off by plastic ropes. In it stood four shiny new turret drilling machines, familiar to everyone in the machine tool industry because of the large "B" on the turret heads. They were small Burgmaster "1" models, in many ways unchanged from the prototype that Fred Burg, Joe Burg, and Norm Ginsburg had arduously pieced together almost forty years earlier. A closer look showed, however, that they were not the last machines of their kind to be built in the Burgmaster plant. Rather, they were machines made in Japan for sale in the United States.

It took many months to liquidate the Burgmaster plant after the incomplete success of the January auction. Machines that failed to attract the minimum opening bid had to be priced low enough to get them out of the factory. Burgmaster's parts inventory, meanwhile, was transferred to a building in Cerritos, a nearby Los Angeles suburb. Strippit intended to provide spare parts and service for Burgmaster machines out of this facility for the next several years.

By April 1986, the two horizontal tool changers destined for Hardinge Bros. were sufficiently respectable to be shipped. In the entire plant, only the Italian grinder remained. "It couldn't sell for the longest time," recalled Ken Slawson, Strippit's president, but finally a buyer for even that machine was found.[3] All that remained was to fill in the reinforced concrete foundations that had been poured to keep Burgmaster's machines securely fastened to the earth. These huge, gaping holes, some of them twelve feet deep, pockmarked the factory floor.

For a time, the Northrop Corporation expressed an interest in the plant. But when the aerospace manufacturer failed to win a Defense Department contract for its Tigershark jet fighter, it lost interest in the eleven-acre site. Then, in August 1986, the property was sold for almost $6 million to a private individual. Given its location, just ten minutes down the Harbor Freeway from the Port of Los Angeles, the purchaser thought it would make an excellent bonded warehouse for foreign goods. Plans were made to adapt the plant to the needs of its future occupant, Transport Express, a trucking company.

When TE's vice president, Bill Meroth, drove up to the property for the first time, he did a double take. Although he was familiar with Gardena, the address did not click in his mind at first. But as he drove there, he suddenly realized that 139th and Broadway was near where he used to work. Then, as he came to the intersection, he realized it *was* where he used to work. More than fifteen years before, Meroth had worked in the tool crib at Burgmaster.

When Meroth walked inside, he didn't see an empty factory. The smell of grease and metal rubbing against metal still hung in the air, and it didn't take any imagination to see the machine tools still in their place. He half-expected to see Big Ben Bezdziecki, the foreman of the machine shop, walking down an aisle. "I can't believe I'm here," thought Meroth.[4]

A few months later, after the addition of twenty-six truck bays and a barbed wire fence, the plant was ready for Transport Express to move in. In a short time, what used to be the machine shop was crammed with goods from Taiwan, Indonesia, and Brazil. The imports were not sophisticated, high-value goods, but mostly household and consumer items like furniture, toys, and textiles. The plant was well suited to its new role, although it was intended for more. But only Bill Meroth was the wiser. Where bookcases from Taiwan now stood, stacked twelve feet high, only Meroth knew there used to be a Burgmaster 3BH turret drill, turning out the parts necessary to reproduce itself and, in turn, countless other machines.

Once the cavernous factory created wealth and embodied America's manufacturing prowess. Now it warehoused the industry of others.

The manufacture of the small tools line in Japan ensured that the Burgmaster trademark would persist long after the Gardena plant shut down. Actually, there were two separate agreements with Japanese builders. The bench models would be manufactured by Chukyo, the builder that became a Burgmaster licensee after infringing on the Burgs' patent twenty-five years ago. Meanwhile, NHK, another Japanese builder, had the license to manufacture the larger 1 models. By September 1986, the availability of these

Burgmaster turret drills was being widely advertised at tool fairs and in the trade press.[5]

Eventually Strippit, which owned all Burgmaster rights, also planned to import another, much larger line of Burgmaster turret drills from the Far East. Initially, the licensing agreement with the China Machinery and Equipment Council called for the manufacture of the model "3" turret drills for China's consumption only. But if the Chinese proved up to the task, over time Strippit hoped to import part of their production into the United States. Turret drills were still popular when the versatility of a machining center was unnecessary. Indeed, there was a healthy market for remanufactured, ten to twenty-year-old Burgmaster turret drills. They were often deemed to be no more than electronically obsolete.[6]

While Burgmaster was being reduced to a ghost of its former self, the rest of Houdaille's machine tool group met their respective fates as well. In April 1986, after eight months of negotiations, Stanwich Industries purchased the Powermatic, Universal Engineering, and Penberthy divisions. Stanwich, a private investment and holding firm based in Connecticut, refused to disclose the exact price or its plans. But it employed a familiar device to finance the purchase—a leveraged buyout. The respective managers of Powermatic, Universal, and Penberthy expressed optimism about the future, even though they still had to contend with a substantial debt. At least they were no longer lumped together with much larger divisions whose performance threatened to drown everyone in a tide of red ink. The sale to Stanwich "means business as usual, only better," said Universal Engineering's marketing manager.[7]

By contrast, the planned buyout of Strippit/Di-Acro was not going smoothly. Ken Slawson, Strippit's president, was anxious to run the company on his own. He was firmly convinced that machine tools were "still a very good business," and that under his management, Strippit could service a buyout debt until the pot of gold was within reach.[8] The company did not face the same competition that overwhelmed Burgmaster. In addition, Strippit had been strong enough to attract a Japanese partner, Nisshinbo Industries.[9] If necessary, Nisshinbo could be used to supply parts or entire machines, and give Strippit the margin it needed to survive.

But Slawson could not come up with the $50 million he needed to make the buyout work, despite the high-powered financial advice of the First Boston Corporation. No amount of creative financial engineering could overcome the machine tool industry's bad business press. Investors and lenders were skittish about sinking money into a leveraged tool builder, regardless of the interest offered. After almost a year of trying, Slawson and Houdaille president Phil O'Reilly recognized that the climate wasn't right, and pulled Strippit off the market.[10]

In addition to thwarting Slawson's ambition, the failure to leverage Strippit undermined O'Reilly's grand strategy. By jettisoning most of the machine tool group, Houdaille's CEO had managed to whittle down the debt from 113 percent of the conglomerate's capitalization in 1984 to 103 percent by 1986.[11] Once the conglomerate was pruned of everything save its profitable interest in industrial products, O'Reilly hoped to pull Houdaille out of its debt trap, and put what remained on a stable footing. But that was not to be.

The inability to get rid of Strippit was only part of the problem. Realistically, the roots of Houdaille's predicament went much deeper. A leveraged company reached the pot of gold by reducing the large debt-to-equity ratio incurred at the outset of a buyout. But if it failed the test, it had to pay a steep price, and Houdaille was no exception. The conglomerate found itself sucked into a whirlpool: in a manner typical of LBOs, the Houdaille buyout had been structured so that the heaviest debt payments actually came due in later years.[12]

As a result, over the next eighteen months the conglomerate would have to entertain a dizzying array of proposed deals, buyouts, divestitures, and buybacks. By the time it was all over, Phil O'Reilly would be out of a job and Houdaille would cease to exist for all practical purposes. The company that pioneered the large leveraged buyout became one of its first big casualties, a classic illustration of the consequences of equity transformed into debt.

Initially, Phil O'Reilly and Kohlberg, Kravis, and Roberts, the de facto owners of Houdaille, tried to pull Houdaille out of its tailspin by selling off the conglomerate in one fell swoop in 1986. KKR had much more profitable ways to spend its time than attending to a sickly buyout. The investment bankers wanted to pay off creditors and equity investors who were clamoring about the windfall profits that were promised within five years of the 1979 buyout, but never came. Selling Houdaille seemed a way out because for all its troubles, the conglomerate still included some attractive companies, especially the John Crane mechanical seals division.

Several industrial concerns expressed interest in one or more of Houdaille's subsidiaries once it became known the conglomerate was for sale. But no one was willing to swallow Houdaille whole, and on this point KKR was adamant.[13] It was all or nothing.

The failure to dispose of Houdaille by the summer of 1986 forced KKR's hand, for to some degree its reputation was at stake. After seven years, if KKR could not extricate the original investors without some profits to show for their troubles, it would draw into question KKR's franchise as the premier LBO boutique. So KKR resorted to the best solution short of selling Houdaille outright. It engineered another leveraged buyout, this time for $430 million.

In a sense, the 1986 buyout was not a full LBO because Houdaille was already a private concern. It might be more accurately described as a recapitalization of the leverage from the 1979 deal. Regardless of the name attached to the transaction, however, common shareholders, who paid $2.52 per share for their stock in 1979, received $11 per share in the September 1986 buyout.[14] Thus, every equity participant who wanted out managed to exit

Houdaille with a tidy profit. Those who stayed in the deal realized a handsome dividend in lieu of the pot of gold. The rest of the $430 million went toward repaying bank debt from the first buyout and redeeming preferred stock.

The profits were extracted at a high cost. The second buyout was notable for its financial brinkmanship. Whereas the 1979 deal had been constructed with a pot of gold in mind, this buyout piled debt upon debt and put Houdaille on a precipice from which there was virtually no escape, aside from dismemberment. KKR and Houdaille management, along with a few holdovers from the first buyout, held the equity portion of the 1986 deal, namely, $15 million in preferred stock and $20 million in common stock. To finance the rest of the transaction, though, the newly formed Houdaille borrowed $220 million from banks and issued $175 million in subordinated notes. This meant that Houdaille's debt leverage soared from 103 percent of capitalization to a staggering 152 percent.[15]

That was not all. In order to "quiet the natives," the original equity investors, with $11 cash per common share, the reincarnated Houdaille had to record a $145 million equity deficit on its books. And to attract lenders for its subordinated debt issue, Houdaille's underwriters had to offer interest rates as high as 13.875 percent. This came at a time when banks were charging most business customers less than 10 percent. Standard & Poor's assigned a low CCC rating to the $175 million in subordinated notes (a D rating means bankruptcy), and warned potential investors that the notes could be worth less than par value in the near future. "Cash interest coverage and debt service coverage are very thin," noted an S&P analyst. "Cash flow could become insufficient to service debt if Houdaille's earnings suffer due to an economic downturn."[16]

The single most threatening feature of the second buyout, however, was the repayment schedule of the $220 million bank debt. As with the first LBO, the debt was structured so that the heaviest payments came due later. Houdaille would annually pay between $5 and $15 million on the principal from the debt until 1992; then $25 million would be due in 1993 and 1994. Although such payments were probably manageable, in addition Houdaille faced two balloon payments, of $40 million and $60 million, due in 1989 and 1994, respectively. These hung over Houdaille like the sword suspended over Damocles. Or as Standard & Poor's analyst understatedly put it, "Whenever you have an aggressive LBO and a recapitalized leverage situation on top of it, it's tough to manage."[17]

In November 1986, three months after the recapitalization, Houdaille's fortunes appeared to brighten momentarily. The Reagan administration finally produced the import relief that U.S. tool builders had been clamoring for since 1983. Even though the administration stopped short of approving the NMTBA's national security petition, the net effect on imports was virtually identical. The Commerce Department extracted "voluntary" concessions from

Japan and other tool-exporting countries. For a period of five years, beginning in 1987, these countries agreed to roll back their exports to 1981 levels.[18]

O'Reilly welcomed the news as vindication of Houdaille's lonely struggle, though he was still bitter. He could not help noticing, though, that NC punching machines—like those made by Strippit/Di-Acro—were going to enjoy extraordinary protection under the voluntary agreement. By returning to 1981 export levels, the Japanese were agreeing to cut their share of the market by 56 percent. Strippit could hardly avoid making lots of money again. This was Commerce Secretary Baldrige's way of seeing to it "that justice was finally being done Houdaille," as he personally told O'Reilly.[19]

With this unusual boost, O'Reilly thought for a while that Houdaille might have a chance to survive its second buyout intact. Besides the VRA, there was another reason for optimism. The Reagan administration, after raising the dollar to unconscionably high levels during its first term in office, was now determined to drive the dollar down because of a staggering merchandise trade deficit. Without so much as lifting a finger, Strippit was suddenly 30 to 40 percent more competitive in terms of price than it had been just two years before. Foreign sales were once again possible.

But it took time for a tool builder to recover lost market share at home and lost markets overseas. And the only thing Houdaille had less of than money was time. In any case, Strippit was far too small to generate anywhere near the cash flow Houdaille needed to pull out of its tailspin. In April 1987, seven months after the recapitalization, Houdaille filed a securities registration statement with the SEC. The conglomerate warned that it might prove unable to make the $40 million balloon payment due in 1989, in which case it would have to divest itself of additional assets.[20]

In midsummer, in a move to economize, O'Reilly shifted Houdaille's headquarters from Fort Lauderdale to a suburb near Chicago. In a way, Houdaille was coming home. The company started out as a small, midwestern industrial concern that was a stepchild to the auto industry. From there it grew, and by necessity diversified, until it was a highflying conglomerate, with a corporate headquarters in a sunny clime, far removed from the manufacturing heartland. Now, somewhat humbled, it was returning to Illinois, to be closer to its John Crane division. But Houdaille had not only come full circle. The circle was about to close.

In August 1987, Houdaille announced that Phil O'Reilly was retiring from active management, effective immediately. The abrupt departure caught industry observers by surprise. Few CEOs were more vigorous than the high-profile O'Reilly, and at age sixty-one, he was well short of normal retirement. Don Boyce, his successor, never gave a clue as to the reason for O'Reilly's departure. Indeed, Boyce attempted to paint a picture of business as usual. The restructuring and consolidation of Houdaille was now over, he said, and no major changes were anticipated. In fact, he spoke about selective acquisitions in the near future if everything continued to break Houdaille's way.

"Economic statistics indicate there will be an improvement in the capital markets we serve," said Boyce, "so we are expecting that things should improve for us as well."[21]

Three weeks later, the other shoe dropped. In late August a British industrial conglomerate, Tube Investments (TI) Group, announced that it was going to buy Houdaille outright, and then dismember it, keeping only the John Crane unit. A year earlier, in 1986, when KKR put Houdaille on the market, TI tried to buy the Crane division. It already owned 51 percent of Crane's British subsidiary, and dearly wanted the whole company. But KKR insisted on selling all of Houdaille, and TI could not afford to buy it. After a year spent restructuring its own operations, however, TI now had the cash to pull off its coup. It acquired Houdaille by assuming its entire $338 million debt, and paying $112 million in cash to Kohlberg, Kravis, Roberts & Co.[22]

On September 28, TI Group announced that it had found a buyer for the Houdaille divisions it did not want—Kohlberg, Kravis, and Roberts, in partnership with the management from those divisions. This announcement naturally raised speculation about a prior understanding between KKR and TI as to the true nature of their August deal. When asked why Houdaille didn't simply sell Crane to TI in the first place, a Houdaille spokesman cited "tax and legal" reasons, but declined to be more specific.[23] Whether or not a prior understanding existed, no doubt certain tax advantages did accrue from consummating the deal in such a roundabout fashion. For once again, the Houdaille divisions TI didn't want underwent a leveraged buyout, this time for $220 million. The IDEX Corporation was born.

Houdaille was now a shadow of its former self, reduced to a holding company for John Crane. For all intents and purposes, it had passed into oblivion as an industrial manufacturer.

In stark contrast to Houdaille's lot stood the fortunes of Kohlberg, Kravis, Roberts & Co. Houdaille had been only the first in a remarkable string of buyouts that were changing the face of corporate America, and making KKR's partners extremely wealthy in the process.

KKR still tried to shroud its undertakings in a "Garbo-like secrecy," as *The Wall Street Journal* put it. In early 1986, when the *Journal* wanted to run a long, front-page profile of the firm that could "not be ignored," KKR politely but repeatedly rejected numerous requests for an interview.[24] KKR was hardly keeping its guard up because it was concerned about inspiring competition. On the contrary, KKR's success was one of the worst-kept secrets on Wall Street. KKR, in fact, had helped sire a whole new industry.

Buyouts were no longer the exclusive preserve of such little-known boutiques as KKR, Forstmann Little, Gibbons Green van Amerongen, and Clayton & Dubilier. By 1985, as many as two hundred financial institutions were furiously soliciting buyouts, leading to a record $18 billion worth of LBOs that year. By virtue of their place in the standings—KKR accounted for a full third of the $18 billion—Kohlberg, Kravis, and Roberts were still regarded as the foremost practitioners of the art, unmatched for their creativity in engineering deals.[25] But the field they once had more or less to themselves was now crowded with other banking houses, including such aggressive giants as Merrill Lynch.[26]

Nor were LBOs an isolated financial phenomenon, popular only because of the fantastic profits they promised investors. Buyouts were part of a much broader trend, namely, the great wave of corporate restructuring that was occurring during the 1980s. A resurgence in corporate mergers, takeovers, and divestitures was occurring on a scale not seen since the late 1960s. The Reagan administration's lax attitude toward antitrust enforcement, euphemistically called a "more favorable climate in Washington," was one frequently cited reason for the sudden burst of corporate redeployment.[27] But economics had more to do with the third tidal wave of mergers in U.S. industrial history.

Several economic factors were at work. First, the Reagan administration's deregulation of the financial markets caused commercial banks, thrift institutions, and insurance companies to invade each other's territory in the early 1980s. The increased competition and squeezed earnings sent the institutions scurrying after high-yield investments and imaginative new financial instruments. Junk bonds, of the kind used to finance takeovers and buyouts, offered a yield that more staid investments in stocks or bonds could not match.[28]

In addition, following KKR's lead, Wall Street investment bankers discovered pension funds, a largely untapped and bountiful, institutional source of capital. Scandals nearly a decade earlier had prompted the Congress to tighten the laws governing retirement funds. As a result, many private and state pension funds dropped archaic rules against investing in stocks and bonds. Many observers hoped the workers' funds would become a huge pool of capital for long-term, productive investment. Instead, pension fund managers, under relentless pressure or lured by incentives to produce immediate gains, approached the market with only one goal, quick profit maximization, in mind.[29] In a remarkably short time, institutional investors, by virtue of their aggregate financial power, came to dominate the market. Stock ownership became more concentrated than ever before.[30]

But the concentration of and competition for capital, though a necessary condition, was insufficient to explain the merger mania. The other part of the equation was stagnation in the U.S. economy, coupled with the demonstrable failure of the conglomeration strategy of the 1960s. Corporate America had repeatedly demonstrated the foolhardiness of attempting to run businesses that it knew nothing about, especially in an economy racked by alternating bouts of inflation, recession, both together (stagflation), and increased foreign competition. The most efficient and profitable corporations were ones that had "stuck to their own knitting."[31]

Given the tax advantages gained by turning equity into debt, it was relatively simple to calculate that hundreds of corporations, including scores of *Fortune* 500 companies, were worth more broken up into sundry parts than they were worth whole, *worth* being defined as the price the companies could command on the stock exchange. This judgment was exactly the opposite of the notion that held sway in the 1960s, when a conglomerate was commonly assigned a market value greater than the sum of its parts.

Through its 1979 leveraging of Houdaille, of course, KKR had been one of the very first to try and extract profits from a large, underperforming conglomerate. And where KKR led, a host of others now followed. Not all the players opted to wield KKR's chosen instrument, the LBO. Corporate raiders like Carl Icahn and T. Boone Pickens, for example, became the bane of entrenched managers for mounting unsolicited takeover bids. Stockholders were getting shortchanged, the raiders would cry, by management that was too dumb, fat, and happy. The raiders would then make a bid based on the value of the corporation after divestiture. Often this price would be high enough to attract a majority of the shareholders right away, especially institutional investors always looking for a premium. In other instances, prolonged takeover battles would result, made all the more dramatic by Wall Street's colorful vernacular. "Greenmail," "golden parachutes," "sweeteners," and "poison pills" were just some of the incentives and defenses that sprang up amid the rash of takeovers.

No matter how gentlemanly they appeared by contrast, leveraged buyouts were just the other side of the coin.[32] Instead of wresting control away from the managers of underperforming assets, however, LBOs gave them a generous incentive to bring about the same "efficiencies" demanded by the raiders. As Harvard Business School professor Michael C. Jensen, a leading academic champion of buyouts, claimed, "LBOs are an absolutely ingenious invention. Public companies may grow fat and sloppy. LBOs put management on the razor's edge to create efficiencies so the debt can be paid off."[33] In effect, LBOs bought off a large chunk of the corporate community that otherwise would have fallen prey to raiders or sought deals-curbing legislation from Washington. They acquiesced because LBOs promised to make the managers rich beyond their wildest expectations. As Henry Kravis would assert on more than one occasion, "Management buyouts are very good for corporate America. What is wrong with management making a lot of money?"[34]

Huge pools of concentrated capital, swollen and unfocused corporations, and the rise of takeover and buyout "artists" all helped fuel a bull market on Wall Street of a kind not seen since the 1920s. In many respects, the parallels between the boom that began in 1982 and its earlier cousin were uncanny, as John Kenneth Galbraith pointed out. The particulars differed, but in essence both markets rose atop inverse pyramids of endlessly imaginative and highly lucrative debt.[35] One Wall Street economist likened investors' inexhaustible willingness to buy up debt to playing with a roulette wheel. "People will keep putting their money on a number and when they hit the jackpot, they will do it again. As long as there are people with money, the wheel will keep spinning."[36]

If one company in an industry was taken over or leveraged at a premium, the stock of nearly every company in that industry would immediately be pushed upward by investors anticipating other bids. "Breakup value" became the measure of a corporation's worth, and corporate cash flow (enhanced by Reagan's 1981 tax cuts) replaced earnings as a key factor in any valuation of how much to bid. Cash flow determined "how much leverage could be picked up;" simultaneously, Wall Street thwarted every effort to rescind the federal tax blessing bestowed on takeovers and buyouts.[37]

With debt cheaper to finance than equity, financial capitalism supplanted managerial capitalism, and speculation replaced enterprise. Only a few voices were raised to protest the perversion of the capital markets into a casino. The federal government, that sometime regulator of unbridled capitalism, was decidedly split among those who worried about the wounding of the economy, those who celebrated Wall Street's creativity, and those who said nothing.

In particular, the SEC's resounding silence spoke volumes. John Shad, now SEC chairman and many years removed from his days on Burgmaster's board of directors, took a monkish approach to the speculation. In a widely noted 1984 speech, Shad warned that "the more leveraged takeovers and buyouts today, the more bankruptcies tomorrow." But he admitted having no desire to "pass on the merits of such transactions," and averred that the marketplace was the best judge. "It would be as wrong to overreact to these issues as it would be to ignore them," concluded Shad, as he consciously steered an agnostic's path between the old world of managerial capitalism and the brave new one of financial capitalism.[38] The SEC, along with the FTC and IRS, did not even bother to perform one of government's most basic functions, which is to collect information. The federal government had virtually no idea about many of the sums involved, such as the total amount of interest deductions that corporations were claiming on monies borrowed to finance mergers.[39]

Among those in the government who wanted to put on the brakes, Federal Reserve Chairman Paul Volcker was perhaps the most vigorous. Three years of watching the bull charge persuaded him that the market run-up was not logical or rational but the perverse result of greed. "We spend our days issuing debt and retiring equity, both in record volumes," said Volcker in late 1985, "and then we spend our evenings raising each other's eyebrows with gossip about signs of stress in the financial system."[40] Volcker wanted to use the Federal Reserve's power to curtail sharply the virtually unregulated ability of shell corporations to issue junk bonds.

His lonely attempt predictably evoked howls of protest from Wall Street—but more significantly, strong opposition from within the Reagan administration. Speaking for the latter, the Justice Department said, "The [Fed's] proposal would destroy the market for corporate control, which disciplines inefficient management and enables stockholders to maximize returns on their investment."[41] Volcker's effort quickly began to wither from lack of support, and the stock market kept roaring.

Around the same time, feeble attempts were made in Congress to dampen the merger mania. Some senators favored wholesale limits on Wall Street's ability to finance takeovers and buyouts with junk bonds; others wanted only to restrict some of the controversial tactics, such as greenmail and poison pills, that had sprung up during hostile takeover battles. Investment bankers, who knew the market spree would soon end if takeovers and buyouts abated, swung into action. For many banking houses, the fees alone from mergers and acquisitions had become their lifeblood. They turned to such well-placed friends as New York Senator Alfonse D'Amato, chairman of a pivotal subcommittee of the Senate Banking Committee and not coincidentally the recipient of $500,000 in campaign donations from Wall Street. Although it is not commonly understood, guaranteeing congressional *inaction* can be easily more important than the passage of special interest legislation. So long as Senator D'Amato chaired the banking subcommittee on securities, no legislation even remotely opposed by the investment banks was going to be reported out of committee.[42]

The market's speculative pyramid kept building, stoked by a seemingly endless supply of takeover and buyout deals. Another shift became evident as well. At the outset of the bull market, takeovers had dwarfed buyouts in both number and size. LBOs accounted for just 5.7 percent of all such transactions, by value, in 1982. By 1986, however, LBOs had almost quadrupled to 21 percent of all takeover and buyout activity by value.[43]

KKR alone was responsible for engineering a total of twenty-nine separate buyouts valued at just under $14 billion during this period. Not all of the deals had matured to the payback, or pot-of-gold stage. But of those that had, the average annual compounded rate of return was an astonishing 47 percent. An institutional investor could entrust $5 million to KKR, and in some instances walk away a few years later with $18 million. By 1986, to participate in one of KKR's buyout pools, investors had to ante up a minimum of $20 million.[44]

Kohlberg, Kravis, and Roberts were catholic and impartial when it came to deciding which corporations were candidates for a buyout. They would just as soon leverage a motel chain (Red Lion Inns) as a machine tool manufacturer (Eaton Leonard); a media chain (Storer Communications) could be as suitable as an oil company (Union Texas Petroleum). And the LBOs got bigger all the time. In 1979, all of Wall Street sat up and took notice when KKR engineered the Houdaille buyout because of its audacious size. By 1986 standards, however, the $355 million Houdaille LBO was just a middling affair. The Storer and Union Texas buyouts were priced at $2.4 billion and $2.1 billion, respectively. In March 1986, KKR topped itself and consummated a buyout of truly mammoth proportions: Beatrice Cos. went private for $6.2 billion. KKR's fee alone for arranging that deal came to $45 million, then the largest single investment advisory fee on record.[45] Sheer size offered less and less immunity against a buyout.

The lives of the KKR partners were changing almost as much as the balance sheets of corporate America. According to Wall Street estimates, the buyout boutique's three senior partners were now worth between $150 million and $500 million each. In 1985, KKR's taciturn elder statesman, Jerome Kohlberg, bought a home in exclusive Westchester County, not too far from similar estates owned by Ivan Boesky and Carl Icahn, two other new Wall Street titans.[46]

But the widest swath was cut by Henry Kravis, who was also emerging more and more as KKR's spokesman. The same year Kohlberg purchased his Westchester estate, Kravis moved into a sixteen-room, $5.5 million, two-fireplace apartment in a Park Avenue building that once boasted John D. Rockefeller, Jr., as a tenant. Soon afterward, the *New York Times Magazine* brought its readers into Kravis's new apartment, "revealing an opulent temple of materialism that might have stirred envy in a 19th-century robber baron."[47]

Kravis and his wife, Carolyn Roehm, began to crop up regularly in Manhattan society columns. Kravis joined the boards of the New York City Ballet, Mount Sinai Hospital, and WNET/Channel 13, the city's public television station. An avid art collector, specializing in nineteenth-century European painting, Kravis personally donated $10 million to help the Metropolitan Museum of Art complete its master expansion plan. By doing so, he attained what passes for immortality in social Manhattan—the new addition was to be named the Henry R. Kravis Wing. In a *New York Times* social page article entitled "New Stars on the Circuit," Miss Roehm offered a succinct explanation for her husband's charitable impulses. "Henry says if you have money you have an obligation to share it and your time with the community."[48]

As more and more bankers sought to emulate the success of Henry Kravis, ever more baroque forms of speculation appeared. Takeover and buyout artists dominated the deal making, but soon a new breed captured the imagination—the risk arbitrageur, personified by Ivan Boesky. His aim, of course, was simply to profit from the next outbreak of takeover or buyout fever. As the funds at the command of risk arbitrageurs grew to an estimated $15 billion though, so did their power.[49] They could even put corporations into play in some instances, a rather shrewd way to take the risk out of the arbitrage. But there was no mistaking that although their chosen instruments differed, and they operated at varying levels of respectability, corporate raiders like Carl Icahn, risk arbitrageurs like Ivan Boesky, and investment banking boutiques like KKR were all engaged in exploiting the same situation.

"Nothing so gives the illusion of intelligence as the personal association with large sums of money," John Kenneth Galbraith wrote near the height of the bull market.[50] And so it was with Boesky, who was admired, feted, and invited to speak at college commencements before his fall from grace in November 1986. Boesky's excesses revived moribund congressional interest in curbing the speculation mania. The Wall Street investment banks braced for another round on Capitol Hill, and began madly hiring Washington consultants and lobbyists to protect their highly profitable takeover business.

KKR, for one, hired the Washington firm of Foley & Lardner to forestall any adverse legislation "pertaining to mergers and acquisitions and leveraged buyouts."[51]

The investment bankers quickly sought to draw distinctions. As far as insider abuses went, they argued that more stringent self-regulation would be the best protection against the aberrations. But takeovers and buyouts were another matter. The bankers added a new twist to their already finely honed argument about the positive effects of corporate asset redeployment. Now such transactions were helping to make America more competitive. "A leveraged buyout is like taking the corporation to the health club and getting it into better shape," one Wall Street analyst argued.[52] Enormous debt was not a burden, but good discipline for management. Buyouts in particular encouraged management to dismiss deadwood employees, sell underutilized assets, and make decisions without regard to short-term movements in stock prices.

Yet by 1987, Jerome Kohlberg, KKR's elder statesman and bellwether, was beginning to be troubled by several trends. First, he was becoming more and more disturbed over the ever-increasing size of the LBOs being engineered by KKR. The $6.2 billion Beatrice buyout in 1986 had been followed rather quickly by a $4.25 billion leverage of Safeway Stores. KKR, Kohlberg believed, was drifting far from the four or five guidelines that he thought were vital for a successful buyout. LBOs were being used to defend against hostile takeovers, something that was unthinkable just a few years before. His partners were even contemplating the idea of mounting unsolicited buyouts after secretly acquiring toeholds in target companies. In sum, KKR itself seemed to be caught in the speculation fever and Kohlberg feared that reason no longer prevailed. He found himself increasingly at odds with Henry Kravis and George Roberts.[53]

He also was having some doubts about the very nature of some leveraged buyouts. None was sufficient to dissuade him entirely. But a few years before, whenever he had been asked about what economic or social benefits LBOs provided to justify such enormous rewards, Kohlberg had had a ready answer. Buyouts promoted economic efficiency by giving managers a stake in the business. Now he was less of an unalloyed booster. Perhaps he had Houdaille in mind when he told the *New York Times*, "It's not all black-and-white."

> This is not all good. I can understand the problems some people have, especially when they've been building something all of their lives. But a lot of companies have gotten too big and less competitive. I guess you could say that we've been the balance wheel to the conglomeratization that came before us.[54]

In early 1987, Kravis and Roberts expressed their desire to solicit a buyout fund of $5 billion, which, unlike earlier buyout pools, could be used to make unfriendly offers. Kohlberg realized that his "philosophical" differences with his partners were now so big that it was time for a parting of the ways. The year before, KKR had raised $2 billion for buyouts in what was then the largest fund ever assembled for that purpose. The $5 billion figure was a clear signal that his partners intended to do ever-bigger deals, despite his reservations. In May 1987, Kohlberg announced his withdrawal from active participation in KKR during a private speech to the firm's investors. He took the occasion to comment on the decline of ethics on Wall Street and the "overpowering greed that pervades our business life." He also insisted that without a resurgence of values "we will kill the golden goose."[55]

Five months after Kohlberg's farewell address, it looked indeed as if the goose had been cooked. Black Monday saw the biggest one-day plunge in stock market history. The *Times* labeled it a "Stunning Blow to a Gilded, Impudent Age," and suddenly there seemed to be almost unanimous agreement that things had gotten a little too much out of hand. "There's a certain goofiness about having kids decide the future of a company when they've never even walked a plant floor," noted one business professor.[56] Corporate executives breathed a collective and almost audible sigh of relief. In the wake of the traumatic crash, no one doubted that the junk bond market would shrink significantly, bringing about a slowdown in the takeover and buyout frenzy.[57] No less than five public and private post-mortems on the crash also suggested that a semblance of sanity was about to return to the capital markets.

But in fact, the first tangible result from the crash was that an intimidated Congress dropped, like a hot potato, its plan to curb takeovers and buyouts. Several weeks before the crash, Congressman Dan Rostenkowski proposed a $5 million limit on tax deductions for interest incurred to finance takeovers and buyouts. This plan would have put Wall Street's speculation orgy under a very cold shower.

Instead of earning praise, however, in the wake of Black Monday Rostenkowski found himself in the unenviable position of being blamed for the market meltdown. "It wasn't an accident. This was what knocked the props out from underneath the market," said one arbitrageur. "Somebody pulled the plug on one of the major reasons for the bull market—the restructuring of corporate America. Somebody found the Achilles heel. . . . It was irresponsible."[58] Virtually overnight, the Democrats reversed their political field, and jettisoned the whole idea of curbing takeovers and buyouts. "A number of us agreed that [the proposed takeover curbs] were not only bad for the operation of the free market, but also that they were shaking up Wall Street," said Congressman Tom Downey, a liberal from New York.[59] Congress was thoroughly cowed.

If a basic cause for Black Monday was going to go uncorrected for the moment, it was nevertheless reasonable to expect that the crash post-mortems would draw some necessary lessons. Nothing of the kind happened. As these studies trickled in, they invariably singled out for blame such derivative speculation instruments as options, computerized program trading, and stock index futures. All the reports exhaustively examined the technical intricacies of the crash itself, as if they were the sole root of the debacle. The question of why, in the first place, the market had been driven to its super-heated, overvalued state—which was of at least equal importance—was neatly evaded.[60]

Little wonder that by January 1988, less than three months after the crash and shortly after Wall Street had finished weeding out some of its own extraneous and overpaid personnel, takeovers and buyouts began making a comeback. In less than two months $50 billion worth of deals were on the table. Merger mania's obituary had been written prematurely. Although the tax code had changed appreciably since the precedent-setting 1979 buyout of Houdaille, debt was still cheaper than equity as a means of corporate financing.[61] In effect, the U.S. Treasury still subsidized takeovers and buyouts, although some restraints had been slapped on corporate raiders. But the slack they left was more than enough for the corporate establishment itself and "power investors" on Wall Street. As *Business Week* observed in March, "Mergers and acquisitions have become an ingrained way of doing business, an important method of dislodging lackadaisical managements, an easy opportunity to make money, and [ostensibly] a prime means of staying competitive."[62] As these transactions made a comeback, the stock market recouped some of its lost paper value.

Simultaneously, Wall Street investment houses underwent their own restructuring. Takeover and buyout "superstars" at established firms like First Boston suddenly left to form their own boutiques, for much the same reason that Kohlberg, Kravis, and Roberts left Bear, Stearns in 1976. "Everyone wants to be like Kohlberg, Kravis, Roberts & Co. or one of the other top firms that have minted money by specializing in arranging buyouts of companies," said one *New York Times* article. By the fall of 1988, buyout artists had reportedly raised equity pools totaling $25 to $30 billion, meaning that $250 to $300 billion was available to finance buyouts.[63]

KKR was bound to face more competition than ever. But Henry Kravis exuded nothing less than complete confidence, even though his firm would have to meet its competitors sans Jerome Kohlberg. Washington had been beaten back after the market plunge. Reportedly, KKR refused an invitation to testify before a congressional panel investigating takeovers and buyouts, and there wasn't the will or the votes to subpoena the investment bankers. Kravis, in fact, was already planning for the post-Reagan era. Six weeks after the market crash, he arranged a fund-raising lunch for George Bush that netted $550,000. Moreover, as finance chairman of the Bush campaign in New York, Kravis would surely have the ear of a Bush administration. Nor would he have to do much persuading. During the campaign, Bush declared—not surprisingly—that he favored a "pro-stockholder, free-market approach" to corporate takeovers and buyouts.[64]

Meanwhile, KKR's new buyout pool was oversubscribed. Kravis, in fact, had managed to raise $5.6 billion rather than the $5 billion planned, which meant that the lull in the junk bond market would have little or no effect on KKR's deal making. The October plunge, asserted Kravis, was not a disaster, just a mixed bag. "We got lucky, fat and happy over the last few years. Now we're going to go back to the old days when we turned to banks for financing and held our positions for five or seven years."[65]

Ten months later, KKR launched an unsolicited $20 billion offer for RJR Nabisco, the nineteenth largest industrial company in America.

15
EPILOGUE

G iven American culture, which venerates success and great wealth, it was not surprising when Ivan Boesky became an icon for the mid-1980s. By the end of the decade, however, a different mood came over the nation.

For the first time during the Reagan presidency, in 1988 polling data revealed a sense of uneasiness about the future unmatched since the most troubled days of the Carter administration. This time the cause was not hostages, but a sense that America was no longer in control of its economic destiny, that there was something about the economic arrangement that was seriously out of kilter.[1]

Reagan's chief legacy was to leave the United States the world's biggest debtor, and with a severely diminished capacity to direct its economic and social destiny. Yet the unease that gripped many citizens had little to do with the fantastic numbers generated by a nation living beyond its means. Instead, the disquiet probably arose from what could be seen daily and in every American city: poverty, homeless people, decrepit public schools, and soup kitchens that were reluctantly thriving. Just as important, these phenomena were occurring in the midst of an economic windfall for a very few. It is almost un-American to begrudge or look askance at generous rewards to an elite if everyone else seems to benefit as well. But while institutional investors, brokers, investment bankers, arbitrageurs, and some corporate managers became extraordinarily wealthy, 10.8 million Americans lost their prime blue-collar jobs from 1981 to 1985.[2] Billions of dollars worth of assets were reshuffled, but the only parties that were truly better off seem to be the ones who dealt and shuffled. More than anything, the unease stemmed from a sense that inequality was on the rise in America, and it was a perception more than borne out by the statistics.[3]

The public's latent anxiety manifested itself in other ways besides polls: concern over America's economic vulnerability in the world marketplace; criticism of foreign investment; a rising clamor for "managed trade" or other forms of protection; and simple Jap-bashing. It was surely evident during the

presidential campaign as well, even though some of the candidates most identified with "economic nationalism" went down to defeat. The mood was also
inextricably linked to the flourishing debates over solvency, "imperial over-
stretch," and the erosion of American power. Economists debated whether
there would be a sudden, jarring crash or just a gradual but inexorable
decline.[4]

Apologists, beneficiaries, and some politicians claim that several of these
phenomena do not exist, or if they do, they are unrelated. In particular, they
dispute one of the most important correlations, namely, the link between
domestic economic ills and the decline of American industry.[5] The shift from a
manufacturing-based economy to one dominated by services should be little
cause for concern, goes the argument, for such a transformation is an inevitable, even desirable evolution. In 1984, for example, the New York Stock Exchange asserted that "a strong manufacturing sector is not a requisite for a
prosperous economy." That claim was followed in 1985 by the Reagan administration's declaration that the "progression of an economy such as
America's from agriculture to manufacturing to services is a natural change."[6]

But manufacturing has not lost its central function in a modern economy.
Even though there is an ongoing technological transformation in the means of
manufacture, it heralds a shift from one kind of industrial economy to another,
not a diminution of manufacturing's importance. A strong service economy is
a complement to manufacturing, not a substitute for or successor to it. The
notion of an American economy devoid of manufacturing is a recipe for
domestic impoverishment, social injustice, national insecurity, and global
discord.[7]

And if manufacturing still matters, then the machine tool industry cap-
tures, in many ways, the American predicament. Political primacy, economic
wealth, and preeminence in machine tool production have always coincided
because "mother machines" are the heart of any industrial economy. The correspondence between the rise in the American tool industry, which began
before the turn of the century and reached a peak in the early 1960s, and
American politico-economic power was not mere happenstance. In like manner, the tool industry parallels the decline of the American economy since
then. The U.S. share of world production was almost halved between 1965
and 1982.[8]

The axiom of this book is that the demise of one machine tool builder may
be a lens that reveals what has befallen a key industry and the manufacturing
economy. Of course, the rise and fall of Burgmaster is a unique story in several
respects, and any conclusions have to be drawn with care. At the same time,
the uniqueness of the saga does not make it parochial. It represents a veritable
panorama of the many complicated factors involved in the decline of an industry, American manufacturing, and the economy as a whole. Its meaning even
extends to international issues, most obviously the friction-filled American
relationship with Japan.

In its first two decades of existence, Burgmaster exemplified American capitalism as it is supposed to work. The Burgs were entrepreneurs who paid good wages and gave satisfying employment to hundreds of workers. In the process of creating wealth for themselves, they enhanced the productivity and ultimately the wealth of the entire economy. When Burgmaster became a publicly traded corporation in 1961, enterprise was rewarded as the capital markets performed their societal and economic function. The Burgs received a personal windfall, and obtained needed funds to reinvest in their business. In exchange, public investors now had an opportunity to share in the Burgs' enterprise. Wall Street, for its role in arranging the mutually beneficial relationship between entrepreneur and investor, profited too.

From a management point of view, Burgmaster thrived because the Burgs knew their business. All the reasons for the company's extraordinary success from 1946 to 1965 flowed from this simple yet vital fact. Burgmaster first designed and manufactured the turret drill because Fred Burg recognized, from his own experience, that it promised to be a significant advance. But even after that first blush of success, there was no assurance that Burgmaster would become the largest tool builder west of the Mississippi. It became a company to be reckoned with because the Burgs operated their enterprise on the maxim that a machine tool builder is only as good as its workers. They cultivated a work force that was second to none in its productivity and dedication to quality.

Of equal importance, and as a consequence, Burgmaster never stood still. Innovation did not just sound like a good idea; it was considered pivotal. The Burgs constantly developed new variations on their basic invention, made improvements, and adopted the latest technology when feasible. Numerical control, the single greatest advancement in machine tool technology since the turn of the century, was a commercial failure because the air force R&D subsidy produced a system that was wholly impractical. It remained for builders like Burgmaster to make it work on an economical basis.

A few other points stand out from those first twenty years. There was virtually no foreign competition. Better still, Burgmaster had all the benefits of a relatively sound national economy. Inflation was low, and although the economy on occasion sputtered, it generally grew at a steady rate. That was important because it meant that a well-invested dollar in plant, equipment, or R&D was likely to yield a handsome return.

To a greater or lesser degree, the machine tool industry as a whole enjoyed the same advantages until the mid-1960s. Then, because of their solid profits and apparently captive hold over the world's largest market, U.S. tool builders became enticing targets for conglomerates. Houdaille's acquisition of Burgmaster in 1965 was not an isolated phenomenon, but typical of a broad merger and takeover trend that affected perhaps two-thirds of the industry.[9] Large, diversified corporations raced to enter the industry that made the machines that make all machines. They were quite right to find so attractive the solid firms that underpinned the most productive industrial economy in the world.

Several things then proceeded to happen, all of them adverse to Burgmaster and the tool industry. There is nothing written anywhere that says a conglomerate cannot per se run a tool builder well. Indeed, on the face of it, the resources of a great corporation and the cyclic nature of the machine tool industry should make for a good fit. The recognition that Burgmaster had to develop a whole new generation of machining centers, in fact, was a major reason behind the Burgs' decision to sell.

But the union with Houdaille did not produce a better Burgmaster. Houdaille's management compared to the Burgs' was deficient, and the very characteristics that were responsible for Burgmaster's success began to erode. Burgmaster lost its reputation as a work place with good people in every area, where everyone had a job to do and did it well, or wasn't tolerated. The Houdaille takeover marked the introduction of a management that sought to confine workers' participation, despite all the slogans aimed at them. A distant, managerial capitalism replaced entrepreneurial capitalism, and Burgmaster was much the worse for it.

As one scholar of the machine tool industry, David Noble, has pointed out, under managerialism, "management control is the *sine qua non* of efficient production, and it leads typically to the single-minded pursuit of management control as an end in itself."[10] This atmosphere was radically different from the way the company operated under the Burgs. There was no doubt about the Burgs' authority over production, of course, or over every single aspect of Burgmaster. Yet their supreme control, as opposed to mere ownership, emanated from a partnership with the work force and their own intimate understanding of the business. Houdaille's alternative was to make time studies and employ other management fads as they came along, in an endless and ultimately futile search for a better formula. No formula was a substitute for management involvement on the shop floor.

The "Houdaille way" first took hold on the factory floor, but gradually seeped into every department. Dedicated, outspoken employees were cast aside in favor of those more amenable to the corporate ethic. Meeting the monthly quota became success, rather than simply a measure of it. Burgmaster lost its vitality, and acquired layers of new management obsessed with procedure and prestige rather than function and need. The sense of everyone working together, as efficiently as possible, was suffocated by a mushy, bureaucratic environment.

Burgmaster continued to make money for Houdaille long after the takeover, and in some years chalked up sizable profits. But success, such as Burgmaster enjoyed from 1966 to the mid-1970s, derived more from past accomplishments than contemporary ones. Philosophically, Houdaille was committed to the notion that Burgmaster had to innovate to remain a force in the industry. It sanctioned the expenditure of time, energy, and resources. But

Burgmaster's striving to remain a state-of-the-art manufacturer was a litany of mistakes and delays. Managerialism had drained Burgmaster of its once-formidable capacity to innovate and its technological prowess.

Burgmaster and other tool builders similarly beset might have stumbled along this path indefinitely but for one thing. By the late 1970s, the Japanese builders they had licensed ten years earlier began to make deep inroads into the U.S. market.

The issue is not whether the licensing agreements were "abused." Given Japan's explicit intention of gaining industrial parity with the West, a state-of-the-art machine tool industry was an irreducible goal, and Japan was bound to become competitive. Japanese builders eventually would have caught up through reverse engineering even if U.S. tool builders had been stingy with their technology. Mimicry has been an unavoidable part of the machine tool industry ever since the Round Foundry imitated the machines built by the Soho Foundry in nineteenth-century England. Patents offer only minimal protection. In short, the only genuine recourse for U.S. builders was to continue to outengineer and outproduce the competition.

Since they later became a point of so much contention, the factors that enabled the Japanese to catch up bear reiterating. To be sure, MITI played a significant role. During the 1950s and 1960s, the ministry protected and nurtured domestic builders. But as one expert on Japan has observed,

> The central lesson of the Japanese industrial policy experience is not, as some Americans argue, that government "guidance" of industry works better than traditional market economies. Unfettered supply and demand determine the direction of growth in Japan at least as much as they do in the United States. The lesson of Japan is that a government can truly aid private industry if and only if it coherently plans *its* ordinary activities on the basis of a vision of the economy's future.[11]

In other words, the most important step that the government could take, and did, was to foster an economic climate in which builders like Okuma and Yamazaki could thrive. It provided a soundly managed economy and an educated work force, probably the two most important "ordinary" tasks of government. Although MITI tried to do more on occasion, no amount of bureaucratic guidance or promotion transformed Yamazaki and Okuma into world-class builders. The truly vital qualities were to be found inside their respective machine shops and engineering departments. "Promote high technology and maintain good labor relations" were the bylaws at Okuma.[12] It does not seem coincidental that Burgmaster also thrived in the years when it followed the same precepts, and did not just mouth them.

Another striking contrast between American and Japanese builders was in the attention they paid to each other's markets. Here Yamazaki Machinery, a builder once linked to Burgmaster, is the best example. Despite formidable handicaps, such as a language barrier, the lack of a service network, and long-standing consumer-supplier relationships, Yamazaki was dogged in its determination to succeed in the American marketplace. By contrast, U.S. builders were casual in their attempt to penetrate the Japanese market.

This is not to minimize the difficulties in exporting to Japan. But in contrast to the hungry and aggressive Yamazaki brothers, U.S. builders were a complacent lot. They approached business in Japan as if it were simply a more exotic version of business in the United States. In Japan, as opposed to the United States, service and longstanding business ties tend to outweigh simple calculations like price. By licensing their Japanese counterparts, U.S. builders opted for a less taxing but temporarily profitable route, falsely content with the belief that the world's largest and most lucrative market—their own back yard—was captive.

If these were the most pertinent reasons for Japan's success, they nevertheless fall short of answering the most important question. Why, once the Japanese began penetrating the American market by the late 1970s, were U.S. builders so woefully vulnerable? Why weren't they able to compete at *home?*

Again, conglomerate management was certainly one factor that hindered Burgmaster's ability to respond. It was no longer the lean, innovative company that Houdaille acquired in 1965. Burgmaster's malaise, moreover, was not rare among tool builders absorbed by conglomerates. It was replicated over and over, judging from the number of conglomerates, including Textron, Colt, and Bendix, that beat a retreat from the machine tool industry in the 1980s.

According to the original logic of conglomeration, conglomerate-owned tool builders should have been among the fittest to meet the challenge from overseas. But the converse proved true. One reason was that the corporate ladder to the top was increasingly dominated by executives with legal or accounting backgrounds rather than managers versed in production. A willingness to innovate and be daring comes from hands-on experience. It was not surprising to see these qualities sacrificed to such concepts as "profit centers" and "return on investment," given the backgrounds of the new corporate elite.[13] One of the enduring ironies here, of course, is that MITI greatly feared American conglomeration, and tried in vain to get Japanese builders to adopt a similar "rationalization" strategy.

The generalization about corporate management is an incomplete explanation though. Many independent builders, unfettered by conglomeration, also lost substantial market share. There were two other significant factors involved. One was the failure of U.S. builders as a whole to invest in new technology during the 1970s. The other was the adverse impact of military spending on technological innovation in the industry. Both, in turn, skewed engineering, manufacturing, and marketing strategies.

There are diverse opinions regarding the failure to invest during the 1970s. Some observers attribute it to builders' innate conservatism. Historically, builders are slow to adopt the same advanced machines they are eager for others to buy. Others believe that tool builders failed to modernize because they did not properly calculate the benefits that would accrue from greater automation.

Both of these were in all likelihood true, but they obscure the reason most germane. The unpredictable economic climate of the 1970s, on top of the industry's normal cycles, was not conducive to capital investment and risk. Economic uncertainty first appeared in the guise of inflation in the late 1960s. It was followed in short order by devaluation, and then by varying doses of recession, more inflation, stagnation, and then stagflation. For almost a decade there was little assurance that a dollar invested today would yield sufficient profit, quickly enough, tomorrow.

As a result, independent builders were more leery than ever about upgrading their manufacturing processes. Meanwhile, for the builders owned by conglomerates, the all-powerful bottom line dictated caution. The short-term, hard-nosed demands of the quarterly report drove management, not what their subsidiaries had to do to be a force in the machine tool industry over the next ten years. Long-term investments were seen as irresponsible. For both independent builders and conglomerates alike, it was far safer to stick with an older machine tool, still within its useful life, and hire more workers who could be dismissed.

The Japanese were buffeted by some of the same financial shocks during the 1970s. Indeed, in some instances, such as oil price hikes, their economy was far more vulnerable. But Japan proved more adaptable, and found a formula that returned the economy to solvency. Investment in advanced technologies could continue at a much faster rate in Japan, and productivity grew as well. The bottom line was that with newer tools, Japanese builders were eventually able to manufacture at levels of efficiency that neither Burgmaster nor most American builders could match.

The last factor responsible for the abrupt loss of U.S. competitiveness was the impact of military spending on the industry. Burgmaster was more vulnerable than most builders by virtue of its location. It fought for engineers and machinists in a tight market, Southern California, where the pool of these individuals is dominated by defense-related industries. Whereas competitors in Japan benefited from the best of their engineering and manufacturing talent, Burgmaster saw the best minds and hands invariably drawn to the more lucrative aerospace industry. Defense contractors, with the Pentagon's backing, could pay far higher salaries than any tool builder could afford.

For most other builders, which were located in the East, the impact of Pentagon spending was more subtle. In a sense, the phenomenon was akin to what happened during the development of NC, except that it was multiplied a thousandfold. Builders were more eager than ever to sup at the Pentagon's table of guaranteed profits during a decade of economic instability. The Pentagon functioned as a perverse and much more powerful MITI, through its procurement policies. The direct and indirect machine tool purchases of the Defense Department, which absorb in peacetime between 20 and 30 percent of domestic output, lured the industry into two-tiered R&D.[14] Its best efforts were devoted to engineering and building custom machines. But even though the U.S. industry could still boast about its technical sophistication, the exotic, custom systems subsidized by the Pentagon did not result in commercially competitive machines.

The supreme irony here is that Pentagon spending exists in the first place to ensure a vital machine tool industry that can be mobilized in case of an emergency. Instead, and in the context of an uncertain economy that exaggerated risk and discouraged investment, the Pentagon helped skew the machine tool industry toward a commercially disastrous strategy. Guaranteed profits for machines with bells and whistles caused American builders to neglect the large market for standardized, economical NC machines. Meanwhile, Japanese builders were accustomed to building such machines, largely in response to the demands of their auto industry. They stepped into the breach left by American builders, and the end result was the impoverishment of U.S. commercial industrial capacity, and the defense industrial base. Incredibly, advocates for increasing the Pentagon's economic role abound, notwithstanding the sorry track record of military spending. [15]

Still, it cannot be said that Burgmaster's fate was signed and sealed by the late 1970s. Faced with the Japanese challenge, Houdaille could have modernized its equipment and expanded its plant, redirected its marketing strategy toward standardized machines (the very concept Burgmaster fleetingly adopted in the late 1960s), and tried to outperform foreign builders in quality and service. But at a crucial juncture, Burgmaster and Houdaille underwent a sea change in ownership and ultimately in goals.

In 1979, at the very moment Japanese builders were throwing down the gauntlet, Houdaille underwent a leveraged buyout. It was arguably the first large industrial concern to undergo the transformation from managerial to financial capitalism. The new owners, men trained in law and finance, did not look upon Burgmaster, or Houdaille for that matter, as a concern that earned a tidy profit by producing goods needed by the economy. Instead, the conglomerate was a vehicle for taking advantage of complex tax rules in an utterly ingenious way, and existed primarily to pay off a huge gamble. If everything broke according to the investment bankers' plan, there would be fantastic profits for themselves, holdover management, and institutional investors. If not, they would still manage to squeeze profit from a combination of going private, going separate, and going bankrupt.

Perhaps the only aspect more self-serving than the LBO itself was the rhetoric spewed out by the interests involved. In May 1984, even as his machine tool group, or some 25 percent of the company, was headed for the chopping block, Houdaille president Phil O'Reilly could still be found dutifully praising leveraged buyouts. Among the joys cited by O'Reilly was that as CEO of a private company, answerable only to select institutional investors, he could "look out at a longer horizon."[16]

It would be difficult to fashion a more disingenuous picture of what was really going on inside Burgmaster. Even the quarterly and annual horizon that dominated Burgmaster during the Saltarelli era was a model of long-term planning compared to the exigencies of the buyout. Decisions were taken that could only be justified in terms of the debt, because they were incompatible with managing the company as if there were a tomorrow. The LBO exacerbated Burgmaster's managerial problems, brought out its worst instincts, misallocated corporate resources, and made it impossible to take the steps necessary to meet the competition. Burgmaster came to epitomize the corporate consequences of an economic environment where debt is more profitable than equity, speculation more lucrative than enterprise.

This does not mean that without the LBO, Burgmaster would have survived. Its existence was in question in any case because of Japanese competition, its own inadequacies, and external penalties such as a grossly overvalued dollar. Other tool builders, many of whom were not subject to the strictures of an LBO, succumbed to just these factors by the mid-1980s. The number of shellshocked builders (both independent and conglomerate-owned) that closed down a large part or all of their domestic operations included some of the industry's most prestigious names: Brown & Sharpe, Jones & Lamson, and LaSalle. Even giants like Cross & Trecker and Cincinnati Milacron were forced into major retrenchments. Overall, perhaps 25 percent of the industry evaporated before the 1986 voluntary restraint agreement slapped a limit on imports. That staunched the hemorrhage of indigenous machine tool capacity, for the time being.

Nevertheless, as far as Burgmaster was concerned, the LBO, far from being an elixir that rejuvenated the company, enfeebled it. Even if the exact combination that produced Burgmaster's demise was not quite typical of the tool industry, there seems little doubt that Burgmaster was a harbinger of buyout bankruptcies to come in manufacturing and other sectors of the economy. According to one economist, U.S. corporations today devote, on average, more than 50 percent of their earnings to finance their debt. And in 1987, with the economy still growing, corporate defaults soared to an unprecedented $9 billion.[17] Unless inflation becomes rampant, no one doubts that scores of leveraged companies will totter into bankruptcy at the next recession. Corporations with equity can suspend dividend payments if need be. But debt has to be serviced.

In recent years, about 50 percent of all leveraged buyouts have occurred in the broad category of manufacturing.[18] Perhaps if these companies were going deeply into hock to replace outmoded equipment or otherwise modernize, the debt they have to service would be worth assuming. Instead, they have undertaken a calculated, federally subsidized gamble that results in either corporate survival and exorbitant profits or puts the entire company at risk. Moreover, for those companies that reach the pot of gold, it may take years before it will be known whether the sacrifices they made to pay off their debt carried long-term consequences. Perhaps that deferral in capital spending or reduction in R&D will not matter. Then again, it may matter greatly.[19]

One fact is indisputable. When the "real money" is to be made by anticipating mergers and investing in buyout pools, capital becomes more expensive. Corporations are forced to raise the yields on their bonds, and new stock offerings are viewed with distaste. Altogether, there is less capital to invest in the companies and technologies necessary for American goods to compete in world markets. As the Nobel Prize–winning economist James Tobin noted three years before the 1987 crash, "We're throwing more and more of our resources, including the cream of our youth, into financial activities remote from the production of goods and services, into activities that generate high private rewards disproportionate to their social productivity."[20] Never have so few people made so much money for doing so little.

Not surprisingly, even the oldest names in U.S. manufacturing are drawn by the lure of unbeatable profits being dangled by financial capitalism. For decades, the slogan "You can be sure . . . if it's Westinghouse" signified that industrial giant's commitment to the manufacture of high-quality consumer and durable goods. But the well-worn phrase has taken on a whole new meaning in the unbridled speculation of the 1980s, as one large advertisement in *The Wall Street Journal* recently illustrated.

> Westinghouse is no longer making steam irons, but we can certainly help smooth out the complexities of your next acquisition.
> Westinghouse Credit is an innovative resource for all kinds of corporate financing—from leveraged buyouts to capital for expansion to recapitalizations. Our network of skilled specialists offers the in-depth knowledge you need to get the job done. And since every deal is different, our broad range of capabilities and services is designed to encourage flexibility. We'd like to help you iron out your next corporate financing deal.[21]

Another one of the more curious and disturbing features of the buyout and junk bond frenzy is the pivotal role played by state-managed pension funds. On the surface, the funds would seem to be a quintessential middle America vehicle, dedicated to obtaining moderate and steady returns— precisely the kind that result from and promote long-term growth. When these bountiful funds first began to attract notice in the mid-1970s, in fact, many observers hailed them as a serendipitous source of capital for the revitalization of American manufacturing. Then KKR and other buyout boutiques discovered pension funds and used them as an indispensable element for LBOs The promise of a 40 percent return on investment enticed pension fund managers in Oregon, Iowa, Washington, and Minnesota to participate eagerly in buyout pools. What should have been a wellspring for industrial revitalization became one of the chief instruments for speculation.

Because it serves their interest, corporate raiders and buyout artists like to present a dilemma: the choice is between their brands of corporate restructuring and mediocre, flabby managerialism. The choice almost makes their case appear reasonable, because the corporate establishment is under attack from many sides. Ralph Nader-style liberals were the first to rail publicly against "corpocracy," but the refrain against "bloated, risk-averse, inefficient and unimaginative" corporate management was also and most prominently echoed by the Reagan administration, including that business redoubt the Commerce Department.[22]

Yet widespread agreement about corporate ills should not unthinkingly translate into a green light for antisocial behavior and supposed market forces to work their will. There is nothing marketlike about the tax breaks KKR buys or protects in Washington, except that they cost money.[23] Mergers, acquisitions, and buyouts would not be as ubiquitous without the tax considerations that make or break the deals. Congress did not have leveraged buyouts in mind when it came up with the concept of capital goods depreciation. The main purpose of depreciation was, and has always been, to spur *new* capital investment, not make the reshuffling of assets endlessly profitable.

In a capitalist society, the managers and owners of productive economic assets must operate under a compact. They are permitted large rewards in exchange for employing those assets in an economically productive, socially responsible, and environmentally sound manner. The precise definitions of the terms may change over time. But gambling with and manipulating productive assets ought to be viewed with the same intolerance as polluting a river or firing a worker because of race. Something is fundamentally dysfunctional when companies are allowed to use their future earnings to finance debt and profits for a few, rather than build something useful.

This appraisal is reinforced by the growing evidence of an alternative between corpocracy and speculation, and Japanese companies are providing it. The machine tool industry is a good example in fact. Yamazaki established its U.S. foothold long ago. But since the 1982 Houdaille petition and the subsequent voluntary restraint on tool imports, many more Japanese builders have made major direct investments in U.S. plant and equipment. By 1988, nine Japanese machine tool plants were in operation on American soil—including a large plant in North Carolina owned by Okuma, the builder that spurned Houdaille's plea to acquire Burgmaster. Although some of these subsidiaries simply assemble kits manufactured in Japan, other factories rely on an American production component of 50 percent or more.[24] At least some of these plants are proof that the choice served up by Wall Street, between corpocracy and speculation, is a self-serving and false one.

Direct foreign investment in machine tools, which is an infinitesimal part of the more than $1 trillion of overseas capital that has been streaming into the United States in recent years, can be interpreted several ways.[25] Some observers hail it as an unmitigated good: an organic integration of markets, a desirable division of labor, or a quick way to refurbish the U.S. industrial base. Others worry that it necessarily entails a loss of political sovereignty and American control over its own economic destiny—or worse.[26] In 1984, then CIA Director William Casey characterized the Japanese presence in the U.S. semiconductor industry as a "Trojan Horse ... a dangerous course in a national security context as well as in a commercial context."[27]

There would be little reason for concern if indigenous American companies seemed to be holding their own in a more integrated, competitive market. The problem is, they are not. And that is at the root of why foreign ownership raises a gnawing fear. Unchallenged superiority in manufactures, such as this country blissfully enjoyed until the 1960s, is out of reach for the United States. But the inability to sustain an indigenous manufacturing capability that is at least on a par with any other country raises a host of issues. If it cannot be first, indeed if there is no first, the United States can nevertheless ill afford to be a distant second.

The United States will assume the position of being a permanent economic supplicant to Japan unless it can sustain an indigenous, advanced industrial base that builds something other than the implements of war. For all their direct investment in the United States, the Japanese will take care to reserve for their own economy the first-rate technologies and means of manufacture. The days when Japan was ostensibly dependent on the inventiveness of others and incapable on its own are long past, as one recent analysis of U.S. patent data has shown.[28] It's pertinent to note too that despite their recent spate of machine tool investments, Japanese builders for the most part are keeping their advanced flexible manufacturing systems (FMS) technology at home, where it is rapidly spreading.[29]

Unless U.S. manufacturing can keep pace, there will be not only a chronic imbalance between the economies of the two countries but also an "awkward, ominous and potentially explosive" relationship, as one American scholar of Japan, John Dower, put it.[30] This is another lesson from the Burgmaster saga. The Houdaille petition, precisely because it failed by the narrowest of margins, illustrates vividly just how brittle that relationship is under the current circumstances.

Credit for Houdaille's near accomplishment is due Richard Copaken, a savvy and zealous advocate who displayed a consummate understanding of how trade politics are played in Washington. Houdaille's "compelling case" was an admixture of fact and fancy that did not support the main thesis, namely, that the Japanese government had commanded a machine tool cartel. Yet neither the executive branch nor Congress, during consideration of the petition, ever understood the combination of factors that prompted Houdaille's petition. Perhaps it is too much to expect of government. Perhaps it is naïve to think the occasion of the petition might have been used to explore either the managerialism, the financial legerdemain, or the government's own insolvent economic policies over two decades, all of which combined to produce Houdaille's predicament. It was infinitely easier and more palatable to blame others, to prey on Americans' conspiratorial suspicions about Japan's trade and industrial practices. Copaken not only shrewdly capitalized on this tendency—he banked on it.

The role of the media merits at least passing comment, since it played an overly sympathetic and therefore instrumental part in Copaken's grand scheme. Though there was criticism, particularly in editorial columns, by and large the media unhesitatingly funneled to the public a great amount of misinformation. The obvious connection between Houdaille's leveraged buyout and the unprecedented petition was not seriously raised in one article during the eleven months the petition was under consideration. There was no attempt to explore the reasons for Japan's success from the perspective of its tool builders. The entire debate was more or less conducted within the bounds and language set by Copaken. Even though the government failed, the press might have tried to find out why Houdaille could not compete.

Nothing that has happened since the petition offers much ground for optimism. In the summer of 1987, four congressional representatives engaged in a spectacle calculated to appeal to the same instincts aroused by Copaken. After it was revealed that a machine tool subsidiary of the Japanese electronics conglomerate Toshiba had sold a sophisticated milling machine to the Soviet Union, the four representatives ostentatiously smashed a Toshiba radio with sledgehammers on the steps of the Capitol. (Significantly, no one smashed a tin of sardines to protest a Norwegian company's involvement in the transaction.) In addition, bitter disputes arose between the United States and Japan over semiconductors, telecommunications, supercomputers, construction—even forklifts. Virtually no foreign or domestic issue, for that matter, seems immune from the "Japan-bashing" virus. When a Massachusetts congressman, Chet Atkins, visited Vietnam in January 1988, for example, he suggested that if Hanoi did not cooperate on the M.I.A. issue, the United States might seek to retaliate by obtaining sanctions against Japanese trade with Vietnam. "Any kind of Japan-bashing plays better and better in American politics as time goes on," he observed.[31]

Racism may well play a role in Japan-bashing. Even so, the wellspring is a nationalist fear engendered by what appears to be an unstoppable industrial juggernaut. If the United States and Japan are to remain competitors and not become adversaries, genuine equality and reciprocity will have to mark the relationship. And some semblance of economic balance is imperative for that to happen.

Both countries need to make adjustments. Japan, the greatest beneficiary of the free trade regimen, also exhibits some unflattering, nativist elements that could compromise its hard-won gains. It needs a measure of internal reform so that it is not simply a trading machine pointed in one direction. Recently, there has been considerable evidence of a shift to domestic-led economic growth. Nor will the necessary changes be that difficult, for Japan has the luxury of making adjustments in an economy that is generating real wealth, not just paper profits for an elite.

Between the two countries, the United States has the far greater task. It will be more difficult to put America's house in order, and ensure that public and private debt is incurred for productive investment. Meanwhile it is unbecoming, and surely self-defeating, for America to shrilly blame the Japanese when the fault lies squarely at the United States' own doorstep.[32]

Here then, is the final lesson from Burgmaster's forty years. For who can deny, after examining that history, that the United States has a de facto industrial policy. It is evident every single day, in the most ordinary of the government's policies. When the government chooses to subsidize speculation instead of productive investment; when the government militarizes the manufacturing and research base of the economy; when the government proves incapable of educating a large number of its citizens; and above all, when the government proves incapable of managing the economy responsibly, it is formulating an industrial policy that manufacturers have to contend with, whether it is recognized as such or not.

Current U.S. industrial policy is a debacle. Any nation that cannot define, much less assemble, a coherent role for the government in its economy is in trouble.

Financial Performance of Burgmaster Corporation, 1954–1964

	1954	1955	1956	1957	1958	1959	1960	1961	1962	1963	1964
Net sales	573,641	1,143,755	1,793,755	1,904,206	1,756,202	3,415,239	4,440,822	4,815,737	6,294,484	6,817,614	7,433,854
Pretax income	60,673	126,134	240,294	182,918	81,608	530,307	736,427	878,531	988,619	859,838	1,032,030
Net income for the year	35,093	63,252	115,458	95,057	43,506	246,728	350,491	433,531	479,890	426,838	547,030
Net income per share	.07	.13	.23	.19	.09	.50	.71	.88	.97	.86	1.11
Working capital	69,257	123,854	232,087	335,338	586,609	702,486	875,132	1,950,794	2,191,391	2,422,370	2,796,024
Net worth	113,716	176,968	292,426	457,483	500,989	747,717	1,098,207	2,562,989	3,035,799	3,459,066	3,928,740
Number of shareholders	3	3	3	3	3	3	3	1987	2047	1641	1573
Number of employees	45	62	74	66	70	139	155	205	227	222	240

All figures are in unadjusted, current dollars for the fiscal years ending October 31 except where noted. Net income per share based on 494,810 shares as of 31 October 1964. A 2.5 percent stock dividend was paid during 1961 and 1962, and a 5.0 percent dividend in 1963 and 1964.

Source: Burgmaster Corporation, "Annual Reports," for years ending 31 October 1963 and 31 October 1964.

Appendix B

Financial Performance of Houdaille Industries, 1965–1978

	1965	1966	1967	1968	1969	1970	1971
Net sales ($000)	174,809	189,470	192,946	203,465	203,231	187,950	201,171
Pretax income ($000)	16,051	20,573	21,737	25,327	24,358	11,954	14,467
Net income ($000)	8,775	11,216	11,911	13,020	12,770	6,775	8,128
Common shares outstanding	7,259,196	7,358,756	7,622,278	8,290,962	8,316,328	8,323,645	8,327,923
Income per common share ($)	1.02	1.32	1.38	1.50	1.47	.76	.92
Cash dividends per share ($)	.45	.54	.63	.75	.80	.75	.60
Working capital ($000)	45,086	55,772	64,713	73,009	75,331	70,902	72,781
Cash and securities ($000)	13,686	19,835	21,455	25,806	18,396	19,671	25,269
Long-term debt ($000)	20,892	30,563	30,478	30,226	30,394	28,944	27,600
Depreciation, etc. ($000)	6,828	7,438	7,695	7,791	7,420	7,501	7,524
Capital expenditures ($000)	7,908	11,395	8,345	7,538	9,171	11,397	9,671
Stock price: high-low	11⅜-7⅝	13⅜-8⅜	17¾-9⅛	25⅞-14½	24-13⅝	15⅞-8⅝	15⅞-11
Assets ($000)	89,560	107,329	120,592	134,420	140,234	141,008	144,641
Equity ($000)	49,746	55,112	69,042	82,274	88,320	88,420	90,946
Net profit as % of sales	4.6	5.4	6.1	6.6	6.5	3.6	4.1
Net profit as % of equity	14.4	16.3	16.3	16.3	14.8	7.7	9.2
Number of employees	5,000	6,377	6,377	7,500	8,229	7,400	6,685
Sales per employee	24.2	26.0	26.0	27.6	24.7	25.4	30.3
Machine Tool Group							
Sales ($000)	43,300	59,600	41,147	44,496	45,700	39,100	31,300
% of total	25	31	21	22	22	21	16
Industry rank by shipments	25	20	7	10	11	15	18
Pretax income ($000)	N.A.	N.A.	4,369	3,230	1,999	(1,729)	(1,226)
% of total	N.A.	N.A.	20	13	8	(14)	(8)

	1972	1973	1974	1975	1976	1977	1978
Net sales ($000)	247,437	305,204	317,657	291,522	332,845	385,786	409,583
Pretax income ($000)	23,014	30,883	32,854	31,711	45,201	49,284	50,754
Net income ($000)	12,804	17,230	18,184	17,361	24,821	27,055	28,454
Common shares outstanding	8,368,141	8,370,141	8,370,141	8,370,141	8,375,641	8,426,641	8,463,141
Income per common share ($)	1.48	2.01	2.12	2.02	2.88	3.14	3.32
Cash dividends per share ($)	.70	.80	.85	.85	.90	1.00	1.20
Working capital ($000)	74,109	83,595	92,784	96,256	97,333	113,342	125,000
Cash and securities ($000)	21,473	22,013	17,846	33,997	28,556	35,439	41,132
Long-term debt ($000)	27,650	27,700	26,500	25,300	23,985	22,555	20,425
Depreciation, etc. ($000)	7,970	8,344	8,933	9,098	9,544	9,727	10,607
Capital expenditures ($000)	7,211	10,461	12,232	10,686	17,545	12,770	20,341
Stock price: high-low	16⅜-12¼	16⅛-8	11¼-6	10¾-7¼	17¾-10¼	18⅜-14⅝	14½-33⅞
Assets ($000)	158,463	170,182	178,771	189,655	213,107	236,386	263,579
Equity ($000)	95,755	105,881	116,523	N.A.	N.A.	N.A.	180,298
Net profit as % of sales	5.2	5.6	5.7	6.0	7.5	7.0	6.9
Net profit as % of equity	13.4	16.3	17.2	N.A.	N.A.	18.9	17.6
Number of employees	7,500	7,500	8,400	N.A.	N.A.	7,700	8,100
Sales per employee	33.0	33.0	37.8	N.A.	N.A.	50.1	50.6
Machine Tool Group							
Sales ($000)	43,500	54,600	65,100	62,175	61,340	89,031	109,761
% of total	18	18	20	21	18	23	27
Industry rank by shipments	8	11	11	N.A.	N.A.	N.A.	9
Pretax income ($000)	3,390	5,417	8,577	6,200	6,502	14,785	20,950
% of total	15	17	26	20	14	26	35

All dollar figures are in unadjusted, current dollars for the year ending December 31. In some instances there were discrepancies between the figures reported by Houdaille and those reported by *American Machinist*. The Houdaille figures were considered more authoritative. The category "Industry rank" includes all publicly traded machine tool builders, but excludes privately held builders. The 1965 and 1966 figures for the machine tool group are somewhat inflated. During these years, Houdaille included in its machine tool group several divisions that were tangential. Later these divisions were separated out into an industrial products group. Conversely, in 1977 Houdaille shifted its Universal division, which averaged about $9 million in sales, from its industrial products group to its machine tool group. One-third of the large increase in 1977 sales resulted from this reclassification.

Sources: Houdaille Industries, "Annual Reports," for years ending 31 December 1972 through 31 December 1977; Houdaille Industries, Form 10-K Annual Report to the Securities and Exchange Commission, 1971–1978; "The Blue Bulletin," *American Machinist*, 1966–1979 (not published 1976–1978).

Houdaille Industries after the Leveraged Buyout, 1979–1986

Business segment data				—Year ending July 31, 1985—		
(Mil. $)	Sales	Oper. income	Deprec.	Oper. cash flow	Cap. exp.	Assets
Industrial products	232.5	35.6	10.7	46.3	3.8	210.8
Fluid handling	85.6	16.3	4.2	20.5	2.0	66.7
Machine tools	54.9	1.5	3.0	4.5	0.5	42.5
Total	373.0	53.4	17.9	71.0	6.3	320.0

(%)	% of Sales	Sales growth	Oper. income growth	Oper. margin	Oper. ret. on assets	Asset growth
Industrial products	62.3	(2.5)	34.3	15.3	16.9	(5.3)
Fluid handling	23.0	15.1	7.9	19.0	24.4	(5.1)
Machine tools	14.7	(8.8)	114.3	2.7	3.5	(20.4)
Total	100.0	0.3	26.0	14.3	16.7	(7.6)

Financial statistics			—Year ended July 31—		
(Mil. $)	1986*	1985*	1985	1984	1983
Net inc. from cont. oper.	5.2	7.5	8.0	(7.3)	(38.5)
Funds from oper.	21.4	12.7	19.2	17.0	(1.0)
Capital expend.	4.6	6.4	7.9	7.2	7.3
Total debt	267.1	N.A.	354.4	373.0	366.0
Preferred stock	23.5	23.5	23.5	23.5	23.5
Total stockholders' equity	(31.8)	N.A.	(56.8)	(65.5)	(47.9)
Oper. inc. % of sales	16.3	18.6	18.7	16.4	12.1
Pretax interest coverage (x)	1.40	1.40	1.36	0.92	0.08
Funds from oper./total debt (%)	N.M.	N.M.	6.6	4.6	N.M.
Pretax return on perm. cap. (%)	N.M.	N.M.	10.4	10.2	0.9
Total debt/cap. (incl. STD) (%)	103.2	N.A.	110.4	112.7	107.3

*For nine months to April 30.
N.A.—Not available.
N.M.—Not meaningful.

Information about Houdaille's financial performance from 1979 to 1982 is not available from public documents.
Source: Standard & Poor's Creditweek, 18 August 1986.

NOTES ▬▬▬▬▬▬▬▬▬▬▬▬▬▬▬▬▬▬▬▬▬▬▬▬▬▬▬▬▬▬

Introduction

1. Frederick V. Geier, "The Machine Tool Industry," *The Analysts Journal*, Third Quarter (1950), pp. 27–29.

2. E. Sciberras and B.D. Payne, *Machine Tool Industry* (Essex, England: Longman Group, 1985), p. 31; National Machine Tool Builders' Association, *Economic Handbook of the Machine Tool Industry, 1987–1988* (McLean, VA: NMTBA, 1987), p. 165 (hereafter cited as NMTBA, *Economic Handbook*); and "Machine-Tool Makers Lose Out to Imports Due to Price, Quality," *The Wall Street Journal*, 17 August 1987.

3. See Marvin J. Wolf, *The Japanese Conspiracy* (New York: Empire Books, 1983); Julian Gresser, *Partners in Prosperity* (New York: McGraw-Hill, 1984); Robert Kuttner, *The Economic Illusion* (Boston: Houghton Mifflin, 1984); Steven Schlossstein, *Trade War* (New York: Congdon and Weed, 1984); Ezra F. Vogel, *Comeback Case by Case* (New York: Simon and Schuster, 1985); Douglas F. Lamont, *Forcing Our Hand* (Lexington, MA: Lexington Books, 1986); Gary R. Saxonhouse and Kozo Yamamura, eds., *Law and Trade Issues of the Japanese Economy* (Seattle: University of Washington Press, 1986); Stephen S. Cohen and John Zysman, *Manufacturing Matters* (New York: Basic Books, 1987); Clyde V. Prestowitz, *Trading Places* (New York: Basic Books, 1988); and David Friedman, *The Misunderstood Miracle* (Ithaca, NY: Cornell University Press, 1988). Wolf and Schlossstein cite the Houdaille case as evidence for their conspiratorial views. Aside from Saxonhouse and Yamamura, the most scholarly and devastating critique is Friedman's. Prestowitz's book is perhaps the most sympathetic to Houdaille, which is understandable given his role in the Commerce Department when the petition was under review. The rest of the books fall between these points of view.

1: The Founding of Burg Tool (1943–1954)

1. The account of Burg's early life is based on interviews with Fred Burg (21 April 1979 and 25 August 1987); Blanche and Norm Ginsburg (6 January 1986, 16 June 1987, 25 August 1987), and Joe Burg (11 May 1987 and 26 August 1987).

2. There are many different ways to classify metal-cutting machine tools, but the simplest is to categorize them by the relative motions of the workpiece and cutting tool. (The workpiece is the raw piece of metal being machined to conform to specifications; the tool is that part of the machine tool which comes into contact with the workpiece and, by doing so, cuts or otherwise shapes it.) In turning, the workpiece is rotated and the cutting tool, remaining stationary, produces the desired cylindrical shape; the process is similar to paring an apple to produce a peel. A lathe operates in this manner. In drilling, the cutting tool is rotated while the workpiece remains stationary; the tool moves in a spiral, thereby cutting a hole in the workpiece. Making a hole with a drill press is the most familiar application of this operating principle. In milling, the workpiece is traversed by a rotating tool. Milling machines typically make the cuts on all flat-sided metal stock. In grinding, a rotating abrasive wheel removes metal; typically, grinders are used to remove small amounts of material after milling. The final mode of operation, planing, is rarely used today. In it a stationary cutting tool is traversed by the workpiece, much as cheese is pulled along a grater.

3. "Gear Shifting Mechanism," No. 1,905,635, Patented 25 April 1933, by Fred Ginsburg, U.S. Patent Office, Washington, DC. Burg's original surname was Ginsburg. He shortened it to Burg shortly after moving to California.

4. "Flexible Tool Holder," No. 2,525,646, Patented 10 October 1950, by Fred Burg, U.S. Patent Office, Washington, DC.

5. A spindle is a powered shaft that rotates and imparts motion to whatever it holds, be it a tool (on a drill press) or a workpiece (on a lathe).

6. Robert S. Himes, "A Study of the Machine Tool Industry, with Emphasis on the Problem of Stability" (Ph.D. diss., American University, 1962), p. 202. See also Harless D. Wagoner, *The U.S. Machine Tool Industry from 1900 to 1950* (Cambridge, MA: MIT Press, 1968), pp. 318–319.

7. Interview with Robert French, 11 May 1987.

8. L. T. C. Rolt, *A Short History of Machine Tools* (Cambridge, MA: MIT Press, 1965), p. 83.

9. Ibid., pp. 243–244.

10. "Burgmaster Growth Plan," Houdaille Industries, Inc., 1966. This internal document was written shortly after Houdaille acquired Burgmaster, and briefly traces Burgmaster's history.

11. "Machine Tool of the Drill Press Type Having Multiple Rotary Tools," No. 2,670,636, Patented 2 March 1954, by Fred Burg, U.S. Patent Office, Washington, DC.

12. Daniel Yergin, *Shattered Peace* (Boston: Houghton Mifflin, 1977), p. 400.

13. Cited in ibid., pp. 342–343.

14. D.F. Fleming, *The Cold War and Its Origins, 1917–1960,* 2 vols. (Garden City, NY: Doubleday, 1961), 1:516, 537, and Wagoner, *Machine Tool Industry,* p. 344.

15. Yergin, *Shattered Peace,* p. 408, and Himes, "Machine Tool Industry," p. 204.

16. Cited in U.S. Congress, Senate, Committee on Banking and Currency, *Review of Voluntary Agreements Program under the Defense Production Act: Expansion of Machine-Tool Industry, Report Dated February 10, 1958 by the Attorney General,* 85th Cong., 2d sess., 1958, p. 6.

17. Ibid.

18. Ibid., pp. 6–8.

19. Letter, Kenyon Instrument Company to Acme Saw & Supply, 30 March 1953. Acme was a Burgmaster dealer.

20. Burg Tool Manufacturing Company, "Burgmaster Model 6000," undated. Another "special" typical of the Korean War period was the "Burgmaster Gun Barrel Drilling and Tapping Machine."

21. "Burgmaster Growth Plan," Houdaille, 1966.

22. "Burg in 4th Expansion," *Los Angeles Examiner,* 12 September 1954.

2: Success Story (1954–1959)

1. Robert S. Himes, "A Study of the Machine Tool Industry" (Ph.D. diss., American University, 1962), p. 299. Total shipments of machine tools fell from a wartime peak of $1.2 billion in 1953 to $892 million in 1954, and $670 million in 1955. But shipments recovered and hovered around $865 million for the next two years. By contrast, after 1945, when shipments stood at $424 million, they fell to $335 million, $306 million, $288 million, and $249 million over the next four years. The figures cited are given in current (then-year) dollars.

2. Robert H. Ferrell, ed., *The Eisenhower Diaries* (New York: W.W. Norton, 1981), p. 195.

3. Cited in Himes, "Machine Tool Industry," p. 204.

4. Ibid., pp. 204–205. To be fair, as Himes notes, the economic situation prevailing after the Korean War differed substantially from what existed after 1945. In 1953–1954, the machines were disposed of practically one at a time. That would have been impractical after World War II because of the inflationary demand for civilian production.

5. Ibid., pp. 212–213.

6. Burgmaster Corporation, "Annual Report," for the year ending 31 October 1963. See also Appendix A for a table of figures on Burgmaster's financial performance from 1954 to 1964.

7. Ginsburg interview, 6 January 1986.

8. "Burgmaster Growth Plan," Houdaille Industries, Inc., 1966.

9. For example, while overall machine tool shipments underwent a sharp contraction from 1956 to 1958, Burg Tool's sales remained steady. See Appendix A and NMTBA, *Economic Handbook*, p. 42.

10. As Wagoner points out, machine tool demand roughly falls into two classes: orders resulting from industrial expansion and orders resulting from replacement of worn-out or obsolete tools. The first class can be further divided into peacetime and wartime expansion. Weapons production inevitably causes huge surges in production, whereas civilian expansion is usually more modest, since it depends on the invention, development, and manufacture of new products, or increased production of existing products. Traditionally, the second class, replacement demand, has also been modest, although when technology advances it can be more sustained. In the 1950s and 1960s, the working life of a machine tool was generally assumed to be from fifteen to twenty-five years, depending on its size, the tasks it had to perform, and how well it was maintained. See Harless D. Wagoner, *The U.S. Machine Tool Industry from 1900 to 1950* (Cambridge, MA: MIT Press, 1968), pp. 92–93.

11. French interview, 5 May 1987.

12. Ibid.

13. Ibid.

14. Ibid.

15. Ibid.

16. Ibid.

17. Except for Burg Tool and the Axelson Manufacturing Company, a builder of heavy-duty lathes for the railroad and mining industries, there were no Western-based machine tool builders with a national reputation.

18. In the regions where the machine tool industry was concentrated, it also encountered competition for skilled workers, chiefly from the automobile industry. But the wage gap there was rarely as wide as the one between the machine tool and the aircraft industries.

19. French interview, 5 May 1987.

20. Interview with Edward Merk, 27 August 1987.

21. French interview, 5 May 1987. See also Memo from A. Raiha, chief engineer, to J.L. Burg, president, Burgmaster Corporation, 11 December 1961. In this correspondence Raiha criticizes the inadequate budget and staff that he has to work with, along with the constant push for new machines.

22. French interview, 5 May 1987.

23. Ibid.

24. Ibid., 11 May 1987.

25. Ibid., 5 May 1987, and Ginsburg interview, 6 January 1986.

26. French interview, 5 May 1987, and Ginsburg interview, 6 January 1986. Each employee received a fixed percentage of profits, and the formula rose incrementally so that workers who earned more also had higher percentages.

27. Interview with Sandor Forizs, 9 June 1985, and French interview, 5 May 1987.

28. Interview with Bernhard Holland, 12 August 1987.

29. Fred Burg interview, 25 August 1987. The Burgs' approach bore a close resemblance to a seminal work on management that was first published in 1960. See Douglas McGregor, *The Human Side of Enterprise* (New York: McGraw-Hill, 1985).

McGregor, a president of Antioch College from 1948 to 1954, initially outlined his ideas in a 1957 address that became widely known as the "Theory Y" speech.

30. Richfield Oil Corporation, "Success Story," transcript, 18 May 1956.

31. French interview, 5 May 1987.

32. Richfield Oil, "Success Story," 18 May 1956.

33. Joe Burg interview, 11 May 1987.

34. Interview with Pete Ives, 18 January 1985.

35. A typical sales brochure from the late 1950s describes these different models: the O, 1-D, 1-DHT, 2B, 2BL, 2BR, 2BH, 2BHT, 2BHT-L, 2BHT-TH, 25AH, 25AHT, 25AHT-L, 25AHT-XL, 3BH, 3BHT-B, and 3BHT-L.

36. "Feed Control System for Machine Tools," No. 2,776,584, Patented 8 January 1957; "Speed Control System for Machine Tools," No. 2,767,598, Patented 23 October 1956; "Cyclically Operable Power Transmission Mechanism," No. 2,795,307, Patented 11 June 1957; "Machine Tool Having a Turret Head," No. 2,870,659, Patented 27 January 1959; "Quick Setting Adjustable Stop," No. 3,037,404, Patented 5 June 1962, all by Fred Burg, U.S. Patent Office, Washington, DC.

37. Richfield Oil, "Success Story," 18 May 1956.

38. French interview, 5 May 1987, and Ginsburg interview, 25 August 1987.

39. French interview, 5 May 1987. On the issue of circumventing patents, see Himes, "Machine Tool Industry," pp. 61–62. On the diffusion of ideas for new machines, see L.T.C. Rolt, *A Short History of Machine Tools* (Cambridge, MA: MIT Press, 1965), especially chapter 8.

40. "Quint Turret Drills," *Machinery*, April 1915, p. 27.

41. Joe Burg interview, 11 May 1987, and French interview, 5 May 1987.

42. Rolt, *Machine Tools*, pp. 223, 237. See also David F. Noble, *Forces of Production* (New York: Alfred A. Knopf, 1984), pp. 33, 70. Noble's work describes in detail the development and adoption of NC. He also posits a provocative thesis about the motivation behind management's push for automatic control.

43. Jacob Sonny, "Technological Change in the U.S. Machine Tool Industry, 1947–1966" (Ph.D. diss., New School for Social Research, 1971), p. 69. Sonny cites patent claims made by the LeBlond Company and the Bullard Company that antedate Parsons's work. Noble shows, however, that Parsons was perhaps the most forceful advocate of the idea.

44. Noble, *Forces of Production*, pp. 101–105.

45. Ibid., pp. 113–130.

46. Ibid., pp. 134–138, 199–200.

47. Ibid., pp. 195–202.

48. Ibid., pp. 219–226.

49. Sonny, "Technological Change," p. 70. From 1954 to 1958, only 173 NC units were shipped.

50. Noble, *Forces of Production*, pp. 220–221.

51. Ibid., p. 216. MIT pioneered what was called continuous path NC, which enabled machines to produce any shape. Point-to-point positioning NC, the kind employed in the Burgmaster, was less capable but quite suitable for drilling and similar operations.

52. "What's New in Drilling," *American Machinist*, 11 November 1963. See also Stephen S. Heineman and George W. Genevro, *Machine Tools* (San Francisco: Canfield Press, 1979), p. 373, and Kearney & Trecker v. Houdaille Industries, Inc., "Plaintiff's Answers and Objections to Defendant Houdaille's Interrogatories," Civil Action 70-C-3123, U.S. District Court, Northern District of Illinois, Eastern Division, 6 February 1973.

53. Nathan Rosenberg, cited in Noble, *Forces of Production*, p. 212.

3: Heydays (1960–1964)

1. NMTBA, *Economic Handbook,* p. 42, and John Diebold, "The Revolution That Fails to Take Place," Address before NMTBA, 3 May 1963, Cincinnati, Ohio. The machine tool percentage of new plant and equipment sales had declined from 3.6 percent in 1939 to about 1.5 percent by the early 1960s.

2. Robert S. Himes, "A Study of the Machine Tool Industry" (Ph.D. diss., American University, 1962), pp. 208–214, and David F. Noble, *Forces of Production* (New York: Alfred A. Knopf, 1984), p. 9. Just before the Korean armistice an ambitious plan for stabilizing the machine tool industry was put forward in a report to the Office of Defense Mobilization. The Vance committee recommended annual expenditures of almost $500 million to keep the machine tool industry vibrant. Nothing like this level of support was ever achieved. Procurement fell from about $100 million in 1954 and 1955 to $22 million by 1961.

3. "64 Percent of Machine Tools Are Over-Age," *American Machinist,* 10 June 1963.

4. Industry protests reached a peak in 1954 and 1958, both recession years. See "Machine Tool Makers Ask Faster Write-Offs for Their Customers," *The Wall Street Journal,* 28 April 1958, and Memorandum by Frederick Geier, "The American Machine Tool Industry," Commission on Foreign Economic Policy (2), Box 588, Official Files, Dwight Eisenhower Library, Abilene, Kansas.

5. Himes, "Machine Tool Industry," p. 183, and *The Wall Street Journal,* 28 April 1958. Although the United States was the world's leading producer, West Germany was the leading exporter, selling a greater percentage of its production to other countries.

6. Robert Triffin, *The World Money Maze* (New Haven, CT: Yale University Press, 1966), pp. 96–98.

7. "Capital Goods Exports and the International Competitive Position of U.S. Machinery Manufacturers," *Capital Goods Review,* Machinery and Allied Products Institute, No. 58, June 1964, Washington, DC.

8. *American Machinist,* 11 November 1963. See also Edward G. Merk, "Tough Jobs Made Easy with Numerical Control and Turret Drilling," Technical Paper No. 548, American Society of Tool and Manufacturing Engineers, 1964.

9. "NC Cuts Reactor Manufacturing Costs," *American Machinist,* 6 August 1962. The fact that the stainless steel castings were first drilled, then bored and reamed indicates that a high degree of precision was required. Chamfering is a machining operation that removes a small amount of metal at the entrance of a hole, usually at a 45 degree angle to the hole's axis.

10. Advertising Brochure, Burgmaster Corporation, Gardena, California, 1 January 1962. Tooling costs usually refer to the need for custom-made jigs, fixtures, or templates for machining. A jig or fixture is a device that holds the workpiece in a manner that reduces the number of setups to a minimum and ensures accuracy. A template is a thin plate of metal that serves as a guide or gauge during machining.

11. Noble, *Forces of Production,* pp. 253–256.

12. "Burgmaster Growth Plan," Houdaille Industries, Inc., 1966. Brown & Sharpe ranked as a competitor on hand-operated machines only. Later in the 1960s, Giddings & Lewis and Kearney & Trecker also developed into major competitors.

13. Burgmaster Corporation, Registration No. 2-18270, Securities and Exchange Commission, Washington, DC, pp. 7–8, 10. In 1960, the Burgs each received $2,048 out of the $50,000 set aside for profit sharing. This sum amounted to 5 percent of Fred Burg's salary ($43,000), and 6 percent of Joe Burg's and Norman Ginsburg's salary

($36,000). All three also received year-end bonuses given to all directors and officers of the company; those amounts are included in the salary figures.

14. Ibid., p. 8.

15. Ibid., pp. 6–7. In 1960, after the 54 percent of total sales owed to NC machines, the next highest category was manual machines, which constituted 14 percent. Sales of hydraulic models accounted for about 12 percent, and bench models added up to 5 percent. Custom-built machines accounted for only about 13 percent of total sales. The balance of the company's business, 2 percent, came from sales of the Tool-flex.

16. Harless D. Wagoner, *The U.S. Machine Tool Industry from 1900 to 1950* (Cambridge, MA: MIT Press, 1968), pp. 107–108, 114.

17. Joe Burg interview, 11 May 1987.

18. Documents obtained under the Freedom of Information Act, 14 September 1987, National Labor Relations Board, Washington, DC.

19. Even if a machinist at Burg Tool was red-lined, however, he did not receive as much as a worker doing the same job in the aerospace industry.

20. Ginsburg interview, 6 January 1986, French interview, 11 May 1987, and Holland interview, 4 May 1987. Later, after Burg Tool was organized, the union would do an about-face and inform the Burgs it favored red-lining. It boosted the high end of the wage structure.

21. See note 20.

22. Ginsburg interview, 6 January 1986, and 25 August 1987.

23. Ibid.

24. Burgmaster Corporation, Registration No. 2-18270, SEC, p. 6.

25. Ginsburg interview, 6 January 1986.

26. By the 1980s, class members would be top executives at Bloomingdale's, Zayre's, Xerox, Capital Cities/ABC, and Johnson & Johnson, among other companies. Shad, who later earned a law degree from NYU, would do very well too. In 1963, he left Shearson for a vice presidency at E.F. Hutton. There he consummated corporate financings and mergers worth billions of dollars, and, in the process, earned tens of millions for himself. A staunch backer of the Republican party, in 1981 he was appointed head of the SEC by President Reagan, reportedly at the suggestion of William Casey. He served in that post longer than any of his twenty-one predecessors. In 1987, he became the U.S. ambassador to the Netherlands. See Ronald Brownstein and Nina Easton, *Reagan's Ruling Class* (Washington, DC: Presidential Accountability Group, 1982), pp. 715–721.

27. Interview with John Shad, 31 August 1987. Shad responded in writing to questions about Burgmaster.

28. Burgmaster Corporation, Registration No. 2-18270, SEC, p. 10. Before the company went public, Fred Burg owned 126,750 shares, or 39 percent of Burg Tool; the families of Joe Burg and Norm Ginsburg each held 100,125 shares, or about 30 percent.

29. Cited in Robert Sobel, *The Last Bull Market* (New York: W.W. Norton, 1980), p. 66.

30. "Firm Voids 1st Public Stock Sale 2 Weeks after Offering; Prospectus Error Found," *The Wall Street Journal*, 29 May 1961.

31. "Burgmaster Again Files Common Stock Offering It Withdrew Earlier," *The Wall Street Journal*, 12 June 1961.

32. Burgmaster Corporation, Registration No. 2-18270, SEC, p. 2.

33. Shad interview, 31 August 1987.

34. Ginsburg interview, 25 August 1987.

35. *The Wall Street Journal*, 29 May 1961.

36. Shad interview, 31 August 1987.

37. Burgmaster Corporation, "Annual Report," for the years ending 31 October 1962 and 31 October 1963.

38. Ibid.

39. "Additions to Its Product Line Help Burgmaster's Drive to Peak Net," *Barron's,* 12 October 1964.

40. "Burgmaster Corp. Drilling a Big Niche in Machine Tool Industry," *Los Angeles Times,* 4 November 1964. As always, the selling price of a machine tool depended finally on what the market could bear, not the cost of production. When Burgmaster's competitors lowered their prices, Burgmaster had no choice but to follow. A 2BH-TXL with GE Mark II numerical controls, for example, sold for $40,000 in 1961; a year later, despite rising production costs, the same machine was quoted at $36,070. On price competition and cost cutting, see transcripts of Monthly Staff Meetings, Burgmaster Corporation, 3 May and 14 June 1962.

41. Burgmaster Corporation, "Annual Report," for years ending 31 October 1962 and 31 October 1963. See also *Barron's,* 12 October 1964. In a sliding head machine, the turret head assembly, instead of being fixed, could move up and down, greatly increasing the machine's versatility. A traveling column machine followed much the same principle except that the column moved horizontally rather than vertically. The two movements could also be combined in a sliding head/traveling column machine.

42. *Barron's,* 12 October 1964.

43. Judging from transcripts of monthly staff meetings, during the early 1960s quality control of new machines was a chronic problem. See Monthly Staff Meetings, Burgmaster Corporation, 3 May and 14 June 1962.

44. Ives interview, 18 January 1985 and 6 May 1987.

45. Ibid.

46. Ginsburg interview, 6 January 1986, and Joe Burg interview, 11 May 1987. No one can recall exactly how Burgmaster learned about the patent infringement.

47. Ginsburg interview, 6 January 1986, and Joe Burg interview, 11 May 1987.

48. Ibid. See also Monthly Staff Meetings, 3 May and 14 June 1962, and Ginsburg interview, 25 August 1987. Ginsburg recalled that the damages amounted to $50,000, but two years passed before Burgmaster received any money.

49. Burgmaster Corporation, "Annual Report," for year ending 31 October 1963.

50. French interview, 11 May 1987.

51. "Burgmaster Growth Plan," Houdaille Industries, Inc., 1966. See also "Metalworking Man of the Month," *Western Metalworking,* March 1963. One of the directors on Burgmaster's board was an Ex-Cell-O vice president. Undoubtedly his presence facilitated the overseas link between the two companies.

52. Noble, *Forces of Production,* p. 212, and "On the Job, Automatic Tools Prove Virtuosos," *Business Week,* 14 March 1959. On the predecessors to K&T's tool changer, see "Special Report 763: Machining Centers," *American Machinist,* February 1984.

53. *Business Week,* 14 March 1959. See also "New Tape-Controlled Tools Help Automate Low Production Plants," *The Wall Street Journal,* 14 October 1959. Besides the number of tools, another factor that contributed to the M-M's edge was that it featured an indexing table. This allowed its horizontal spindle to address each of four faces of a cube-shaped workpiece without refixturing.

54. *The Wall Street Journal,* 14 October 1959.

55. Burgmaster Corporation, "Annual Report," for year ending 31 October 1963.

56. French interview, 5 May 1987.

57. Ibid.

58. "Twenty Tools without a Changer," *American Machinist,* 7 June 1965.

59. *Los Angeles Times,* 4 November 1964.

4: Takeover (1965)

1. "Ralph Peo Dies; Industrialist, 69," *New York Times,* 30 November 1966.
2. Ibid.
3. Until 1955, Houdaille was known as the Houdaille-Hershey Corporation.
4. Interview with Phillip O'Reilly, 17 March 1987.
5. "Houdaille Industries, Inc.," *Moody's Industrial Manual* (New York: Moody's Investors Service, 1958), pp. 1293–1296, and interview with Gerald Saltarelli, 27 March 1987.
6. Saltarelli interview, 27 March 1987, and *New York Times,* 30 November 1966. The barrier was not actually part of the bomb but was used to enrich uranium.
7. Saltarelli interview, 27 March 1987.
8. "Frontier Industries," *New York Times,* 26 February 1955.
9. Saltarelli interview, 27 March 1987. One reason subcontracted parts cost more was that the United Auto Workers insisted on "pattern plus" from companies like Houdaille. If Ford Motor, for example, agreed to a pattern-setting contract that gave its auto workers a ten-cent raise, pattern plus required subcontractors to pay eleven cents.
10. Ibid., and "Houdaille-Hershey," *New York Times,* 20 May 1955. At the height of its relationship with auto makers, Houdaille was manufacturing nineteen different parts in twenty-one plants. Shock absorbers and automobile bumpers were the largest items in terms of dollar volume, but Houdaille also produced everything from camshafts and crankshafts to locks, ignitions, fender skirts, and air cleaners.
11. Saltarelli interview, 27 March 1987.
12. "Expansions," *New York Times,* 24 October 1955, and "Houdaille-Hershey," *New York Times,* 20 May 1955.
13. *New York Times,* 30 November 1966, and "Houdaille Industries," *Moody's Industrial Manual,* 1966, p. 1875. See *Moody's* for Houdaille's acquisitions from 1956 to 1962.
14. Saltarelli interview, 27 March 1987.
15. Ibid.
16. Ibid. Saltarelli may not have intended to include himself, but in an interview, he talked freely about how "this country's industry has tended to pick financial men and lawyers as CEOs. . . . I'm glad but in looking back it was overdone. U.S. industry missed something, an in-depth knowledge of how something is made. Lawyers are best at picking out important facts. . . . [it's best] when the people running operations are engineers and come from the factory floor." On the management trend that Saltarelli reflected, see Robert H. Hayes and William J. Abernathy, "Managing Our Way to Economic Decline," *Harvard Business Review,* July–August 1980, pp. 74–75.
17. Saltarelli interview, 27 March 1987. One of the biggest blows fell in 1957. Little more than one year after Houdaille spent $2 million on new auto bumper facilities, Ford notified Houdaille that as of 1958, it would be bending its own bumpers.
18. Jon Didrichsen, "The Development of Diversified and Conglomerate Firms in the United States, 1920–1970," *Business History Review* 46 (1972): 202–219. See also Robert Sobel, *The Age of Giant Corporations* (Westport, CT: Greenwood Press, 1972), pp. 196–197, and Barry Bluestone and Bennett Harrison, *The Deindustrialization of America* (New York: Basic Books, 1982), p. 124. Didrichsen traces the rise of conglomerates back to 1953. Sobel cites a 1948 Federal Trade Commission report to show that aside from a few pharmaceutical conglomerates, as a form of corporate organization con-

glomeration was rare until the late 1950s. Bluestone and Harrison cite a Senate study that shows conglomerate-type mergers accounted for between 60 and 80 percent of all merger activity during the 1960s as opposed to 20 percent in the 1940s, and between 40 and 50 percent in the 1950s. In *The Last Bull Market* (New York: W.W. Norton, 1980), p. 51, Sobel suggests that the species "conglomerate" eluded simple definition. Nevertheless, "Wall Street knew a conglomerate when it saw one."

19. Sobel, *Bull Market*, p. 51, and *Giant Corporations*, pp. 205–208.

20. David J. Ravenscraft and F. M. Scherer, *Mergers, Sell-Offs, and Economic Efficiency* (Washington, DC: Brookings Institution, 1987), pp. 214–215.

21. Sobel, *Giant Corporations*, pp. 202–204, and Didrichsen, "Conglomerate Firms," pp. 216–218.

22. Sobel, *Giant Corporations*, pp. 202–203.

23. Ibid., p. 197.

24. Didrichsen, "Conglomerate Firms," p. 219.

25. In the late 1960s, at the height of the conglomerate fever, it was not unusual for corporations to pay an average premium of 25 percent more than the market value of the target company's stock. "The Agglomeration of America," *New York Times*, 12 July 1981.

26. Sobel, *Bull Market*, pp. 145–146, and *Giant Corporations*, pp. 205–208. Also Saltarelli interview, 27 March 1987. The so-called P/E multiple is the spread between a stock's selling price and its expected earnings. Litton achieved one of the highest multiples ever for a conglomerate in 1960, when its P/E multiple was fifty. Houdaille's never rose above ten for most of the decade. On the link between P/E ratios and conglomerate takeovers, see Paul M. Sweezy and Harry Magdoff, *The Dynamics of U.S. Capitalism* (New York: Monthly Review Press, 1972), pp. 68–87.

27. Saltarelli interview, 27 March 1987.

28. Ibid.

29. Jacob Sonny, "Technological Change in the U.S. Machine Tool Industry, 1947–1966" (Ph.D. diss., New School for Social Research, 1971), pp. 51–52, and Robert S. Himes, "A Study of the Machine Tool Industry" (Ph.D. diss., American University, 1962), pp. 270–272. Generally, diversification did not help builders compensate for cyclic demand. It was too expensive to use underemployed machinists to make relatively crude products; and often, diversification simply increased capital risk without relieving the cyclic problem. Most machine tool companies that tried to diversify ended up regretting their attempt to make bottle labelers (Norton Company), plastic-molding machines (Giddings & Lewis), and golf balls (LeBlond).

30. Harless D. Wagoner, *The U.S. Machine Tool Industry from 1900 to 1950* (Cambridge, MA: MIT Press, 1968), p. 49.

31. Sonny, "Technological Change," p. 30.

32. Editorial, *American Machinist*, 29 March 1965, and 25 October 1965.

33. Editorial, *American Machinist*, 22 November 1965.

34. Houdaille Industries, Inc., "Annual Report," for year ending 31 December 1967.

35. Sonny, "Technological Change," p. 24, and Burgmaster Corporation, "Annual Report," for year ending 31 October 1963. Burgmaster, with 222 employees in 1963, fit into the category of builders employing 100 to 249 workers. According to the 1963 *Census of Manufactures* cited by Sonny, the average value of shipments per worker for a company that size was $20,349. Burgmaster's sales amounted to $30,709 per worker.

36. Saltarelli interview, 27 March 1987.

37. "Burgmaster Growth Plan," Houdaille Industries, Inc., 1966.

38. Ginsburg interview, 6 January 1986.

39. Ibid.

40. Shad interview, 31 August 1987.

41. Ibid. Preferred stock also gave Burgmaster stockholders first call on Hou-

daille's future dividends. See also John S.R. Shad, "The Financial Realities of Mergers," *Harvard Business Review,* November–December 1969, pp. 134–135. The advantages of swapping common for convertible preferred shares diminished once the SEC, during the height of the conglomerate fever, required conglomerates to report their earnings per common share as if preferred stock had been converted.

42. Shad interview, 31 August 1987.

43. "Houdaille Agrees to Buy Burgmaster for Stock Valued at $8.5 Million," *The Wall Street Journal,* 7 June 1965.

44. "Houdaille Industries Increases Its Price Offered for Burgmaster," *The Wall Street Journal,* 28 July 1965, and Joe Burg interview, 11 May 1987.

45. Merk interview, 27 August 1987.

46. *The Wall Street Journal,* 7 June 1965.

5: The Houdaille Way (1966–1967)

1. French interview, 11 May 1987.

2. "Burgmaster Growth Plan," Houdaille Industries, Inc., 1966, and Letter from J. L. Burg to Burgmaster employees, "Growth Requires Growth," 1 February 1967.

3. "Burgmaster Growth Plan," Houdaille, 1966.

4. The Broadway plant's specifications are cited in a sales brochure prepared by Grubb & Ellis, industrial realtors, in 1986.

5. "Burgmaster Growth Plan," Houdaille, 1966.

6. Ibid. Burgmaster's situation was not unique; in fact, the backlog in the machine tool industry as a whole exceeded $1 billion. But Burgmaster's production bottlenecks were undoubtedly worse than those of most other tool builders.

7. Ibid.

8. Ibid.

9. Ibid., and O'Reilly interview, 27 March 1987.

10. Ginsburg interview, 25 August 1987.

11. Joe Burg interview, 11 May 1987.

12. Saltarelli interview, 27 March 1987.

13. Ibid.

14. French interview, 5 May 1987.

15. Merk interview, 27 August 1987.

16. Saltarelli interview, 27 March 1987.

17. Ibid.

18. Interview with Tom Norton, 12 April 1987.

19. Saltarelli interview, 27 March 1987.

20. Ginsburg interview, 6 January 1986.

21. Interview with Ben Bezdziecki, 11 January 1986.

22. Ibid.

23. Ibid.

24. "Burgmaster Growth Plan," Houdaille, 1966. The document noted that "the most acute needs of the moment are reliable internal controls."

25. Ibid.

26. Ibid.

27. French interview, 5 May 1987.

28. Joe Burg interview, 11 May 1987.

29. Bezdziecki interview, 11 January 1986.

30. Paul Goodman, *Growing up Absurd* (New York: Random House, 1956), p. xiii.

31. "Twenty Tools without a Changer," *American Machinist,* 7 June 1965, and Bezdziecki interview, 11 January 1986.

32. "Soviet Delegation Tours L.A. Plant; Eyes U.S. Tape Units," *Industrial News*, 2 January 1967. The one time Burgmaster had inquired about exports to communist countries, the Commerce Department replied with a flat no.

33. Ibid.

34. Houdaille Industries, Inc., "Annual Report," for year ending 31 December 1967, p. 12.

35. Saltarelli interview, 27 March 1987.

36. Norton interview, 12 April 1987.

37. Joe Burg interview, 11 May 1987.

38. Letter from J. L. Burg to Burgmaster employees, 1 February 1987.

39. Powermatic Brochure, Houdaille Industries, 1966.

40. "Busy Burgmaster: Preps to Handle Small Tool Line, Dualcenter," *Metalworking News*, 23 March 1970.

41. "Burgmaster Growth Plan," Houdaille, 1966, and Ginsburg interview, 6 January 1986.

42. Norton interview, 12 April 1987.

43. Ibid.

6: Under New Management (1968)

1. *Feedback*, Burgmaster, May 1968. *Feedback* was a company newsletter.

2. Robert Sobel, *The Last Bull Market* (New York: W.W. Norton, 1980), pp. 218–219.

3. Ibid.

4. Saltarelli interview, 27 March 1987.

5. Houdaille Industries, Inc., "Annual Report," for year ending 31 December 1967, pp. 22–23.

6. Barry Bluestone and Bennett Harrison, *The Deindustrialization of America* (New York: Basic Books, 1982), pp. 122–123, and David J. Ravenscraft and F.M. Scherer, *Mergers, Sell-Offs, and Economic Efficiency* (Washington, DC: Brookings Institution, 1987), pp. 21–24. According to FTC statistics cited by Ravenscraft and Scherer, the volume (in constant 1972 dollars) of manufacturing and mineral firm mergers in 1968 exceeded $15 billion, the highest level ever; 44 percent of all the 1950–1977 merger activity occurred within the five-year period 1966–1970; and more than 80 percent of all mergers from 1966 to 1968 were conglomerate in nature. See also John M. Blair, *Economic Concentration* (New York: Harcourt Brace Jovanovich, 1972), pp. 285–298.

7. "Trends," *American Machinist*, 28 February 1966.

8. Ibid., 19 December 1966, and 28 February 1966.

9. Ibid., 18 December 1967.

10. NMTBA, *Economic Handbook*, p. 42. Although total output during the 1950s was slightly greater (in constant 1986 dollars, $57.2 billion versus $56.3 billion during the 1960s), in the 1960s, the industry enjoyed six straight years of growth, a postwar record.

11. Walter Adams and James W. Brock, *The Bigness Complex* (New York: Pantheon, 1986), pp. 42–43, 183.

12. David Calleo, *The Imperious Economy* (Cambridge, MA: Harvard University Press, 1982), pp. 20–24.

13. Bluestone and Harrison, *Deindustrialization*, p. 114, and Sobel, *Bull Market*, p. 124.

14. "A Remembrance of Interest Rates—and an Editor—Past," *The Wall Street Journal*, 5 July 1983, and Calleo, *Imperious Economy*, pp. 26–28.

15. IRS figures cited in Bluestone and Harrison, *Deindustrialization*, pp. 147–148.

16. Sobel, *Bull Market,* p. 198. In 1968, the assets of acquired companies as a percentage of new investment was more than 44 percent. A decade earlier, the same figure was less than 9 percent.

17. "Special News Bulletin," *American Machinist,* 14 May 1969. See also Ravenscraft and Scherer, *Mergers,* p. 39.

18. Sobel, *Bull Market,* p. 197.

19. "Special News Bulletin," *American Machinist,* 7 June 1967, and 14 May 1969. This ranking did not include privately owned builders.

20. Editorial, *American Machinist,* 19 May 1969.

21. See Appendix B.

22. "J. L. Burg Appointed by Houdaille," *Buffalo Courier-Express,* 30 August 1967.

23. Ginsburg interview, 25 August 1987.

24. Holland interview, 20 January 1986.

25. Saltarelli interview, 27 March 1987.

26. Norton interview, 12 April 1987.

27. Ibid.

28. Ibid.

29. Ibid.

30. Ibid.

31. Ibid.

32. Interview with Gene Dobmeier, 4 May 1987.

33. French interview, 5 May 1987.

34. Holland interview, 4 May 1987, and *Feedback,* Burgmaster, April 1968.

35. French interview, 11 May 1987.

36. Dobmeier interview, 4 May 1987.

37. Douglas McGregor, *The Human Side of Enterprise* (New York: McGraw-Hill, 1985), pp. 33–35, and David F. Noble, *Forces of Production* (New York: Alfred A. Knopf, 1984), pp. 33–34.

38. Joe Burg interview, 11 May 1987.

39. Ibid.

40. Merk interview, 27 August 1987, and Bezdziecki interview, 11 January 1986.

41. Merk interview, 27 August 1987.

42. 20T Advertising Brochure, Burgmaster division, February 1967.

43. Norton interview, 12 April 1987.

44. Joe Burg interview, 11 May 1987.

45. Ginsburg interview, 25 August 1987.

46. Editorial, *American Machinist,* 23 October 1967, and "Kearney & Trecker Corp. v. Giddings & Lewis, Inc.," *United States Patents Quarterly* 171 (October–December 1971): 652–653.

47. Merk interview, 27 August 1987.

48. Norton interview, 12 April 1987.

49. Ibid., and *Feedback,* Burgmaster, April 1968.

50. NMTBA, *Economic Handbook,* p. 42. The figures given are in constant 1986 dollars.

51. See Appendix B. The decline is masked by the fact that Houdaille added two new acquisitions, Logan Engineering and Kaufman Tool and Engineering, to its machine tool group in 1969.

52. French interview, 11 May 1987.

53. Norton interview, 12 April 1987, and Merk interview, 27 August 1987.

54. Ginsburg interview, 25 August 1987.

55. Ibid.

7: Cutting Edge Lost (1969–1970)

1. Interview with Allan Folger, 20 January 1986.
2. "The Blue Bulletin," *American Machinist*, 29 May 1968, and 14 May 1969.
3. Norton interview, 12 April 1987.
4. Folger interview, 20 January 1986.
5. Norton interview, 12 April 1987.
6. Interview with Dave Balbirnie, 29 August 1987.
7. Bob Doyle interview, 27 August 1987, and Merk interview, 27 August 1987.
8. Burgmaster Auction Brochure, National Industrial Services Incorporated, St. Louis, MO, 15 January 1986. The brochure printed by the auctioneers who liquidated the Burgmaster plant listed every machine in the factory, along with the year it was acquired.
9. Norton interview, 12 April 1987, and Balbirnie interview, 29 August 1987.
10. U.S. Congress, House, Select Committee on Small Business, *Problems Facing the Tool and Die Industry*, 91st Cong., 1st sess., 1969, p. 182.
11. "Trends," *American Machinist*, 18 July 1966.
12. Norton interview, 12 April 1987, and Balbirnie interview, 29 August 1987.
13. Folger interview, 20 January 1986.
14. "Pepsico Entering Restaurant Field," *New York Times*, 24 January 1969.
15. Memo, A. B. Folger to Burgmaster supervisors, 22 August 1969, and Memo, Alf Celinder to engineering personnel, 25 August 1969.
16. "Kearney & Trecker Corp. v. Giddings & Lewis, Inc.," *United States Patents Quarterly* 171 (October–December 1971): 653, and Folger interview, 20 January 1986.
17. Folger interview, 20 January 1986.
18. Ibid.
19. Dualcenter Machining Center Brochure, Burgmaster, June 1970.
20. O'Reilly interview, 17 March 1987.
21. Kearney & Trecker v. Houdaille Industries, Inc., "Answer and Counterclaim," Civil Action No. 70-C-3123, U.S. District Court, Northern District of Illinois, Eastern Division, 7 May 1971.
22. Ibid.
23. Merk interview, 27 August 1987.
24. MT-3 and MT-3A Machining Center Installations, Burgmaster, n.d.
25. Ibid.
26. French interview, 11 May 1987.
27. Editorial, *American Machinist*, 23 October 1967.
28. "Kearney & Trecker Corp. v. Giddings & Lewis, Inc.," *United States Patents Quarterly* 171 (October–December 1971): 653, 665. In addition to its control of the all-important Brainard patent, K&T had tightened its grip on the technology by purchasing from IBM the rights to a competitive design, the so-called Morgan patent, in 1963.
29. Folger interview, 20 January 1986.
30. Ibid.
31. "Busy Burgmaster: Preps to Handle Small Tool Line, Dualcenter," *Metalworking News*, 23 March 1970.
32. "Patent Suit Is Won by Kearney & Trecker," *The Wall Street Journal*, 19 November 1969.
33. "Strippit Improves Computer Control," *American Machinist*, 29 June 1970. Houdaille was not alone in developing its own control units. During the 1960s, about ten machine tool builders and five outside suppliers developed NC systems. Nearly all were incompatible with one another, relatively complex, and expensive. See David

Collis, "The Machine Tool Industry and Industrial Policy, 1955–82," in A. Michael Spence and Heather A. Hazard, eds., *International Competitiveness* (Cambridge MA: Ballinger, 1988), p. 92.

34. Any references to NC machines in the text from this point on should be taken to mean CNC machines as well.

35. French interview, 5 May 1987, and interview with Socrates Lenders, 6 May 1987.

36. *Metalworking News,* 23 March 1970.

37. Ibid.

38. Dobmeier interview, 4 May 1987.

39. Ibid.

40. Ibid.

41. See corporate listings in *Moody's Industrial Manual,* 1970.

42. Dennis Encarnation, "Cross-Investment: A Second Front of Economic Rivalry," in Thomas K. McCraw, ed., *America versus Japan* (Boston: Harvard Business School Press, 1986), pp. 119–125, 134–137.

43. Ibid., pp. 121–124, and Mira Wilkins, *The Maturing of Multinational Enterprise* (Cambridge, MA: Harvard University Press, 1974), pp. 349–350.

8: The Rise of Yamazaki (1945–1970)

1. Cited in Peter Duus, "Japan: Taking Off," *The Wilson Quarterly,* Winter 1982, p. 119.

2. *Mazak* (Japan: Yamazaki Machinery Works, Ltd., 1983), p. 3, and Ezra F. Vogel, *Comeback Case by Case* (New York: Simon and Schuster, 1985), p. 76.

3. Ibid., pp. 61, 76, and "New in Japan: The Manless Factory," *New York Times,* 13 December 1981.

4. Patricia Hagan Kuwayama, "Japan: Success Story," *The Wilson Quarterly,* Winter 1982, p. 134, and Vogel, *Comeback,* p. 61.

5. Vogel, *Comeback,* p. 76, and David Friedman, *The Misunderstood Miracle* (Ithaca, NY: Cornell University Press, 1988), pp. 73–74.

6. Vogel, *Comeback,* pp. 61–62, and James Crowley, "Japan: An Empire Won and Lost," *The Wilson Quarterly,* Winter 1982, p. 132. See also Thomas McCraw and Patricia O'Brien, "Production and Distribution," in McCraw, ed., *America versus Japan* (Boston: Harvard Business School Press, 1986), pp. 84–85.

7. Friedman, *Misunderstood Miracle,* pp. 73–74.

8. Ibid., pp. 75–76. See also Leonard H. Lynn and Timothy J. McKeown, *Organizing Business* (Washington, DC: American Enterprise Institute for Public Policy Research, 1988), pp. 10, 28–30, 69–74. Several "outsiders" were not considered sufficiently important to be invited to join the JMTBA.

9. Duus, "Taking Off," p. 110.

10. Cited in Michael Schaller, *The American Occupation of Japan* (New York: Oxford University Press, 1985), p. viii.

11. Thomas McCraw, "From Partners to Competitors," in McCraw, ed., *America versus Japan,* pp. 6–7.

12. "U.S. Far from Prescient on Japan 31 Years Ago," *Washington Post,* 24 May 1985.

13. McCraw, "From Partners to Competitors," pp. 10–21, and Terutomo Ozawa, "Japanese Policy toward Foreign Multinationals," in Thomas A. Pugel and Robert G. Hawkins, eds., *Fragile Interdependence* (Lexington, MA: Lexington Books, 1986), p. 146.

14. Martin Fransman, "International Competitiveness, Technical Change and the

State: The Machine Tool Industry in Taiwan and Japan," *World Development* 14 (1986): 1383.

15. Vogel, *Comeback*, p. 70. Japanese companies were required to prove that a domestic tool could not perform a needed function before they could obtain foreign exchange to buy an imported tool.

16. Friedman, *Misunderstood Miracle*, pp. 77–78. See also Susumu Watanabe, "Market Structure, Industrial Organization and Technological Development: The Case of the Japanese Electronics-Based NC-Machine Tool Industry," World Employment Programme Research Working Paper WEP2-22/WP.111 (Geneva: International Labor Organization, February 1983), p. 53.

17. Vogel, *Comeback*, pp. 65–66.

18. Ibid., pp. 67–68.

19. Friedman, *Misunderstood Miracle*, p. 116.

20. Ibid., p. 79.

21. Ibid., pp. 79–80, 118. The tariff for machines with no Japanese equivalent was 10 percent.

22. Ibid., p. 77.

23. Ibid., p. 85.

24. Harless D. Wagoner, *The U.S. Machine Tool Industry from 1900 to 1950* (Cambridge, MA: MIT Press, 1968), pp. 74–75. The JMTBA was certainly not the first trade association to advocate such discipline in the marketplace. Its American counterpart, the NMTBA, had urged similar actions when U.S. industry was plagued by fierce competition and sagging demand in the 1920s.

25. Kozo Yamamura, "Success That Soured," in Yamamura, ed., *Policy and Trade Issues of the Japanese Economy* (Seattle: University of Washington Press, 1982), p. 80.

26. Vogel, *Comeback*, p. 69.

27. Ibid.

28. Ibid., p. 76.

29. McCraw, "From Partners to Competitors, " pp. 16–17.

30. "Japan Makes Its Bid for World Machine Tool Markets," *American Machinist,* 1 June 1959.

31. Vogel, *Comeback*, p. 74.

32. Ibid., pp. 62–63.

33. Friedman, *Misunderstood Miracle*, pp. 82–83.

34. Fransman, "Machine Tool Industry," pp. 1382–1383, and Watanabe, "NC-Machine Tool Industry," p. 10.

35. Watanabe, "NC-Machine Tool Industry," pp. 34–35, and Vogel, *Comeback*, pp. 80–81.

36. Vogel, *Comeback*, pp. 80–81.

37. Ibid., Watanabe, "NC-Machine Tool Industry," p. 10, and Friedman, *Misunderstood Miracle*, p. 122.

38. Watanabe, "NC-Machine Tool Industry," p. 34.

39. Fransman, "Machine Tool Industry," p. 1383, and Friedman, *Misunderstood Miracle*, p. 116.

40. Friedman, *Misunderstood Miracle*, pp. 97–98.

41. *Hahanaru Kikai: San-ju nen no Ayumi* (Mother Machines: A Thirty Year History) (Tokyo: Seisanzai Marketing, 1982), p. 58.

42. Vogel, *Comeback*, p. 76.

43. Ibid., pp. 73, 76–77.

44. Ibid., pp. 76–77.

45. Ibid., p. 77.

46. Ibid.

47. Ibid.

48. *Mazak*, p. 3.
49. Mark Zimmerman, *How to Do Business with the Japanese* (New York: Random House, 1985), pp. 134, 141, 150–151, and McCraw, "Conclusions and Implications," in McCraw, ed., *America versus Japan*, p. 377.
50. Vogel, *Comeback*, p. 75.
51. Ibid., p. 73.
52. Fransman, "Machine Tool Industry," p. 1383.
53. Cited in Mira Wilkins, *The Maturing of Multinational Enterprise* (Cambridge, MA: Harvard University Press, 1974), p. 349.
54. Thomas A. Pugel, "Japan's Industrial Policy," *Journal of Comparative Economics* 8 (1984): 428–429.
55. Ozawa, "Foreign Multinationals," pp. 146–148, and Dennis Encarnation, "Cross-Investment: A Second Front of Economic Rivalry," in McCraw, ed., *America versus Japan*, p. 122.
56. McCraw, "From Partners to Competitors," p. 18.
57. Vogel, *Comeback*, p. 73.
58. Friedman, *Misunderstood Miracle*, pp. 99–100.
59. Ibid., pp. 82–85.
60. Ozawa, "Foreign Multinationals," p. 149.
61. Chalmers Johnson, *MITI and the Japanese Miracle* (Stanford, CA: Stanford University Press, 1982), p. 276.
62. Ibid., p. 277.
63. Friedman, *Misunderstood Miracle*, p. 100.
64. Quote cited in ibid.
65. Ibid., pp. 100–102, and Vogel, *Comeback*, p. 78.
66. Statement of National Machine Tool Builders' Association, Hearings on the Future of United States Foreign Trade Policy before the Trade Information Committee, Office of the Special Representative for Trade Negotiations, Washington, DC, 6 June 1968, p. 12.
67. "More Machine Tools from Overseas Flow into the U.S. Market," *The Wall Street Journal*, 25 May 1965.
68. NMTBA statement, 6 June 1968, p. 11.
69. "Foreign Machine Tool Builders Capitalize on Long Delivery Times of U.S. Concerns," *The Wall Street Journal*, 25 May 1965.
70. NMTBA statement, 6 June 1968, p. 17.
71. Ibid., p. 12, and Vogel, *Comeback*, p. 81.
72. Vogel, *Comeback*, p. 78.
73. *The Wall Street Journal*, 6 September 1967.
74. Editorial, *American Machinist*, 4 November 1968.
75. NMTBA statement, 6 June 1968, Appendix K, pp. 4, 32.
76. Ibid., pp. 6–9.
77. Ibid.
78. Kuwayama, "Success Story," p. 138.
79. NMTBA, *Economic Handbook*, pp. 126, 134, 198.
80. Gary R. Saxonhouse, "Why Japan Is Winning," *Issues in Science and Technology*, Spring 1986, p. 77, and Vogel, *Comeback*, p. 73.
81. Friedman, *Misunderstood Miracle*, pp. 105–107.
82. Ibid.
83. Pugel, "Japan's Industrial Policy," pp. 429–430.
84. NMTBA statement, 6 June 1968, Appendix K, p. 5, and Fransman, "Machine Tool Industry," p. 1383.
85. Saltarelli interview, 27 March 1987.
86. "Agreement between Houdaille Industries, Inc., and Yamazaki Machinery

Works, Ltd.," 23 June 1970, Papers filed under Investigation No. 337-TA-34, U.S. International Trade Commission, Washington, DC. The life of the agreement was twelve years for the Dualcenters, ten years for all other machines.

87. Ibid. This estimate was calculated by taking the average list price of all Burgmaster machines, as stipulated in the agreement, and assuming that Yamazaki could sell about 170 machines annually.

9: Stagnation (1971–1978)

1. Doyle interview, 27 August 1987.

2. See Appendix B.

3. See Michael J. Piore and Charles F. Sabel, *The Second Industrial Divide* (New York: Basic Books, 1984), especially chapter 7.

4. David F. Noble, *Forces of Production* (New York: Alfred A. Knopf, 1984), pp. 224–225. The diffusion of NC machines to small businesses was so slow that in 1971 a Senate subcommittee held hearings on what was considered to be a serious manufacturing problem. See U.S. Congress, Senate, Select Committee on Small Business, Subcommittee on Science and Technology, *Introduction to Numerical Control and Its Impact on Small Business,* 92nd Cong., 1st sess., 24 June 1971.

5. Turret Machining Centers, Brochure, Burgmaster, 1972.

6. Kearney & Trecker v. Houdaille Industries, Inc., "Plaintiff's Reply," Civil Action 70-C-3123, U.S. District Court, Northern District of Illinois, Eastern Division, 21 September 1972.

7. See Appendix B.

8. NMTBA, *Economic Handbook,* p. 42.

9. "Special News Bulletin," *American Machinist,* 18 May 1971, and 19 May 1972.

10. "Houdaille to Phase Out Auto-Parts Division," *The Wall Street Journal,* 29 August 1974.

11. U.S. Congress, House, Committee on Banking, Finance and Urban Affairs, Subcommittee on Economic Stabilization, *Industrial Policy—Part 2,* 98th Cong., 1st sess., 1983, p. 628.

12. Editorial, *American Machinist,* 22 January 1973.

13. David P. Calleo, *The Imperious Economy* (Cambridge, MA: Harvard University Press, 1982), p. 64.

14. Merk interview, 27 August 1987.

15. "Meeting the Machine-Tool Boom," *American Machinist,* 14 October 1974.

16. See Appendix B.

17. In then-year dollars, profits from Houdaille's machine tool group rose 59 percent from 1972 to 1973, and another 59 percent from 1973 to 1974. In constant 1986 dollars, however, the increases were only 48 percent and 34 percent, respectively. See Appendix B.

18. "Machine-Tool Industry, Mired in Doldrums, Has Hope—But Only a Bit—of Improvement," *The Wall Street Journal,* 27 December 1971, and "Corporate Profitability Rising, Reversing 15-Year Downturn," *New York Times,* 30 November 1987.

19. "VTC Emphasis Is Mechanical," *American Machinist,* 15 September 1975, and *Feedback,* Burgmaster, December 1975.

20. Telephone interview with James Cameron, November 1987. Cameron was a former Ford Motor executive hired by Houdaille as a manufacturing consultant.

21. The Houdaille-Kearney & Trecker suit was settled with prejudice, meaning that neither party could return to the courts with the same complaint. Ultimately, all three of Kearney & Trecker's costly efforts to protect its technological lead in the courts proved futile.

22. Forizs interview, 9 January 1986.

23. Merk interview, 27 August 1987, and *American Machinist*, 15 September 1975. Only 27 percent of Burgmaster's 1976 production was devoted to tool changers.

24. French interview, 5 May 1987.

25. Merk interview, 27 August 1987.

26. Bezdziecki interview, 11 January 1986.

27. Ibid.

28. French interview, 5 May 1987.

29. Mazak-Burgmaster Brochure, circa 1971.

30. For a description of Yamazaki's manufacturing philosophy, see Seymour Melman, *Profits without Production* (New York: Alfred A. Knopf, 1983), pp. 140–141. See also Lawrence Livermore Laboratory, "Trip Report on the Technology of Machine Tools in Japan," Department of Energy Contract W-7405-Eng-48, February 1980, pp. 59–63.

31. *American Machinist*, 25 November 1974.

32. General Electric's failure to match FANUC's innovative use of microprocessor technology (which was first introduced in the United States in 1972) was a major reason why American builders lost their edge in NC. See Ezra F. Vogel, *Comeback Case by Case* (New York: Simon and Schuster, 1985), p. 83, and E. Sciberras and B. D. Payne, *Machine Tool Industry* (Essex, England: Longman Group, 1985), pp. 30, 40–41.

33. Sciberras and Payne, *Machine Tool Industry*, pp. 34, 40, 42–43; Watanabe, "NC-Machine Tool Industry," p. 20 (see chapter 8, note 16); Fransman, "Machine Tool Industry," pp. 1383–1384 (see chapter 8, note 14). See also Seymour Melman, *The Permanent War Economy* (New York: Simon and Schuster, 1974), p. 41.

34. Marvin Wolf, *The Japanese Conspiracy* (New York: Empire Books, 1983), pp. 61–64, and Judge Myron Renick, "Recommended Determination in the Matter of Certain Numerically Controlled Machining Centers and Components Thereof," Investigation No. 337-TA-34, 19 December 1977, United States International Trade Commission, Washington, DC.

35. Folger interview, 20 January 1986. Many other American builders that had licensing agreements with the Japanese shared the sentiment. The Japanese sought licenses to learn, but had no intention of permanently accepting inferior status.

36. NMTBA, *Economic Handbook*, p. 126.

37. Cited in Morton Research Corporation, "The Machine Tool Industry January 1979: An Economic, Marketing, and Financial Study Document of the Metal Forming, Metal Cutting, and Machine Tool Accessories Industry" (Merrick, NY: Morton Research Corp., 1979), p. 270.

38. Ibid., p. 271.

39. Telephone invterview with James Mack, NMTBA, 9 July 1987.

40. U.S. General Accounting Office, *United States-Japan Trade: Issues and Problems* (Washington, DC: GAO, September 1979), pp. 120, 122.

41. Holland interview, 4 May 1987.

42. Merk interview, 27 August 1987.

43. "Machine-Tool Orders Declined 1.5% in February," *The Wall Street Journal*, 27 March 1978.

44. "Houdaille Plans to Sell Some of Its Operations," *The Wall Street Journal*, 25 October 1977.

45. "Retooling Would Force Closing at Houdaille," *Herald-Dispatch* (Huntington, WVA), 18 November 1978.

46. Richard J. Schonberger, *Japanese Manufacturing Techniques* (New York: Free Press, 1982), p. 234.

47. Merk interview, 27 August 1987.

48. Doyle interview, 27 August 1987.

49. "Burgmaster Cost Reduction Program Purpose and Objective," Burgmaster, 14 June 1978.

10: Buyout (1979–1980)

1. Quoted in Clifford W. Fawcett, "Factors and Issues in the Survival and Growth of the U.S. Machine Tool Industry" (Ph.D. diss., George Washington University, 1976), p. 180.

2. "Takeover Hope and Houdaille," *New York Times*, 7 July 1978.

3. Saltarelli interview, 27 March 1987.

4. Houdaille Industries, Inc., "Prospectus," 19 April 1979, SEC, p. 33.

5. "Corporate Profitability Rising, Reversing 15-Year Downturn," *New York Times*, 30 November 1987.

6. *New York Times*, 7 July 1978.

7. Ibid.

8. Ibid.

9. Saltarelli interview, 27 March 1987.

10. *New York Times*, 7 July 1978.

11. Houdaille Industries, Inc., "Proxy Statement," 3 April 1979, SEC, pp. 2–3.

12. "Houdaille to Get Offer Totaling $347.7 Million," *The Wall Street Journal*, 26 October 1978.

13. "Finding Happiness in Buyout," *New York Times*, 26 May 1984.

14. "Buyout Pioneer Quits the Fray," *New York Times*, 19 June 1987, and "How the Champs Do Leveraged Buyouts," *Fortune*, 23 January 1984. As used here, the term "cash flow" means earnings plus depreciation and amortization minus capital spending.

15. *Fortune*, 23 January 1984.

16. *New York Times*, 19 June 1987, and "Funds Galore for LBO Prospects," *Euromoney* (Special Supplement), December 1986, p. 3.

17. *Fortune*, 23 January 1984.

18. Ibid. See also Nicholas Wallner, "Leveraged Buyouts: A Review of the State of the Art, Part II," *Mergers & Acquisitions*, Winter 1980, p. 25.

19. David J. Ravenscraft and F.M. Scherer, *Mergers, Sell-Offs, and Economic Efficiency* (Washington, DC: Brookings Institution, 1987), pp. 123, 157, and *Euromoney* (Special Supplement), December 1986, p. 3.

20. *Fortune*, 23 January 1984.

21. Ibid., and "King of the Buyouts, Kohlberg Kravis Helps Alter Corporate U.S.," *The Wall Street Journal*, 11 April 1986.

22. *Fortune*, 23 January 1984, and *New York Times*, 19 June 1987. See also Federal Election Commission, "Selected List of Receipts & Expenditures," 1983–1984, Washington, DC.

23. Federal Election Commission, "Selected List," and *Fortune*, 23 January 1984.

24. *Fortune*, 23 January 1984, and *The Wall Street Journal*, 11 April 1986. KKR's first three deals were buyouts of A.J. Industries, U.S. Natural Resources, and L.B. Foster. By 1985, KKR's four partners and nine executives were sharing fees estimated at $160 million.

25. *Euromoney* (Special Supplement), December 1986, p. 4.

26. "A Leveraged Buyout: What It Takes," *Business Week*, 18 July 1983.

27. U.S. Congress, House, Committee on Energy and Commerce, *Leveraged Buyouts and the Pot of Gold: Trends, Public Policy, and Case Studies*, 100th Cong., 1st sess., 1987, Committee Print 100-R, pp. 7–8. See also Nicholas Wallner, "Leveraged Buyouts, Part I," *Mergers & Acquisitions*, Fall 1979, pp. 4–7.

28. *Euromoney* (Special Supplement), December 1986, p. 3.

29. *Fortune*, 23 January 1984.

30. Saltarelli interview, 27 March 1987.

31. *Fortune,* 23 January 1984; Houdaille, "Proxy Statement," p. 5; and U.S. Congress, House, Committee on Energy and Commerce, *Merger Activity and Leveraged Buyouts: Sound Corporate Restructuring or Wall Street Alchemy?* 98th Cong., 2d sess., 1984, Committee Print 98-FF, pp. 22–26. Generally speaking, the revaluation of capital assets after a buyout was across-the-board, except in certain instances. If the company previously took a lot of depreciation or used substantial investment tax credits on a particular asset, it could be hit with a "tax recapture" under the tax laws. That could outweigh the benefits of re-depreciation, in which case the gambit was avoided.

32. Wallner, "Leveraged Buyouts, Part I," p. 6.

33. Interview with Kenneth Slawson, 24 April 1987.

34. Saltarelli interview, 27 March 1987.

35. Cited in U.S. Congress, House, *Pot of Gold,* p. 1.

36. *The Wall Street Journal,* 26 October 1978.

37. "Takeover of Houdaille May Be Completed in 4 Months, Firm Says," *The Wall Street Journal,* 12 January 1978.

38. "Houdaille Agrees to Be Purchased for $338.5 Million," *The Wall Street Journal,* 6 March 1979.

39. Ibid.

40. "Houdaille Purchase by Group of Investors Approved by Holders," *The Wall Street Journal,* 4 May 1979.

41. *New York Times,* 19 June 1987.

42. Saltarelli interview, 27 March 1987, and Houdaille, "Prospectus," 19 April 1979, p. 46.

43. "Houdaille Shifts Officers," *New York Times,* 30 May 1979.

44. Norton interview, 12 April 1987.

45. *New York Times,* 26 May 1984. According to the *Times,* O'Reilly received about $1.5 million from the LBO. His equity share in the reorganized Houdaille was 1.8 percent of the new common stock, at a total purchase price of $504,000.

46. *New York Times,* 30 May 1979.

47. Folger interview, 20 January 1986.

48. Ibid.

49. Ibid.

50. "Machine Tools: Uproar over a Bottleneck," *New York Times,* 26 February 1978, and Japan Economic Institute, "JEI Report," No. 36A, 21 September 1984.

51. "JEI Report;" Merk interview, 27 August 1987; and NMTBA, *Economic Handbook,* pp. 126–127.

52. Burgmaster Auction Brochure, National Industrial Services Incorporated, St. Louis, MO, 15 January 1986.

53. Interviews with Slawson, 24 April 1987, Jo Kelly, 11 May 1987, and Jack Finch, 7 May 1987.

54. Balbirnie interview, 19 August 1987.

55. Interview with George Delaney, 10 April 1987.

56. Dobmeier interview, 4 May 1987.

57. Kelly interview, 11 May 1987.

58. Delaney interview, 10 April 1987, and Dobmeier interview, 4 May 1987.

59. Delaney interview, 10 April 1987.

60. Interview with Ed Rubenstein, 11 May 1987.

61. Ibid., and Finch interview, 7 May 1987.

62. Kelly interview, 11 May 1987.

63. Dobmeier interview, 4 May 1987.

64. Finch interview, 7 May 1987.

65. Holland interview, 4 May 1987.

11: Turning to Washington (1981–1982)

1. "Houdaille Industries to End Auto-Bumper Output in Oshawa," *The Wall Street Journal*, 11 June 1980.
2. "Boyce Named CEO of Houdaille, Succeeds O'Reilly," *Metalworking News*, 10 August 1987, and Houdaille Holdings Corp., *Standard & Poor's Creditweek*, 18 August 1986. Houdaille did not release any financial details about its purchase of Crane.
3. Thomas Ferguson and Joel Rogers, *Right Turn* (New York: Hill and Wang, 1986), pp. 118–119.
4. NMTBA, *Economic Handbook*, p. 79.
5. "How Competition Led Houdaille to Ask Trade Curb," *New York Times*, 29 December 1982.
6. NMTBA, *Economic Handbook*, pp. 126–127.
7. *New York Times*, 29 December 1982.
8. NBC Reports, "Japan vs. USA: The Hi-Tech Shoot-out," broadcast 14 August 1982.
9. Richard Copaken, "The Houdaille Petition," *George Washington Journal of International Law and Economics* 17 (1983): 212–213.
10. Actually, O'Reilly's suggested remedy was far short of the penalty necessary to make a dent in Japanese imports. Greater productivity in Japan, lower costs, plus an artificially high dollar probably nullified the 15 percent advantage O'Reilly sought.
11. David P. Rapkin, "Industrial Policy and Trade Conflict in the Machine Tool Industry: The Houdaille Case," Department of Political Science, University of Nebraska, 1984, p. 28.
12. "Covington & Burling," *The American Lawyer Guide* (New York: The American Lawyer, 1983–1984), pp. 602–603.
13. Ibid., p. 601.
14. Margot Cohen, "Making Rain in the Caribbean," *The American Lawyer*, March 1986, p. 17.
15. Ibid.
16. Ibid., pp. 18–19. See also Mark J. Green, *The Other Government* (New York: Viking, 1975), pp. 256–258.
17. Cohen, "Making Rain," pp. 21–22.
18. Copaken, "Houdaille Petition," pp. 217–219.
19. If that standard had prevailed, Section 103 would have had a very short life. After vigorous foreign protests, Nixon removed the 10 percent surcharge two weeks after the Revenue Act became law.
20. Ferguson and Rogers, *Right Turn*, p. 75, and Copaken, "Houdaille Petition," pp. 217–219.
21. Copaken, "Houdaille Petition," p. 222. Section 103's precise description of unfair trade practices cited the definition contained in Section 252(b) of the Trade Expansion Act of 1962. It defined such practices as "nontariff trade restrictions, including variable import fees, which substantially burden United States commerce in a manner inconsistent with provisions of trade agreements," or "discriminatory or other acts (including tolerance of international cartels) or policies unjustifiably restricting United States commerce."
22. Richard Copaken, "The Politics of Trade Law Proceedings," unpublished manuscript, 8 March 1984, p. 22.
23. Ibid.
24. Copaken, "Politics of Trade Law," p. 23.
25. Ibid., pp. 23–24.
26. "Nimble Soldiers of the Commercial Wars," *New York Times*, 16 November 1987.

27. Ferguson and Rogers, *Right Turn,* p. 112.

28. Ibid., and Ronald Brownstein and Nina Easton, *Reagan's Ruling Class* (Washington, DC: Presidential Accountability Group, 1982), p. 84.

29. "White House Considers Plea to Penalize U.S. Firms That Buy Tools from Japan," *The Wall Street Journal,* 13 January 1983.

30. Cited in Rapkin, "Houdaille Case," p. 29.

31. Copaken, "Politics of Trade Law," p. 12.

32. The debate over Japan, of course, persists to this day. See Chalmers Johnson, "The Japanese Political Economy," *Ethics & International Affairs* 2 (1988): 79–97.

33. Thomas Rohan, "U.S. May Have Found Potent Import-Fighter," *Industry Week,* 15 November 1982, and "Machine-Tool Charges against Japanese Split U.S. Industry, Officials," *The Wall Street Journal,* 29 March 1983.

34. Cohen, "Making Rain," p. 20.

35. Marvin J. Wolf, *The Japanese Conspiracy* (New York: Empire Books, 1983), p. 131.

36. Covington & Burling, *Petition to the President of the United States through the Office of the United States Trade Representative for the Exercise of Presidential Discretion Authorized by Section 103 of the Revenue Act of 1971,* submitted on behalf of Houdaille Industries, Inc., 3 May 1982, Washington, DC, pp. 1–15.

37. Ibid., pp. 55–63, 77, 91.

38. Ibid., pp. 122–123.

39. Copaken, "Politics of Trade Law," p. 21.

40. Robert Herzstein and Patrick Macrory, "The Houdaille Case—An Attack on Japanese Industrial Policy," June 1982, pp. 8–11, manuscript obtained under the Freedom of Information Act (hereafter referred to as FOIA), United States Trade Representative (USTR). Herzstein and Macrory were lawyers at Arnold & Porter, which represented the Machine Tool Importers Association of America.

41. Copaken, "Politics of Trade Law," p. 3.

42. Ibid., p. 5.

43. Ibid., p. 6.

44. Rohan, "Potent Import-Fighter."

45. Interview with Richard Copaken, 31 March 1987, and Copaken, "Politics of Trade Law," p. 25.

46. O'Reilly Letter, Houdaille Industries, Inc., 29 April 1982, obtained under FOIA, USTR.

47. Copaken, "Politics of Trade Law," pp. 25–26.

48. Herzstein and Macrory, "The Houdaille Case," pp. 3–4.

49. Letters received at the USTR, May-August 1982, obtained under FOIA, USTR.

50. Ibid.

51. Ibid.

52. Ibid.

53. "Wender Murase & White," *Martindale-Hubbell Law Directory,* Vol. 5 (Summit, NJ: Martindale-Hubbell, 1982), pp. 1709B–1713B.

54. "'Japan-Bashing' Becomes a Trade Bill Issue," *New York Times,* 28 February 1988.

55. Wender Murase & White, *Comments in Opposition to the [Houdaille] Petition,* submitted on behalf of Japan Machine Tool Builders' Association et al., 29 July 1982, Washington, DC, pp. iii–ix.

56. Ibid., pp. 78–82, 111–114.

57. Copaken, "Politics of Trade Law," pp. 8–9.

58. Ibid.

59. Copaken got his first inkling about the race track proceeds from an English-

language book. See Ira C. Magaziner and Thomas M. Hout, *Japanese Industrial Policy* (Berkeley, CA: University of California, Institute of International Studies, 1981), p. 98.

60. Covington & Burling, *Comments by the Petitioner*, submitted on behalf of Houdaille Industries, Inc., 31 July 1982, Washington, DC, pp. 1–6, 18–21.

61. NBC Reports, "Japan vs. USA: The Hi-Tech Shoot-out," 14 August 1982, pp. 35–40.

62. Ibid., p. 63.

63. Matthew Marks to Jeanne Archibald, "Additional Comments on Behalf of the Japanese Machine Tool Builders' Association," 31 August 1982, pp. 8–10, Appendix D, obtained under FOIA, USTR.

64. Letter, Copaken to Jeanne Archibald, USTR, 28 September 1982, obtained under FOIA, Department of Commerce (DOC).

65. Covington & Burling, *Comments by the Petitioner*, p. 7.

66. Interview with Carl Green, 1 April 1987.

67. U.S. Congress, Senate, Committee on Foreign Relations, *U.S. Trade Relations with Japan,* 97th Cong., 2d sess., 14 September 1982, pp. 61–63.

12: Blame the Japanese (1982–1983)

1. Quoted in Ronald Brownstein and Nina Easton, *Reagan's Ruling Class* (Washington, DC: Presidential Accountability Group, 1982), pp. 32–33.

2. "The Cabinet's Trade Hawk Earns His Spurs," *New York Times,* 19 May 1987.

3. "An Obscure, Elite Agency Marks 25 Years' Survival," *Washington Post,* 16 November 1987.

4. On Commerce Department attempts (concurrent with the Houdaille petition) to heighten concern over the trade deficit with Japan, see Clyde V. Prestowitz, *Trading Places* (New York: Basic Books, 1988), pp. 14–18.

5. Brownstein and Easton, *Reagan's Ruling Class*, p. 30, and *New York Times,* 19 May 1987.

6. "U.S. Official Favors Blunt Talk in Negotiations with Japan," *National Journal,* 15 June 1985.

7. Letter, Copaken to Prestowitz, 9 September 1982, obtained under FOIA, DOC.

8. Several of Copaken's unedited videos were screened for the author in the Covington & Burling offices in May 1987.

9. See note 8.

10. "Houdaille, Japan Tool Dispute Escalates," *American Metal Market/Metalworking News,* 22 November 1982.

11. Letters in opposition to the Houdaille Petition, October 1982, obtained under FOIA, USTR.

12. Letter, Carl Green to author, 1 June 1988.

13. "Industrial Deception?" *National Journal,* 16 October 1982, p. 1763, and "A Bad Trip," *National Journal,* 8 January 1983, p. 77.

14. Brownstein and Easton, *Reagan's Ruling Class*, p. 72.

15. Green to author, 1 June 1988.

16. Memo, 15 October 1982, obtained under FOIA, DOC.

17. Prestowitz, *Trading Places*, p. 224.

18. Memo, Waldmann to Olmer, undated, obtained under FOIA, DOC.

19. "Houdaille Plea on Imports Falls Short of White House," *American Metal Market/Metalworking News,* 1 November 1982.

20. "Reagan Is Urged to End Credits on Japan Tools," *Los Angeles Times,* 19 October 1982.

21. Green to author, 1 June 1988.

22. Thomas Rohan, "U.S. May Have Found Potent Import-Fighter," *Industry Week,* 15 November 1982.

23. "U.S. Move Worries Japanese," *New York Times,* 27 December 1982.

24. Slawson interview, 24 April 1987.

25. *American Metal Market/Metalworking News,* 22 November 1982.

26. Thomas Ferguson and Joel Rogers, "The Great Japan Debate," *The Nation,* 13 February 1982, p. 169, and "Trading on Good Connections," *Newsweek,* 22 December 1986, p. 48.

27. Prestowitz, *Trading Places,* p. 60.

28. "Foreigners Hiring Reagan's Ex-Aides," *Washington Post,* 16 February 1986. In addition to the JMTBA, by 1984 Anderson had been retained by the Communications Industries of Japan and the Electronic Industries Association of Japan for about $350,000 annually. Many more Reagan administration insiders followed in Anderson's footsteps. Although trading on governmental connections was hardly an invention of the Reagan administration, it was more pronounced than ever during the 1980s. The phenomenon was undoubtedly a consequence of the administration's protectionist tinge and its lax attitude toward lobbying by former insiders. By 1984, Japan would be spending $14.3 million annually on lobbyists. "People," *National Journal,* 3 May 1986, p. 1070.

29. "Choosing Winners and Losers," *National Journal,* 26 February 1983, p. 445. Motorola's ad campaign may have been linked to the fact that a former executive, Lionel Olmer, was then one of Baldrige's top Commerce Department deputies.

30. Letter, Copaken to deKieffer, 10 November 1982, obtained under FOIA, USTR.

31. "U.S. Nearing a Decision in Crucial Case on Imports of Japanese Machine Tools," *Asian Wall Street Journal Weekly,* 27 December 1982.

32. "Playing Games with Protectionism," *New York Times,* 8 November 1982.

33. "A U.S. Company's Case against Japan," *New York Times,* 19 November 1982.

34. Phillip O'Reilly, "United States Import Laws: A Critical Examination—The Houdaille Petition," speech given before the National Association of Manufacturers, 3 November 1982, p. 2.

35. "Reagan Urged to End Machine Tool Breaks," *Washington Post,* 23 December 1982.

36. "I Am a Video Camera," *Fortune,* 7 February 1983, and Margot Cohen, "Making Rain in the Caribbean," *The American Lawyer,* March 1986, p. 20.

37. Review of unedited videotapes at Covington & Burling offices, May 1987.

38. *Fortune,* 7 February 1983, and Richard Copaken, "The Politics of Trade Law Proceedings," unpublished manuscript, 8 March 1984, p. 30.

39. *American Metal Market/Metalworking News,* 22 November 1982.

40. Copaken, "Politics of Trade Law," p. 13.

41. "Industrial Policy: An Unfair Trade Practice?" *Congressional Quarterly,* 29 January 1983.

42. U.S. Congress, Senate, *Congressional Record,* 97th Cong., 2d sess., 21 December 1982, pp. S 15961 to S 15962. The Democratic cosponsors were Senators Lawton Chiles (Florida), Alan Dixon (Illinois), Walter Huddleston (Kentucky), Ernest Hollings (South Carolina), Paul Tsongas (Massachusetts), Lloyd Bentsen (Texas); the Republicans included Alfonse d'Amato (New York), Roger Jepsen (Iowa), John Heinz (Pennsylvania), Paula Hawkins (Florida), Robert Dole (Kansas), Jake Garn (Utah),

Charles Percy (Illinois), Robert Kasten (Wisconsin), John Danforth (Missouri), Rudy Boschwitz (Minnesota), and Mack Mattingly (Georgia).

43. Copaken, "Politics of Trade Law," p. 33.

44. *Congressional Quarterly*, 29 January 1983, p. 213.

45. *Asian Wall Street Journal Weekly*, 27 December 1982.

46. Copaken, "Politics of Trade Law," p. 34.

47. Ibid., p. 35.

48. *Congressional Quarterly*, 29 January 1983.

49. Robert Herzstein and Patrick Macrory, "Houdaille Case—An Attack on Japanese Industrial Policy," June 1982, p. 29, obtained under FOIA, USTR.

50. Rohan, "Potent Import-Fighter," and *Asian Wall Street Journal Weekly*, 27 December 1982.

51. "Irresolute Resolution," *New York Times*, 25 December 1982. A month later, one Republican senator, Steven Symms of Idaho, stood up on the Senate floor and criticized the "dangerous" resolution. He suggested that the Houdaille petition raised more questions than it answered, and introduced into the record the entire NMTBA report of its mission to Japan in June 1981. See U.S. Congress, Senate, *Congressional Record*, 98th Cong., 1st sess., 26 January 1983, pp. S 66 to S 78.

52. *New York Times*, 29 December 1982.

53. NMTBA, *Economic Handbook*, pp. 42, 126, and Memo, Prestowitz to Olmer, 10 March 1983, obtained under FOIA, DOC.

54. Central Intelligence Agency, "The World Machine Tool Industry in Transition: Growing Role of Japanese Producers," February 1983, obtained under FOIA, CIA.

55. National Academy of Sciences, *The U.S. Machine Tool Industry and the Defense Industrial Base* (Washington, DC: National Academy Press, 1983).

56. United States International Trade Commission, "Competitive Assessment of the U.S. Metalworking Machine Tool Industry," USITC Publication 1428 (September 1983), pp. 47–55, 127. When the study was finally printed, it tended to vindicate Houdaille's opponents rather than Copaken.

57. Copaken interview, 31 March 1987.

58. "Meeting the Japanese Challenge," Prepared by the Japanese Study Mission of the National Machine Tool Builders' Association, 14 September 1981.

59. Leonard H. Lynn and Timothy J. McKeown, *Organizing Business* (Washington, DC: American Enterprise Institute for Public Policy Research, 1988), p. 121.

60. "Machine-Tool Move Hit by Trade Aide," *Washington Post*, 25 December 1982.

61. *National Journal*, 26 February 1983, p. 423.

62. "Japan Limits Machine-Tool Exports," *Los Angeles Times*, 4 March 1983.

63. *New York Times*, 27 December 1982.

64. *Congressional Quarterly*, 29 January 1983, pp. 212–213, and *National Journal*, 26 February 1983, pp. 417, 441–443. See also Thomas Ferguson and Joel Rogers, *Right Turn* (New York: Hill and Wang, 1986), pp. 156–157. When the Democrats' Center for National Policy finally unveiled its "reindustrialization" plan in late 1983, it pleased almost no one.

65. *National Journal*, 26 February 1983, p. 442.

66. *New York Times*, 27 December 1982.

67. "Machine-Tool Charges against Japanese Split U.S. Industry, Officials," *The Wall Street Journal*, 29 March 1983.

68. *National Journal*, 8 January 1983, p. 77, and *Congressional Quarterly*, 29 January 1983, p. 213.

69. *Asian Wall Street Journal Weekly*, 27 December 1982, and Memo, Prestowitz to Olmer, 29 December 1982, obtained under FOIA, DOC.

70. "White House Considers Plea to Penalize U.S. Firms That Buy Tools from Japan," *The Wall Street Journal,* 13 January 1983.

71. *Fortune,* 7 February 1983.

72. Letter, Wender Murase & White to deKieffer, 10 December 1982, and Letter, Marks to Archibald, 21 December 1982, both obtained under FOIA, USTR. Also Green interview, 1 April 1987.

73. Letter, Marks to Archibald, 23 December 1982, obtained under FOIA, USTR.

74. Letter, Marks to Brock, 4 January 1983, obtained under FOIA, USTR.

75. "Trade Battle with Japan Shows Policy Confusion," *Washington Post,* 15 August 1983.

76. Ibid.

77. Memo, Brock to Trade Policy Committee, 1 February 1983, obtained under FOIA, DOC.

78. "Tax Credit Decision on Japan Tools Delayed," *American Metal Market/ Metalworking News,* 17 January 1983, and Memo, Prestowitz to Olmer, 5 January 1983, obtained under FOIA, DOC.

79. *National Journal,* 8 January 1983, p. 77, and 26 February 1983, p. 432. The most complete résumé of federal government subsidies is contained in ITC, "Competitive Assessment of the U.S. Metalworking Machine Tool Industry," pp. 36–46.

80. Memo, Kendall to Donnelly et al., 18 January 1983, obtained under FOIA, Department of Defense (DOD), and Prestowitz, *Trading Places,* pp. 224–225. Prestowitz says this TPC meeting occurred on January 16.

81. Memo, Prestowitz to Olmer, 5 January 1983. To be fair, some elements within the Commerce Department had trouble with the remedy proposed by Houdaille.

82. Memo, Kendall to Donnelly, 18 January 1983.

83. Memo, Prestowitz to Olmer, 5 January 1983.

84. Memo, Kendall to Slowey, 27 January 1983, obtained under FOIA, DOD.

85. U.S. Congress, House, Committee on Ways and Means, *Overview and Compilation of U.S. Trade Statutes,* 100th Cong., 1st sess., 6 January 1987, pp. 56–57, 295–296.

86. Memo, Prestowitz to Olmer, undated, obtained under FOIA, DOC. Another problem posed by Section 201 was that presidential action could only follow a finding of "serious injury" by the International Trade Commission. The ITC standard of "serious injury" is very difficult to prove, and would have meant delaying a resolution of the Houdaille case by eight months. Carl Green always believed that a Section 201 finding posed the greatest threat to Japanese tool imports. Copaken undoubtedly eschewed this route because the process was too insulated from the political pressures he intended to bring to bear.

87. Ibid.

88. Briefing Memorandum, under secretary for international trade to the secretary, undated, obtained under FOIA, DOC.

89. Memo, Prestowitz to Olmer, undated. Countervailing duty investigations are used to determine whether foreign producers receive unfair subsidies. If substantial subsidies are proven, and U.S. producers are thereby injured, the Commerce Department must impose countervailing duties equal in amount to the subsidies.

90. Memo, Prestowitz to Olmer, 2 February 1983, obtained under FOIA, DOC.

91. David P. Rapkin, "Industrial Policy and Trade Conflict in the Machine Tool Industry: The Houdaille Case," Department of Political Science, University of Nebraska, 1984, p. 67.

92. Prestowitz, *Trading Places,* pp. 226–227; *Washington Post,* 15 August 1983; and Copaken, "Politics of Trade Law," pp. 37–38.

93. *Washington Post,* 15 August 1983.

94. Ibid., and "U.S. Moves Closer to Machine Tool Ruling," *Los Angeles Times,* 25 March 1983. Also Memo, Prestowitz to Olmer, 15 February 1983, obtained under FOIA, DOC.

95. *Washington Post,* 15 August 1983, and "Draft," 22 February 1983, obtained under FOIA, DOC.

96. Memo, Robinson to Prestowitz, 16 February 1983, obtained under FOIA, DOC.

97. Copaken, "Politics of Trade Law," p. 39, and *Los Angeles Times,* 4 March 1983. See also "MITI Official Denies Tool Export Limit to U.S.," *Foreign Broadcast Information Service,* 5 March 1983.

98. *Washington Post,* 15 August 1983.

99. Quoted in the *National Journal,* 26 February 1983, p. 419.

100. Copaken, "Politics of Trade Law," p. 37.

101. Letter, Copaken to Archibald, 25 February 1983, obtained under FOIA, DOC.

102. Letter, Green to Archibald, 7 March 1983, obtained under FOIA, DOC, and Green interview, 1 April 1987.

103. Memo, Blaker to under secretary of defense, 10 March 1983, obtained under FOIA, DOD. In *Trading Places,* Prestowitz writes that the Pentagon belonged to the White Hats. But FOIA documents suggest that at the very least, the Pentagon was divided internally over the petition.

104. Memo, Prestowitz to Olmer, 10 March 1983.

105. Memo, Prestowitz to Olmer, 7 March 1983, obtained under FOIA, DOC.

106. Memo, Blaker to under secretary of defense, 10 March 1983, and Information Memorandum, under secretary to the secretary, 4 April 1983, obtained under FOIA, DOC.

107. "Trade Panel Rejects Tool Imports Curbs," *Washington Post,* 22 March 1983, and Copaken, "Politics of Trade Law," p. 38.

108. Memo, Prestowitz to Olmer, 2 February 1983.

109. U.S. Congress, House, Committee on Ways and Means, Subcommittee on Trade, *United States-Japan Trade Relations,* 98th Cong., 1st sess., 10 March 1983, p. 160.

110. "Tool Makers Ask Quotas on Imports," *Washington Post,* 11 March 1983.

111. Letter, Copaken to McNamar, 29 March 1983, obtained under FOIA, USTR.

112. *The Wall Street Journal,* 29 March 1983.

113. Ibid.

114. Prestowitz, *Trading Places,* p. 226.

115. *The Wall Street Journal,* 29 March 1983, and Green interview, 1 April 1987.

116. Letter, Copaken to McNamar, 29 March 1983.

117. Information Memorandum, under secretary to the secretary, 4 April 1983.

118. "Houdaille Loses Import-Relief Bid," *Los Angeles Times,* 26 April 1983.

119. *Washington Post,* 15 August 1983, and Prestowitz, *Trading Places,* pp. 227–228.

120. Letter, Richman to McNamar, 5 April 1983, obtained under FOIA, USTR.

121. Ibid., and Letter, Copaken to McNamar, 11 April 1983, obtained under FOIA, DOC.

122. Review of unedited videotapes at Covington & Burling offices, May 1987.

123. Letter, Copaken to McNamar, 12 April 1983, obtained under FOIA, USTR.

124. *Washington Post,* 15 August 1983.

125. Ibid.

126. "Insider's Intimate Portrait of a First Lady's Power," *New York Times,* 3 February 1988.

127. *Washington Post,* 15 August 1983.

128. Ibid.

129. Prestowitz, *Trading Places,* p. 229.

130. *Washington Post,* 15 August 1983.

131. Ibid.

132. Ibid.; Prestowitz, *Trading Places,* p. 229; and CBS News, "60 Minutes: A Fair Trade?" broadcast 6 November 1983.

133. *Los Angeles Times,* 26 April 1983.

134. USTR, "Brock Announces Decision on Houdaille Petition," 22 April 1983.

135. "Houdaille Loses Plea on Imports," *New York Times,* 27 April 1983; and "Tool Maker May Try a New Tack in Battle with Japanese," *Washington Times,* 29 April 1983.

136. Cohen, "Making Rain," p. 20.

137. Ibid.

13: Demise (1983–1985)

1. Green interview, 1 April 1987.

2. "Administration Split on Trade Relief," United Press International, 17 June 1983, and Richard Copaken, "The Politics of Trade Law Proceedings," unpublished manuscript, 8 March 1984, pp. 40–41.

3. *Washington Post,* 15 August 1983.

4. "No Messages," *Washington Post,* 12 September 1983.

5. CBS News, "60 Minutes: A Fair Trade?" broadcast 6 November 1983. Copaken reportedly told Senator Grassley that he accompanied the 60 Minutes production team to Japan. This curious journalistic procedure may have been one reason why the broadcast was so biased.

6. Ibid., and Copaken, "Politics of Trade Law," p. 20.

7. U.S. Congress, House, Committee on Ways and Means, Subcommittee on Trade, *United States-Japan Trade Relations,* 98th Cong., 1st sess., 10 March 1983, pp. 286–287.

8. U.S. Congress, Joint Economic Committee, *The Machine Tool Industry and the Defense Industrial Base,* 98th Cong., 1st sess., 7 June 1983, pp. 126–143; Senate, Committee on Banking, Housing and Urban Affairs, Subcommittee on International Finance and Monetary Policy, *Foreign Industrial Targeting,* 98th Cong., 1st sess., 7 July 1983, pp. 89–105; House, Committee on Banking, Finance and Urban Affairs, Subcommittee on Economic Stabilization, *Industrial Policy—Part 2,* 98th Cong., 1st sess., 26 July 1983, pp. 595–610; Senate, Committee on Foreign Relations, *U.S. Machine Tool Industry,* 98th Cong., 1st sess., 28 November 1983, pp. 136–141; House, Committee on Small Business, Subcommittee on Antitrust and Restraint of Trade Activities Affecting Small Business, *Impact of International Trade Practices on Small Business,* 98th Cong., 2d sess., 23 March 1984, pp. 143–159; Senate, Committee on Finance, *Improving Enforcement of Trade Agreements,* 100th Cong., 1st sess., 17 March 1987, pp. 52–63, 130.

9. U.S. Congress, House, *Impact of International Trade Practices,* p. 159.

10. Folger interview, 20 January 1986, and Lenders interview, 6 May 1987.

11. Holland interview, 4 May 1987.

12. Doyle interview, 27 August 1987.

13. Delaney interview, 10 April 1987.

14. Ibid.

15. U.S. Department of Commerce, Bureau of the Census, *U.S. Imports for Consumption, TSUSA Commodity by Country,* 1983.

16. Ives interview, 18 January 1986.

17. "March Run-off of Plant Visitors," Burgmaster, 22 February 1982.

18. Letter, Star Machinery to Pete Ives, 27 January 1982. The letter from Star Machinery, a Burgmaster distributor in Seattle, describes various problems and "excessive down time" on three Burgmaster vertical machining centers at Boeing Aerospace.

19. Ives interview, 18 January 1986.

20. Memo, "Information on the Metalworking Machine Tool Industry," U.S. International Trade Commission, 26 January 1983.

21. Interview with Shohichi Kato, 5 January 1986.

22. Ives interview, 18 January 1986, and Forizs interview, 9 January 1986.

23. "Something New in Machine-Tool Firms," *American Machinist,* April 1983, and Delaney interview, 10 April 1987.

24. Delaney interview, 10 April 1987.

25. Ibid., and Balbirnie interview, 29 August 1987.

26. Doyle interview, 27 August 1987, and Balbirnie interview, 29 August 1987.

27. Doyle interview, 27 August 1987.

28. Letter, Hernandez to sales executives, Burgmaster, 17 January 1983.

29. Letter, Pico Metal Products, Inc., to Burgmaster, 28 January 1983.

30. Balbirnie interview, 29 August 1987. Ironically, Houdaille would always cite the purchase of the Italian grinder as evidence of Burgmaster's ability to make capital improvements despite the leveraged buyout.

31. Ibid.

32. Letter, Paul Bromley to author, 16 July 1987.

33. Delaney interview, 10 April 1987.

34. Marvin J. Wolf, *The Japanese Conspiracy* (New York: Empire Books, 1983), p. 67.

35. "Burgmaster Company Proposals, Economic Issues," United Steelworkers of America, Local Union No. 2018, 8 June 1983.

36. "Japan Inc., U.S.A.," *The New Republic,* 26 November 1984; "Houdaille Industries Considers Venture in Machine Tools with Japanese Concern," *The Wall Street Journal,* 27 March 1984; and "A U.S. Toolmaker Cozies Up to Its Former Foes," *Business Week,* 16 April 1984.

37. O'Reilly interview, 17 March 1987.

38. Ibid.

39. Ibid.

40. *Business Week,* 16 April 1984.

41. *The Wall Street Journal,* 27 March 1984.

42. "A Machine-Tool Dynasty," *New York Times,* 5 September 1985.

43. Delaney interview, 10 April 1987.

44. "Japanese Machine-Tool Makers Are Seen Raising Output in U.S. to Avoid Friction," *The Wall Street Journal,* 19 February 1980, and "Japan Grinds Down the Competition," *The Economist,* 13 December 1980.

45. *New York Times,* 5 September 1985.

46. "Houdaille Explores Overseas Connections," *American Machinist,* May 1984.

47. "Houdaille Talks to Okuma on Tool Venture," *American Metal Market/Metalworking News,* 10 September 1984, and "Houdaille Explores Overseas Connections," *American Machinist,* May 1984.

48. Delaney interview, 10 April 1987.

49. Slawson interview, 24 April 1987.

50. Copaken interview, 18 April 1987.

51. O'Reilly interview, 17 March 1987.

52. Delaney interview, 10 April 1987.

53. *American Machinist,* May 1984, and "Making Machine Tools Increasingly Re-

quires Ties to Foreign Firms," *The Wall Street Journal,* 4 September 1984. Houdaille's efforts at internationalization were not limited to Burgmaster. In 1983, Strippit entered into a production agreement with the French builder Promecam, and the Universal Engineering division signed up with West Germany's Krupp Widia.

54. See Appendix C.

55. Clyde V. Prestowitz, *Trading Places* (New York: Basic Books, 1988), pp. 242–245, and Leonard H. Lynn and Timothy J. McKeown, *Organizing Business* (Washington, DC: American Enterprise Institute for Public Policy Research, 1988), pp.121–122.

56. "A Survival Fight in Machine Tools," *New York Times,* 8 July 1984, and NMTBA, *Economic Handbook,* p. 126.

57. "Foreign Tool Cos. Invade Systems," *American Metal Market/Metalworking News,* 10 September 1984.

58. Forizs interview, 9 January 1986.

59. Balbirnie interview, 29 August 1987.

60. Ibid.

61. Ibid.

62. *New York Times,* 26 May 1984.

63. "Some Builders Give Up," *Industry Week,* 14 October 1985.

64. Copaken interview, 18 April 1987.

65. Balbirnie interview, 29 August 1987.

66. Holland interview, 20 January 1986.

67. Memo, Ives to Delaney, Burgmaster, 2 April 1985.

68. Figures cited in National Academy of Engineering, *The Competitive Status of the U.S. Machine Tool Industry* (Washington, DC: National Academy Press, 1983), p. 31.

69. "Houdaille, Okuma Reach Deal," *American Metal Market/Metalworking News,* 19 November 1984.

70. Ibid.

71. Delaney interview, 10 April 1987.

72. "Okuma Machinery Said Delaying Houdaille Pact," *American Metal Market/Metalworking News,* 11 February 1985.

73. O'Reilly interview, 17 March 1987, and Balbirnie interview, 29 August 1987.

74. Slawson interview, 24 April 1987.

75. Statement, Houdaille Industries, Inc., 24 September 1985, and "Houdaille Puts Tool Divisions on the Block," *American Metal Market/Metalworking News,* 30 September 1985.

76. "Houdaille to Drop Machine Tools," *Los Angeles Times,* 1 October 1985, and *Industry Week,* 14 October 1985.

14: Workers, Managers, and Alchemists (1986–1987)

1. Merk interview, 27 August 1987.

2. Interview with Tom Ruiz, 15 January 1986.

3. Slawson interview, 24 April 1987.

4. Interview with Bill Meroth, 6 May 1987. In August 1988, Transport Express moved to another location and an associated trucking company moved into the former Burgmaster plant.

5. "Burgmaster Drill Has Six Spindles," *American Machinist,* September 1986, and O'Reilly interview, 17 March 1987.

6. Slawson interview, 24 April 1987, and "Three Firms Join for Machine Updating," *American Machinist,* April 1984.

7. "Houdaille Sells Divs. to Stanwich," *Metalworking News,* 28 April 1986, and Delaney interview, 10 April 1987.

8. The proposed buyout of Strippit/Di-Acro was to include the Hydraulics division of Houdaille as well.

9. Slawson interview, 24 April 1987, and "Houdaille: Auction and Foreign Tie," *American Machinist*, February 1986. Three U.S. manufacturers, one of which was Strippit/Di-Acro, accounted for 100 percent of domestic punching machine production. Strippit also faced only one main Japanese competitor, Amada.

10. "Houdaille Divisions Sale Estimated at $50 Million," *Business First-Buffalo*, 30 September 1985, and Slawson interview, 24 April 1987.

11. See Appendix C.

12. "Perils of LBO Seen Exemplified by Sale of Debt-Burdened Firm," *Metalworking News*, 31 August 1987.

13. "Houdaille Saga at End," *Metalworking News*, 31 August 1987.

14. O'Reilly interview, 27 March 1987, and "Houdaille Holdings Corp. Announces Public Offering of Subordinated Notes for Recapitalization of Houdaille Industries Inc.," PR Newswire, 9 September 1986.

15. *Standard & Poor's Creditweek*, 18 August 1986.

16. Ibid.

17. Ibid.

18. "Japan to Cut Share of U.S. Market for Machine Tools," *The Wall Street Journal*, 21 November 1986. Shortly after Japan, Taiwan also signed a voluntary restraint agreement (VRA) limiting its tool exports to the United States. But the next largest exporters, West Germany and Switzerland, refused to sign. Subsequently, in December 1986, the Reagan administration put them and seven other countries (Britain, Spain, Italy, Sweden, Brazil, South Korea, and Singapore) on notice that it would restrict imports if these countries allowed shipments to exceed the levels recorded in 1985.

19. Office of the Press Secretary, "Statement by the President," White House, 16 December 1986, and Copaken interview, 31 March 1987.

20. *Metalworking News*, 31 August 1987.

21. "Boyce Named CEO of Houdaille, Succeeds O'Reilly," *Metalworking News*, 10 August 1987.

22. "TI to Acquire Houdaille from Kohlberg for $112 Million, Assumption of Debt," *The Wall Street Journal*, 26 August 1987.

23. "Houdaille Execs Buy Back Six Units from TI," *Metalworking News*, 5 October 1987. Within a week or two of the sale of Houdaille to the TI Group, several U.S. companies made offers for one or more of the six Houdaille units ostensibly up for sale. But at least one company was told that the units had already been sold. This led to speculation about a prior understanding.

24. "King of the Buyouts, Kohlberg Kravis Helps Alter Corporate America," *The Wall Street Journal*, 11 April 1986.

25. Ibid., and "King Henry," *Business Week*, 14 November 1988.

26. "Merrill Lynch Leads Wall Street's Buy-Out Business," *The Wall Street Journal*, 5 August 1987.

27. "A Frenzy of Mergers," *Washington Post*, 12 August 1981.

28. "Buyouts Altering Face of Corporate America," *New York Times*, 23 November 1985, and Harry Magdoff and Paul M. Sweezy, *Stagnation and the Financial Explosion* (New York: Monthly Review Press, 1987), p. 18.

29. Peter Drucker, "A Crisis of Capitalism," *The Wall Street Journal*, 30 September 1986.

30. By 1985, banks, insurance companies, and pension funds accounted for more than 70 percent of all the trading on the New York Stock Exchange, up from 20 percent in 1960. They also held an estimated 35 percent of all outstanding corporate stocks. See U.S. Congress, House, Committee on Energy and Commerce, Subcommittee on

Telecommunications; Consumer Protection, and Finance, *Restructuring Financial Markets*, 99th Cong., 2d sess., July 1986, p. 269.

31. "After Wave of Mergers, Analysts Debate Pluses," *New York Times*, 31 May 1982.

32. "The Birth of the Financial Entrepreneur," *The Wall Street Journal*, 4 March 1987, and "New Type of Owner Emerges in Wave of Company Buyouts," *New York Times*, 8 November 1988.

33. *The Wall Street Journal*, 11 April 1986. Jensen explains his view in detail in John Coffee, Louis Lowenstein, and Susan Rose-Ackerman, eds., *Knights, Raiders, and Targets: The Impact of the Hostile Takeover* (New York: Oxford University Press, 1988), pp. 314–354.

34. "Big Players in 1985," *New York Times*, 29 December 1985.

35. John Kenneth Galbraith, "The 1929 Parallel," *The Atlantic Monthly*, January 1987, pp. 64–65.

36. *New York Times*, 23 November 1985.

37. *The Wall Street Journal*, 11 December 1987, and "Takeovers: A Friendly Climate," *New York Times*, 5 November 1988.

38. "The Leveraging of America," *The Wall Street Journal*, 8 June 1984.

39. U.S. General Accounting Office, *Information on Interest Deducted for Financing Mergers Is Not Available* (Washington, DC: GAO GGD-88-58, March 1988).

40. "The Peril Behind the Takeover Boom," *New York Times*, 29 December 1985. See also U.S. Congress, House, Committee on Energy and Commerce, *Leveraged Buyouts and the Pot of Gold*, 100th Cong., 1st sess., 1987, pp. 34–35.

41. Ibid.

42. "Sen. D'Amato wins Wall Street's Favor—And Contributions," *The Wall Street Journal*, 25 September 1986, and "D'Amato Accused on Anti-Takeover Bill," *New York Times*, 25 November 1986. From 1981 to 1986, D'Amato received $500,000 in contributions from a veritable who's who among investment banking houses, including Drexel Burnham Lambert, Morgan Stanley, and Kidder, Peabody.

43. U.S. Congress, House, *Pot of Gold*, p. 21.

44. *The Wall Street Journal*, 11 April 1986.

45. Ibid.

46. "Wall Street's Top Salary: $125 Million," *Washington Post*, 9 June 1987, and *The Wall Street Journal*, 11 April 1986.

47. "Speculative Fever Ran High in the 10 Months Prior to Black Monday," *The Wall Street Journal*, 11 December 1987.

48. "New Stars on the Circuit," *New York Times*, 20 May 1986.

49. *The Wall Street Journal*, 17 February 1987.

50. Galbraith, "1929," p. 65.

51. "Companies, Securities Firms Enlist Top Lobbyists for Showdown over Bid to Tighten Takeover Law," *The Wall Street Journal*, 9 March 1987, and "Lobby Registrations," *Congressional Quarterly*, 22 August 1987.

52. *New York Times*, 23 November 1985.

53. "Buyout Pioneer Quits the Fray," *New York Times*, 19 June 1987. On the evolution of LBOs, see Dr. Carolyn Kay Brancato, "The Current Economic Climate for Leveraged Buyouts," unpublished paper, 18 March 1988, Weil, Gotshal & Manges, New York, and "Violating Our Rules of Prudence," *The Wall Street Journal*, 25 October 1988.

54. Ibid.

55. Ibid., and "Kohlberg Is Raising $5 Billion," *New York Times*, 10 July 1987.

56. "For Many Business School Students Wall Street Loses a Lot of Its Magic," *The Wall Street Journal*, 10 March 1988.

57. "Leveraged Buy-Outs Are Facing Downturn after Crash," *The Wall Street Journal,* 6 November 1987, and "Crash Could Weaken Wall Street's Grip on Corporate America," *The Wall Street Journal,* 29 December 1987.

58. "What Killed Stock Boom? Some Point at Tax Idea," *Washington Post,* 13 December 1987.

59. "House Drops Plans to Tax Takeovers," *New York Times,* 17 December 1987, and "Hill Reluctant to Take Lead on Market Regulation," *Congressional Quarterly,* 21 May 1988.

60. "Galbraith on Market's 'Pixilation,'" *The Wall Street Journal,* 1 March 1988. The three major federal studies were the *Report of the Presidential Task Force on Market Mechanisms* (the so-called Brady Commission); the SEC study, *The October 1987 Market Break;* and a GAO report entitled *Financial Markets: Preliminary Observations on the October 1987 Crash.*

61. U.S. Congress, House, *Pot of Gold,* pp. 35–36.

62. "A New Strain of Merger Mania," *Business Week,* 21 March 1988, and "Power Investors," *Business Week,* 20 June 1988.

63. "Infighting Is on Rise at Troubled Firms after Stock Plunge," *New York Times,* 4 February 1988, and "Takeover Boom Is Expected to Continue Through 1988 After a Strong First Half," *The Wall Street Journal,* 5 July 1988.

64. "Bush's Money Machine," *Washington Post,* 15 May 1988, and "Who's Giving to Whom," *Left Business Observer,* February 1988.

65. "Buyout Artist Kravis Had a High-Ticket Year," *New York Times,* 4 January 1988, and "All Dressed Up and No Place to Go?," *New York Times,* 7 August 1988.

15: Epilogue

1. "Poll Finds Less Optimism in U.S. on Future, a First under Reagan," *New York Times,* 21 February 1988.

2. "Stocks' Five-Year Rise Has Showered Benefits Unevenly in Economy," *The Wall Street Journal,* 10 August 1987.

3. Frank Levy, *Dollars and Dreams* (New York: Russell Sage Foundation, 1987); Thomas Edsall, "The Return of Inequality," *The Atlantic Monthly,* June 1988, pp. 86–94; and "Wage Stagnation Termed an Issue Beyond Campaign," *New York Times,* 4 September 1988.

4. See "Economic Nationalism Shapes Democratic Campaign Debate," *New York Times,* 22 March 1988, "Losing Its Grip?" *National Journal,* 6 February 1988; "The Wake of the Cold War," *Washington Post,* 14 June 1988; and "Long-Term View: Gloomy Forecasts," *New York Times,* 5 August 1988.

5. Many economists challenge the "anecdotal" notion of such a decline, citing figures that portray manufacturing as a more or less constant percentage of the nation's production of goods and services. But some economists have begun to dispute the methodology of government statistics that show a stable manufacturing sector. See "Is U.S. Manufacturing Really Stable? Some Say Reports May Mask Decline," *Washington Post,* 5 June 1988, and "U.S. Economic Statistics Off the Mark?" *National Journal,* 3 September 1988.

6. Cited in Stephen S. Cohen and John Zysman, *Manufacturing Matters* (New York: Basic Books, 1987), pp. 5, 265.

7. Ibid. See also Bruce R. Scott and George C. Lodge, eds., *U.S. Competitiveness in the World Economy* (Boston: Harvard Business School Press, 1985), pp. 480, 493. As Lodge and Crum conclude, if loss of manufacturing continues, the United States will "face prolonged high unemployment, a stagnant or declining real standard of

living, and possible social unrest.... Ultimately, even our national security could be undermined due to cuts in funding for defense or the loss of productive capability."

8. E. Sciberras and B.D. Payne, *Machine Tool Industry* (Essex, England: Longman Group, 1985), p. 31.

9. "Industry Report—Machine Tools," *Tooling & Production,* June 1985, pp. 66–67. This estimate includes mergers that occurred within the industry as well as acquisitions by conglomerates.

10. U.S. Congress, House, Committee on Banking, Finance and Urban Affairs, Subcommittee on Economic Stabilization, *Industrial Policy—2,* 98th Cong., 1st sess., 1983, p. 568.

11. Cited in Ray Marshall, *Unheard Voices* (New York: Basic Books, 1987), p. 279.

12. "A Machine-Tool Dynasty," *New York Times,* 5 September 1985. See also Robert H. Hayes, "Why Japanese Factories Work," *Harvard Business Review,* July–August 1981, pp. 56–66.

13. Robert H. Hayes and William J. Abernathy, "Managing Our Way to Economic Decline," *Harvard Business Review,* July–August 1980, pp. 67–77.

14. U.S. Congress, House, Committee on Banking, Finance and Urban Affairs, Subcommittee on Economic Stabilization, *Industrial Policy—2,* 98th Cong., 1st sess., 1983, p. 625.

15. Daniel Charles, "Reformers Seek Broader Military Role in Economy," *Science,* 12 August 1988, and "Bigger Role Urged for Defense Dept. in Economic Policy," *New York Times,* 19 October 1988.

16. "Finding Happiness in Buyout," *New York Times,* 26 May 1984.

17. "Takeover Trend Helps Push Corporate Debt and Defaults Upward," *The Wall Street Journal,* 15 March 1988, and "Fed Tells Banks To Weigh How Loans for Buyouts Would Fare in a Recession," *The Wall Street Journal,* 27 October 1988.

18. U.S. Congress, House, Committee on Energy and Commerce, *Leveraged Buyouts and the Pot of Gold,* 100th Cong., 1st sess., 1987, p. 22.

19. *The Wall Street Journal,* 15 March 1988. This article cites the Burlington Industries buyout as one example where capital spending was strictly limited to $75 million annually. Prior to the buyout, such spending averaged $180 million.

20. "The Age of 'Me-First' Management," *New York Times,* 19 August 1984.

21. *The Wall Street Journal,* 16 March 1988.

22. Mark J. Green and John F. Berry, *The Challenge of Hidden Profits* (New York: William Morrow, 1985), and "Baldrige Joins Attack on U.S. Firms," *Washington Post,* 13 November 1986.

23. See "Lobbyists Rally to Kill Proposal in Tax Overhaul That Could Undercut Many Corporate Takeovers," *The Wall Street Journal,* 29 July 1986, and "Two Ex-Senate Staffers, Longtime Pals, Face Off in Lobbying Effort over Takeover Tax Breaks," *The Wall Street Journal,* 15 December 1987.

24. "Japanese Firms Open U.S. Plants," *American Machinist,* June 1987, and Linda M. Spencer, *American Assets: An Examination of Foreign Investment in the United States* (Arlington, VA: Congressional Economic Leadership Institute, 1988), p. 1.

25. "Foreign Investment in U.S. Mutes Trade Debate," *New York Times,* 8 February 1987. About $250 million of the $1 trillion has been invested in manufacturing and assembly plants.

26. "Money Talks: How Foreign Firms Buy U.S. Clout," *Washington Post,* 19 June 1988, and "Japan's Clout in the U.S.," *Business Week,* 11 July 1988.

27. "Japanese Investment, a New Worry," *New York Times,* 6 May 1984.

28. "Novel Technique Shows Japanese Outpace Americans in Innovation," *New*

York Times, 7 March 1988.

29. "The 21st-Century Factory," *National Journal,* 13 February 1988, and Ramchandran Jaikumar, "Postindustrial Manufacturing," *Harvard Business Review,* November–December 1986, pp. 69–76.

30. John Dower, "The End of Innocence," *The Nation,* 12 September 1987.

31. "As Refugees Get Vote, Politicians Go to Vietnam," *New York Times,* 11 January 1988.

32. "New Pride Changes Japan's View of U.S.," *New York Times,* 28 June 1988.

BIBLIOGRAPHY AND SOURCES

Books

Adams, Walter, and Brock, James W. *The Bigness Complex: Industry, Labor, and Government in the American Economy.* New York: Pantheon, 1986.

Allen, G.C. *The Japanese Economy.* New York: St. Martin's, 1981.

Blair, John M. *Economic Concentration: Structure, Behavior and Public Policy.* New York: Harcourt Brace Jovanovich, 1972.

Bluestone, Barry, and Harrison, Bennett. *The Deindustrialization of America: Plant Closings, Community Abandonment, and the Dismantling of Basic Industry.* New York: Basic Books, 1982.

Blumberg, Paul. *Inequality in an Age of Decline.* New York: Oxford University Press, 1980.

Brownstein, Ronald, and Easton, Nina. *Reagan's Ruling Class: Portraits of the President's Top 100 Officials.* Washington, DC: Presidential Accountability Group, 1982.

Calleo, David P. *The Imperious Economy.* Cambridge, MA: Harvard University Press, 1982.

Chandler, Alfred D., Jr. *The Visible Hand: The Managerial Revolution in American Business.* Cambridge, MA: Harvard University Press, Belknap Press, 1977.

Cohen, Stephen S., and Zysman, John. *Manufacturing Matters: The Myth of the Post-Industrial Economy.* New York: Basic Books, 1987.

Davies, David G. *United States Taxes and Tax Policy.* Cambridge: Cambridge University Press, 1986.

Deyo, Frederic C., ed. *The Political Economy of the New Asian Industrialism.* Ithaca, NY: Cornell University Press, 1987.

Dore, Ronald. *Flexible Rigidities: Industrial Policy and Structural Adjustment in the Japanese Economy 1970–1980.* London: Athlone Press, 1986.

Dumas, Lloyd J. *The Overburdened Economy: Uncovering the Causes of Chronic Unemployment, Inflation, and National Decline.* Berkeley: University of California Press, 1986.

Dumas, Lloyd J., ed. *The Political Economy of Arms Reduction: Reversing Economic Decay.* Boulder, CO: Westview Press, 1982.

Federal Reserve Bank of Kansas City. *Industrial Change and Public Policy.* Kansas City: Federal Reserve Bank, 1983.

Ferguson, Thomas, and Rogers, Joel. *Right Turn: The Decline of the Democrats and the Future of American Politics.* New York: Hill and Wang, 1986.

Friedman, Benjamin M., ed. *The Changing Roles of Debt and Equity in Financing U.S. Capital Formation.* Chicago: University of Chicago Press, 1982.

Friedman, David. *The Misunderstood Miracle: Industrial Development and Political Change in Japan.* Ithaca, NY: Cornell University Press, 1988.

Frost, Ellen L. *For Richer, For Poorer: The New U.S.-Japan Relationship.* New York: Council on Foreign Relations, 1987.

Gansler, Jacques S. *The Defense Industry.* Cambridge, MA: MIT Press, 1986.

Gilpin, Robert. *The Political Economy of International Relations.* Princeton, NJ: Princeton University Press, 1987.

Green, Mark J. *The Other Government: The Unseen Power of Washington Lawyers.* New York: Viking, 1975.

Green, Mark J., and Berry, John F. *The Challenge of Hidden Profits: Reducing Corporate Bureaucracy and Waste.* New York: William Morrow, 1985.

Gresser, Julian. *Partners in Prosperity: Strategic Industries for the United States and Japan.* New York: McGraw-Hill, 1984.

Harrison, Bennett and Bluestone, Barry. *The Great U-Turn: Corporate Restructuring and the Polarizing of America.* New York: Basic Books, 1988.

Heineman, Stephen S., and Genevro, George W. *Machine Tools: Processes and Applications.* San Francisco: Canfield Press, 1979.

Herman, Edward S. *Corporate Control, Corporate Power.* Cambridge: Cambridge University Press, 1981.

Inoguchi, Takashi, and Okimoto, Daniel I., eds. *The Political Economy of Japan: The Changing International Context.* Vol. 2. Stanford, CA: Stanford University Press, 1988.

Johnson, Chalmers. *MITI and the Japanese Miracle: The Growth of Industrial Policy, 1925–1975.* Stanford, CA: Stanford University Press, 1982.

Katzenstein, Peter J., ed. *Between Power and Plenty: Foreign Economic Policies of Advanced Industrial States.* Madison: University of Wisconsin Press, 1978.

Kelley, Maryellen R., and Brooks, Harvey. *The State of Computerized Automation in U.S. Manufacturing.* Cambridge, MA: Kennedy School of Government, Harvard University, October 1988.

Kennedy, Paul. *The Rise and Fall of the Great Powers: Economic Change and Military Conflict from 1500 to 2000.* New York: Random House, 1987.

Kuttner, Robert. *The Economic Illusion: False Choices Between Prosperity and Social Justice.* Boston: Houghton Mifflin, 1984.

Lamont, Douglas F. *Forcing Our Hand: America's Trade Wars in the 1980s.* Lexington: MA: Lexington Books, 1986.

Lawrence, Robert Z. *Can America Compete?* Washington, DC: Brookings Institution, 1984.

Levy, Frank. *Dollars and Dreams: The Changing American Income Distribution.* New York: Russell Sage Foundation, 1987.

Lodge, George C. *The American Disease.* New York: Alfred A. Knopf, 1984.

Lodge, George C., and Vogel, Ezra F., eds. *Ideology and National Competitiveness: An Analysis of Nine Countries.* Boston: Harvard Business School Press, 1987.

Lowenstein, Louis. *What's Wrong with Wall Street: Short-term Gain and the Absentee Shareholder.* Reading, MA: Addison-Wesley, 1988.

Lynn, Leonard H., and McKeown, Timothy J. *Organizing Business: Trade Associations in America and Japan.* Washington, DC: American Enterprise Institute for Public Policy Research, 1988.

Magdoff, Harry, and Sweezy, Paul M. *The Deepening Crisis of U.S. Capitalism.* New York: Monthly Review Press, 1981.

_____. *The End of Prosperity: The American Economy in the 1970s.* New York: Monthly Review Press, 1977.

_____. *Stagnation and the Financial Explosion.* New York: Monthly Review Press, 1987.

Marris, Stephen. *Deficits and the Dollar: The World Economy at Risk.* Washington, DC: Institute for International Economics, 1987.

Marshall, Ray. *Unheard Voices: Labor and Economic Policy in a Competitive World.* New York: Basic Books, 1987.

McCraw, Thomas K., ed. *America versus Japan.* Boston: Harvard Business School Press, 1986.

McGregor, Douglas. *The Human Side of Enterprise.* New York: McGraw-Hill, 1985.

Meek, Christopher; Woodworth, Warner; and Dyer, W. Gibb. *Managing by the Numbers: Absentee Ownership and the Decline of American Industry.* Reading, MA: Addison-Wesley, 1988.

Melman, Seymour. *The Permanent War Economy: American Capitalism in Decline.* New York: Simon and Schuster, 1974.

_____. *Profits without Production.* New York: Alfred A. Knopf, 1983.

Melnyk, Stephen; Carter, Phillip L.; Dilts, David M.; and Lyth, David M. *Shop Floor Control.* Homewood, IL: Dow Jones-Irwin, 1985.

Mishel, Lawrence. *Manufacturing Numbers: How Inaccurate Statistics Conceal U.S. Industrial Decline*. Washington, DC: Economic Policy Institute, 1988.

Montgomery, David. *The Fall of the House of Labor: The Workplace, the State, and American Labor Activism, 1865–1925*. Cambridge: Cambridge University Press, 1987.

National Academy of Engineering. *The Competitive Status of the U.S. Machine Tool Industry: A Study of the Influences of Technology in Determining International Industrial Comparative Advantage*. Washington, DC: National Academy Press, 1983.

National Machine Tool Builders' Association. *Economic Handbook of the Machine Tool Industry, 1987–1988*. McLean, VA: NMTBA, 1987.

National Research Council. *Toward a New Era in U.S. Manufacturing: The Need for a National Vision*. Washington, DC: National Academy Press, 1986.

_____. *The U.S. Machine Tool Industry and the Defense Industrial Base*. Washington, DC: National Academy Press, 1983.

Noble, David F. *Forces of Production: A Social History of Industrial Automation*. New York: Alfred A. Knopf, 1984.

Ozaki, Robert S. *The Control of Imports and Foreign Capital in Japan*. New York: Praeger, 1972.

Patrick, Hugh, ed. *Japan's High Technology Industries: Lessons and Limitations of Industrial Policy*. Seattle: University of Washington Press, 1986.

Patrick, Hugh T., and Tachi, Ryuichiro, eds. *Japan and the United States Today: Exchange Rates, Macroeconomic Policies, and Financial Market Innovations*. New York: Center on Japanese Economy and Business, Columbia University, 1986.

Peet, Richard, ed. *International Capitalism and Industrial Restructuring: A Critical Analysis*. Boston: Allen and Unwin, 1987.

Pempel, T.J. *Policy and Politics in Japan: Creative Conservatism*. Philadelphia: Temple University Press, 1982.

Peterson, Wallace C. *Our Overloaded Economy: Inflation, Unemployment, and the Crisis in American Capitalism*. Armonk, NY: M.E. Sharpe, 1982.

Phillips, Kevin P. *Staying on Top: The Business Case for a National Industrial Strategy*. New York: Random House, 1984.

Piore, Michael J., and Sabel, Charles F. *The Second Industrial Divide: Possibilities for Prosperity*. New York: Basic Books, 1984.

Prestowitz, Clyde V. *Trading Places: How We Allowed Japan to Take the Lead*. New York: Basic Books, 1988.

Pugel, Thomas A., and Hawkins, Robert G., eds. *Fragile Interdependence: Economic Issues in U.S.-Japanese Trade and Investment*. Lexington, MA: Lexington Books, 1986.

Ravenscraft, David J., and Scherer, F.M. *Mergers, Sell-Offs, and Economic Efficiency*. Washington, DC: Brookings Institution, 1987.

Reich, Robert B. *The Next American Frontier*. New York: Times Books, 1983.

Rolt, L. T. C. *A Short History of Machine Tools*. Cambridge, MA: MIT Press, 1965.

Rosenberg, Nathan. *Perspectives on Technology*. Armonk, NY: M.E. Sharpe, 1976.

_____. *Technology and American Economic Growth*. New York: Harper and Row, 1972.

Saxonhouse, Gary R., and Yamamura, Kozo, eds. *Law and Trade Issues of the Japanese Economy: American and Japanese Perspectives*. Seattle: University of Washington Press, 1986.

Schlossstein, Steven. *Trade War: Greed, Power, and Industrial Policy on Opposite Sides of the Pacific*. New York: Congdon & Weed, 1984.

Schonberger, Richard J. *Japanese Manufacturing Techniques: Nine Hidden Lessons in Simplicity*. New York: Free Press, 1982.

Sciberras, E., and Payne, B.D. *Machine Tool Industry: Technical Change and International Competitiveness*. Essex, England: Longman Group, 1985.

Scott, Bruce R., and Lodge, George C., eds. *U.S. Competitiveness in the World Economy*. Boston: Harvard Business School Press, 1985.

Shaiken, Harley. *Work Transformed: Automation and Labor in the Computer Age.* New York: Holt, Rinehart and Winston, 1984.

Smith, Merritt Roe, ed. *Military Enterprise and Technological Change: Perspectives on the American Experience.* Cambridge, MA: MIT Press, 1985.

Sobel, Robert. *The Age of Giant Corporations: A Microeconomic History of American Business 1914–1970.* Westport, CT: Greenwood Press, 1972.

———. *The Last Bull Market: Wall Street in the 1960s.* New York: W.W. Norton, 1980.

Spence, A. Michael, and Hazard, Heather A., eds. *International Competitiveness.* Cambridge, MA: Ballinger, 1988.

Spencer, Linda M. *American Assets: An Examination of Foreign Investment in the United States.* Arlington, VA: Congressional Economic Leadership Institute, 1988.

Stone, I.F. *Business As Usual: The First Year of Defense.* New York: Modern Age Books, 1941.

Sweezy, Paul M., and Magdoff, Harry. *The Dynamics of U.S. Capitalism: Corporate Structure, Inflation, Credit, Gold, and the Dollar.* New York: Monthly Review Press, 1972.

Thurow, Lester C. *The Zero-Sum Society: Distribution and the Possibilities for Economic Change.* New York: Basic Books, 1980.

Thurow, Lester C., ed. *The Management Challenge: Japanese Views.* Cambridge, MA: MIT Press, 1985.

Triffin, Robert. *The World Money Maze: National Currencies in International Payments.* New Haven, CT: Yale University Press, 1966.

Vatter, Harold G. *The U.S. Economy in the 1950s: An Economic History.* Chicago: University of Chicago Press, 1985.

Vogel, Ezra F. *Comeback Case by Case: Building the Resurgence of American Business.* New York: Simon & Schuster, 1985.

Wagoner, Harless D. *The U.S. Machine Tool Industry from 1900 to 1950.* Cambridge, MA: MIT Press, 1968.

Wilkins, Mira. *The Maturing of Multinational Enterprise: American Business Abroad from 1914 to 1970.* Cambridge, MA: Harvard University Press, 1974.

Wolf, Marvin J. *The Japanese Conspiracy: The Plot to Dominate Industry Worldwide— and How to Deal with It.* New York: Empire Books, 1983.

Yamamura, Kozo, ed. *Policy and Trade Issues of the Japanese Economy: American and Japanese Perspectives.* Seattle: University of Washington Press, 1982.

Yamamura, Kozo, and Yasuba, Yasukichi, eds. *The Political Economy of Japan: The Domestic Transformation.* Vol. 1. Stanford, CA: Stanford University Press, 1987.

Yoshida, Mamoru. *Japanese Direct Manufacturing Investment in the United States.* New York: Praeger, 1987.

Zimmerman, Mark. *How to Do Business with the Japanese.* New York: Random House, 1985.

Zysman, John. *Governments, Markets, and Growth: Financial Systems and the Politics of Industrial Change.* Ithaca, NY: Cornell University Press, 1983.

U.S. Government Publications (Government Printing Office, Washington, DC, unless otherwise noted).

Presidential Task Force on Market Mechanisms. *Report of the Presidential Task Force on Market Mechanisms.* January 1988.

U.S. Congress, Congressional Budget Office. *Using Federal R&D to Promote Commercial Innovation.* April 1988.

U.S. Congress, House, Select Committee on Small Business. *Problems Facing the Tool and Die Industry.* 91st Cong., 1st sess., 1969.

U.S. Congress, House, Committee on Armed Services. *The Ailing Defense Industrial Base: Unready for Crisis.* 96th Cong., 2d sess., 1980.

U.S. Congress, House, Committee on Banking, Finance and Urban Affairs, Subcommittee on Economic Stabilization. *Industrial Policy—Part 2.* 98th Cong., 1st sess., 1983.

U.S. Congress, House, Committee on Ways and Means, Subcommittee on Trade. *United States-Japan Trade Relations.* 98th Cong., 1st sess., 1983.

U.S. Congress, House, Committee on Energy and Commerce. *Merger Activity and Leveraged Buyouts: Sound Corporate Restructuring or Wall Street Alchemy?* 98th Cong., 2d sess., 1984.

U.S. Congress, House, Committee on Energy and Commerce, Subcommittee on Telecommunications, Consumer Protection, and Finance. *Corporate Takeovers: Public Policy Implications for the Economy and Corporate Governance.* 99th Cong., 2d sess., 1986.

U.S. Congress, House, Committee on Energy and Commerce, Subcommittee on Telecommunications, Consumer Protection, and Finance. *Restructuring Financial Markets: The Major Policy Issues.* 99th Cong., 2d sess., 1986.

U.S. Congress, House, Committee on Energy and Commerce. *Leveraged Buyouts and the Pot of Gold: Trends, Public Policy, and Case Studies.* 100th Cong., 1st sess., 1987.

U.S. Congress, House, Committee on Ways and Means. *Overview and Compilation of U.S. Trade Statutes.* 100th Cong., 1st sess., 1987.

U.S. Congress, House, Committee on Small Business, Subcommittee on Antitrust and Restraint of Trade Activities Affecting Small Business. *Impact of International Trade Practices on Small Business.* 98th Cong., 2d sess., 1984.

U.S. Congress, Joint Economic Committee. *The Machine Tool Industry and the Defense Industrial Base.* 98th Cong., 1st sess., 1983.

U.S. Congress, Office of Technology Assessment. *The Defense Technology Base: Introduction and Overview.* March 1988.

———. *Technology and the American Economic Transition: Choices for the Future.* May 1988.

———. *Paying the Bill: Manufacturing and America's Trade Deficit.* June 1988.

U.S. Congress, Senate, Committee on Banking and Currency. *Review of Voluntary Agreements Program under the Defense Production Act: Expansion of Machine-Tool Industry, Report Dated February 10, 1958 by the Attorney General.* 85th Cong., 2d sess., 1958.

U.S. Congress, Senate, Select Committee on Small Business, Subcommittee on Science and Technology. *Introduction to Numerical Control and Its Impact on Small Business.* 92nd Cong., 1st sess., 1971.

U.S. Congress, Senate, Committee on Banking, Housing and Urban Affairs, Subcommittee on International Finance and Monetary Policy. *Foreign Industrial Targeting.* 98th Cong., 1st sess., 1983.

U.S. Congress, Senate, Committee on Foreign Relations. *U.S. Trade Relations with Japan.* 97th Cong., 2d sess., 1982.

———. *U.S. Machine Tool Industry: Its Relation to National Security.* 98th Cong., 1st sess., 1983.

U.S. Congress, Senate, Committee on Finance. *Improving Enforcement of Trade Agreements.* 100th Cong., 1st sess., 1987.

———. *Mastering the World Economy—Part 2.* 100th Cong., 1st sess., 1987.

U.S. Department of Commerce. *An Assessment of U.S. Competitiveness in High Technology Industries.* February 1983.

———. *A Competitive Assessment of the U.S. Flexible Manufacturing Systems Industry.* July 1985.

U.S. Department of Energy. *Trip Report on the Technology of Machine Tools in Japan.* Prepared by Lawrence Livermore Laboratory (UCID-18591), Livermore, CA, February 1980.

U.S. General Accounting Office. *United States-Japan Trade: Issues and Problems.* GAO,

Washington, DC, September 1979.

_____. *Industrial Policy: Japan's Flexible Approach.* GAO/ID-82-32, Washington, DC, June 1982.

_____. *Foreign Industrial Targeting—U.S. Trade Law Remedies.* GAO/NSIAD-85-77, Washington, DC, May 1985.

_____. *Combating Unfair Foreign Trade Practices Under Section 301.* GAO/NSIAD-87-100, Washington, DC, March 1987.

_____. *Financial Markets: Preliminary Observations on the October 1987 Crash.* GAO/GGD-88-38, Washington, DC: January 1988.

U.S. International Trade Commission. *Competitive Assessment of the U.S. Metalworking Machine Tool Industry.* USITC Publication 1428, Washington, DC, September 1983.

U.S. Securities and Exchange Commission. *The October 1987 Market Break.* SEC, Washington, DC, February 1988.

Dissertations

Fawcett, Clifford W. "Factors and Issues in the Survival and Growth of the U.S. Machine Tool Industry: With Emphasis on the Impact of Computer Based Automation and Foreign Machine Tool Technology." George Washington University, 1976.

Himes, Robert S. "A Study of the Machine Tool Industry, with Emphasis on the Problem of Stability." American University, 1962.

Sonny, Jacob. "Technological Change in the U.S. Machine Tool Industry, 1947–1966." New School for Social Research, 1971.

Legal Submissions

Covington & Burling. *Petition to the President of the United States through the Office of the United States Trade Representative for the Exercise of Presidential Discretion Authorized by Section 103 of the Revenue Act of 1971.* Submitted on behalf of Houdaille Industries, Inc., 3 May 1982, Washington, DC.

_____. *Petition under the National Security Clause, Section 232 of the Trade Expansion Act of 1962 for Adjustment of Imports of Machine Tools.* Submitted on behalf of the National Machine Tool Builders' Association, 1983, Washington, DC.

Cravath, Swaine & Moore. *Computer-Aided Manufacturing: The Japanese Challenge.* Comments submitted to the U.S. International Trade Commission on behalf of Cincinnati Milacron, December 1982, Washington, DC.

Wender Murase & White. *Comments in Opposition to the [Houdaille] Petition.* Submitted on behalf of Japan Machine Tool Builders' Association et al., 29 July 1982, Washington, DC.

Articles

Copaken, Richard. "The Houdaille Petition: A New Weapon against Unfair Industry Targeting Practices." *George Washington Journal of International Law and Economics* 17 (1983): 211–295.

_____. "United States Import Laws: A Critical Examination—The Houdaille Petition." Address before the Electronic Industries Association, 11 October 1982.

_____. "The Politics of Trade Law Proceedings." Unpublished manuscript, 8 March 1984.

Cremeans, John E., and Dalton, Donald H. "The U.S. Machine Tool Industry and International Competition." *Industrial Economics Review* 1 (1982): 1–10.

Didrichsen, Jon. "The Development of Diversified and Conglomerate Firms in the United States, 1920–1970." *Business History Review* 46 (1972): 202–219.

Dornbusch, Rudiger; Poterba, James; and Summers, Lawrence. "The Case for Manufacturing in America's Future." Eastman Kodak Company, 1988.

Edsall, Thomas. "The Return of Inequality." *The Atlantic Monthly*, June 1988, pp. 86–94.

Epstein, Gerald. "The Triple Debt Crisis." *World Policy Journal* 2 (Fall 1985): 625–657.

Faux, Jeff. "The Austerity Trap and the Growth Alternative." *World Policy Journal* 5 (Summer 1988): 367–413.

Fransman, Martin. "International Competitiveness, Technical Change and the State: The Machine Tool Industry in Taiwan and Japan." *World Development* 14 (1986): 1375–1396.

Gansler, Jacques S. "Needed: A U.S. Defense Industrial Strategy." *International Security* 12 (Fall 1987): 45–62.

Googins, Brian A., and Greene, James A. "The Industrial Targeting Practices of Japan and the Domestic Machine Tool Industry." *Case Western Reserve Journal of International Law* 15 (Summer 1983): 469–487.

Green, Robert T., and Larsen, Trina L. "Only Retaliation Will Open up Japan." *Harvard Business Review*, November–December 1987, pp. 22–28.

Hadley, Eleanor M. "Industrial Policy for Competitiveness." *Journal of Japanese Trade & Industry*, September 1982, pp. 45–49.

Hayes, Robert H. "Why Japanese Factories Work." *Harvard Business Review*, July–August 1981, pp. 57–66.

Hayes, Robert H., and Abernathy, William J. "Managing Our Way to Economic Decline." *Harvard Business Review*, July–August 1980, pp. 67–77.

Herrigel, Gary. "Industrial Order in the Machine Tool Industry: A Comparison of the United States and Germany." Center for European Studies, Harvard University, 1988.

Jaikumar, Ramchandran. "Postindustrial Manufacturing." *Harvard Business Review*, November–December 1986, pp. 69–76.

Johnson, Chalmers. "The Japanese Political Economy: A Crisis in Theory." *Ethics & International Affairs* 2 (1988): 79–97.

Knoll, David D. "Section 232 of the Trade Expansion Act of 1962: Industrial Fasteners, Machine Tools and Beyond." *Maryland Journal of International Law and Trade* 10 (Spring 1986): 55–88.

Kurth, James R. "The Political Consequences of the Product Cycle: Industrial History and Political Outcomes." *International Organization* 33 (Winter 1979): 1–34.

Morse, Ronald A. "Japan's Drive to Pre-Eminence." *Foreign Policy*, Winter 1987–1988, pp. 3–21.

Norton, R.D. "Industrial Policy and American Renewal." *Journal of Economic Literature* 24 (1986): 1–40.

Pempel, T.J. "Japanese Foreign Economic Policy: The Domestic Bases for International Behavior." *International Organization* 31 (Autumn 1977): 139–190.

Pugel, Thomas A. "Japan's Industrial Policy: Instruments, Trends, and Effects." *Journal of Comparative Economics* 8 (1984): 420–435.

Pyle, Kenneth B., ed. "A Forum on the Trade Crisis." *Journal of Japanese Studies* 13 (Summer 1987): 239–429.

Rapkin, David P. "Industrial Policy and Trade Conflict in the Machine Tool Industry: The Houdaille Case." Department of Political Science, University of Nebraska, 1984.

Reich, Robert B. "Beyond Free Trade." *Foreign Affairs* 61 (Spring 1983): 773–804.

Saxonhouse, Gary R. "Why Japan Is Winning." *Issues in Science and Technology*, Spring 1986, pp. 72–80.

Sayle, Murray. "Japan Victorious." *New York Review of Books*, 28 March 1985, pp.

33–40.

Shad, John S.R. "The Financial Realities of Mergers." *Harvard Business Review,* November–December 1969, pp. 133–146.

Stokes, Bruce. "The 21st-Century Factory." *National Journal,* 13 February 1988, pp. 382–387.

———. "Living with a New Japan." *National Journal,* 12 March 1988, pp. 657–662.

Sweezy, Paul, and Magdoff, Harry. "The Stock Market Crash and Its Aftermath." *Monthly Review,* March 1988, pp. 1–13.

Trezise, Philip H. "Industrial Policy Is Not the Major Reason for Japan's Success." *Brookings Review,* Spring 1983, pp. 13–18.

van Wolferen, Karel. "The Japan Problem." *Foreign Affairs* 65 (Winter 1986/87): 288–303.

Watanabe, Susumu. "Market Structure, Industrial Organization and Technological Development: The Case of the Japanese Electronics-Based NC-Machine Tool Industry." World Employment Programme Research Working Paper WEP2-22/WP.111, Geneva: International Labor Organization, February 1983.

Periodicals

American Machinist
American Metal Market/Metalworking News
Barron's
Business Week
Foreign Affairs
Foreign Policy
Harvard Business Review
International Organization
Los Angeles Times
National Journal
New York Times
The Wall Street Journal
Washington Post
World Policy Journal

Interviews with Burgmaster and Houdaille Personnel

Burgmaster executives and employees (years with the company)

Dave Balbirnie (1962–1986)
Ben Bezdziecki (1959–1974)
Fred Burg (1946–1967)
Joe Burg (1946–1970)
Gene Dobmeier (1966–1976; 1980–1981)
Bob Doyle (1967–1971; 1977–1980)
Jack Finch (1973–1983)
Allan Folger (1969–1980)
Sandor Forizs (1959–1961; 1966–1985)
Robert French (1956–1978)

Norman Ginsburg (1946–1969)
Bernhard Holland (1953–1982)
Pete Ives (1957–1985)
Shohichi Kato (1956–1985)
Jo Kelly (1973–1981)
Socrates Lenders (1959–1981)
Edward Merk (1958–1983)

Houdaille executives (years with the company)

George Delaney (1967–1987)
Tom Norton (1947–1980)
Phillip O'Reilly (1960–1987)
Gerald Saltarelli (1941–1979)
Kenneth Slawson (1965–1987)